EERL With...
Surplus/Duplicate

DATE DUE

PUBLICATIONS OF THE DEPARTMENT OF
ROMANCE LANGUAGES
UNIVERSITY OF NORTH CAROLINA

General Editor: ALDO SCAGLIONE

Editorial Board: JUAN BAUTISTA AVALLE-ARCE, PABLO GIL CASADO, FRED M.
CLARK, GEORGE BERNARD DANIEL, JANET W. DÍAZ, ALVA V. EBERSOLE, AUGUSTIN
MAISSEN, EDWARD D. MONTGOMERY, FREDERICK W. VOGLER

NORTH CAROLINA STUDIES IN THE
ROMANCE LANGUAGES AND LITERATURES

ESSAYS: TEXTS, TEXTUAL STUDIES AND TRANSLATIONS: SYMPOSIA

Founder: URBAN TIGNER HOLMES

Editor: JUAN BAUTISTA AVALLE-ARCE
Associate Editor: FREDERICK W. VOGLER

Other publications of the Department: *Estudios de Hispanófila, Hispanófila,
Romance Notes, Studia Raeto-Romanica*

Distributed by:

INTERNATIONAL SCHOLARLY BOOK SERVICE, INC.

P. O. BOX 4347
Portland, Oregon   97208
U. S. A.

NORTH CAROLINA STUDIES IN THE
ROMANCE LANGUAGES AND LITERATURES
Essay 3

STUDIES IN TIRSO, I:

The Dramatist and his Competitors,
1620-26

STUDIES IN TIRSO, I:

The Dramatist and his Competitors, 1620-26

BY

RUTH LEE KENNEDY

*Professor Emerita of Spanish in Smith College
and in The University of Arizona*

PQ
6436
K4
v.1

CHAPEL HILL

NORTH CAROLINA STUDIES IN THE ROMANCE
LANGUAGES AND LITERATURES

U.N.C. DEPARTMENT OF ROMANCE LANGUAGES

1974

THE ELMER E. RASMUSON LIBRARY
UNIVERSITY OF ALASKA

Library of Congress Cataloging in Publication Data

Kennedy, Ruth Lee, 1895
    Studies in Tirso, I

    (North Carolina Studies in the Romance Languages and Literatures.
Essays, no. 3)
    1. Téllez, Gabriel, 1580?-1648-Contemporaries. 2. Téllez, Gabriel, 1580?-
1648-Contemporary Spain.
    I. Title. II. Series.

PQ6436.K4   862'.3   74-3444
ISBN 0-88438-003-3

I.S.B.N. 0-88438-003-3

PRINTED IN SPAIN

IMPRESO EN ESPAÑA

DEPÓSITO LEGAL: V. 2.451 - 1974

ARTES GRÁFICAS SOLER, S. A. - JÁVEA, 28 - VALENCIA (8) - 1974

To the memory of
some friends and scholars
who, from across their teachers' desks,
shared with me their love and knowledge
of Spain, its people, and its culture:
Lilia M. Casis
James Pyle Wickersham Crawford
Sylvanus Griswold Morley
Miguel Romera Navarro
Rudolph Schevill

OUTLINE

PREFACE

In his essay, "Intellect," Emerson wrote that "all our progress is an unfolding, like the vegetable bud." The unfolding has, in the case of my Tirsian studies, been a slow one. I began them with what I expected to be the relatively modest task of establishing the chronology of Gabriel Téllez's theatre, one I erroneously believed would call for some five years of my time. Never was there worse miscalculation on the part of a not inexperienced scholar! I have, during more than thirty years, devoted such hours as my teaching would permit to Tirso, and only now is the end in sight.

In trying out various norms that would help me establish Tirso's chronology, I soon realized the necessity of studying the many allusions in his theatre to the sumptuary decrees of 1623. These references, together with the knowledge acquired of their historical background, led to a series of three articles, printed in the *Hispanic Review* (1942-1943). While analyzing these superficial reflections of a reform movement in the dramatist's theatre, I reached the conviction that Tirso's part in that movement extended to far more important aspects of the political and social world about him than were indicated in the ephemeral effects of such decrees; and this realization would, in 1945-1946, lead to a series of lectures which I gave in England (six in Oxford and two in Cambridge) on the "Reform Movement of 1617-1625 and its Reflections [political, economic, social, etc.] in Tirso's Theatre." From this general study, it was but a step to a monograph of 1948 on "Tirso's *La prudencia en la mujer* and the Ambient that Brought it Forth." Therein I sustained the thesis that Tirso, under cover of a historical play dealing with María de Molina, had written nothing less than a mirror for princes in dramatic form, one that was directed against Philip IV and his regime. (Other long studies, still in manuscript, make evident that Tirso, in the years that followed, grew increasingly bitter toward his young monarch and the royal alter-ego that was the Conde-Duque de Olivares.)

No one can get very far into Tirso's works without coming to the conclusion that his relations to the literary movements and the *literati* of Madrid — to Lope, Alarcón, the Aristotelians, the Gongorists, etc.— are of primary importance to our understanding of this Mercedarian and his theatre. It was not, however, until around 1962 that I began to suspect the identity of some of the specific targets at whom Tirso's satire was being aimed: when re-reading *La fingida Arcadia,* for at least the tenth time, I came to the realization that he was satirizing Vélez de Guevara as head of the Andalusian drama of spectacle and was linking the dramatist's fate with that of the man who was adulterating the coin of the realm, i.e., Olivares.

From this time on, the unwinding would proceed somewhat more rapidly. This discovery was the silken thread which would lead me through the maze of satirical comments that are found in Tirso's plays and stories. I began my study of the Mercedarian's relations to other individual dramatists —to Vélez de Guevara, to Ruiz de Alarcón, to Lope de Vega Carpio— and these investigations, in turn, indicated the necessity for re-study of certain Tirsian plays which seemed to link up with the very years of the dramatist's banishment from Madrid in 1625, or with the year that immediately followed.

In making analyses, which were essentially chronological, of such plays as *No hay peor sordo, Desde Toledo a Madrid, La ventura con el nombre, El amor médico,* and *Escarmientos para el cuerdo,* as well as of Tirso's relations to the dramatists named, I began to glimpse little by little the importance of the well-known abusive quatrain which linked Tirso to Alarcón. At the same time, I started to re-study the many references to "literary envy" in Tirso's *Cigarrales* and in his plays. These last investigations ultimately suggested consideration of the plays of Tirso's *Primera parte* of 1626-1627 *as a single unit,* as well as a re-evaluation

of the symbolic satire one encounters in the *Cigarrales* of 1624,
a miscellany which had been sent to press by October 8, 1621. In
it, I found satire that must have been inserted after the book
first went to press; and in the plays of the *Parte I* (1627), some
of which had been played in the Palace in 1622-1623, there were
references that could not possibly have been included at the time
they were originally written. Indeed, some of the barbs of the
Primera parte must necessarily have been added after the *Junta
de Reformación* had banished Tirso from Madrid in 1625. Certain
other plays containing equivocal satire were now re-examined and
the knowledge gained from this further study was then added to
that I had acquired in reviewing his *Primera parte* and his *Cigarrales*. I could finally understand, in large measure, the satire
directed against an envious *cortesano!* With these pieces of the
jig-saw puzzle in hand, I was at long last in a position to connect
up the various blocks that I had assembled over the years; and
the colorful design of Tirso's life and work in Madrid seemed
now reasonably clear!

I say "reasonably clear," for this book makes no claim to
having solved all the problems of Tirso's years in the capital. Nor
will any such claim be made when the second and the third volumes of the series come forth — volumes in which I plan 1) to
study his political plays, and 2) to continue my investigations of
Tirso's relations to other literary schools and personalities of his
time: to Góngora and gongorism, to the Aristotelians, to Mira de
Amescua, etc.

Some of the conclusions which I have reached in this first
volume will perhaps appear controversial to some of my colleagues, the more so because it has not previously been recognized
that Tirso refashioned so many of his *comedias*. Yet, as the above
resumé of my efforts makes evident, they were not reached
hastily nor lightly. My Tirsian studies have indeed been long in
the making. I have had not only to study such works of other
poets as could offer grist to my mill, but to bury myself in the
day-by-day historical accounts of the epoch. Tirso was a very
communicative dramatist; he was, moreover, one who drew heavily from the milieu that surrounded him, particularly during his
Madrid period. For confirmation of the chronology I assigned this

or that play, I sought parallels in the *belles lettres*, in the diaries, in the portraits of the time. What I have not been able to do to the extent I should have liked is to make myself acquainted with Luis Vélez's theatre. A former student of mine, Dr. Vern Williamsen of the University of Missouri, is, I am happy to say, going to undertake it.

If in my search I have been wedded to any particular conviction, to any particular bias, I have not known it. It seems to me that I have striven only to keep in mind two warnings of my revered professors, S. Griswold Morley and Miguel Romera-Navarro: 1) "Have a respect for facts!" and 2) "You'll always find the answer if you just keep looking long enough!" I have sought for facts regardless of where they might lead me.

Nevertheless, as time goes on, more facts that have a bearing on the situation will be found. Some of them will, I believe, substantiate my general conclusions; others, no doubt, will call into question some of those I suggest — or even negate them. I can only hope that the succeeding generation of Tirsian students will find that the foundations which I have thought to leave them are *essentially* solid. Of them, I beg that they reserve judgment until I can get all my evidence into print.

My debt in many directions is a large one, so large and so extended over the years that were I to start listing names here, I should, with the bad memory of my years, fail to include some of the distant past which should unquestionably be included. Let me accordingly paraphrase Enrico's question of *El condenado por desconfiado* in this form:

> ¿Quién podrá ahora acordarse
> de tanta obligación vieja?

In a word, I throw myself on the clemency of my many early creditors for not thanking them here one by one. Many are the kind librarians, many the kind archivists, both here and abroad, who put their time and their treasures at my disposal; many are the colleagues of Smith College and elsewhere who have, at one point or another, held out a helping hand. Even so, I have drawn far more heavily from Tirso's own works than from books or manuscripts about him.

I, at least, can here make specific acknowledgment to the foundations that made available the wherewithal to continue my studies: to the A.A.U.W., who twice came to my aid, to the University of Pennsylvania, and to the Guggenheim Foundation. I should like, as well, to give thanks to Tirsian scholars of the past: to Hartzenbusch; to my good friends, Cotarelo and Ángel González-Palencia; to Sra. de los Ríos, whose conclusions as to chronology I have frequently had to reject even while recognizing her intimate knowledge of Tirso's theatre. Much information is available to the Tirsian scholar of today that was not available to her. Chaucer pointed out long ago in his *Parliament of Fowls:*

> ... out of olde feldes, as man sayth,
> cometh al this newe corn fro yer to yere;
> and out of olde bokes, in good feyth,
> cometh al this newe science that men lere.

I must, as well, acknowledge my debt to some younger Tirsian scholars who, with their perspicacity, have pointed out my errors and thereby set my course in other directions: to Miss Margaret Wilson, who, with the introduction to her edition of *Antona García,* made me realize that the biographical elements found in that play must have been added after Tirso was banished from Madrid; and to Dr. Alan K. G. Paterson, whose study, "Tirso de Molina: Two Bibliographical Studies," convinced me that the edition of the *Cigarrales* in 1624 was the *princeps* of that work, that there was no edition of 1621, as I had argued.

Debts incurred, even since I reached the point of actual composition of this book, are many. My gratitude is due to Professor J. B. Avalle-Arce of the University of North Carolina, who — with his broad erudition and his very precise knowledge of the genealogy of Spain's noble families — has, as editor of *Studies in the Romance Languages and Literatures,* saved me from more than one pitfall. It goes, as well, to Professor Alexander A. Parker, of the University of Texas, not only for the early faith he displayed in my ability to carry my task to a successful conclusion but for many valuable suggestions he gave me over a period of months; to Dean Herbert Rhodes, Professor Raymond Thompson, Mr. Marshall Townsend, all of the University of Arizona, and to Professor

D. Lee Hamilton, formerly of this same university, for lending sympathetic ears to my problems on more than one occasion; to Professors Dolores Brown, Robert ter Horst, and Agapito Rey (retired), of the University of Arizona, who took long hours out of busy days to read my manuscript when it was still in a very primitive form and to give me the advantage of their disinterested advice; to Mrs. Edmund L. King of Bryn Mawr, who like-wise read the manuscript in an early stage of its development, and made very pertinent comments; and finally to Professor Bruce Wardropper, of Duke University, who, with his very incisive mind and his tremendous loyalty to his friends, proved a veritable tower of strength in moments when I had real need of one.

I should like also to express my warm thanks to three of our graduate students, Sherman L. Asay, Bernadette Komonchak, and Linda E. Haughton, who helped me overcome both clerical and physical shortcomings. Finally to Miss María Araujo, once of the *Seminario de Lexicografía* of the Real Academia Española, and now of our Serials Department in the University of Arizona Library, my debt is more that due to a collaborator than to a secretary: she has not only put at my disposal her very thorough classical and liturgical background but has given me clerical help in days when it necessarily represented a drain on her strength.

ABBREVIATIONS

Acad.	*Obras de Lope de Vega,* published by la Real Academia Española, 1890-1913, 15 vols.
Acad. N	*Obras de Lope de Vega,* published by la Real Academia Española (nueva edición), 1916-30, 13 vols.
BAE	*Biblioteca de Autores Españoles*
BCom.	*Bulletin of the Comediantes*
BHS	*Bulletin of Hispanic Studies*
BNM	Biblioteca Nacional, Madrid
BNL	Biblioteca Nacional, Lisbon
BRAE	Boletín de la Real Academia Española
Dif.	*Comedias de diferentes o varios autores,* 7 vols.
Esc.	*Comedias escogidas de los mayores ingenios de España* (1652 1705), 48 vols.
HR	*Hispanic Review*
M-B	Morley y Bruerton. *Cronología de las comedias de Lope de Vega*
NBAE	*Nueva Biblioteca de Autores Españoles*
NRFH	*Nueva Revista de Filología Hispánica*
PMLA	*Publications of the Modern Language Association of America*
RABM	*Revista de Archivos, Bibliotecas y Museos*
RBAM	*Revista de la Biblioteca, Archivo y Museo del Ayuntamiento de Madrid*
R-C	H. A. Rennert y A. Castro. *La vida de Lope de Vega Carpio*
S-S	Spencer and Schevill. *The Dramatic Work of Luis Vélez de Guevara*
Varios	See above under *Dif.*

BACKGROUND FOR THE STUDY

I

TIRSO IN AN ERA OF REFORM
AND RAPID CHANGE

Tirso's span of literary activity in Madrid was short. It could have covered, at most, from early 1620 — around which time he evidently made a brief visit to the capital — to July of 1626, by which date we know he was acting as "comendador" of the Mercedarian convent in Trujillo. His actual residence in Madrid was even briefer: he would soon to have been officially transferred to his Mercedarian house there in the early months of 1621 and to have left Madrid sometime in March of 1625 after the *Junta de Reformación* had recommended that he be banished from the city to one of the distant convents of his Order. There is good evidence, nevertheless, that he spent some months in the capital in the first half of 1626. [1]

The five years or so that the dramatist lived in the metropolis were years of rapid flux. They were years in which even the most experienced of old-timers often found it difficult to steer a steady

---

[1] These first pages are a running account, intended as background for the more specific information that follows. In succeeding ones, I shall, of course, give documentary authority for all general statements such as the ones made in the first and second paragraphs. The same will hold for other general summaries that follow.

All quotations from Tirso's works in this study are to E. Hartzenbusch's *Comedias escogidas de Fray Gabriel Téllez* (*BAE*, V) and E. Cotarelo y Mori, *Comedias de Tirso de Molina* (*NBAE*, IV and IX), unless it is stated otherwise. *Complete bibliographical information for all titles used in both text and notes will be found in the bibliography, placed in the concluding pages of this volume.*

course in the dangerous waters that lay about, years in which the most flexible of the young often lost their footing. "Mar de Madrid" is a phrase found over and over in the literature of the day. Tirso's previous literary experience had been largely in the relatively quiet waters of old Toledo. After some ten years there, he had spent two in distant Santo Domingo (1616-1618), helping to reorganize the Mercedarian house on that island. The three years following his return from Santo Domingo must have been given largely to study and to official duties in connection with his Order. Thus, he was, in early 1621, around forty [2] before he entered the swirling waters of the court.

The metaphor of the preceding paragraph, though hackneyed today by long use, was suggested by one of Tirso's own. He has left for us in his *Cigarrales de Toledo* [3] a description of an aquatic fête, one that supposedly took place on the Tagus of the Imperial City. In it, he first makes clear the spirit of envy that he had met in Madrid — even though he was "a son of the Manzanares" — and contrasts it with the spirit of generosity and good will that had characterized his literary relations in Toledo. This he follows with a description of his own entry in the aquatic fête. It is a passage of less than 200 words which we shall have occasion to quote in full in the chapter that follows. [4] For the moment we need only stress the autobiographic importance of that sustained bit of symbolism, which has not as yet been understood. It indicates not only that Tirso was striving for the laurel wreath of fame but that he was meeting opposition from a competitor who was, to him, as ignorant as he was envious. This autobiographic passage — which was not likely to have been written until the dramatist had experienced for some time the envy to which he

---

[2] It would now seem to be fairly well established that Tirso was born in 1580-1581 since, on January 25, 1638, the Mercedarian himself declared that he was 57 years old. See G. E. Wade, "The Year of Tirso's Birth," *Hispanófila*, VII (1963), no. 19, 1-9. In his study, Prof. Wade has summed up the conclusions that Sr. Guillermo Guastavino Gallent had previously published in *RABM*, LXIX (1961), 817-820. I agree with Sr. Guastavino and Prof. Wade that 1580 seems the more probable year of Tirso's birth.

[3] *Los Cigarrales de Toledo*, ed. Espasa-Calpe (Madrid, 1942), I, 116-117. All references to the *Cigarrales* will be to this same edition.

[4] See p. 142.

points — must, we believe, have been added to the *Cigarrales* sometime between the time that miscellany was originally sent to press, around October 8th, 1621, and the time it was released in March, 1624.

If we are to understand the full import of Tirso's words, they will first have to be studied in connection with a symbolic engraving, found on the title page that prefaces the first edition of his *Los cigarrales de Toledo* (1624). [5] It will be our contention that these two bits of symbolism were *indirectly* the cause of Tirso's troubles with the *Junta de Reformación*, which, on March 6, 1625, recommended that he be banished from his convent in Madrid to one of the distant ones of his Order and that he be forbidden to write further plays or poems. If we are to prove our thesis, we must, after analysing the implications of the aforesaid symbolism, study them in connection: 1) with a passage from *La república al revés*, added when that play was retouched in 1621; 2) with certain references, found in various places of Tirso's works, to "envious poets," rich in worldly goods, who have the name of being "discreet," yet can't keep their mouths shut; 3) with other allusions to "escribanos" who are so many "cats" with very long claws; 4) with an "epistle" from one Lope de Vega Carpio, written around September of 1623, to don Antonio de Mendoza; 5) with satire of Tirso, hidden away in Mendoza's theatre; 6) with the well-known passage of Ruiz de Alarcón's *Las paredes oyen* which satirizes Lope's "princesses of León"; 7) with the abusive *copla* which links Ruiz de Alarcón's name with that of "el fraile de la Merced"; 8) with a rhymed bit of doggerel, sent to Philip IV in early 1626 by Luis Vélez de Guevara, which ends with a curse on one "Arceo" and "el fraile de la Merced"; 9) and even with an effort on Olivares part to suppress the Mercedarian Order in 1626.

With the chain of evidence forged by study of these various documents, we shall be led to the conclusion that Gabriel Téllez, known to the literary world as "Tirso," was locked in struggle

---

[5] For 1624 as date of the *princeps*, see Dr. Alan K. G. Paterson, "Tirso de Molina: Two Bibliographical Studies", 43-68. I had argued previously for a *princeps* of 1621, but Dr. Paterson's article convinced me that I was mistaken. The description of the title page is found on p. 43.

with don Antonio Hurtado de Mendoza — behind whom stood
the all-powerful Olivares and his appointed *Junta de Reformación* — as well as with Luis Vélez de Guevara, who was a close
friend of Mendoza's and, like him, an *hechura* of the *privado*.
Into this struggle would be drawn Lope de Vega Carpio on the
side of Mendoza. It would ultimately involve, as well, don Juan
Ruiz de Alarcón, though the part of the Mexican in this fight
is far from being as clear as is that of the other dramatists.

This study, in sum, seeks to unravel the intermeshed lives of
Tirso, Antonio Hurtado de Mendoza, Lope de Vega Carpio, Luis
Vélez de Guevara, and Juan Ruiz de Alarcón — primarily during
the years 1621-1627, although the fight broke out again in the
thirties. In making our analysis, we shall hope not only to reveal
the tragi-comedy of their interwoven existences but to comprehend the temperaments that brought about the conflict. We shall
realize, too, the importance of Tirso's political outlook, as a mo-
tivating force in the fight. As the drama unfolds, we shall see
Tirso grow in moral courage, if not in worldly discretion. Saurina
was certainly speaking for Gabriel Téllez (i.e., Tirso) when she
stated in *El bandolero:* [6] "Mejor me acomodo al espíritu temerario que al pusilánime." Tirso not only challenged the combined
forces of his opponents; he even warned them in advance of the
war he was intending to wage against them!

But Gabriel Téllez's position was much less secure than it
would have been in earlier days. Shielded though the Mercedarian was by a far-flung religious Order that was nearly four
hundred years old (and one of royal origin), that Order was
so little in Olivares' favor that the *privado* would, in 1626, even
try to dissolve it. Moreover, the Lopean *comedia*, which Tirso
championed so warmly on reaching Madrid in 1621, was in 1625
faced with more serious opposition than it had been in the earlier
year. There were, as we shall see, men on that commission who
were not only of very stern mold, but were under the domination
of Olivares. There were, moreover, in the Palace those who
wanted a theatre that was written, not to catch the fancy of the

---

[6] Gabriel Téllez, *El bandolero,* 77. All references to *El bandolero* will
be to Viada y Lluch's edition, unless otherwise stated.

vulgo, but instead one that would meet the more sophisticated tastes of the court. This new group was added to others who had long found the *comedia* unsatisfactory: to the Aristotelians who criticized it not only because of its sprawling structure but because they felt the Lopean *capa y espada* play was "paja todo"; and to the stern "Catones," many of them grave prelates, who saw, in the Lopean formula of love and honor, a menace to the morals of the young.

Moreover, this opposition was buttressed by the gravity of both the national and the international situation. Spain was at the crossroads. The more serious-minded of her citizens saw only destruction ahead unless her ship of state could be steered on a safer course. It could not have taken long for such men to recognize the political realities of this new regime: they had for king a youth "whose only business was pleasure" and a power-loving *privado* "whose only pleasure was business." Bitter strife between Catholics and Protestants had already begun in Italy and Bohemia before the regime of Philip III had ended, strife to which Spain, as Defender of the Faith, could not be indifferent, strife which would eventually engulf most of Europe and leave her prostrate. The truce which Spain had made with Holland would end in 1621 and would, in the very first days of a new regime, have to be renewed or rejected; what is more, there were "hawkish" forces in both countries which were urging rejection — with the new war-front it implied. Yet Spain's national treasury was as bare as was Mother Hubbard's cupboard of nursery rhyme; worse still, her income from one source or another was pledged to foreign bankers for years to come. She could no longer count on the same immense quantities of bullion from the New World which had once helped her solve her fiscal problems: it came now in an ever-diminishing flow, and even that which was mined often did not reach Spain because of pirates from England. If it did, much of it had to be sent on its way to Holland or Milan, there to pay for the costly fripperies which elegantly dressed Spaniards thought indispensable.

Even Nature herself had been uncooperative: there had been a bad drought in 1616, and the Government had found it necessary to lower for one province after another the assessments for a

tax commonly known as "millones," at the very moment when
the national treasury was in desperate straits. The situation was
not improved by the lack of rains in 1617 and again in 1621-1623.
The African locusts had come to be a tremendous scourge and
continued to multiply — as did the official bureaucracy in Madrid,
and as did the poverty-stricken who flowed in from the starving
provinces and managed to live in the capital by hook or by crook.

With such conditions, attempts at change were inevitable, and
it was, ironically enough, one phase of the reform movement which
would, in its backlash, seek to banish Tirso from Madrid in 1625
and forbid him to write "comedias ni otro ningún género de versos profanos." As the very perceptive study of Professor Margaret
Wilson [7] has pointed out:

> Something clearly happened to the Spanish theatre in
> 1625... Whatever may be the full story behind the edict
> against Tirso, it seems fairly clear that 1625 was the
> year in which the views of the moralists finally prevailed
> to the extent that the *comedia* could henceforth only
> survive by coming to terms with them.

In her surmise, Professor Wilson is, I believe, eminently correct. At
least she is, in so far as her analysis of the spirit that motivated
the *Junta de Reformación* in its recommendations is concerned,
and in regard to the profound effects of their *acuerdo*. But the
weapons that body used against Tirso were forged by political
and literary forces of the moment that were far from being as
admirable as were those that moved the *Junta*.

Let us study first the spirit which animated 1617-1625, for if
we are to understand the zeal of that *Junta* we must move back
in time to the closing years of Philip III's regime. In the last years
of that gentle monarch's reign, the spirit of reform that characterized Spain's more thoughtful citizens was as intense as it was
deep. [8] This held for members of the *Cortes*, meeting from Feb-

---

[7] Margaret Wilson, *Spanish Drama of the Golden Age*, 149.

[8] I read many years ago those volumes of the *Actas de las Cortes de
Castilla* (XXX-XXXV) which covered the *Cortes* of 1617-1620 and took full
notes on them. Through force of circumstances, the *Cortes* of 1617-1620
accomplished little, but I should like to insist here—from my first-hand
knowledge of those tomes—on the deadly earnestness, the deep intensity

ruary 9, 1617 to the end of March, 1620; for those men of the Royal Committee, appointed by Philip III on June 6, 1618, which handed in its recommendations by February of 1619; for certain elements of the literary and clerical groups who wanted literature to take more seriously its slogan of "enseñar deleitando..."

These different groups naturally threw stress on different facets of reform. The Cortes' basic *raison d'être* was to take care of the Royal Treasury, and this inevitably implied that its members were interested in taxes and in all matters relating to their origin and collection. They were only too well acquainted with the government's reliance on borrowing and with the money-lenders who were always willing to let a spendthrift government have what it asked — at a price. They had had experience, too, with various fiscal devices, such as an adulterated coinage which, if it gave the government the quick money it was asking, could be counted on to bring inflation in its trail. And knowing such things, they fought, with bulldog tenacity, in the Cortes of both 1617 to 1620 and again in that short session of 1621, to keep the purse-strings in their hands. In the former Cortes, they were determined to check-mate a rapacious Lerma, minister and favorite to Philip III, but it was in vain. True, he was forced to retire on October 18, 1618, and even to don a cardinal's hat in an effort to save himself from physical harm; but the disloyal son, i.e., the Duque de Uceda, who helped bring about his father's fall, was a weakling, one in no way equal to the problems that faced the nation. These Cortes of 1617-1620 were, moreover,

---

of the drive that animated that body. Around 1945 I gave at Oxford University in England lectures which dealt at some length with the history of this reform movement and its reflections in Tirso's theatre. Here I have had necessarily to reduce the original study to the bare bones of history so that what emerges can be found in almost any history of Spain. See, for instance, R. Trevor Davies', *The Golden Century of Spain, 1501-1621*, in particular, 229-294.

The report of don Diego de Corral y Arellano's committee will be found in Sempere y Guarino's *Historia del lujo*, II, 115-116. Velázquez painted don Diego's portrait (Prado Museum, no. 1195). In the museum's catalogue (of 1952), he is characterized as follows: "jurisconsulto y juez íntegro; votó en contra de la sentencia de muerte de D. Rodrigo Calderón". Phrased in other terms, this means he was not under the domination of Olivares. See n. 21 of this same chapter for further analysis of his character.

twice forced to give ground in the matter of *vellón:* on September 23, 1617 they gave permission to the government to coin 18,000,000 *ducados* of *vellón* and again when Philip III lay dying, to issue another 800,000.

The Crown, faced with criticism from the Cortes, asked for a "general reform of customs:" "reformación de costumbres" became a set phrase, heard in every direction. What little is known of this reform movement is limited to the report of the Committee which was appointed on June 6, 1618 to study conditions of the realm, particularly "the causes of the depopulation of the provinces and the illness which this poor andy needy republic is suffering." Armed with royal authority, the Committee, under the direction of its fine chairman, don Diego de Corral y Arellano of the Royal Council, went to work with a will and by February of the following year, i.e., 1619, was ready with its well-known report. It was nothing, if not forthright! Warning Philip III that cities, kingdoms, and monarchies perish, as do men and all other things in this world, it made broad recommendations that called for nothing less than a national housecleaning of heroic proportions. At the same time it implied the existence of conditions that were anything but creditable to those responsible. The Committee granted that the stringent remedies it was suggesting would, at first sight, appear difficult and almost impossible, but the national illness was, in its opinion, so extremely grave that it could be cured by nothing less than severe measures. It was, they felt, a question of cutting off the arm to save the body, so great was the economic distress and so profound the political and social corruption which were destroying the republic. We can not here give, even in outline, the recommendations of that body. They were not of the nit-picking variety! Indeed, they were so all-encompassing as to make shiver a lethargic king past forty, who had hated the thought of any decisive action from the moment he had inherited the throne from Philip II in 1598. As a result of the report, he and his weakling minister, Uceda, took flight for Portugal.

From this point on until the end of the reign of Philip III, things were at a virtual standstill. This was even more true when the king, as he was returning from Lisbon to Madrid, fell

gravely ill in the little town of Casarrubios. For weeks a distress-
ed nation despaired of his recovery. Those who had been
deputized by the monarch to hold things together in his absence
were men of great probity, but they naturally felt their authority
limited. Partial sumptuary decrees were passed in October of
1619 and re-affirmed in March of 1620, [9] but they served only to
increase public enthusiasm for the things forbidden and to offer
pabulum for satire to the pens of the poets. In any attempt,
however, to gauge final results of the Committee's recommendations, it should be remembered that the famed reforms, initiated
by Philip IV in 1623, took as their point of departure the report
which had been prepared for his father in 1618-1619. One Fernández de Navarrete glossed it for the new regime that picked
up the reins of government on the night of March 31, 1621.

From night to morning, the political picture changed. Young
Philip, five days short of his sixteenth birthday, ascended the
throne, and with him the Count of Olivares, who — even before
Philip III's death — had promised his sovereign that he would
free the Royal Treasury from debt. Under the most favorable
circumstances it would have been a promise difficult to keep.
When the new *privado* immediately refused to renew the twelve-
year pact with Holland, [10] one that had brought peace with that
country since April 9, 1609, and, in refusing, helped bring on
the heavy costs of international conflict, it became a pledge that

---

[9] See my study, "Certain Phases of the Sumptuary Decrees of 1623
and their Relation to Tirso's Theatre", 91-92, n. 3.

[10] See Gregorio Marañón, *El Conde-Duque de Olivares*, 299. That excellent historian evaluated Spain's war with Holland in the following terms:
"... la guerra de Holanda, y el racimo de las que se le fueron enzarzando,
se debió a un brote de imperialismo territorial y religioso, animado por un
conductor delirante [i. e., Olivares], lleno, eso sí, de buena intención; y
secundado por el ambiente propicio del pueblo entero". Nevertheless, it
should be remembered that Baltasar de Zúñiga, uncle to Olivares and supposedly "el todo" at that moment in the government of Spain, had favored
the *renewal* of the twelve-year pact of peace with Holland. C. H. Carter
—in *The Secret Diplomacy of the Habsburgs. 1598-1625* (Chapters 19-21)—
makes evident that certain forces in Holland were quite as determined to
end the truce as was Olivares.
    Granting Gabriel Téllez's glorification of Philip III and the peace he had
given his kingdom, it is logical to assume that he would have held the same
point of view as Zúñiga.

no man could have kept. The country-side was in woeful condition,
partly as a result of absent landlords and thieving tax-collec-
tors, partly because of a series of droughts, in combination with
African locusts. Yet again, Olivares had inherited, along with his
role of favorite and minister, the responsibility of a young king
who wanted to play a role of princely munificence. Worse still,
the new *privado* was an "antipático" with a passion for power
that led him to trample underfoot any and all opposition which
came from the camp of those loyal to Philip III's memory. Some
of his opponents were merely despoiled of authority, others were
banished from Madrid; one — the luckless don Rodrigo Calderón, who had risen from page in Lerma's household to a position
of almost boundless authority but was languishing in prison when
Philip III died — had, on October 21, 1621, lost his head on the
scaffold. Such violent measures on the part of Olivares and his
new bureaucracy, coming as they did from the very forces which
had been so loud in their denunciation of his predecessor's avarice
and profligacy, divided Philip's subjects at the beginning of his
reign into warring camps: those favorable to the new regime and
those against it. Moreover, when Olivares accepted one *merced*
after another from his sixteen-year old king, the "outs" felt that
his attitude in condemning Calderón was inconsistent and hypocritical.

Yet again, in his attempts to free the Royal Treasury from
debt and to meet the ever-increasing costs of what would become
known to history as the Thirty Years War, he resorted in desperation to one unpopular measure after another. Hopefully, he
summoned new *Cortes* in early 1621 [11] to help him resolve the
fiscal problems of the new regime, but he found them even more
inflexible than had been the preceding ones in matters of taxation
and *vellón*. The outstanding figure in this new House of Deputies
was a man from Granada, named don Mateo de Lisón y Biedma. [12]
Having assumed the mantle of leadership given him by his
fellow members, he had ready by July 28th of that summer a

---

[11] See Vol. XXXVI of the *Actas de las Cortes de Castilla*, which covers
the meetings of the group from June 19, 1621 to November 19, 1621.

[12] I have given some idea of don Mateo's role in my study, "*La prudencia
en la mujer* and the Ambient that Brought it Forth," 1141-1147.

list of thirteen matters which, as he saw it, called for change, and
he begged that the Cortes appoint a committee which would present them to the king as a memorial. That body promptly followed
his suggestion and named one — with Lisón y Biedma as chairman.
In making their plea to the king, these representatives of the *Cortes* asked that he appoint a *Junta* of his own to confer with them
as to ways and means. The king duly named his *junta,* as
requested, but it was not destined to discuss matters with the
group from the Cortes. The king unexpectedly dissolved that
body on November 19, 1621, in order to go hunting! He was,
nevertheless not done with don Mateo de Lisón y Biedma. That
worthy stayed on in Madrid and put into print the memorial
which he had already given orally to his irresponsible young
monarch. To it he would later add a second and even a third
memorial, the last of which is a veritable *de regimine principum,*
an impassioned one in which he frankly states he was writing it
without much hope of making Philip understand the desperate
straits of his people. With these reports, we shall have occasion
to deal at some length when studying Tirso's politico-economic
plays. I must, as well, leave until that time all consideration of
the various measures used by Olivares in his attempts to get
money with which to wage an all-European war. The Cortes
were not summoned again until April 4, 1623. In this session,
there is no Lisón y Biedma from Córdoba. On the other hand, one
finds among the new deputies a Gaspar de Olivares from Madrid.

The *Junta* that Philip IV appointed had, at once, more and
less power than the one named by his father. This new one had
no authority to deal with political or economic problems, as
had that of don Diego de Corral y Arellano. Its royal orders, dated
May 1, 1621, were: "reformación, no sólo en esta corte, sino
en estos mis reinos, en materia de vicios, abusos y cohechos." [13]
The President of the Council of Castile, don Francisco de Contreras, was its chairman. He was undoubtedly a distinguished man,
as were its other members, but they were a stern group, made up,
for the most part, of churchmen, who would take most seriously
the duties assigned them. What is more, they were, as we shall

---

[13] See Ángel González Palencia, "Quevedo, Tirso y las comedias ante
la Junta de Reformación", 43.

see, very closely in touch with Olivares, the man who necessarily approved their appointment. Their first task was to get ready the *capítulos de reformación*. These were proclaimed by the town crier on February 11, 1623 and appeared in print on February 14. These decrees had not only been heralded by some five years of agitation, but, before reaching final form, they had been preceded by more than three months of discussion, during which time the government strove to sound out public opinion and to make such modifications as it might deem advisable. In a letter dated November 16, 1622, Almansa y Mendoza [14] outlines the provisions as they were at the moment contemplated, then adds that the king had ordered that "copies be sent to many gentlemen (i.e., of the court) and to each city ... in order that their aldermen and other persons of wisdom and conscience should make such recommendations as they might see fit."

As these decrees finally came off the press, they included twenty-two provisions, [15] no one of which dealt with what the Cortes had considered the basic problem, i.e., taxation. Eight of the provisions sought to curb various luxuries in dress; a ninth was intended to prevent importation of manufactured goods; yet another was calculated to close the brothels of the realm. Various others strove to alleviate the state of the over-crowded cities and at the same time to solve the reverse problem of the depopulated provinces. For instance, it was forbidden that anyone should abandon the kingdom without permission of the king or that anyone should leave his holdings to take up residence at court or in the crowded cities of Sevilla or Granada. To improve the agricultural situation, all absentee landlords were ordered to return to their estates, etc.

Fate itself now intervened to make virtually null and void many of the provisions. It was a Fate wearing the garb of an English prince, who, accompanied only by his friend, "Steenie" (the Duke of Buckingham), had come to woo Spain's princess in a fashion as extravagantly romantic as that of the most idealistic

---

[14] Andrés de Almansa y Mendoza, *Cartas*, 145-147.
[15] The *BAE* (XXV) has "la gran consulta", and with it, Fernández de Navarrete's "Conservación de monarquías y discursos políticos ...", first printed in Barcelona (Sebastián de Cormellas, 1621) as *Discursos políticos*.

lover of a cape and sword play. Such an occasion demanded a show of splendor: how impress their English visitors with the opulence, the generosity, the might of Spain when the court had gone in for Quaker-like simplicity? Impossible! And so by March 22, the town crier was again called into action, this time to tell the people that certain of the new laws concerning dress were suspended until after the departure of their royal wooer — this, to the great joy, no doubt, of the effeminate gallants of the day, but to the dismay certainly of those sterner souls, who, like Lisón y Biedma, dreamed of turning Spain back from her paths of self-indulgence.

The Prince of Wales, with his "Steenie," had hardly crossed the Segovian bridge which led out of the Castilian capital when there was a new pronouncement from the town crier which stated that the suspension, granted as a token of the delight which the nation felt over the visit of Prince Charles, was now over and that the sumptuary decrees, proclaimed on February 11 were once more in force. [16] So little resonance did this new pronouncement occasion that Almansa y Mendoza's letter, covering "events of this court from August 15 to the end of October," does not even mention it; nor does it appear, in so far as I know, in any history, contemporary or modern. The last gasp of this particular reform movement has been recorded in León Pinelo's *Historia:* [17] there we learn that on February 8, 1625, the people were given one more year in which to use up such clothes as had been prohibited by the decrees of February 11, 1623.

It was in this same year of 1625, on March 6, [18] that the *Junta de Reformación del Consejo de Castilla,* i.e., the Council of which we have heard so much, recommended that Tirso be banished from Madrid because he was writing plays "of evil incentive and example" and that he be forbidden henceforth

---

[16] There is, in the *Varios* of the Biblioteca de Sevilla, a "Ley o pregón sobre trages o adornos en 15 de Septiembre de 1623", one which suggests this, though I have found no record of the *pregón* being given in Madrid. See no. 1284 in Francisco Escudero y Perosso's *Tipografía hispalense,* 376.

[17] Antonio de León Pinelo, *Historia de Madrid* (ms.), under date of February 8, 1625, according to *BAE,* XIV, 668a.

[18] See Ángel González Palencia, "Quevedo, Tirso y las comedias ante la Junta de Reformación", 83-84, also 77-78.

to write "comedias or any other kind of profane verses." That
Junta, its work on the sumptuary decrees ended, had, in fact,
turned its attention to the reform of the theatre (and all those
connected with it) as early as March 24, 1624. On that date, its
members concerned themselves with the religious who were attending the presentation of plays in the public *corrales.* Tirso
was, probably, one of the guilty, though his name was not
mentioned at that time. [19]

The Committee appointed by Philip III, i.e., the one headed
by Diego de Corral y Arellano, had been broader-minded, more
tolerant in such matters than was this one named by Olivares:
it had not raised, directly or indirectly, the question of the
theatre. The truth is that the earlier body was more concerned
with the sins of those who were governing than it was with
those of the people. Olivares' directions to his committee, as
we have seen, did not encourage investigation of the government:
its purpose was to reform the morals of the *people;* and members
of that *Junta* interpreted their task, no doubt, in terms of the
stern ideals of Philip II, ideals which, at the beginning of the new
regime, took hold in official circles and became a concrete slogan
for those forces which took the helm at Philip's III's death on
March 31, 1621. Just what that ideal was was spelled out by
Quevedo in his *Grandes anales de quince días:* [20] "Those who
serve today promise us … that they will return to Philip II's
principles of government, adjusting their procedure to his norms."
They presumably took as their text-book Cabrera de Córdoba's
life of that king, [21] published in 1619, which was, in that stern

----

[19] I am assuming this, partly because it seems likely from Tirso's *El
Caballero de Gracia* (I, v) that he and another dramatist (probably Lope)
had attended the *ensayo* of a *comedia* together: "… me dijo, viendo el ensayo de una *comedia* famosa…". Moreover, the assumption is in keeping
both with Tirso's love of the *comedia* (for him, "princesa de las artes libe-
rales") and with his very independent spirit.

[20] *Anales de quince días, BAE,* XXIII, 193-220.

[21] In asking the *Cortes* for money to publish his *Historia de Felipe II*
(Madrid, 1619), Cabrera stated: "Presento a V. S. la historia del Señor Rey
de España, don Felipe II, asunto grande, *verdadera regla para saber reinar."*
He entitles him "el perfecto" and compares his talents as king with those
of all the famous monarchs of history, Biblical and profane. When dedicating
it to the future Philip IV, he says: "Haga imitador a V. A. el ejemplo de
quien sangre y obligaciones tiene para que sucediendo en ellas, nos le

historian's own prologue, proclaimed a "mirror for princes." This same Cabrera de Córdoba was now one of the influential members of the *Junta* appointed by Olivares. Such — in skeleton-outline — were the attempts at reform, made by the Cortes and the Royal Council, in the years 1617 to 1625.

Let us now turn our attention to those who were interested specifically in reforming the Lopean *comedia*, for if officialdom in Philip III's time was not seriously concerned with the theatre and its effects on the morals of the young, there were undoubtedly those in the literary world of 1617-1620 who were interested in just that! They consisted of two different groups: the "Catones" (usually *clerics*), as Tirso dubbed them, and the Aristotelians whom Lope de Vega normally satirizes as the *críticos*. The Aristotelians would go into action the same year as did the Cortes, 1617, but it would not be until three years later that the clerics would find a powerful spokesman. In early 1620, while the

---

represente cual desea y espera su imperio". He makes clear that his ideal king was a prince at once "temido y amado". Tirso will, in his portrait of Primislao II, found in his *La ventura con el nombre* (I, vi), give his model king in which he interprets the tag of Cabrera de Córdoba as "temido al tiempo que amable, / amoroso con los suyos, / con extraños formidable...".

Matías de Novoa in his *Memorias*, states (373): "Don Alonso de Cabrera [era] hombre sin ningún género de humanidad y misericordia en sus acciones...". Elsewhere (*Ibid.*, 341), he calls him "hombre duro de condición". These characterizations should be contrasted with the one Novoa gives of don Diego de Corral y Arellano, who refused to be "led" in the matter of don Rodrigo Calderón's death. Novoa wrote of Corral's role on that occasion (372): "no venía en ella, ni la firmaba, ni lo haría por ningún caso y que éste era su parecer. Pues no era esto por falta de letras, virtud y buena intención y rectitud. Pocos hombres había mejores que éste en el Consejo. ¿Pocos, dije? Ninguno ni que se le igualasen en el caudal de buenos estudios y estimación que hacía dél aquel senado y la que hizo el piadoso y católico rey, don Felipe III (que goza de Dios) cuando recibió de su talento aquella consulta... Esta determinación de D. Diego del Corral hizo notable ruido en la corte y en las orejas de los poderosos, y desengañó a muchos...".

Novoa indicates that *first* Contreras (who early became "Presidente del Consejo de Castilla" under Philip IV and headed up the *Junta de Reformación*) and *then* Luis de Salcedo (also a member) changed their votes in Calderón's trial under pressure, presumably of Olivares. So the *Junta* which condemned Tirso to "banishment" had on it the stern Cabrera de Córdoba and two of the same men who had sentenced Calderón to execution. And behind all three stood the inflexible Olivares.

Cortes were still in session and the people were expecting new sumptuary decrees, there was a clear-cut effort on the part of some of the clerics to close the theatres or, if that were impractical (as they feared), to bring them under close supervision. It is evident that they were seeking to have incorporated in the expected decrees provisions against the *comedia* as well as against those priests who were writing plays and against such of them as were attending theatrical performances. I had occasion to study the aims of this group, [22] so admirably summed up in the anonymous *Diálogos de las comedias,* in an article of 1966, one which sought to make clear that the *Junta de Reformación,* appointed by Philip IV, was merely taking up where these earlier forces had left off. The *Junta's* members were, in purpose at least, spiritual successors to those men of 1620 who, forced by circumstances over which they had no control, had had, at the moment, to lay aside their efforts. The *Diálogos* were undoubtedly aimed at Lope, "*lobo* carnicero de las almas, tan celebrado de los críticos," but when the fight was enjoined against the theatres in 1624-1625, it was Tirso, his loyal disciple, who was chosen for the sacrifice. Lope had not attacked the new administration; Tirso was, on the other hand, an openly avowed enemy to it. Lope had been careful to cultivate not only the good will of Olivares and his family, but that of the poets near him and near the king. Tirso had told all the world that *he* was climbing for the laurel wreath of fame; what is more, he indicated that, willy-nilly, in spite of Envy's efforts, he expected to get it.

Those years of 1617 to 1625 were, it seems to me, far more important for Spanish literature than has yet been realized. They were years so favorable to the exemplary short story which Cervantes had sired by 1613 that this genre began to flourish like the proverbial bay tree around the year 1620. [23] They were years

---

[22] See my "Attacks on Lope and his Theatre in 1617-1621", 57-76.

[23] The years 1620-1625 produced the following volumes of short stories: Diego de Agreda y Vargas, *Novelas morales* (1620); Juan Cortés de Tolosa, *Lazarillo de Manzanares, con otras cinco novelas* (1620); Antonio Liñán y Verdugo, *Guía y avisos de forasteros* (1620); Alonso Gerónimo de Salas Barbadillo, *Casa de placer honesto* (1620); Lope Félix de Vega Carpio, *Las fortunas de Diana,* included with *La Filomela* (1621); Francisco de Lugo y Dávila, *Teatro popular: novelas morales* (1622); Gonzalo de Céspedes y Meneses, *Historias peregrinas y ejemplares* (1623); José Camerino, *Novelas*

in which the agitation for change threw into clear, sharp relief the political decay, the economic disorder, and the social corruption that were rotting the national fabric and thus gave inexhaustible material to corrosive pens like Quevedo's, Góngora's, or Villamediana's. For us it is particularly important that they were years that to many seemed to cry aloud for a more serious theatre than was offered by the Lopean formula of love, honor, and intrigue — one that should perform the corrective function that had, at least in theory, been allotted that genre since the days of Aristotle and Horace. It should be noted, too, that this demand came in days so inherently dramatic, by virtue of the very political events that were taking place [24] (events that were themselves closely related to the reform movement), that they offered the basic stuff from which classical drama had ever been fashioned.

There was yet another factor which cannot be disregarded, if we are to get an accurate picture of the literary world at this time. One must not forget that between 1616 and 1621 the greatest talents of Spain were being drawn to Madrid as though by a magnet, some of them after long years abroad. There they

---

amorosas (1624); Juan Pérez de Montalván, Sucesos y prodigios de amor en ocho novelas ejemplares (1624); Juan de Piña, Novelas ejemplares y prodigiosas historias (1624); Matías de los Reyes, El curial del Parnaso (1624); Gabriel Téllez, Los cigarrales de Toledo (1624); Lope Félix de Vega Carpio, La Circe, con otras rimas y prosas [i. e., three novelas] (1624); Alonso de Castillo Solórzano, Tardes entretenidas (1625); Baltasar Mateo Velázquez, El filósofo del aldea (1625).

Virtually all of these came out in Madrid, and many of them include in their descriptions the word "exemplares", "morales", etc.

[24] Madrid's citizens, in October of 1621, were eye-witnesses to the violent revolutions of tragedy's wheel of fortune. The death of Rodrigo Calderón on the scaffold, which represented to many the terrible example of Fortune's fickle ways, had within it the very essence of classic tragedy and the wheel of fortune that symbolized her rapid changes. His fate represented a clear-cut turning-point for many (among others, for Tirso) in their attitude toward Olivares. G. Marañón (El Conde-Duque de Olivares, 50), having commented on Calderón's death and "sus fechorías, no mayores, por cierto, que las de cualquier otro de sus contemporáneos de la corte española", then adds: "Fenómeno muy propio de la psicología popular española fue el viraje sentimental de aquel pueblo, que pidió a gritos la cabeza del ministro durante tanto tiempo y que, de repente, al ver su gesto magnífico ante el cadalso de la Plaza Mayor de Madrid, lo trocó en su ídolo... acusando de verdugo cruel al nuevo Valido." I am sure that Tirso, even before Calderón's death, would have voted with Diego de Corral against Calderón's execution.

formed a galaxy so brilliant that it dazzles even at this distance
in time. To a constellation which had been gradually growing in
sparkle ever since the court had been brought back from Valladolid in 1606 — one which already included such literary lights
as Lope de Vega Carpio, Vélez de Guevara, Ruiz de Alarcón,
Suárez de Figueroa, and Salas Barbadillo — there were, in this
brief span of six years, suddenly added seven other stars, some
of them of first magnitude. Mira de Amescua appeared in 1616;
Góngora and the Conde de Villamediana in 1617; Quevedo in
1618; Guillén de Castro was there by early 1619; Tirso, by
early 1621. The last to arrive was probably the Prince of Esquilache in 1621.

This poet had not been back from Peru a year when Lope
complained, in the dedication to his play, *La pobreza estimada*, [25]
that Madrid's poets were now divided into bands like the
Guelphs and the Ghibellines. But this was really no new state
of affairs; the atmosphere in Madrid's literary circles had been
stormy for at least five years when this complaint was made. At
the very center of the various winds that raged stood an aging
Lope who was fending off attacks from various directions — at
the same time that he was dealing blows which belied his nearly
sixty years. In one direction he, as a *llano*, was tilting with Góngora, a Góngora who, in syntax, lexicon, and figures of speech,
was asking for a poetry aimed at the elite, not at the *vulgo*; in
another, he was waging a fight (for the most part along personal
lines) with the Mexican "Terence," Ruiz de Alarcón; in yet a
third, he was warring with the Aristotelians who were condemning
his ideas on dramatic purpose, at the same time they were
demanding a theatre which observed classical precepts of form;
in a fourth he was having to meet the indictment of certain
elements of the reform movement who had long seen in the Lopean
comedia a menace to public morals. When history ushered in the
new reign of Philip IV and Olivares, there would be added to
Lope's enemies a fifth group — and to Tirso's even a sixth one.

---

[25] Printed in the *Decimaoctava parte de las comedias de Lope de Vega
Carpio*. The book's *aprobación* by Espinel is dated June 22, 1622, though
it did not actually come off the press until early 1623.

We cannot, in this volume, take up Tirso's role in Lope's struggles with Góngora. Neither can we, at this point, deal with his part in Lope's fight with the Aristotelians — a not inconsiderable one, as we shall show on another occasion — even though we shall presently have to make clear that for this study the Aristotelians cannot, in the years 1617-1625 at least, be separated in their chief aim from the group that Tirso dubs the severe "Catones." With the history of Tirso's relations to Lope and to Ruiz de Alarcón, we shall, in the chapters that follow, be concerned, and even more with the court groups who, with the favor of the new regime, assumed an importance out of proportion to their literary worth.

Before taking up these new literary circles that would take on lustre with the rise to power of Philip and Olivares, we must show the relationship that existed between the Aristotelians and the "Catones" in 1617-1625. In insisting on this bond, I am aware that Menéndez y Pelayo, having sketched the conflict that arose between Aristotelian concepts of drama and the practices of Lope and his school, rigorously dismissed all discussion of related ethical problems. He wrote in his *Ideas estéticas*,[26] first published in 1886:

> Nada he dicho en esta obra de los escritores que en pro o en contra discurrieron sobre la licitud de las representaciones dramáticas y sobre su valor ético... En rigor, esta cuestión no pertenece a la Estética... sino a la ciencia de las costumbres, a la Ética. Lo contrario sería involucrar dos criterios distintos, haciendo que el uno y el otro padeciesen y se' maleasen de resultas de la mezcla.

That clerics, in general, had a focus on the drama different from that of the Aristotelians is, of course, true.

Yet from the very first there had been a connection between the Aristotelians and ethical reform. As Américo Castro [27] had occasion to observe in his work on Cervantes' thought (pp. 28-29),

---

[26] Menéndez y Pelayo, *Historia de las ideas estéticas*, II, 323-24, n. 2. The pages dealing with López Pinciano and his *Philosophía antigua poética* cover 327-351.

[27] Américo Castro, *El pensamiento de Cervantes*, 28-29.

> el Renacimiento propiamente dicho (fines del siglo xv y
> primera parte del xvi) no tiene en cuenta la *Poética* de
> Aristóteles ... Pero ... hacia 1550... Aristóteles se tor-
> na casi un doctor de la Iglesia, y la literatura, infiltrada
> del espíritu de la Contrarreforma, tendrá que armonizar-
> se con finalidades éticas y racionales. En 1548 surge con
> Robortelli la primera edición crítica de la *Poética* de
> Arisóteles y de esa suerte el preceptismo neoclásico apa-
> rece como un fenómeno en conexión con Trento, al in-
> tentar restablecer la síntesis medieval mediante la unión
> del arte con la vida y por tanto con la moral.

Castro points out further that one Italian preceptor after another
followed Robortelli: Maggi published his *Poetics* in 1550, Varchi
his *Lessons on Poetry* in 1553, and Scaliger his *Poetics* in 1561.
[There were yet others that dealt with Aristotelian poetics, as
Spingarn pointed out some decades ago.]

Américo Castro does not, either for Italy or Spain, pursue this
relationship between the Aristotelians and the reform spirit, but
that it continued to exist, at least in Spain, is indicated when one
makes a comparison of the didactic literature of that country
directed against the theatre with the recurring attempts to bring
economic, social, and moral reform that characterized the early
decades of the seventeenth century. There was, it seems to me,
during the last years of Philip II's reign, and throughout
Philip III's, almost perfect synchronization of the two movements.
With a break of only 19 days in 1598, the House of Deputies was
in continuous session from May 3, 1592 to February 28, 1601;
from January 7, 1602 to June 30, 1604; from April 6, 1607 to
February 2, 1611; and from February 4, 1617 to March 28, 1620.
It also met for a few fleeting months in the winter and spring of
1611-12 and again for a brief stretch in 1615. Except for two
short periods when the Cortes were dissolved before the reform
spirit could get well under way, the pattern would seem to have
followed the same design: an empty national treasury; the
summons of new Cortes to find the wherewithal for a wasteful
and rapidly expanding bureaucracy; a fight on the part of the
members of that body to cede such funds only in exchange for
fiscal and economic reform; an attendant struggle for social and
moral betterment that culminated in sumptuary decrees, calculated

to check the frivolous trend of the times. Normally, the question of the theatre's influence was raised; normally, too, there were accusations and apologies from both clericals and seculars; normally, the Aristotelians [28] came forward with their plea for a drama that conformed to classic precepts.

We can not trace here, even in outline, the various skirmishes between Lope and the Aristotelians that prefaced the battle of 1617-1621. The reader must, however, if he is to comprehend the turn of events, know something of the issues at stake. The struggle first became acute in Spain around 1596 when López Pinciano published his *Philosophia antigua poética.* [29] Therein he challenged the dramatic formula of Lope — without ever mentioning the latter's name — with a book that is nothing less than a complete philosophic presentation of classic tenets. It should be noted in passing that it came out while the Cortes were in session and that just a year later the theatres were closed temporarily, following deaths in the royal family. In the following year, as a result of the pleas of the clergy, it was announced that they were to be closed permanently. Significantly, Lupercio Leonardo de Argensola, a classicist who "was angered at any frivolous or trivial use of poetry" and could conceive of it — to quote Menéndez Pelayo — "only as a Celtiberian matron armed with iron, the moral law on her lips," joined the clerical forces in their condemnation of "amorous comedies," as well as in their attempts to keep the public theatres closed.

López Pinciano, having first accepted for all imaginative literature the Aristotelian principles of *imitation* and *verisimilitude,* straightway goes on to declare that the arts were invented "to give both delight and doctrine." Tragedy, he defines in true Aristotelian terms as "the imitation in suave language of an action that is grave, perfect and of suitable grandeur, one made to cleanse the soul of its passions, not through narration, but rather through pity and fear." As for comedy — while this preceptor himself preferred to think of this genre as "a portraiture of the

---

[28] See Lily B. Campbell's *Shakspere's Tragic Heroes,* which gives in the first chapter an outline of English writers who stressed the moral purpose of tragedy. She quotes Seneca as well and on various occasions.

[29] Menéndez y Pelayo, *Historia de las ideas estéticas,* II, 223.

ridiculous which rests on ugliness and stupidity" — he concedes
that others prefer to define it either "as a story which, by showing forth the passions, makes manifest what is useful and what
harmful to human life" or as "an imitation for representation, so
fashioned as to purge the soul of its passions through joy and
laughter." As the struggle between the Aristotelians and the Lopean theatre became accentuated, the very serious among the
classically-minded were naturally more and more inclined to such
definitions as stressed its ethical purpose and would accordingly
find themselves marching shoulder to shoulder with the clerical
forces.

This latter group, taken as a whole, could have cared little
for the aesthetics of the Aristotelian preceptors, aesthetics which
were concerned primarily with the oft-used word "imitation." For
although the relationship may not at first glance be clear to a
modern, the crux of the whole question, whether the stress was
on the ethic or the aesthetic, came to lie in the much battered
word *imitation*. What was "true imitation" — for poetry? Had one
the right to demand of the poet the fidelity to fact that was
demanded of the historian, that is, a verisimilitude of detail that
today would be termed a photographic reproduction of the individual case? Or should he strive rather for a composite picture of
truth which represented an idealization of a more general reality?
López Pinciano interpreted Aristotle as insisting on this *universal*
realism which could reach to the soul of things, not on a pedestrian
accuracy of detail to the individual case — in which beauty,
harmony, and even real truth might well be lost. By way of
support, López Pinciano, the Aristotelian, could quote Aristotle's
statement: "It is not the office of the poet to tell things as they
actually happened, but as they *ought* to have happened, or as
should be credible." Imitation, then, consisted not in telling the
particular truth of what occurred on a given occasion but rather
in so fashioning and blending the various elements of one's story
that the whole might *seem* truthful and reasonable. Indeed, in
the doctrine of Aristotle, according to Pinciano's interpretation of
it (339), "the poet must put aside the possible, if it be not credible,
and follow the credible, though it be impossible." And precisely
because the poet was seeking a harmonious, ideal truth that was

universal rather than an adherence to objective fact — such as we expect of the historian, no matter how incongruous or even immoral might be the result — poetry was, in the opinion of the philosopher, superior to history. Given such conclusions, it naturally followed that one should concede the poet some freedom in his use of historical material. History, according to López Pinciano, was but the warp of the cloth that the poet was weaving; the woof was imitation, but an imitation which would permit him to weave his whole so as to conform with this idealized reality.

The struggle thus initiated between the historian and the poet was fought out bitterly in both Italy and Spain. It was a conflict, as Américo Castro pointed out, [30] which did not acquire importance in Italy until after the Counter Reformation set in — and, with it, the interest in Aristotelian precepts of literature. Henceforth, he added, "the moralists censured the purely imaginative literature of autonomous art." A *true* literature was needed, one that was at the same time exemplary — and they took as their point of departure the statement from Aristotle that we have already quoted: i.e., that "it is not the office of the poet to relate things as they actually happened, but as they *ought to have happened* or as should be probable."

The conflict, as is evident then, rested on two different ideas as to imitation, two different approaches to poetic truth. As social decay more and more preoccupied the austere of soul, as one reform movement followed another in Philip III's reign, as the tensions became ever greater, tensions that would end in the Thirty Years War, stress on the didactic naturally increased, and that Aristotelian "ought" became more and more a moral imperative — particularly for theatrical art.

For it was drama which caught the brunt of the storm, and naturally enough because of its very hold on the minds of the people. Here was one point on which every Spaniard could agree, no matter in which camp he might be found: the historian, the imaginative poet, the stern cleric, all alike conceded the bewitching power of the drama as a literary form and its tremendous potentiality for good or evil. There was nothing inherently wrong with dramatic representation, as all parties would have agreed.

---

[30] Américo Castro, *El pensamiento de Cervantes*, 29.

All would readily have granted Aristotle's claims that "imitation is natural to man from childhood," that "it is also natural for all to delight in works of imitation." Few would have quibbled with Horace's statement: "Less vividly is the mind stirred by what finds entrance through the ears than by what is brought before the trusty eyes." No one would have had any quarrel with Cicero's oft-quoted definition of the comedy as "an imitation of life, a mirror of customs, an image of truth," provided the poet kept in mind Horace's injunction "to join profit with delight." All would have agreed enthusiastically with Euripides' " answer to Aeschylus in the *Frogs*. [31] Asked "on what ground a poet should claim admiration," Aristophanes made Euripides answer: "if his art is true and his counsel sound, and if he brings help to the nation by making men better in some respect."

But here was the rub, in seventeenth century Spain, as in the Greece of Aristophanes' time. Just as Aeschylus straightway called into question Euripides' claim to admiration on any such score, implying that this dramatist had "upon good and strong men the effect of making them weaker and worse," so the more serious Spaniards, at least, questioned the effect of the Lopean comedy on public behavior. What is more, like Dionysius who had overheard the tilt, some of them would have been quite willing to condemn to figurative galleys any dramatist who failed to keep in mind his social responsibility. To Sir Philip Sydney's attitude [32] that the poet is "the right popular philosopher" who entices men to do well by showing forth the ills of the social body, their instant reply would have been that *should* be his role — but was the Lopean comedy fulfilling its mission? They thought not.

A tragedy which portrayed the awful fate overtaking those of high estate who conquered not such passions as overweening ambition, lust, hatred, etc., would have received instant approval from both cleric and Aristotelian critic. The Jesuits, in their many schools scattered throughout Europe, had for decades stressed the importance of the stage in their struggle against evil, had even laid unusual emphasis on stagecraft precisely because of their

---

[31] Aristophanes, *The Frogs*, translated by Gilbert Murray, ed. 1925, p. 74.
[32] For an analysis of Sir Philip Sydney's *An Apologie for Poetrie* (1595, but written c. 1583), see Lily B. Campbell, *Shakspere's Tragic Heroes*, 28-31.

recognition of the power of vision in connection with the spoken word. Even a comedy which held up for gentle raillery and fitting punishment such foibles of the lower social classes as envy, vanity, gluttony, etc., would probably have met little, if any protest; a general satire, like the *vetus comoedia* of ancient Greece, [33] which presented for scorn and contempt the shortcomings of either social class — for instance, one such as Ben Jonson had tried out in England when the Archbishop of Canterbury in 1599 issued his famous restraining order against the satires of the time — would no doubt, have been met with real welcome.

For teaching by *exempla* was a time-honored method which had behind it all the weight of classic and medieval tradition. It was one still recognized by many in the 1620's. One reads, for instance, in *Alonso, mozo de muchos amos*, [34] a picaresque novel by the physician, J. de Alcalá Yáñez y Ribera, a curious passage in which the author makes crystal clear his point of view as to what constituted a moral literature at that time. When the Vicar demands a theatre that is "exemplary" and "decent," Alonso makes answer:

> Está ya, padre, tan depravada la naturaleza y condición de los hombres que ... en no siendo la representación de fabulosas, mentirosas, amorosas, enredos [sic], invenciones y casos que admiren los ingenios y entendimientos de los oyentes, no dan gusto ni hay quien las vea ... En otros tiempos [las comedias] eran la sal de la república, el espejo de la vida, la entrada y lección de los ignorantes, y el desengaño y luz de los que poco sabían. Víase en ellas un mozo libre, vicioso y perdido, sin respetar a

---

[33] For the *vetus comoedia*, see O. J. Campbell, *Comicall Satyre* (3-8) and Mariana, *Juegos públicos* (420-421). According to the former, the "antigua comedia" of Athens would seem to have been, in so far as intention was concerned, similar to the satires of the Spanish academies around 1625. He quotes Cordatus as saying: "that which we call *comoedia* was at first nothing but a simple and continued satyre, sung only by one person." Satires of the *Academy of Madrid* were, of course, read, not sung.

[34] Called also *El donado hablador*. See *BAE*, XVIII. Tirso wrote a *décima* for Jerónimo de Alcalá Yáñez y Ribera's *Verdades para la vida cristiana, recopiladas de los santos y graves autores*, Valladolid, 1632. Doctor Alcalá referred to Tirso as "Difinidor general de la Orden de Nuestra Señora de la Merced y Lector en Teología" in the heading of his *Milagros de Nuestra Señora de la Fuencisla*.

padres, ciego tras sus locos devaneos, en breves años sin
hacienda y salud, puesto en un hospital; la dama feste-
jada del vulgo, servida de todos, enamorada de su hermosura y mocedad, como otro Narciso, en la flor y verdor
de sus años, desengañada de tiempos ... olvidada ya de
los que más celebraron sus dichos, estimaron sus des-
víos y desdenes, y, como sin seso, adoraron sus favo-
res. Hallábase en ellas un criado mentiroso, un despen-
sero ladrón, con más bolsas que Judás, un amigo fingido,
un gracioso desvergonzado, adulador y descubridor de
faltas agenas y que no se sabían; un hablador maldiciente, mentiroso; una fingida hipócrita llorona; una
casada descuidada de sus hijas, y un padre sin cuidado
de criar bien y refrenar la libertad de sus hijos; un
gobernador que se descuidaba del ... buen gobierno de
su república; y una criada destruidora del honor y hacienda de sus amos. Estas eran las comedias antiguas y
representaciones ejemplares, libros que enseñaban a bien
vivir y en cada palabra decían una sentencia, con que
satisfecho el entendimiento, viendo a la vista ya el premio, ya el castigo, seguía el uno por evitar el otro.

To such a conception of comedy, the vicar takes no exception.
Nor would the Aristotelians have done so. Indeed, as the quotation
from *Alonso, mozo de muchos amos* makes evident, the same
thing may be said for dramatic theory in Spain that Professor
Lily B. Campbell [35] said of it in England:

> The theory of the drama in England during the Renais-
> sance was largely the result of the engrafting of the
> rediscovered classical doctrine of imitation upon ... [a]
> tradition, continued from the Middle Ages, of teaching
> by *exempla*.

Both the Aristotelians and the clerics were quite as concerned
over what they considered the frivolous nature of Lope's art, its
lack of true realism, its dearth of decorum in character, the
absence of a sententious, doctrinal tone, as they were with its
failure to comply with classical canons of form. Churchman and
Aristotelian alike wanted a stage that would take more seriously
its duty as social policeman. Only the more rabid of the clerics

---

[35] Lily B. Campbell, *Shakspere's Tragic Heroes*, 25.

would have rejected the idea that pleasure and profit should go hand in hand: *Deleytar aprovechando* ("to delight while profiting"), *enseñar deleytando* ("to teach while delighting"): such were the oft-repeated tags that summed up what they both granted to be the double purpose of literature. But in periods when the reform spirit was running high, both groups felt the *lopistas* were *de manga muy ancha* in interpreting such tags.

They were particularly indignant in 1617-1621 when the Cortes made clear just *how* badly things were going in Spain. The attack of the Aristotelians was initiated by Suárez de Figueroa, a bald-headed, full-faced doctor of jurisprudence, stern of soul and venomous of pen, who had come to Madrid from Valladolid. Once in the capital, he formed a friendship with one Torres Rámila (a tailor's son of pompous manner and frog-like appearance, if we may believe his enemies), who had studied grammar, arts, and theology at Alcalá de Henares. Between the two of them, they managed to loose one of the greatest literary fights in Spanish history. It is one which Professor Entrambasaguas [36] studied some years ago with a richness of documentation, a thoroughness that leaves no need for further study in such areas as his work covered. But in *Una guerra literaria del Siglo de Oro,* that scholar's primary concern was the *Spongia* (the work of Suárez de Figueroa and Torres Rámila) and the furious answers it elicited from Lope and his followers. Since that Latin work had been concerned primarily with Lope's sins as an epic writer, and not as a writer of *comedias,* Sr. Entrambasaguas' study naturally did not go into the attacks on Lope's theatre, except tangentially.

Yet the attack had, from the first, been two-pronged; and if the *Spongia* had not attacked his *comedia,* it was because Suárez de Figueroa had, in *El pasajero* [37] (1617), made clear his contempt for the formula of Lope's *capa y espada* play. Lope's friends would go into action immediately. The *Expostulatio Spongiae,* in fact, closes with countless panegyrics to the Master, some of which had been printed before, some of which had not.

---

[36] Entrambasaguas, "Una guerra literaria del Siglo de Oro", found in *Estudios sobre Lope de Vega,* I and II.

[37] *El pasajero,* 123-138.

Only one of these, that of Alonso Sánchez de Moratalla, professor of Greek at Alcalá, deals with his theatre. It is a chant of glory to Lope as the creator of a new school, the Monarch of the Spanish Theatre, who as such has the right to set his own laws. In the fervor of his enthusiasm, he cries out: [38]

> Tenemos arte, tenemos preceptos que nos obligan, y el precepto principal es imitar a la naturaleza, porque las obras de los poetas expresan la naturaleza, las costumbres y el ingenio del siglo en que se escribieron. Sólo por su modestia no quiere arrogarse Lope el título de creador de un arte nuevo, aunque haya podido formular preceptos con la misma autoridad que Horacio ... Pero a ti, gran Lope, ¿qué te importa la comedia antigua, puesto que tú solo has dado a nuestro siglo mejores comedias que todas las de Menandro y Aristófanes? Conserven ellos su gloria; a ti te la dan inmortal los siglos presentes y te la darán los futuros ... Tu pueblo te ha dado el cetro y reinas con pleno derecho y soberanía sobre los poetas ... Al monarca pertenece dar leyes y no recibirlas.

Even more substantial, if less dithyrambic support, came to Lope from another direction. In the next year of 1618, one Francisco de la Barreda [39] finished what is a truly remarkable apology of the Lopean comedy, though he did not publish it until 1622 as part of his commentaries to the translation he makes of Pliny's panegyric to Trajan. In the drama, la Barreda sees a genre which is "poetry's perfect sphere, since therein are inscribed all other forms of poetry." It is, he agrees, a genre which has a moral pur-

---

[38] Alfonso Sánchez de Moratalla's defense is found in the "Appendix ad Expostulationem Spongiae". Menéndez y Pelayo, *Historia de las ideas estéticas* (II, 306-07), analyses it in some detail. I have used the summary found in Menéndez y Pelayo's *Historia...*

[39] Francisco de la Barreda, *El panegírico de Plinio*. Its *princeps* came out in Madrid, 1622, but it would seem to have been written in 1618. In *Discurso IX* (starting p. 249 of that edition) he begins his "Invectiva a las comedias que prohibió Trajano y apología por las nuestras". Tirso may well have known La Barreda's apology, as well as Sánchez de Moratalla's. When in *El vergonzoso en palacio* (II, xiv), Tirso is quoting "epithets" that he has found in his reading to describe the *comedia*, one is "esfera del pensamiento". La Barreda calls it "un orbe perfecto de la poesía". Tirso and la Barreda were both in the *Academia de Madrid* in early 1625. See below, p. 89, n. 34.

pose, and he recalls Aristophanes' statement, already quoted, concerning its function. Elsewhere, he states:

> El fin de los antiguos siempre fue enseñar; éste es el principal oficio de la poesía, como hemos dicho. Bien es verdad que inventaron modos de mucho gusto ... mas esto fue para vestir el fin principal, que es la doctrina.

However, the theatre has its own methods and "there is no reason why it should be converted into a tribunal or a pulpit ... It is enough if it advises as a friend — without its threatening as judge." And — he goes on to add significantly — "I am not sure but what the serene semblance of the friend may accomplish more than the terrifying one of the judge."

For the purpose of poetry, la Barreda says, is nothing more nor less than to make us know ourselves, a difficult task, since self-love blinds us all. As with the man in Aesop's fable, we all tend to carry two packs, one in front for our neighbor's faults, another behind for our own. In accomplishing this task of self-recognition, the poets have fashioned no form of literature so calculated to give excellent results as the drama; be it tragedy, comedy, or satire. With tragedy, the Greek poets of old punished severely the vices of the princely and powerful; in comedy, those of the masses through contempt; and in satire, the one or the other with insulting laughter.

If poetry is, in Aristotle's words, an imitation and, in Horace's, a painting; if its purpose be to make men better by making them know themselves; and if dramatic form is recognized as the most telling instrument through which to inculcate such knowledge — one that is more vivid than either history or moral philosophy — surely one has the right to ask of the poet that the mirror which is held up to nature shall be a faithful one.

La Barreda, then, in defending Lope, brandishes the very weapon of imitation which the preceptors had handed him, but he demands straightway that it should be a "true imitation in which are mirrored *the customs of the poets' own days,* not those of the Greeks and the Romans." He declares that it must be so, if plays are to give pleasure to Spaniards of the seventeenth century. And he reminds the critics of the Lopean comedy that Horace had reserved the crown of laurel for those dramatists who gave pleasure in addition to doctrine. Having defended also with this same weapon of imitation the mixture of the tragic and the comics, as well as the inobservance of the unities of time and place, he concludes: "In summation, one precept alone suffices: i.e., the realization that all poetry is imitation. That poem will be perfect then ... which imitates the action that it mirrors with sure propriety. It accordingly guards the rules of art."

But war would come from another source in 1620, and it was from a direction to which neither Lope nor Tirso could be indifferent. The theologians had in 1620 added their fulminations to those of Suárez de Figueroa in the anonymous *Diálogos de las comedias*. [40] Written in early 1620, the "theologian" speaks at one point of "las premáticas que ahora se trazan" (p. 230a) and at another of the *Cortes* that were still in session (p. 217a). He, in fact, hopes to bring action through this latter body, for he declares to the *regidor:* "... yo me resuelvo, pues hay ahora Cortes y os cabe ir a ellas, que muy seriamente se tratase de que se quitase este modo que se usa de comedias." The *regidor* in question had stated earlier (p. 211) — when asking the theologian's opinion on this matter of the *comedias* — that he wanted it "para saber de una vez y de raíz la verdad y dar mi voto cuando allá en nuestro regimiento se tratare." Thus, there was a clear, well-defined effort in 1620 to close the theatres or to force them into a mould that would be more acceptable to the very serious-minded. Now the author of the dialogues — poet as well as cleric, since he speaks of "my verses" — was an admirer of the classical school of drama. Asked to suggest authors who would lend their pens to this attempt to reform the theatre, he mentions but three, all of them recognized representatives of that school, the two Argensolas and Francisco López de Zárate — and all of them, I may add, deriving in part their dramatic ideals from Seneca. [41]

---

[40] E. Cotarelo y Mori, *Bibliografía de las controversias sobre la licitud del teatro en España*, 210-231. I have analysed at some length these attacks on the Lopean theatre in "Attacks on Lope and his theatre in 1619-1621," 57-76.

[41] La Barreda, while respecting Senecan tragedy, says frankly (268-269): "Dignas son de veneración las [tragedias] de Séneca; mas no se acuerdan

Significantly, too, the theologian who wrote the *Diálogos de las comedias* quotes Seneca, and on more than one occasion.

The circle was now complete. Lupercio Leonardo de Argensola[42] in 1598, when the struggle had begun, had joined the clerical forces in their condemnation of "amorous comedies," as well as in their efforts to keep the public theatres closed. In 1620, the cleric who wrote the *Dialogues of the Comedies* condemns a theatre whose subject matter he claims is limited to love tangles and asks for one of classic tradition, such as the Argensolas or Francisco López de Zárate would have written. Between 1617 and 1620, then, both *churchmen* and Aristotelians were asking for a theatre which should give instruction in something other than the *ars amandi*, one that would take seriously as they saw it, its moral responsibility toward the people. Both wanted one that would measure up artistically. Both would have found acceptable the Senecan tragedy.

The effects of such deep-seated conflict on the drama of the time were, I believe, greater than has been realized. The attacks of Suárez de Figueroa and even of the theologian who wrote the *Diálogos* had been highly personal in their satire both of Lope and Alarcón. The former had, after outlining satirically a typical *capa y espada* play of Lopean mold, termed it "todo paja"; and the theologian had called Lope "aquel lobo carnicero de almas." Lope was in no position to answer the severe theologian because of his personal life, but he returned blow for blow with his Aristotelian critic — as he did with Juan Ruiz de Alarcón. In this war of personalities, Salas Borbadillo, Tirso, and others soon entered. Salas, in the second part of *El caballero puntual*,[43] which went to press by January 1619, tells of having witnessed a play wherein the author "satirized the customs of Terence and Plautus under cover of an allegory so flimsy that it was as clear to the audience as if he had referred to them by their own names." Present among the spectators were two Aristotelians [probably

---

que la poesía no basta que enseñe, si no deleita. Olvidóse su severidad de lo segundo."

[42] For the attitude of Lupercio Leonardo de Argensola, see Otis H. Green, *The Life and Works of Lupercio Leonardo de Argensola,* 54-55, 146-149.

[43] *El caballero puntual,* II, 296-297.

Suárez de Figueroa and Torres Rámila] who were the objects
of attack. What is more, they [Lope and his cohorts?] had filled
the theatre with their friends and had even distributed "among
those of the pit some trouble-makers, who at the least sign would
sound their vile instruments..." [44] The author then goes on to add
through his character:

> Yo culpé su inmodestia cuando el que estaba a mi lado me
> satisfizo diciendo que los dos le habían provocado con
> iguales y aun mayores injurias. Admiré mucho que entre
> los ingenios grandes se hiciese la guerra con armas tan
> indignas de su autoridad, enseñando ellos mismos el ca-
> mino al vulgo por donde les ha de perder el respeto.

The anonymous author of the *Diálogos de las comedias* not only
confirms Salas' observations (p. 220) but makes clear that the
satire had extended to the political arena: "The dramatists were
presenting to the public," said that critic, "all those things that
were being gossiped of in Madrid, now of the king's minister and
favorite [Uceda?], now of those who were governing, now of
certain *envied* gentlemen, now of certain *envious* ones." In short,
the Aristotelians and the Lopean school, having first washed for
each other's benefit their soiled linen, were now making "free
mock and jest of everything." The theatre had become "a camp

---

[44] Guillén de Castro, both in *Pretender con pobreza* and in *El ayo de su
hijo*, complains of the audiences of the time. In the latter, the *gracioso* has
written a play entitled, *El amante bachiller*. Speaking of the uncertain fortune that may await it, he says (II, 452-453): "...imagino/ que ya es más
dicha que ingenio;/ a las obras me remito/ pues vi muchas parecer/ mal
y ser buenas y he visto/ en infinitas muy malas/ andar como un rayo el
vítor./ Pienso que es según le viene/ al auditorio el capricho/ de bueno
u de mal humor,/ o estar bien quisto o mal quisto/ el poeta, pues si está/
con mosqueteros amigos/ o sin damas obligadas/ llueve a su comedia silbos."
He, moreover, confirms the delight the *mosqueteros* felt on hearing poets
satirize each other: "Diré que un sastre es poeta;/ con que es seguro y
preciso/ ver, habiendo tantas bocas/ arrojar la risa a gritos;/ diré que es
loco un poeta/ y sucederá lo mismo."
In *Pretender con pobreza* (II, 438), he paints the bad manners of the
women: "...por Dios que está vulgar/ el auditorio en la corte:/ estar oyendo y hablando,/ juzgar las cosas por fe,/ reír sin saber por qué,/ celebrar sin
saber cuándo;/ y luego por contratreta/ un silbo tan penetrante/ que aturda
un representante/ y descompone un poeta", etc.

of slander" — to the delight of the *mosqueteros* who were not slow to pick up the unmannerly ways of their betters.

Aside from this highly critical, bitterly satirical atmosphere which resulted from the infighting in literary circles — a spirit that was perhaps the natural concomitant of attempts to bring reform — there were, I believe, other results, some of them felicitous, which I shall have time only to list:

1. The *gracioso*'s role grows more significant as a result of the satirical spirit that animated the *comedia*. He becomes more the social commentator, more the critic of customs, for it was through his mouth that the poet usually sent forth his satirical shafts. The *comedia* of this day is, therefore, as a mirror of the outlook of the times, extraordinarily rich — and extraordinarily personal.

2. There is, at the same time, a more serious note in the drama of the time, one that reveals itself, in part, in the return to favor of tragedy. Cristóbal de Mesa [45] had ironically protested around 1611 (as Lupercio Leonardo de Argensola had done in the earlier conflict of 1598) that the writer of comedy was ever able to gather in the box receipts, while the epic and the tragic poet were dying of hunger. To be sure, there were factors other than the demand for tragedy on the part of the Aristotelians which led in the early 1620's to a revival of the buskined art, among others political, social, and religious conditions. Nevertheless, this revival can hardly fail to be, in part, a result of the oft-repeated demands of the Aristotelians for a more serious theatre.

3. We shall find, as well, I suspect, that there was at the beginning of Philip IV's reign some attempt to revive the typically Senecan conflict wherein a tyrant, impelled by evil desire, misuses his power as monarch to bring tragedy to his innocent vassals. There were mirrors for princes, in dramatic form, written by authors who believed with Hamlet that "the play's the thing with which to catch the conscience of the king." Back of this attempt to revive the Senecan conflict must lie at times (as in *La Estrella*

[45] See Menéndez y Pelayo, *Historia de las ideas estéticas*, II, 285-86.

de Sevilla) [46] the temperament of a young sensual monarch (such as Philip IV), as well as the whole *de regimine principum* literature and the Senecan tradition of tragedy. There were other conflicts, other types of characters, who grew out of the ambient of the moment.

4. We find, too in this epoch more careful workmanship [47] in various directions — particularly in matters of basic structural unity. Plays, in general, probably tended to become shorter. Such improvement was, I believe, due in part to the increasing emphasis on thesis and character portrayal, which, of course, serve as unifying factors; but it would seem logical that part of the credit should go to the Aristotelians. The favor accorded the theatre by the new regime probably played its part as well.

In short, the turmoil of 1617-1625 was far from being the lost cause for literature that the struggle for social and political improvement was for history. I suspect that when we know more about the chronology of Golden Age drama and can throw the plays of this particular period against the ambient that gave them being, we shall find that it gave us some of our most beautiful, most meaningful dramas. If so, it will once more be demonstrated that if history is the record of man's deeds, literature is often the golden web wherein one finds enmeshed his dreams and his aspirations.

In their stress on the didactic, the years 1617-1625 undoubtedly look forward to the Calderonian period, as Miss Margaret Wilson has recently pointed out. Let us again turn to her *Spanish Drama of the Golden Age* for words that in general confirm our belief that the reform movement of 1617-1625 was more important for literature than has been realized: [48]

> The neo-classicists whom Lope defeated are in some measure avenged by Calderón. There is, of course, no question of rigid Aristotelian precepts, nor of any real

---

[46] I have in my files a long study of this play, which is of the same general nature as my study on *La prudencia en la mujer.*

[47] This point has not been as generally recognized as it should be, in my opinion.

[48] Margaret Wilson, *Spanish Drama of the Golden Age,* 150.

modification of the *comedia* form ... [Calderón's] didactic preoccupations undoubtedly link him with *El Pinciano* and with Senecan moral tragedy, and the norms of his theatre are to a large extent those of this temporarily eclipsed genre.

A page or so earlier she had stressed even more Calderón's preoccupation with moral values: [49]

> By raising its own status, by acknowledging itself as an art, whose services, like those of painting, could be put at the disposal of morality and religion, the Spanish theatre ensured its survival for a further generation ... It was above all he [i.e., Calderón] who, allying himself with the wanton *comedia,* made it respectable.

I am in entire accord with Miss Wilson in believing that Calderon's "didactic preoccupations link him with *El Pinciano* and with Senecan moral tragedy ...," but I believe there was recognition on both Mira's and Tirso's part that the theatre was "an art whose services ... could be put at the disposal of morality and religion." Such *comedias* as the *Don Alvaro* plays, *El condenado por desconfiado, La prudencia en la mujer, La mujer que manda en casa,* and *Tanto es lo de más como lo de menos,* are surely eloquent proof of the sincerity of their desire to make the theatre a vehicle for reform.

Miss Wilson, [50] in contrasting the attitude of Lope toward monarchy with that of Calderón, observes that in the drama of the latter "kings are only too fallible," that the "king is no longer the vice-roy of God, the minister of divine justice among men," as he had been in Lope's theatre. Tirso's rulers are not ony fallible; they are *only too often* actual weaklings, dominated by their own lusts and passions. And if the very fountain-head of authority is frivolous or evil, his vassals can be counted upon to imitate him in his shortcomings: as is the monarch, so are his people. Or the ruler muy be under the power of a cynical favorite; and Tirso wanted no all-powerful *privado* to stand between the sovereign and his vassals. In short, our dramatist sought to do in various

---

[49] *Ibid.,* 149.
[50] *Ibid.,* 159-160.

comedias what Lisón y Biedma was striving to do with his memorials: reform the sovereign and weaken the power of his *privado*. But a theatre which sought to improve leadership in the reign of a Philip IV and an Olivares was doomed to failure. It . could create no school, especially not after the Mercedarin's banishment!

In yet another direction, i.e., that of the *pundonor*, Tirso was (in such plays as *El celoso prudente*, *La vida y muerte de Herodes*, and *Escarmientos para el cuerdo*) using his theatre to get across a message. What is more, he spoke out more clearly than did Calderón. As Miss Wilson has pointed out [51] in her *Spanish drama ...*, "in the attempts which have been made to dissociate Calderón from a harsh and an un-Christian moral code, another dramatist [i.e., Tirso de Molina] has perhaps not received his due." And she points to Gabriel Téllez's treatment of the "sterner aspects of *pundonor*" in such plays as *El celoso prudente* and *Escarmientos para el cuerdo*. In the former, the husband, who is doubtful of his wife's fidelity, "prudently investigates" before killing her and finds her innocent. Thus he is spared the necessity of carrying out a vengeance, demanded by "las leyes fieras del mundo, / de las de Dios embarazo." This contrast of the cruel laws of this world and the more clement ones of God is made even stronger in Tirso's *Escarmientos para el cuerdo* where Leonor's father, fully aware of his daughter's transgressions against the *pundonor*, nevertheless rejects this world's laws in favor of Heaven's clemency: "Venganza, sólo sois vos / ley del mundo sin prudencia; / ley de Dios sois vos, clemencia."

In *La vida y muerte de Herodes*, Tirso took the history of Herod, as his life is given in Plutarch, and made of him a husband so crazed by jealousy that he not only orders the death of his innocent wife but appears in the play's last scene "abrazando a los desnudos cuerpos ensangrentados de dos tiernos infantes, víctimas de su vesánico furor." [52] The theologian who wrote the *Diálogos de las comedias* in early 1620 had pointed to the pernicious

---

[51] *Ibid.*, 160-161. Miss Wilson gives the same quotations that I quote here for both *El celoso prudente* and for *Escarmientos para el cuerdo*.

[52] The phrase is taken from Sra. de los Ríos, *Obras dramáticas completas de Tirso,...* I, 1456.

effect on public customs of the Lopean comedia: [53] "¿Qué se puede seguir de ver un enredo de amores lascivos y deshonestos? ...
otro de *venganzas, pundonores vanos, enormes crueldades?*" Tirso
wrote in 1621 both *El celoso prudente* and *La vida y muerte de
Herodes* against the background of such protests. He was, in
general, a defender of the Lopean *comedia*, but he, no more than
the theologian of the *Diálogos*, wanted a theatre of "venganzas,
pundonores vanos, enormes crueldades." It is significant for the
interpretation of such themes in Calderón's theatre that he also
dealt with a Herod who was maddened by jealousy. When the
problems of the *comedia* as a vehicle for reform are better understood, I suspect that it will be discovered that Calderón found,
as Tirso did not, the indispensable formula that would let him
instruct without *offending* either his dramatic audience or his political masters. He accomplished it possibly by so removing his
theatre from reality that Prof. Parker [54] found it "a mistake to
apply any lingering criteria of realism to the action of such a
work [as *La devoción de la Cruz*]." Tirso was, by temperament,
too concrete in his thinking to have found the formula. Calderón
used it only at the expense of clarity.

In the *comedia* of intrigue which called for such stage
mechanics as to baffle the poor actors for the time being — it
was one that necessarily called for brevity of time — Gabriel
Téllez was also the forerunner of such swift Calderonian comedies as *Casa con dos puertas* and *La dama duende*. Tirso's *Los
balcones de Madrid* and his *En Madrid y en una casa* are both
comedies of *tramoya* which depend on stage craft. Tirso, following
Lope's lead, had satirized the use of *tramoyas* in *La fingida
Arcadia*, but he would soon realize its value for the swiftly-
paced comedy of intrigue that we are likely to think of as
Calderonian.

---

[53] I study briefly *El celoso prudente* against the background of the
Diálogos de las comedias in a chapter of this volume, "Tirso de Molina's
Relations to Lope and his Theatre Reappraised." See below, p. 179. See
also my "Tirso's *La vida y muerte de Herodes*: its Date, its Importance, and
its Debt to Mira's Theatre," *RABM* (LXXVI), 121-148. The play was written
against the same background as *El celoso prudente*.

[54] See Alexander A. Parker, *The Approach to the Spanish Drama of the
Golden Age*; also Miss Margaret Wilson's, *Spanish Drama...*, 168.

For his thematic images, Calderón probably turned to Mira de Amescua more than to Tirso, who also borrowed from that Andalusian. [55] It is a point that needs further development than we can give it here. What can be pointed out at this moment is that Tirso used for lyrical passages the pyramidal structure, so characteristic of Calderón, in such a play as *La fingida Arcadia* (II, xiii). In this pastoral play, Lucrecia, "de pastora bizarra" having first addressed herself, one by one, to the "montes, fresnos, robles, murtas, jazmines, mosquetas, trébol, noches, día, aurora, tarde, palabras en papel, obras, deseos," ends her address with this summation:

> ¡Montes, fresnos, robles, murtas,
> jazmines, mosquetas, trébol,
> noche, aurora, día, tarde,
> papeles, obras, deseos!
> ¡todos me habéis, por adoraros, muerto!

There are plenty of other examples in Tirso's theatre of this pyramidal structure.

When don Pedro Calderón de la Barca approved Tirso's *Quinta parte* [56] on July 16, 1635 and pointed to the "muestras de ciencia, virtud y religión [que] ha dado [Gabriel Téllez] a aprehender a los que deseamos imitarle," he was, I believe, speaking with all sincerity. Tirso's theatre, like Mira's was in some ways a transitional one between the Lopean and the Calderonian.

As it happened, Tirso was in Madrid when the Cortes were still in session. First summoned in February of 1617, they were not dissolved until late March of 1620. What is more, he must have been in the capital when, on February 9, 1620, [57] the frail Philip III made his first visit to Atocha, there to give — after

---

[55] See Karl Gregg, "A Metaphor in Mira de Amescua," 36-38; also Vern Williamsen, "The Development of a *décima* in Mira de Amescua's Theatre," 32-36.

[56] Quoted from Cotarelo, *Comedias de Tirso...*, I, p. lxvii.

[57] Date taken from *Noticias* of Antonio de León (ms. 2395, BNM under date given.

months of serious illness — thanks to Heaven for the tenuous hod on life granted him. In a passage that he included in *La villana de Vallecas* (I, vi), Tirso has recorded what was, for him, undoubtedly a very moving experience. In it he sketches for us a picture of his frail sovereign, one that offers sharp contrast, not only to those portraits of that ruler which historians have left us, but to various others that Tirso himself has afforded us of the son who followed that gentle monarch. It is a contrast which is nothing less than indispensable background for much of what Tirso wrote after transferring his residence to Madrid, especially for such essentially political plays as *Privar contra su gusto, La prudencia en la mujer, La mujer que manda en casa, Tanto es lo de más como lo de menos,* and *Los hermanos parecidos.* In some measure, this contrast will, I believe, even explain his theological study. *El mayor desengaño.* Certainly his loyalty to Philip III could hardly have failed to color his attitude toward the Palace and the bureaucracy connected with it in Philip IV's time. Eventually enemies from that Palace were able — with the *Junta de Reformación* as their immediate agent — to restrict his activities as a dramatist, though they could not end them. Tirso was not a man to be cowed easily, and fortunately, for posterity, he believed in the worth of what he had written. "Velint, nolint" (to use his phrase of 1634), [58] he not only succeeded in getting into print the major portion of his plays but even in making clear therein the history of his struggle against the literary envy that lay behind his denunciation to the *Junta.* This volume strives to discover, among other things, the general outlines of what happened to Gabriel Téllez in early March of 1625 and to show his way of meeting the challenge.

Just how warm was the admiration and how deep the affection that Tirso felt for Philip III is abundantly clear from some chit-chat that took place in the little inn of Arganda. It is between one Pedro de Mendoza, just back from Mexico, and one Gabriel de

---

[58] Found in his "Dedicatoria" of the *Parte tercera.* Quoted from Cotarelo, *Comedias de Tirso,* I, p. lvii. In Tirso's *Cigarrales* (I, 116-117), he had used the same phrase in the second person singular when challenging "Envy:" "Velis, nolis."

Herrera, recently arrived from Madrid, both characters in *La villana de Vallecas* (I, vi):

DON GABRIEL: Por buenas nuevas os doy
que el rey ha convalecido.

DON PEDRO: ¡Gracias a Dios!

DON GABRIEL: Y ha salido
a Atocha en público hoy.

DON PEDRO: Habrá la corte con eso
vuelto en sí; que me contaban
que en ella todos andaban
sin color, sin gusto y seso.

DON GABRIEL: Mi palabra os doy que ha sido
la mayor demonstración
de lealtad y de afición
que en historia he leído.
No sé yo que se haya hecho
sentimiento general
con tal muestra y llanto tal
por ningún rey.

DON PEDRO: Muestra el pecho
el reino que a tal rey debe,
que en él goza un siglo de oro.
Sin conocerle, le adoro.

DON GABRIEL: ¿Queréis más, si es que eso os mueve,
que todo el tiempo que ha estado
en contingencia su vida,
hasta la gente perdida
dicen que se había olvidado
de ejecutar la ganancia
de su trato deshonesto?

DON PEDRO: Echó el sentimiento el resto
y conoció la importancia
de la vida de tal rey,
cuya mansedumbre extraña
es causa que goce España
su hacienda, su paz, su ley
sin contrastes ni temores.

DON GABRIEL: ¡Cosa extraña que en veinte años
que reina, ni hambres ni daños
pestes, guerras, ni rigores
del cielo hayan afligido
este reino!

DON PEDRO :   Antes por él
mana España leche y miel.
De promisión tierra ha sido.

DON GABRIEL : No le viene el nombre mal,
pues que en su tiempo ha alcanzado
Castilla el haber comprado
la hanega de trigo a real
y el dar la cosecha a medias
del vino, a quien a ayudar
se atreviere a vendimiar.

Philip III was, for Tirso, in no sense a weakling of atrophied will, but instead a wise and deeply religious ruler, one outstanding for his gentleness and for the purity of his personal life. He was a leader whose spiritual qualities had brought to his people God's richest blessings, making the Spain of his time a veritable promised land of milk and honey, delivering it from the afflictions of famine, disease, war, the harsh inclemencies of Heaven, and making it possible for the nation to enjoy, without opposition or fear, her wealth, her peace, and her religion. The people had had in his reign political and economic stability. More specifically, his economic policies had been so wise, as Tirso saw it, that Castilians had been able to buy their wheat at a *real* the *fanega,* and had harvested their grapes on the halves.

This is the only comment I have noted in Tirso's theatre that could relate to the politico-economic situation that had so moved Spain's House of Deputies and its Royal Council in those last years of Philip III's reign. One finds in his theatre of these years, in so far as I can see, neither praise nor blame for a Lerma or an Uceda, who had filled their own pockets and those of their relatives at the expense of the Royal Treasury, but unless I am mistaken, the *very absence* of tributes speaks eloquently. In this connection we must remember Tirso's very warm praise of Philip III and that of the Archbishop Sandoval y Rojas; let us recall, too, that of the grandnephew [59] of the Archbishop who, on

---

[59] See *No hay peor sordo* (I, 1, 265). For identification of the passage as relating to the Archbishop-Cardinal, Sandoval y Rojas, see A. Nougué, *L'Oeuvre en prose de Tirso de Molina* (148-149). The French critic cites as source of his information J. de Entrambasaguas' *Estudios sobre Lope de Vega* (I, 267-271).

May 17, 1625, [60] inherited the title of Duque de Lerma. Tirso made it a point to give credit where he honestly could, but he could not condemn those two *privados* without hurting men for whom he felt the warmest admiration and affection, i.e., the king and the archbishop. He therefore said nothing. He was quick, however, to take note of the over-night shift of loyalties that took place with the accession of Philip IV and the simultaneous rise to power of Olivares. The year 1621 is marked by Tirso's glorification of loyalty to friendship in moments of adversity. It is evidenced not only by his retouching *Cómo han de ser los amigos* and including it in *Los cigarrales de Toledo*, but by his writing two new plays on the same theme: *El amor y el amistad* and *El honroso atrevimiento*.

Few students of history have seen in the Spain of Philip III's day a land of milk and honey. Moreover, there were plenty of Spaniards, especially in the late years of that monarch's reign, who did not so see it: witness the fight in the Cortes and the famous "Consulta" of 1619 wherein the Royal Junta, appointed by Philip III, outlined the unhappy economic and social conditions prevailing in the realm. Yet Tirso was not as completely myopic as the passage from *La villana de Vallecas* might seem to indicate, nor is his picture an entirely prejudiced one. Indeed, only a few years after Tirso wrote it — when Olivares was at the helm — many of Spain's citizens must have looked back on those days of Philip III's reign as halcyon.

The feelings of love and devotion to Philip III which Tirso has recorded in *La villana de Vallecas* are reaffirmed in various other works of varying date: in the *Cigarrales* [61] (1621-24), in *Las quinas de Portugal* (III, iii), in *Deleytar aprovechando* (1635), and in his *Historia de Nuestra Señora de la Merced* [62] (1638),

---

[60] See *Noticias de Madrid*, 118. Uceda, his son, died May 31, 1624, in Alcalá.

[61] For praise in the *Cigarrales*, see II, 34; for *Las quinas de Portugal*, see III, iii. He twice praised Philip III in his miscellany, *Deleytar aprovechando*. When describing the *quinta* of don Melchor, he calls him (188v.): "La más piadosa majestad que gozó España"; in *No le arriendo la ganancia*, included in *Deleytar aprovechando*, he is "el pacífico Felipe, tercero deste nombre, primero en santidad y pureza de costumbres".

[62] I am indebted to Father Manuel Penedo Rey for both quotations from the *Historia*, a monumental work whose Vol. I is now off press, according

In the last mentioned, a work still partly in manuscript that was not begun until 1638, he contrasts the state of the kingdom under the administration of Philip III and its distressing condition under that of the "new architects" who took over on March 31, 1621 (II, trigésimo octavo, 14.°):

> Vacó la monarquía española con la intempestiva muerte y malograda juventud de Philipo [i.e., Philip III], el manso, el apacible, el santo y el piadoso. Murió con él la paz de su corona, *la abundancia de sus súbditos y el siglo dorado* muchas veces, y de el modo que a la ruina de una grande fábrica cae con ella todo lo suntuoso, lo rico y lo estudiado, ansí con este Rey, nuestras felicidades; y sólo nos quedaron los recuerdos de tanto bien perdido. Vivos permanecerán por edades muchas los llantos, los sentimientos y congojas que ocasionaron esta tragedia irremediable a su inmensa Monarquía, y en especial a su ya huérfana corte.

Shortly thereafter, he pays his respects to the "new architects" who, coming in with Philip IV, had wrought such ruin on the great edifice that had been Spain (*op. cit.,* trigésimo nono, 1.°):

> Murió el católico y piadosísimo Philippo, tercero de este nombre. Desencajáronse las fábricas que con su favor veneraba tanta monarquía. Sucedieron nuevos arquitectos con el Rey nuevo. Deseado han muchos averiguar cuál sea la causa de que, como si fuera efecto necesario de la naturaleza, los príncipes y gobernadores que entran nuevamente en la administración de los Estados, lo primero en que emplean su desvelo es en derribar todos aquellos a quien dio su antecesor la mano, porque si bien la inclinación de sublimar criaturas que solamente de su poder lo sean, parece que puede escusarles de algún modo, con todo eso ni todos los que heredan son tan inadvertidos que muchos no conozcan la importancia de conservar ministros que, diestros con la experiencia de las cosas, prosigan con sus aciertos y no los desbaraten los ímpetus mandones de los modernos. Dejemos esta duda para los estadistas y ... nos sirva de despertador para no poner nuestra esperanza totalmente en los hombres.

---

to recent news. Father Penedo has since published these quotations in his study, *Tirso en Sevilla,* 33-34.

It should be noted, as well, that the news budget which Gabriel de Herrera gives Pedro de Mendoza in *La villana de Vallecas* includes another detail that reflects the interests that were, in March of 1620, uppermost in Tirso's mind. Having satisfied himself as to Philip III's health, don Pedro then continues with another question: "¿Qué hay en Madrid de comedias?" Don Gabriel's answer is that the uncertain state of the king's health was at the moment affecting the theatre. Earlier Pinedo had had tremendous success in *El asombro de la Limpia Concepción*, [63] the best play of that genre. Who had written it? None other than Lope! And then don Gabriel adds proudly: "que no están bien / tales musas sin tal vega."

In March, then, of 1620, the things that were impinging on Tirso's consciousness — aside from the special devotion which both he and his Order felt for the dogma of the Immaculate Conception — were two: 1) the health of his king and the many reasons that Spain had for loving that gentle leader, and 2) the state of the theatre and the great initiator of the "New Comedy," Lope de Vega Carpio.

However, if we take *La villana de Vallecas* as a whole, the play reveals an as-yet largely-unpracticed talent [64] that contact with Madrid's literari had awakened in Tirso, i. e., the tendency to make the theatre a vehicle of literary satire. This play criticizes Ruiz de Alarcón and his *boba*. Tirso had taken note of the fact that the dramatists, with the *comedia* as their conduit, were tearing each other to pieces, and he would decide to imitate them.

---

[63] This is *La limpieza no manchada, Santa Brígida*, written by Lope in 1618, and played by Baltasar Pinedo's company on October 29th of the same year (see Rennert y Castro, *Vida de Lope de Vega*, 472). One wonders if Pinedo did not put it on again in early 1620.

[64] In the eleven plays that we can be reasonably certain Tirso wrote before he went to Santo Domingo, I have noted little, if any, satire of his fellow-dramatists. For Tirso's satire of Alarcón, see the chapter, included in this volume, "Tirso against Juan Ruiz de Alarcón and Luis Vélez."

The "eleven plays" mentioned above, as both the late Courtney Bruerton and I agreed, were: *Cómo han de ser los amigos, La elección por la virtud,* the three *Santa Juana's, Marta la piadosa, Don Gil de las calzas verdes, El vergonzoso en palacio, La peña de Francia, La república al revés,* and *La villana de la Sagra*. See Courtney Bruerton, "*La ninfa del cielo, La serrana de la Vera*, and Related Plays," 63-65, including n. 13a.

It was admittedly a decision on his part that was quite in keeping with his own sense of humor. He would soon learn that satire is a two-edged sword, one which can become exceedingly dangerous when it is in the hands of Envy backed by Power.

The passage of *La villana de Vallecas* is, in fact, curiously prophetic of the interests that would fill Tirso's years in Madrid —and of the reasons why certain forces would, in 1625, strive to remove the literary competition and the political opposition he represented.

I have indicated above that with the new regime of Philip IV and Olivares there would be raised another threat to Lope's supremacy in the dramatic world. To the old forces of opposition — i. e., to Góngora, with his reputation of innovator in the field of stylistics; to Ruiz de Alarcón, with his essentially moralistic theatre; to the united complaints of the Aristotelians and the stern reformists who found Lope's *comedia* "paja todo": to all of these would now be added another threat. It was one headed up by Luis Vélez de Guevara who brought with him the play of spectacle, [65] one that, like that of the Jesuits, depended heavily on stage machinery. This was the play of *tramoyas,* of *apariencias,* one that tended to be linked in the minds of many with the South and the Southeast where the eye apparently played a more important role than did the ear. Cervantes [66] had even made evident in the first *Quijote* his disapproval of *apariencias,* as dramatists were using them in the *comedias de santos,* and later Suárez de Figueroa [67] would do the same in *El pasajero* for "comedias de cuerpo."

The situation would grow acute for Lope in 1621, when Vélez wrote *Más pesa el rey que la sangre,* a play that not only glorified the loyalty of don Alonso Pérez de Guzmán el Bueno (the most famous ancestor of the Olivares branch of the family) to the Spanish monarchy, but also stressed how indebted Philip's

[65] For proof, see study on *La fingida Arcadia,* Ch. IV.
[66] *El Quijote,* I, ch. XLVIII.
[67] Suárez de Figueroa, *El pasajero,* 124.

kingdom was to that branch of the Guzmanes. [68] What is more, Luis Vélez, on writing his play, showed his preference not only for the spectacularism which had long characterized the Andalusian "comedia de ruido" but also for the gongoristic style which the Conde de Olivares was known to favor. This was a situation filled with implications for Lope, as he was quick to realize. He, too, wanted patronage from the all-powerful Olivares and began straightway to see if he could not obtain his favor. He not only dedicated to Olivares himself, in the late summer of 1621, his *Premio de la hermosura* (in which he asks for the role of royal chronicler) but he began to court all the poets near the king and his *privado:* Rioja, Antonio Hurtado de Mendoza, etc. He would later think in terms of winning favor through Olivares' wife, his daughter, his son-inlaw, etc.

To make matters worse for the Phoenix, Olivares was strongly Andalusian in his loyalty to writers from the South. In his role of Maecenas to the literary crew, he consistently favored those from that section over those from other parts of Spain. As Marañón points out in his biography of the *privado:* [69]

> La casa de don Gaspar [de Guzmán] estaba abierta, en los años de esplendor, a todos los sevillanos que ostentaran el título de artistas y hombres de letras, o que, simplemente, presumieran de él; y si había alguna dificultad en la entrada, don Francisco de Rioja [secretario y bibliotecario andaluz de Olivares] se encargaba de que se suavizase.

There was yet another group of poets, i.e., the "repentistas," who flourished in the shadow of the Palace. These would seem to have had the patronage of the king himself, sometimes direct, sometimes indirect. Not only did Philip IV have his own "repentista" in the blind buffoon, Cristóbal, [70] of the Palace, but, at a much higher level, his court poet, don Antonio Hurtado de

---

[68] For my interpretation of this play, see study of *La fingida Arcadia,* included in this volume,

[69] G. Marañón, *El Conde-Duque de Olivares,* 147.

[70] Apparently, Mendocilla was also a poet who wrote "coplas a los ciegos". See *Noticias de Madrid,* 125.

Mendoza, who, in a *romance* addressed to a fellow "ayuda de cámara," calls himself "repentísimo señor." [71] What is more, Mendoza is reputed to have finished in a single day a *comedia de repente*, entitled *Quien más miente medra más*, [72] one written in collaboration with Quevedo. He was given to epigrams: in the three volumes of his poetry, one finds *mote* after *mote*, together with countless eulogies to the Conde-Duque de Olivares [73] and his wife, to Philip IV and Isabel, to the maids-in-waiting in the Palace, etc. His poems, are, for the most part, light in tone, even frivolous. Many are neatly satirical.

In spirit, don Antonio de Mendoza was related to that characterizing the *Academia de Madrid*, a group which in 1625 had for its meeting place the home of Francisco de Mendoza, Secretary to the Conde de Monterrey, who was, as it happened, brother-in-law to Olivares. Like Mendoza, this group was given to *motes* and to *vejámenes*. And though I find no clear proof that the court poet was in 1625 actually attending the meetings of this group, he was a close friend of Luis Vélez de Guevara, who was quite active among its members. Both poets wrote satirical *motes* —Vélez and others termed them "donayres"— which got under the skins of their victims. There were, in that Academy, others of similar bent whose names we shall meet in the pages that follow. In fact, on the very same day, i. e., March 1, 1625, that the *Junta de Reformación* was meeting with the Conde-Duque to discuss plans for banishing Tirso, don Gabriel de Corral was holding forth in the Academy and was satirizing many of his fellow-members by putting them in a mad-house. [74] Among these was young Pantaleón de Ribera. In the former's

---

[71] *Obras poéticas de don Antonio Hurtado de Mendoza*, II, 28-30. The poem is entitled "A Antonio de Alosa, secretario de Cámara, a quien toca guardar los dulces que envían al rey".

[72] La Barrera y Leirado, *Catálogo*, 250. This is, I believe, basically the same play as *Los empeños del mentir*, but here published as the work of Mendoza alone. See below, 132-33. G. A. Davies felt otherwise. See *A Chronology of Antonio de Mendoza's Plays*, 107-109.

[73] There must be a dozen at least—without counting several addressed to Medina de las Torres, son-in-law to the *privado*.

[74] See my study "Pantaleón de Ribera, 'Sirene', Castillo Solórzano, and the *Academia de Madrid* in Early 1625," published in *Homage to John M. Hills*, 189-200.

vejamen, and in those of Pantaleón which quickly followed, we find thumbnail sketches of the various members of the Academy which are invaluable background for this study. Pantaleón was also a "repentista" and, on occasion, must have written *motes* as well. At least we find among his poems one penned in 1627 when he was already "con el pie en la huesa" which is entitled: "escusándose de hacer unos *motes* que le embió a pedir al [sic; el?] excelentísimo Señor Duque de Lerma para Palacio." This new Duque de Lerma was *patrón* to Pantaleón, who openly styled himself a "gongorino," and was, as well, a friend of the classically-minded Torres Rámila.

Lope, as we know, was "anti-gongorino" and he was, in theory at least, "anti-tramoyista" — therefore it should not surprise us that Luis Vélez took no part in the fiestas, captained by Lope, that celebrated San Isidro's canonization — but he was not, in so far as I know, anti-*repentista*. Or if he was, he kept quiet about it, since, as we shall see later, he wouldn't have wanted to anger don Antonio Hurtado de Mendoza, who was so popular with the king. Tirso had no inhibitions in either direction: he satirized the *repentistas* — with abandon! He even slashed away at the king himself and his all-powerful *privado*. [76] What is more, he probably continued to do it, in the case of the *privado,* even after the *Junta de Reformación* had reached its *acuerdo!*

In the year 1621 when, already around forty years of age, Tirso took up residence in Madrid, he had a background different from that of those who would become his enemies of the capital. And, with that background, he had formed a different sense of values. Of his childhood we know nothing for certain, except that he was born in Madrid and that he had a sister living in that city around 1621-1624. She is probably the "doña María de

---

[75] *Obras de Anastasio Pantaleón de Ribera,* II, 105-106.

[76] I sought to prove in 1948 that *La prudencia en la mujer* was a criticism of Philip IV and his ministers ("*La prudencia en la mujer* and the Ambient that Brought it Forth," 1131-1190). Another volume in this series will be concerned with Tirso's political theatre in general. I quite agree with Mr. J. C. J. Metford's "Tirso de Molina and the Conde-Duque de Olivares" (15-27) that *Tanto es lo de más como lo de menos* is a bitter satire directed against the Conde-Duque. I believe, however, that the play in question was rewritten in 1625-1626.

San Ambrosio y Piña, monja en la Magdalena de Madrid," who wrote a laudatory poem for his *Cigarrales,* one that seems, by its tone, to proclaim her sisterly pride in "Gabriel's" achievement. In that same volume, he tells us he had sent her the jewel he had won as a literary prize and he terms her "equal in talents and misfortunes to himself." From his college friend of Alcalá days, Matías de los Reyes, [77] we learn that it was for him pure joy to listen to Tirso talk, and Pantaleón de Ribera would seem to be describing our Mercedarian when he points to one of his fellow-academicians as "hablador de ventaja." That he was of slight stature [78] and immaculately clean and neat in appearance [79] is to be deduced from passages in *El amor médico, Deleytar aprovechando,* and in his *Historia de Nuestra Señora de la Merced.* The roles of Tirso's *graciosos* indicate his enjoyment of broad humor — at times, undoubtedly scatological — but Cervantes also delighted in it on occasion. In the first decade, dramatists were probably more plain-spoken than were those of Philip IV's reign: the new regime, so careless in its moral behavior, was quite restrained in vocabulary.

The dramatist took orders in "Nuestra Señora de la Merced" in Guadalajara, the city of the Mendozas; from there he went

---

[77] Matías de los Reyes, speaking of his desire to return to Madrid, gives as one reason his chats with Tirso: "y cuando este natural amor [a mi patria, i. e., Madrid] no me llamara, la conversación de V. P. (imán de mi voluntad) era bastante para afectar más este mi deseo". Cited from Matías de los Reyes' *Seis comedias* (Jaén, 1629). This *dedicatoria* is, however, dated September 21, 1622. See Gerald E. Wade, "La dedicatoria de Matías de los Reyes a Tirso de Molina", *Estudios,* VIII (1952), Madrid.

[78] See below, p. 89, n. 34; and for his slight stature, see Sra. de los Ríos, *Obras dramáticas completas de Tirso,* II, 966. Tirso undoubtedly defended men of brief stature in *El amor médico* (II, viii), but, in my opinion, the defense must be seen, not against Suárez de Figueroa's strictures of *El pasajero,* but against an occurrence of 1625. See below pp. 256-58.

[79] One deduces the importance of cleanliness and neatness for Tirso in his high praise of the venerable P. Mro. Fray Diego Coronel: "Fue tan extremado en no admitir mancha en el hábito como se afirma del primero [i. e., San Bernardo]; pues si decía San Bernardo que el monje que en lo que se viste consiente algún género de inmundicia, también se descuidará en las del alma, nuestro Mro. Coronel, ya que no lo dijese con la lengua, nos lo amonestaba con las obras, porque le daba en cara cualquiera especie de desaliño". Quoted by E. Cotarelo (*Comedias de Tirso de Molina,* I, xvii) from *Historia de ... la Merced,* II, folios 205 and 206.
Further proof could be cited to prove the point.

to Toledo, city of the Toledos, the Silvas, and of others of Spain's noblest lineages. Its cultural tradition was a long and distinguished one. It was the city, in Tirso's time, of the literary-minded Archbishop of the great Sandoval Rojas family who would receive this talented young dramatist into his literary circle at his beautiful *cigarral, Buenavista,* which overlooked the Tajo. On one occasion, [80] Tirso tells us frankly that he found in Toledo "mejor acogida" than in Madrid where he was born. He speaks of the *llaneza generosa* of the Imperial City and contrasts it with the envy he had met in Madrid: it was presumably a "llaneza", born of distinguished ancestry and established wealth, that felt no need to be on the defensive. Toledo's elite had accepted Tirso as one of their own, their equal by virtue of his outstanding talent, his solid knowledge, his attractive personality, and his position in an old and honorable Order that received Philip III's favor.

When, in official capacity, Tirso went to Santo Domingo in April of 1616 to help reform the Mercedarian house there, these Toledanos on his return most have welcomed him for his broadened point of view and the poise which two years of preaching and of administrative duties in a distant land had brought him. He would straightway begin the ascent within his Order, would become acquainted with its various convents: [81] with that of Valladolid in the summer of 1619; and with Segovia's in the first half of 1620, where we know he was "lector." The latter part of that same year he was, in my opinion, in Aragón and

---

[80] See below, p. 144.

[81] He was in Valladolid on June 14, 1619. See *Estudios,* I (1945), 203. For his presence in Segovia in 1620, see P. Elías Gómez, *Teólogo y asceta: Fray Juan Falconi de Bustemonte (1598-1638),* 1953, p. 72, text and note. Tirso was in Segovia, "de lector", in April of 1620. The note adds this information: "El 29 de mayo, viernes, se le dan unos zapatos al *lector* Téllez". Padre Penedo was so kind as to give me this information in a letter of 1959.

Sra. de los Ríos believed that Tirso was in Portugal in 1619-1620. See in *Reflexión,* 2 (no. 1, vol. I) a study on *El amor médico* and *Escarmientos para el cuerdo* which shows that these plays were written in 1625-1626, not in 1619-1620, as she believed. 1 concluded my study with the remark (30): "Tirso may or may not have made a trip to Portugal in 1619-20, though I admit to being skeptical in the matter."

Cataluña, [82] where he probably came in contact with the Urgeles, the Moncadas, the Alagóns, and other noble families of that region, long known as patrons of his Order. The Mercedarians had, in fact, had their origin in northeast Spain: it was Jaime of Aragón, "el Conquistador," who had founded it; and the mother chapter was in Barcelona. The provinces of Aragón and Cataluña were dotted with its many convents.

Tirso may, or may not, have been of noble blood. [83] I doubt whether it mattered greatly in its effect on his character, for he was the son of a great Order that was royal in origin, and, in his official roles, would have met those on whom his Order had to depend financially. Certainly his sympathies and his understanding were with the nobility — with those ancient families who, throughout the centuries, had so often supplied the nation with its leaders in matters political, military, and religious. His admiration, too, was unbounded for the Pizarros, the Hernán Corteses, the Alburquerques [84] who had extended the borders of the country he loved and, in so doing, set new geographical limits for his faith. From amongst her noble families, too, Spain had often found her cultural leaders, leaders who had glorified knowledge, made it possible for letters to flourish, now within the shadow of the Church, now without. Such men had respect for "noble talent" and for the "studious life" which could bring it to full flower. On the other hand, the smooth courtier could have had little charm for Tirso: the "discreet" man for him was

---

[82] Such works as *El amor y el amistad, La firmeza en la hermosura,* and his novel, *El bandolero,* strongly suggest that he was in Cataluña in 1620. L. C. Viada y Lluch, in the *Prólogo* to his edition of *El bandolero,* declares roundly (p. xvii). "Estuvo, pues, Tirso en Barcelona antes de 1621". I believe he spent the last half of 1620 there.

[83] Sra. de los Ríos has sought to prove that Tirso was of the great Téllez-Girón family. See *Obras dramáticas completas* (I, p. lxxxvi), where she describes the documents that led her to that conclusion. Her "proof" has been questioned repeatedly. See Warren T. McCready's *Bibliografía temática de estudios sobre el teatro español antiguo,* 290-314, in particular nos. 2690, 2691, 2696, 2814, etc. Tirso styles himself (see p. 142) "humilde pastor de Manzanares", precisely when glorifying the "llaneza generosa" of Toledo's families.

[84] See his praise for Hernán Cortés and don Alonso de Alburquerque in the second *Santa Juana* (I, 277). The socalled trilogy of the Pizarros was written to glorify the Pizarros.

not, as we shall see in this study, [85] the socially adaptable *corte-sano;* he was the learned man of St. Isidore of Sevilla, who had identified "el discreto" with "el sabio." Castiglione's *cortesano*, as embodied, for instance, in Antonio de Mendoza, was, for Tirso, one of those whom he derisively calls "sabios por testamentos."

Among the members of this old aristocracy there was often deep love of monarchy, deep loyalty to king, but with the implicit expectation that the ruler would, with his own noble life, set an example to those who would be the nation's future leaders, and could by his own devotion to his Faith, bring many blessings on his nation. Tirso's social organization for the nation was apparently a paternalistic one, a point of view which had probably been nourished by the essentially conservative milieu of Guadalajara and Toledo.

Philip IV, with his frivolous court and with the eternal intrigue that his own lack of moral worth invited, with its envious bureaucracy and its equally envious literary groups, must have represented for Tirso a rude awakening. He was, in the first place, horrified at the two men who held Spain's destiny in their hands (i.e., Olivares and Philip IV), and soon after reaching the court, he quickly turned some of his plays into didactic molds to instruct, now through history, now through the Bible, now through the lives of the saints. [86] His point of view was not unlike that of the writers of traditional "mirrors for princes"; only he would use the theatre as a vehicle for his purpose. Reform should begin *at the top.* It was his aim to reform the governmental reformers.

But he was at the same time fascinated by the multi-faceted, feverish activism, by the cold, hard, brilliance of this mad Madrid — as his many "comedias de costumbres" make evident. And little in the passing scene missed his eagle-eye! He had recognized its madness even on his visit to the capital in early 1620. One of the characters in *La villana de Vallecas* (of 1620) will say (II, ix): "Casa de orates / es la corte." And in the *vejamen*

---

[85] See Ch. II.

[86] In one of the volumes of this series, when dealing with Tirso's political theatre, I shall attempt to make clear just how true this was.

which Tirso's friend, don Gabriel de Corral, pronounced on March 1, 1625, that author points to the need of a very special "hospital" for the poets of the "Academy of Madrid,"— a perennial one, he says, "con hermandad a los Orates de Valladolid y al Nuncio de Toledo." He creates just such a hospital in his *vejamen* and brings down for their treatment no lesser a physician than Apollo himself. No sketch of Tirso is found in the *vejamen*, but we do find, among this same Gabriel de Corral's epigrams, one which speaks of the "vile trick" that had banished from the capital a "discreet" (i.e., a wise) friend. [87] Madrid is the loser, says Corral firmly, not his friend. But posterity was the real sufferer, if we may judge by the very excellent dramas that Tirso was writing in 1625-1626.

---

[87] See pp. 333-34.

TIRSO VERSUS ANTONIO HURTADO DE MENDOZA AND LOPE DE VEGA

II

TIRSO, ANTONIO HURTADO DE MENDOZA, LOPE, AND *THE JUNTA DE REFORMACIÓN*

Tirso and Antonio Hurtado de Mendoza were bitter enemies during many years of their lives, though it is a fact that has not been previously suspected. To be sure, Fernández-Guerra[1] suggested many years ago that certain satire in *Más merece quien más ama* was directed against a scene that Tirso had written, one in which his protagonist was disguised as gardener; but since such scenes were more or less commonplaces in Golden Age drama, and in view of the fact that Mendoza's satire refers as well to some found in Alarcón's *Las paredes oyen*[2] (known to have been in existence by early 1618), the critic's suggestion fell on fallow ground. This chapter seeks to prove that, through Mendoza's actions, Tirso's career as a dramatist came to a virtual close in 1625-26. Before beginning the task of proving it, however, we must first give the reader some background on Antonio Hurtado de Mendoza's life, character, and temperament. Our undertaking will be made the easier by some distinguished studies that Mr. G. A. Davies has recently made of this minor poet and dramatist —

---

[1] Fernández-Guerra y Orbe, Luis. *Don Juan Ruiz de Alarcón y Mendoza,* I, 386-388.

[2] For date of 1617 for *Las paredes oyen, ibid.,* I, 379. Fernández-Guerra saw in it Alarcón's reply to the satire of *El pasajero.* As the latter carries a *tasa* of November 16, 1617, then it would necessarily have been written between that time and February 3, 1618, when Pinedo presented it in the convent of Nuestra Señora de la Victoria. See E. Cotarelo, "Las comedias en los conventos de Madrid en el siglo xvii", *RBAM,* 1925 (II), 461-470.

though we must at times amplify what he has written, if it is to
serve our particular purpose.

According to his contemporary, Antonio Enríquez Gómez, Mendoza "carried off the Palace." [3] Certainly by March 6, 1625, when
the *Junta* recommended that Tirso be banished from Madrid, "el
discreto del palacio," "el lego cortesano," as he was called, had
received honor after honor from the king. In May of 1621 he was
made "guarda-ropa" [4] to his Majesty. On March 10 of 1623, [5] he
was given the title of "Secretario sin ejercicio" to his sovereign;
and in June of that same year, he is listed as "Secretario de su
Majestad y de su Cámara" [6] when taking part in the fiestas for
the Prince of Wales. The king promised, on August 22, 1623, [7] to
make him member of a military order; and on September 24
of that same year, he was given membership in Calatrava, with
Olivares as sponsor for the occasion. [8] In May of 1625 he became
Secretary to the Inquisition, [9] a prestigious position, one may be
sure. During many of these years, at least, he was, as well, *guardadamas* [10] in the Palace, a role that occasioned some jokes at
his expense. He belonged to an illustrious branch of the Hurta-
dos and held seignory, it was said, over Villar del Olmo. Aside
from his inherited wealth, he must have received very handsome

---

[3] La Barrera, *Catálogo bibliográfico y biográfico*, 247.

[4] *Noticias de Madrid*, p. 1. Under [Mayo, año de 1621], one reads:
"... mismo día, juraron por Guarda-ropa del Rey nuestro Señor, don Antonio
de Mendoza y don Antonio Ruiz de la Escalera". G. A. Davies, *A Poet at
Court...*, (27, n. 36) gives the exact date as May 23, 1621.

[5] *Noticias de Madrid*, 49-50.

[6] *Ibid.*, 63.

[7] *Ibid.*, 71.

[8] *Ibid.*, 79. See also G. A. Davies, *A Poet at Court...* (32 with n. 50),
who, when commenting on the importance of this occasion, writes: "certainly for Mendoza the investiture must have symbolized the triumph of
the *arriviste*."

[9] *Noticias de Madrid* (under date of May 17), 118. Antonio de [A]llosa,
who had held that position up to this time, was given "the Secretaría del
Patronato," a place which he would sold apparently only until Sept. 13, 1625.
See below, p. 80.

[10] La Barrera, *Catálogo bibliográfico y biográfico...*, 248. He quotes
Suppico de Moraes as his authority. Tirso's own references in *El melancólico*
and in the "A ti a solas" of his *Parte IV* seemingly confirm Suppico de
Moraes as to Mendoza's role as *guardadamas*.

stipends from his many offices. Measured by the financial state of the penniless poets of the 1620's, he was wealthy indeed. [11]

He had *privanza literaria* with the royal family: it was he who was chosen to write up the fiestas celebrating the king's birthday in 1622; he who, a year or so later, would compose *Querer por sólo querer* for that of the queen; he who wrote up the ceremonies of the oath that the Cortes took to Baltasar Carlos in 1632. His *comedias* are at times *cultas* and of such a nature that they were more pleasing to sophisticated palace tastes than they were to those of the public theatres.

He wrote countless poems in which he flattered people, among others the Conde-Duque, as long as the latter was in favor. When the *privado* fell, he stood apart — a desertion which Gregorio Marañón [12] does not pardon him. In 1643, he apparently had in Zaragoza a quarrel with Olivares' illegitimate son, don Enrique de Guzmán, originally known as "Julián Valcárcel." This quarrel he straightway reported to the king. Marañón's comment on the whole affair is: " ... demuestra, si realmente ocurrió así, la impertinencia de don Julián y la soplonería de don Antonio." Another episode of 1627 points in the same general direction, at the same time

---

[11] It should be noted that he was given "las escribanías de rentas de Ávila y Palencia, Medina del Campo y Carrión de los Condes, que tenía el Conde de Villamediana". See *Noticias de Madrid,* 49-50. The *encomienda* of Calatrava alone meant 10,500 ducats income, according to G. A. Davies, *A Poet at Court,* 33, n. 55.

[12] For the quotations of this paragraph, see G. Marañón, *El Conde-Duque de Olivares,* 143; 182, n. 6; 282; 290, n. 14; 330, n. 190. G. A. Davies (*A Poet at Court* ..., 33), makes a comment on the letter of Mendoza to Olivares that is vital for Tirso's unhappy experiences with the court poet: "One piece of evidence suggests that Mendoza realized that what power he had lay *not in his secretarial office* but in his special relationship with the King's favorite. The occasion was a letter addressed to Olivares from Aranjuez in May, 1627, in which Mendoza tried to dissuade Olivares from allowing Juan de Vera y Figueroa, Count de la Roca (author of a widely read book, *El embajador* [1620], and an old Sevillian acquaintace of the favorite) to be his biographer. Mendoza resorted to calumny and innuendo in order to blacken Roca's name in the eyes of a friend, but the most significant aspect of his venomous letter is what is left unexpressed, that Mendoza probably vented spite on Juan de Vera because of an unwillingness to see someone else engaged on a labour of *pietas* that the poet had probably himself coveted. The limitations to Mendoza's influence with Olivares are indicated by the favorite's refusal to take the hint". Mr. Davies at one time (p. 29) calls Mendoza "Olivares' creature."

that it indicates he may have been jealous of his fellow-writers at court. As Marañón puts it: "Escribió [Mendoza] un alegato, en extremo adulatorio para el valido [Olivares], para que éste no encargase al Conde de la Roca escribir su vida."

Other episodes of 1625 and 1627 not only underline his jealousy of his fellow-workers, but they indicate that he was not above doing them real harm when he could. A case in point is that of one who, like Mendoza, was "ayuda de cámara" to his Majesty. Just how zealously Mendoza was protecting his favor with the king, how ruthlessly he was weeding out any and all competition about that time, is suggested by an episode which both Almansa y Mendoza's *Cartas* and the *Noticias de Madrid* have recorded. In the former source one reads: [13]

> Cayó de su privanza y oficio Antonio de Losa [sic] ayuda de cámara de su Majestad, y *entró en todo* D. Antonio de Mendoza, su compañero, por una cosa bien niña y que esperamos tendrá remedio, *por ser muy buena persona el caído y muy bien quisto*, si bien no lo es menos el que en su lugar ha entrado.

The *Noticias* give us the serious consequences of this "very childish" affair for Alosa: [14]

> A 13 [de septiembre de 1625] mandó el Rey a Antonio de Losa, de su cámara y su secretario, que no entrase en Palacio ni saliese de su casa; después se le dio orden que pudiese ir a misa, pero muy de mañana. Hubo varios discursos acerca de esta orden del Rey.

We do not know what brought about the downfall of Alosa, [15] but it does not require a more than normal amount of malice on the part of the scholar — particularly after reading such suggestive

---

[13] Almansa y Mendoza, *Cartas*, 319.

[14] *Noticias de Madrid*, 124.

[15] His name was Alosa, according to the poems that Mendoza wrote him. See p. 81. G. A. Davies (*A Poet at Court...*, 32-33) says: "It was probably in Zaragoza in January, 1626, that he was promoted to the office of his senior, Antonio de Losa, deposed for a trivial offense." As the *Noticias de Madrid* make evident, it was in Madrid, just before September 13, 1625 that it happened. See p. 124.

comments as those given above — to suspect that Antonio de Mendoza was instrumental in bringing about Alosa's fall through tales he carried to the king. But let us study Mendoza's own words, for we fortunately have two poems from him, written to this same Antonio de Alosa, and both are very revealing. In one poem, entitled "A Antonio de Alosa, estando enfermo el que le escribe," [16] he declares that he envies Alosa his magnificent health, not his new suit: "Si piensas que tengo envidia / a tu verde tafetán, / tu salud me tenga yo / y tus galas Satanás ... / Nada te envidio de tanta / copiosa paternidad, / sino el monte de salud / de tu diluvio carnal." In another, labelled "A Antonio de Alosa, secretario de cámara, a quien toca guardar los dulces que envían al Rey," [17] it is not only Alosa's health, but his "talle tan narcisero" that Mendoza envies: "Y si robusto desprecias / (mal haya su discrición) [sic] / de la sagrada hipocondria / el hipócrita dolor, / vengaránme de tu perra / salud enemigos dos, / las tardes el matrimonio / y las noches el salón." Later, in 1625 (as we have seen above), Mendoza would manage to rid himself of his competitor.

There is yet other proof of Mendoza's envious nature. When the poet Villayzán became the favorite dramatist of the king, Mendoza penned a devastating, if clever, satire against that poet. La Barrera [18] has commented on it in the following terms (p. 491):

> No hubo de ver con mucho gusto "el discreto de Palacio," don Antonio Hurtado de Mendoza, tan marcadas y envidiables distinciones. Evidentemente celoso de ellas, y bajo la apariencia crítica del renombre popular que iba logrando Villayzán, en tal grado que de todas las comedias nuevas *se decía* y divulgaba *que eran suyas*, compuso aquella picante *Letrilla* que anda entre sus obras

Tirso would have granted without discussion that Mendoza was an envious, jealous person; and on March 6 of 1625, he would learn to his misfortune — if he did not know it already — that the poet was a talebearer.

---

[16] See *Obras poéticas de don Antonio Hurtado de Mendoza*, I, 291-293.
[17] *Ibid.*, II, 28-30.
[18] La Barrera, *Catálogo* ..., 491.

But probably the worst of Mendoza's sins from the point of view of our Mercedarian was that "el lego aseado" was the *hechura* of Olivares. Indeed, he must have felt that Mendoza was a turn-coat, one who had won success at court, not through intelligence, talent, and hard study, but through cheap opportunism and compromise. Even his modern biographer [19] is somewhat troubled by the circumstances attending Mendoza's sudden appearance in the new court of Philip IV. How could this mere *segundón*, who had, as late as March 14, 1619, been a 'gentleman' in the court of Saldaña (son to Lerma!), how was it that one suddenly finds him, two months after Philip's accession, 'assistant to the robe' of the new ruler? And it should be noted that he took the oath at the hand of that young monarch's *sumiller de corps*, the Count of Olivares, implacable enemy to the Lermas. How had Mendoza managed to weather the dire misfortune that befell almost all the Sandoval family with Philip III's death to reappear as the *protégé* of the new royal favorite? Mr. Davies goes ahead to add: "The close ties which bound both men together in the years which followed make it likely that Mendoza's appointment was Olivares' personal gift." In 1623, when Mendoza was given the habit of Calatrava at the hands of Olivares — "with great ostentation" — his biographer is willing to concede apparently that the poet was really the *valido* of Olivares rather than of the king. He points out, too, that Mendoza's poetry "reveals the extent to which that triumph was due to assiduous blandishment": in one sonnet the poet proclaims "that nothing on earth would make Mendoza ungrateful to his master." In another epistolary poem to the Count-Duke's son-in law, Medina de las Torres, he declares his loyalty to both and intimates that his crest bears the picture of a slave.

Such terms as "el muy aseado lego," "el lego cortesano," were used to refer to Antonio Hurtado de Mendoza in his own day. That he made a good appearance, one that graced palace halls, that he charmed many around him, can hardly be questioned.

---

[19] G. A. Davies, *A Poet at Court* ..., 27 and *passim*. He suggests (p. 28) the possibility that Mendoza's rapid rise at court, in spite of his previous ties with the Lerma regime, may have been due to the influence of the Duke of Infantado.

Almansa y Mendoza, [20] describing him on the occasion when he was given the habit of Calatrava, mentions "su calidad, su ingenio, su agrado, y buenas partes." La Barrera [21] explains his success with the king in terms of "su excelente tacto cortesano, el feliz ingenio que le adornaba, y su carácter agradable, a la par que franco y desenfadado."

The term "lego" was probably one Mendoza chose for himself, for he shunned consciously the attitude of the professional "littérateur" — probably through instinctive wisdom! Góngora, [22] at least, tells us that don Antonio was "poco adornado de estudios." Mendoza could be pleasantly self-deprecatory to his "betters": for instance, his *comedia Más merece quien más ama*, presented in the Palace, ends:

> Más merece quien más ama;
> y pocas veces os sirve
> su dueño, porque no digan
> "Más yerra quien más escribe."

For all his attitude of dilettante, Mendoza apparently had a clear idea of what should be, for the Palace at least, the *comedia's* aims: he wanted one that should be "a superior form of art," one in keeping with the laws of good taste. The *graciosos* of the man who prided himself on being the perfect *cortesano* are lacking in sparkle and verve — by comparison with Tirso's, for instance — but their humor is such that it could not have brought a blush to the most innocent maiden's cheek. Don Antonio de Mendoza consciously avoided coarseness of expression. His biographer Gareth A. Davies, [23] interprets this fact in terms of "Palace decorum," saying that it "may explain his poetry's total freedom from grossness and obscenity." He goes on to say: "Even when occasionally he is being transparently allusive, he draws over his subject a discreet veil of poetry." Mr. Davies was, at the moment, speaking of Mendoza's poetry, but his statement would hold equally well for his plays. The poet's attitude was perhaps determined in part

---

[20] Almansa y Mendoza, *Cartas*, 219.
[21] La Barrera, *Catálogo* ..., 247.
[22] *Ibid.*, 246.
[23] G. A. Davies, *A Poet at Court* ..., 187-188.

by his Aristotelian leanings. [24] In *Más merece quien más ama,*
he apparently insists on *profit with delight.* Rosauro says (II, fol.
104):

> En sus comedias contemplo
> que las celebran y admiran
> *cuando juntamente miran*
> *al deleite y al ejemplo.*

Mendoza wrote the *entremeses* for Tirso's *El vergonzoso* when
the play was put on at Buenavista. If he attended the performance,
one must wonder what were his sensations on listening to the
gracioso's jokes.

El Conde de la Roca, who shows himself very sympathetic to
Tirso in 1635, has this to say of don Antonio Hurtado de Mendoza: [25]

> Et al Mendoza si dica, che intrigando un tantino di
> più gli argomenti delle sue Comedie, nessuno *discreto* le
> chiamerà lunghe, che ancorche il suo stile non sia l'antico
> Comico è il vero Cortigiano, et il mutarle, sarebbe difetto,
> supposto che in Spagna è già morto il volgo .

Having told Mendoza ironically that by complicating ("intrigan-
do") a bit more his plots, they would not seem so long to the
"discreet," Roca then adds that Mendoza would do quite well
to stay with his courtly plays, for the *vulgo* in Spain was already
dead.

Let us now go to Tirso's travails with the *Junta de Reformación.*

------

[24] His Aristotelian leanings are also evident in *El galán sin dama* (I, 184):
speaking of the many types of *comedias* of the day he says: "Son grandes
imitadoras / de las antiguas que alaban, / pues, *conforme al arte, acaban /
en solas veinte y cuatro horas*". Unless I am mistaken, *El galán sin dama* is,
in its own time element, a play that follows classic rules. My guess is it
was written in 1621-1622 and retouched in 1623 after the changes in costume
due to the sumptuary decrees of February 1623. At one point, don Crisóstomo, who had previously had on "calzas", is wearing a *golilla* (II, p. 197),
at another a "ferreruelo largo" (II, 204).

[25] See his *Ragguaglio,* included in Wido Hempel's study, "In onor della
Fenice ibera", 138-164; in particular, 141.

Since we believe that the *acuerdo* of the *Junta de Reformación* and its setting have not as yet been thoroughly understood, we shall have to reprint it in its entirety, together with two other recommendations made on that same March 6th of 1625. It is a document whose interest extends far beyond Tirso's theatre, one which reads as follows: [26]

> *Maestro Téllez, por otro nombre Tirso, que hace comedias.* Tratóse del escándalo que causa un fraile Mercedario que se *llama el* maestro Téllez, por otro nombre Tirso, con comedias que hace profanas y de malos incentivos y ejemplos. Y por ser caso notorio, se acordó que se consulte a S. M. de que el confesor diga al nuncio (tachado: "que mande a su Provincial") le eche de aquí a uno de los monasterios más remotos de su Religión y le imponga excomunión mayor, *latae sententiae*, para que no haga comedias ni otro ningún género de versos profanos. Y esto se haga luego.

This *acuerdo* relating to Tirso must be interpreted against those general efforts of reform that dated back to March 24 of the preceding year, at which time the *Junta* initiated its campaign: (1) against the performances of *comedias;* (2) against clerics who *attended, wrote,* or *published* them. As early as August 29, 1624, they asked, as well, that the *Consejo de Castilla* consult His Majesty on the advisability of taking up with the *nuncio* (Papal legate) the "exenciones que se dan a Religiosos que acuden a aquel Tribunal [i.e., el Apostólico de Roma] para no estar sujetos a sus Prelados en las licencias para salir fuera y para otras cosas, con que se libran de la obediencia dellos." [27]

---

[26] See Angel González Palencia, "Quevedo, Tirso y las comedias ante la Junta de Reformación," 83. The Junta had been named as early as May 1, 1621, and its first task was to prepare the *Capítulos de Reformación* which were published February 11, 1623. Philip IV's *Junta* was appointed, however, for the "reformación no sólo en esta corte, sino en estos mis reinos, en materia de vicios, abusos y cohechos"; and as early as March 24, 1624, its members took up the matter of the theatre and of the priests who were attending *comedias.* This *Junta,* in its membership, must have been representative of approximately the same forces which in 1620 tried to bring about the reform of the theatre and to prevent such priests as were writing and attending plays from taking part in these worldly practices. See my study, "Attacks on Lope and his Theatre in 1617-1621," 57-76.

[27] González Palencia, "Quevedo, Tirso y las comedias...", 77-78.

The document having to do with Tirso is sandwiched between two others, also dated March 6, 1625. The first of the two deals with *the great number of comedias* and the *frequency of their representations* in the public *corrales;* the second with Tirso's particular case; the third with the attempts of the dramatists of the day to print their plays. Now all three of these problems were taken up on March 1 with the Conde-Duque de Olivares; and the secretary who recorded that conference has done so in most confusing form under the general heading: [28]

> *No se escriban comedias.* Hablóse que se representó a 1 de marzo [de 1625] con el Señor Conde-Duque y pareció a S. E. [i.e., a Olivares] que el Presidente [del Consejo de Castilla], mi señor, y el Consejo, de su oficio, lo hiciesen; y que [en lo de Tirso], S. Ilustrísima [el nuncio] lo podrá mandar así.

In the same minutes there follows a second paragraph that has to do with the third point, one which would soon affect our dramatist Tirso as well as Lope de Vega:

> Y porque se ha reconocido el daño de imprimir libros de comedias, novelas, ni otros de este género, por el que blandamente hacen a las costumbres de la juventud, se consulte a S. M. ordene al Consejo [de Castilla] que en ninguna manera se dé licencia para imprimirlos.

From the above documents, it would seem that the *Junta,* which had originally been appointed by Olivares and was working in closest cooperation with him, took to him three matters: (1) the question as to who should deal with the matter of limiting the influence of plays (their great number and the frequency of their performances). The Conde-Duque's answer was, on March 1st, 1625, that the President of the Royal Council of Castilla, together with members of the Council, could do this by virtue of their office. As to the question of Tirso (since a priest was involved), the *Junta* could get action through the *Nuncio* [29] (the Papal legate).

---

[28] *Ibid.,* 78-79.
[29] The "Nuncio" at this time was Julio Sacchetti. See Espasa Encyclopedia under "nuncio."

[Where doubt was involved, he would presumably take up the question in Rome itself.] In the matter of the printing of books of *comedias*, he suggested that they recommend to his Majesty to give orders to the Council of Castilla that it was, under no condition, to give permission for the printing of such harmful books.

In this maze of conflicting authorities, the *Junta* would walk just as carefully as Olivares had suggested: it would recommend to his Majesty that he *ask his Confessor* to take the matter of Tirso up with the Papal legate. These measures with regard to the theatre were unpopular, and the *Junta* was proceeding with utmost care — but not with enough care, even and so, for it had apparently forgotten that the Order had full authority to deal with its own members. Moreover, priests *still* had the right to go straight to the Apostolic Tribunal of Rome, however much the *Junta* might wish it otherwise. Both the Mercedarians and Tirso would fight zealously for their authority. Now the confessor of the king, fray Antonio de Sotomayor, was almost certainly acquainted with the prerogatives of the Orders and could hardly have been enthusiastic over the task assigned him: Tirso would, years later, in his history of the Mercedarian Order, praise him highly. Possibly the Confessor took it to the Nuncio, as requested, but between them they would have agreed that the rights of the Mercedarian Order were probably involved and that the question would have to be resolved in the Apostolic Council in Rome.

Certainly Fray don Gaspar Prieto, General of the Order, would, in the *capítulo* of the Mercedarians which convened in Seville the last days of April, 1625, fight valiantly for their authority to deal with their own members in civil (as well as religious) matters. Tirso's fate must have been the one in point, but in the records of this chapter, there is no mention of the charge against him. The Mercedarians, at that meeting in Seville, gave orders that "ningún Religioso súbdito saque sus causas a otro cualquier Tribunal, eclesiástico o secular, fuera de los de la Religión (salva semper authoritate [sic] apostólica)." [30] The chapter even threatens the harshest

---

[30] See R. P. Penedo Rey, *Tirso en Sevilla*, 42-44. On March 6, 1627, the Mercedarians were still fighting vigorously for their right to judge their own members in civil cases. What is more, it is evident that this right was recognized by the civil authorities. One reads in the anonymous *Noticias*

punishment for any member who should take his case to *any other tribunal:* "Y assimesmo ordena y manda, pena de privación de voz activa y pasiva, por cuatro años, y de un año de cárcel, y de que en el haga la penitencia de *graviori culpa* ..." Tirso's resume of this, in the history of his Order, is: "Que debajo de justas y rigurosas penas no se litiguen nuestros casos criminales en Tribunal profano [corrected to "extraño"], salvo siempre el apostólico recurso, aunque sean obispos o metropolitanos." It had, in a measure, become a case of *Gaspar* Olivares against *Gaspar* Prieto.

Tirso was meanwhile taking such means of defending himself as were rightfully his. He must have gone directly, or indirectly, to the Apostolic Tribunal of Rome, almost surely with the full approval of the General of his Order, possibly with his *actual aid,* for, as Father Penedo has pointed out,[31] "el general Fr. Gaspar, sobre todo, con quien había convivido [Tirso] en Madrid, según declara repetidamente, desde 1622 a 1625, fue [en la *Historia de Nuestra Sra. de la Merced*] objeto cuidado de su gratitud." Indeed, we have double proof of Tirso's handiwork in Rome. In dedicating his *Parte tercera* (1634) to one Julio Monti, "caballero milanés," Tirso alludes to the "tempestades y persecuciones invidiosas [que]

---

de Madrid (157), under the date indicated above, a curious notice that necessarily brings to mind *El condenado por desconfiado*: "A 6 [de marzo de 1627] llegó nueva que un fraile mercenario [sic], llamado Fray Maldonado, entre Yébenes y Orgaz había muerto ... de un pistoletazo a un arriero por robarle. Prendióle la Santa Hermandad y le llevaron con grillos a Orgaz y *le entregaron a su Religión, que le pidió con grande instancia*; había tres años que andaba fugitivo haciendo robos y muertes con pistolas y coleto y un valiente caballo." Was Fray Maldonado (!) living literature? The matter of *El condenado*'s date of composition is complicated still further by the fact that Juan Acacio had, in his repertoire on March 13, 1627, a play to take to Valencia that was entitled *El condenado por dudar*, one which was, in my opinion, almost certainly *El condenado por desconfiado*. See H. Mérimée's *Spectacles et comédiens à Valencia*, 172, n. 4. There are good reasons for believing that *El condenado* was written in 1622, as I shall show on another occasion.

    I should here like to make acknowledgement of my debt to Father Penedo for comprehension of how the various notes of the *Junta's* meetings should be interpreted. I owe a very real debt also to Miss María Araujo, of the Library of the University of Arizona, who was able to clear up for me some points of conventual practice. Without their aid I should have been lost when interpreting the implications of the *Junta's acuerdo.*

[31] R. P. Penedo Rey, *Tirso en Sevilla*, 35.

procuraron malograr los honestos recreos de mis ocios" and states frankly that, had Julio Monti not played San Telmo in the situation, his bark would have foundered. [32] The reference can hardly be to any storm other than the one he began to ride out in March of 1625.

But, as good fortune has determined it, we probably have a witness of the moment to tell us what Tirso did in those first days after receiving news of the *Junta*'s *acuerdo*. This testimony, as we shall see, has a very strange setting, placed, as it is, in the *vejamen* of a poet of Madrid. One Anastasio Pantaleón de Ribera [33] is, that Lent of 1625, defending himself and his far-from-admirable *cortesana*, "Sirene," against the slurs that Gabriel de Corral had made in his *vejamen*, of March 1, 1625, in the Academy of Madrid. More than defense, it is counter-attack. The very satirical Pantaleón first summons Corral (for he is the "Coriandro" of the very black, bristly beard and the oily skin, whose clothes were seemingly not always so clean as the satirist thought they should be), then demands: [34]

De parte de Dios, mi Musa
que le digas te demanda

[32] Quoted from E. Cotarelo y Mori, *Comedias de Tirso*, I, p. lvii, n. 3.

[33] See my study, "Pantaleón de Ribera, 'Sirene', Castillo Solórzano, and the *Academia de Madrid* in Early 1625," 189-200.

[34] See "Vejamen que dio a los poetas de la *Academia de Madrid*", II, 168-169. It should be noted that the two sketches of Alarcón and Tirso follow immediately the eight verses devoted to "don Abanico de la Iuarreda", identified as Juan [¿Francisco?] de la Barreda in a manuscript of the B. N., according to Gallardo's *Ensayo de una Bib. esp. de libros raros y curiosos*, IV, col. 91-92. In another *vejamen* of Pantaleón's, "Vejamen que el poeta dio en la insigne Academia de Madrid" (II, 28-29), he is "don Abanico de Iurreda". This poet was evidently of very short stature, for he says of himself (II, 30): "Mi talle no es de los buenos, / que da, por lo corto, risa..."; Alarcón was "camello enano"; and Tirso has, in *El amor médico* (II, viii), made a strong defense of short men, one which led Sra. de los Ríos to declare (*Obras dramáticas completas de Tirso*, II, 966): "De modo que Tirso, al defenderse a sí propio, defiende la brevedad de estatura; luego era pequeño...". I quite agree with Sra. de los Ríos that Tirso was short of stature, though not with her conclusion that Tirso was answering Suárez de Figueroa's advice in *El pasajero* (of 1617): "...importa excluir de públicos oficios a sujetos menores de marca, hombrecillos pequeños...". Tirso was answering the men who had linked his name with that of the diminutive Alarcón in the quatrain of 1625. Instinctively, Pantaleón had put the small men of the Academy in a threesome! See below, Ch. VI, pp. 254-58.

si eres alcuza que vives
en penas de hoja de lata.

As witnesses in this very important matter, he calls upon most of
the poets of the Academy of Madrid, summoning each with the
imperative "dígalo"; and in the verses that follow, Pantaleón
manages to give us a thumb-nail sketch of each and every poet.
Having first pulverized Ruiz de Alarcón with the following verses,

Dígalo mi mejicano,
que aunque sin cola ni maza,
es el monazo inventor
del primer "cócale Marta";
el que va a rietar [sic] los toros
de Zamora con su lanza
y su cuartago, hecho un mismo
poeta Ordoñez de Lara;

he then turns to an "hortelano" who is, we believe, Tirso:

Y dígalo el Hortelano
del Prado, [35] que en las palabras

---

[35] The phrase, "el hortelano del Prado" suggests that some play, given
at one of the great estates that lined the Prado, was cause of Tirso's troubles.
For instance, the famous "huerta de Juan Fernández" is described in *Deleytar
aprovechando* in the following terms: "...se ofrece a los ojos, luego que se
entra por la Puerta de Alcalá, presidente a las frescuras *del Prado,* que en
ella tienen principio". It was there that Tirso's *La huerta de Juan Fernández,*
written between March and May of 1626, was played. His novel, *El bandolero,* was read in the so-called "huerta del Duque al Prado", which after
May 17, 1625, at least, must have been the Madrid home of the young
Duque de Lerma whom Tirso has praised warmly in *No hay peor sordo.* One
reads in *Deleytar aprovechando*: "El martes por la mañana ... le tocó a la
generosa huerta del Duque al Prado ... ser el teatro de la nueva fiesta". In the
days of Philip III and Lerma, this *huerta* had often been "teatro de fiestas
reales cuando la privanza de su difunto dueño divertía en él la más piadosa
majestad que gozó España. ... Erigieron ... en el curioso patio ... un capaz
y vistoso tablado. ... Leyóse luego la novela del *Bandolero,* que ocupó toda
la mañana; y el martes por la tarde se ejecutó el auto, *No le arriendo la
ganancia.* ..." (For the quotations from *Deleytar aprovechando,* see Cotarelo,
Comedias de Tirso, I, liii). I note, as well, in La Barrera's *Catálogo* (250):
"Escribieron [Antonio Hurtado de] Mendoza y Quevedo esta comedia [*Quien
más miente medra más*] en el breve término de un día, por encargo del
Conde-Duque de Olivares, *para la magnífica fiesta que dio este célebre ministro a los Reyes la noche de San Juan, del año 1631, en los jardines del*

suele traer ponleví,
siendo hablador de ventaja;
aquel que de allende Roma
casos grita y cuentos ladra
con tal ruido que parece
que los dice una carraca.

Tirso was not taking this "lying down," in the parlance of today. For this sketch is, we believe, of our Mercedarian whose hero had assumed the role of *hortelano* in more than one of his plays, some one of which must have been played near the "huerta del Duque al Prado" shortly before the *acuerdo* was reached. Tirso was undoubtedly a "talker," as his college friend, Matías de los Reyes, [36] makes evident; and he could, on occasion, talk in words of "ponleví" (i.e., high-sounding ones), witness the opening scene of *La mujer que manda en casa*. Tirso was taking his case to Rome, and with all the noise that a rattle or a ratchet brace could make. This *vejamen* of Pantaleón's, as I have shown on another occasion, could not have been written long after Gabriel del Corral's — one which was given around March 1, 1625. [37]

It is interesting to surmise what happened immediately after Tirso received news of the *Junta's acuerdo*. Almost certainly he would pay a call on his friend, the General of the Order, don Gaspar Prieto, possibly one requested by that dignitary, in case the king's confessor, Sotomayor, had already communicated with him. The conversation would have been a long and earnest one; and when it was over, it would probably have been decided at least: (1) that Gaspar Prieto would raise, in the coming *capítulo* of Seville, the question of the Order's authority to deal with all cases of its members (subject only to the Apostolic Council)

---

conde de Monte Rey y del duque de Maqueda, próximos al Prado". Presumably, then, Pantaleón's phrase "el hortelano del Prado" refers to Tirso, who must have put on in early 1625 a play which had as hero a lover who used the disguise of *jardinero*, one that was put on in one of the private theatres belonging to some of the great nobles who had built their palaces near the Prado. I suggest that the play was *La fingida Arcadia*. See p. 130.

[36] For Matías de los Reyes' attitude toward Tirso, see above, Ch. I, n. 77. One may be sure that Pantaleón de Ribera is using derogatively the term, "hablador de ventaja".

[37] See "Pantaleón de Ribera, 'Sirene', Castillo y Solórzano, and the *Academia de Madrid* in Early 1625'," p. 197.

and would seek Rome's backing in the matter; (2) that Tirso
would be present at that chapter in Seville which was to begin
its meetings the last days of April, 1625; and (3) that the dramatist
should consider the various remote convents and decide, if possible,
which of those more distant houses would, from his point of view,
be the more acceptable.

The *acuerdo* of the *Junta*, having branded Tirso's case as
"notorious," had recommended that his banishment from Madrid
begin *immediately (luego)*; and, given the bad relations that already
existed between the Mercedarians and the regime of Olivares, [38]
the Order would not have wanted to anger unnecessarily the *privado* and his Junta. Tirso probably left Madrid as soon as he could
put his house in order. [39] This presumably meant that he must
first do what he could to get his cause before the Apostolic Council
in Rome. That he turned to Julio Monti in 1625 seems doubtful,
for this individual was probably a close relative of the César Monti who was "Patriarch of Antioch and Papal Legate in Spain from
1630-1634." Since Tirso is known to have written his "Acto de
contrición" in 1630, [40] it is probably that same year in which Julio

---

[38] See Sra. de los Ríos (*Obras dramáticas completas de Tirso*, III, 25-26)
for the government's attempt to do away with the Mercedarian and Trinitarian
Orders.

[39] R. P. Penedo Rey believes that Tirso stayed on in Madrid until some
time in April, say the 10th, and that he then accompanied Gaspar Prieto,
Maestro General of the Mercedarians, to Seville (See his "Tirso en Sevilla", 39).
I feel virtually sure that Tirso left Madrid much earlier. When the *acuerdo*
of the *Junta* recommended that his banishment begin *immediately* ("y esto
se haga luego") and when Tirso, through the mouth of the Seventh Castilian
states, in *Antona García* "Vengo de Madrid, huyendo casi", I believe that we
should take seriously the dramatist's words. Moreover, he says it from the
little inn of Mollorido (near Toro and Salamanca where the Mercedarians
had convents), and Tirso's geographical changes are very likely to be recorded
almost immediately in his plays. Later, in *Palabras y plumas*, in a barb added
to the play necessarily after his banishment, he again refers to the inn of
Mollorido. See below, p. 106.

[40] Prof. Vern Williamsen sent me the following information, which he
took from Rinaldi Froldi's edition of "La patrona de las musas" (7, n. 5):
"Fray Manuel Penedo Rey mi ha comunicato desser riuscito a trovare l'*Acto*
[de contrición] che promette di presto pubblicare". Some time before Prof.
Williamsen's letter reached me, Prof. John Reynolds and Prof. Jaime Asensio
had passed on to me the same bit of good news. I am therefore trebly indebted. The *Acto de contricción* has now been published by Fray Manuel
Penedo Rey. See *RABM*, LXXV, 1-2 (1968-1972), 479-509.

Monti became his benefactor. Pantaleón's phrase, "de allende Roma," suggests, in fact, that he first turned to someone "beyond Rome." And Julio Monti was from Milán. Possibly, César Monti was a friend of Gaspar Prieto's and would work on Tirso's behalf at the request of the General. Be the reason what it may be, Tirso eventually turned to Julio Monti, as we have seen above.

Having made ready his defense in Rome, Tirso would presumably ask himself to which of the distant convents of his Order he would prefer going, if leave he must the literary ambient of a Madrid or of a Toledo. I doubt very much indeed that Tirso would have *wanted* to quit the literary circles of those cities: such an atmosphere was nearly as necessary for his poetic survival as oxygen for his physical one. No dramatist ever depended more on the milieu that surrounded him than did Gabriel Téllez. [41] His thoughts would have turned to the West — if for no other reason than that he could not hope to visit those of the East and get back in time to meet his General in Seville by the end of April. He could, on the other hand, go first to the convent in Toro, then to Salamanca's, and from there to Trujillo's, before meeting with Gaspar Prieto and the *capítulo*. In Toro, home of the descendants of Antona García, he would necessarily have friends, for in his play, called *Antona García,* he had defended some two years before the rights of all that family to a tax-free status. It was one which Antona's loyalty to Isabel the Catholic had won for her, — for her and for all her descendants. Then, too, that monastery had nurtured Alonso Monroy, General of the Order at the time that Tirso had professed in Guadalajara. Tirso, however, must have feared from the first that Toro could hardly offer a congenial literary atmosphere. Salamanca would, of course, certainly have much more to offer in that regard, but was there an opening in that university city for him? Trujillo? That was perhaps a possibility. But, for the moment, toward Toro he would go.

---

[41] The importance of the "milieu" for Tirso's theatre is made abundantly evident in his *La prudencia en la mujer,* as I made clear in my study, "*La prudencia en la mujer* and the Ambient that Brought it Forth" of 1948. Such a comedy as *El amor médico,* whose date I have studied in the first number of *Reflexión 2* (a new Canadian review), is likewise proof of it. The same would hold for almost any play that Tirso wrote in 1621-1626. He was extraordinarily "communicative" in his theatre of those years.

Let us admit at the outset that there is no clear documentary proof that Tirso made any such trip through western Spain. [42] In positing it, we are leaning on the frail arm of surmise. Yet it is a surmise made highly plausible, as we shall soon see, by certain autobiographic details that he added to *Antona García* when retouching it in 1625 — probably in the little inn of Mollorido between Medina del Campo and Salamanca, which he had reached after leaving Madrid "almost fleeing." There can hardly fail to be some interrelation between Tirso's phrase, "casi huyendo," and the concluding one of the *Junta:* "y esto se haga luego." As he made his way toward that fortress (on a mule probably that would have been carrying not only Tirso's weight but that of his many manuscripts), the poet would presumably have been mulling over recent events that had overtaken him. If, before leaving Madrid, he had not already ascertained the identity of the person who had denounced him to the *Junta,* that question would presumably have been uppermost in his mind. I'm very inclined to believe, however, that Tirso knew from the first the direction from which his blow had come. At least, he was certain in his own mind by the time he had reached his humble hostel that it was due to envious competitors in the literary world. He had been forbidden to *write comedias,* but nothing had been said that would prevent his refashioning old ones. *Antona García* could serve his purpose: he was in the general vicinity of Toro and could recapture the spirit of its courageous heroine. By retouching scenes in Act III of that play, he could reflect therein the recent storms that had overtaken him. The autobiographical

---

[42] Against my hypothesis that Tirso left Madrid almost immediately and started toward Toro in March of 1625 was the extraordinarily bad weather of that month. The anonymous *Noticias de Madrid* records under the date of March 1st, 1625, a *very* heavy fall of snow, then declares (115): "Y este temporal tan recio y nevar casi ... todos los días duró un mes". Weather notwithstanding, I believe Tirso managed to make the trip to Mollorido and that he probably rewrote his scenes for that play in that very same inn or very shortly after leaving it. I doubt very much, however, that he ever reached Toro, which is perched on a very high cliff that overlooks the Duero. Since Mollorido is between Medina del Campo and Salamanca, both important cities at that time, the roads would presumably have been kept open, but the ascent to Toro may well have been impossible.

changes he chose to make were done hastily. [43] Proof of this lies within the play itself as we have it today. In the changes made, we have almost certainly Tirso's first written reactions to the humiliation he had suffered in Madrid. As altered, this play seems to make evident that from the first he attributed his difficulties to envious competitors in the literary field.

In the war over the succession between Isabel the Catholic and the largely Portuguese forces supporting La Beltraneja — a war which serves as background to *Antona García* — some Castilians and Portuguese are chatting together more or less amicably in the very bad little inn of Mollorido, situated between Salamanca and Medina del Campo. The outcome of the war is of secondary importance to these merchants: their real allegiance is to the theme, "business-as-usual;" or, in the proverb of the time, "Viva quien venza." Having discussed their own wares, one of the salesmen then turns to the "Seventh Castilian" with the question: "Y vos, ¿qué mercaduría vendéis?" The dialogue that follows includes, in almost the same words, some of the ideas found in Tirso's dedication to Monti (III, iii):

CASTELLANO 7: *Vengo de Madrid,*
huyendo casi.

---

[43] Some years ago in studying the date of this play ("On the Date of Five Plays by Tirso", 207, n. 69) I pointed out my reasons for believing that it had suffered changes: "In the third act (sc. iii), it would seem that there must have been some tampering. At the beginning of the scene, one reads the following stage directions: 'Salen los *cuatro* castellanos'. Yet in this scene, *eight* Castilians take part and Tirso himself is clearly speaking through the mouth of the seventh. It is probable, then, that the autobiographical element in this scene was added after its original composition." Unfortunately, I tied my own hands by concluding that the *refundición* was made in 1623. Knowing that *Palabras y plumas* (played in the Palace in 1623) had a similar reference to Mollorido's inn, I decided (erroneously) that Tirso must have spent some time there *in 1623*.

It is difficult to be sure that Tirso did not change some of the other material in this scene —material that is important for its date and that of other plays with similar allusions. For instance, there is included in the list of characters of this *comedia* a "Chinchilla, soldado", and this must have been the very delightful *gracioso* of *El castigo del penséque* and *Quien calla otorga*. In its earlier form, he possibly had included within *Antona García* a virtual *entremés* with Chinchilla as hero. There is a play, *El capitán Chinchilla*, attributed to Enríquez Gómez, which I have not been able to see. See La Barrera, *Catálogo*, 141. Medel's *Índice* does not list it.

PORTUGUÉS 2:	¡Por Dios!
	pues ¿qué os sucedió?
CASTELLANO 7:	*Tener*
	enemigos (y) *envidiosos.*
PORTUGUÉS 3:	Eso es propio de *ingeniosos.*
CASTELLANO 7:	De *ricos* lo había de ser;
	que *el oro* los pone en precio
	de *discretos.*
PORTUGUÉS 3:	No lo ignoro;
	necio debe ser el oro,
	pues siempre acompaña *al necio.*
PORTUGUÉS 1:	Riquezas son estímulos
	de vicios.
PORTUGUÉS 2:	Siempre se ve.

Tirso has left Madrid, almost in flight, because of envious enemies. Envy is the inevitable lot of the talented, as the Second Portuguese sees it. It should be the lot of the rich — retorts the Seventh Castilian. In reality it is only their gold that wins for them the name of "discreet." The Third Portuguese agrees: gold must be very stupid, since it always accompanies the stupid. Thereupon the First Portuguese adds: "Riches are the cause of vice," an observation with which the Second Portuguese is in agreement.

Somewhat later, Tirso will resume his plaints — again through the mouth of the Seventh Castilian (III, iii):

CASTELLANO 7:	Emulos tengo sin "e."
PORTUGUÉS 1:	Emulos, sin "e," son mulos.
CASTELLANO 7:	Pues *¿qué queréis vos que sea*
	quien se pone a reprender
	lo que nunca acertó a hacer
	porque al discreto recrea?

Really his enemies should be termed "mulos" (stupid beasts), not "émulos" (rivals). What else could you call one who reproves a fellow-poet because he is successful in entertaining the *discreet,* — as Tirso felt he had been doing — a thing that his envious rival had never managed to do?

If we are to understand this quotation and much of what follows, we must stop a moment to see just what Tirso meant by

The More Significant Erratas Noted in "Studies in Tirso, I"

	Reads	Should Read
p. 13, 2nd paragraph, l. 3	vo-lumes	vol-umes
p. 16, end of l. 7	like-wise	likewise
p. 28, 2nd paragraph, l. 7	andy	and
p. 40, 1st paragraph, l. 8	Aristóteles	Aristóteles
p. 44, 1st paragraph, l. 10	Eurípides ''	Eurípides'
p. 50, 1st paragraph, l. 5	comics	comic
p. 50, 1st paragraph, l. 9	accondingly	accordingly
p. 51, 3rd paragraph, l. 11	Borbadillo	Barbadillo
p. 56, 1st paragraph, l. 5	Mercedarin	Mercedarian
p. 56, l. 4 from bottom	abrazando	abrazado
p. 59, 1st paragraph, l. 1	hod	hold
p. 59, 1st paragraph, l. 15	study. _El_ ...	study, _El_ ...
p. 60, l. 11 of verse	demonstración	demostración
p. 64, 3rd paragraph, l. 3	literari	literati
p. 66, 1st paragraph, l. 14	son-inlaw	son-in-law
p. 70, 2nd paragraph, l. 3	most	must
p. 78, note 9, l. 3	sold	hold
p. 101, note 52, l. 8	time"....	time:" . . . .
p. 105, note 55, l. 6	in	it
p. 105, note 55, l. 13	wass	was
p. 108, 3rd paragraph, l. 6	di-sections	di-rections
p. 111, note 66, l. 4	Biographical	Bibliographical
p. 115, note 74, l. 3	Penninghis acto	penning his note
p. 115, end of note 74		

	for	read
p. 222, 1st paragraph, l. 15	courtlines	courtliness
p. 226, note 21, l. 6	given their honor	given in their honor
p. 240, note 49, l. 2	Court of Entertainment	Court Entertainment
p. 245, 1st paragraph, l. 11	poet wrote	poet who wrote
p. 249, note 6, l. 4	Andrés	Andrée
p. 250, l. 1	no sé que	no sé qué
p. 281, 2nd paragraph	Inés Guzman	Inés de Guzmán
p. 283, note 38, l. 1	May 19th	May 17th
p. 288, end of second quotation	A todo	A todos
p. 294, 3rd paragraph, l. 7	Conde la Saldaña	Conde de Saldaña
p. 298, note 3, 2nd paragraph, l. 6	port	part
p. 298, note 3, 2nd paragraph, l. 8	will	has
p. 308, l. 9	de mi	de mí
p. 321, l. 12	prowerful	powerful
p. 322, 2nd paragraph, l. 7	whe-reas	where-as
p. 332, note 4	intencinado	intencionado
p. 334, end of Corral's quotation	bastan	basta
p. 340, l. 10	through out	throughout
p. 346, note 46	suggest	suggests
p. 354, l. 8	May 1st	March 1st
p. 354, note 61, l. 2	Nevertheles	Nevertheless
p. 357, note 66, l. 1	hal	had
p. 358, 2nd paragraph, l. 3	plays	play
p. 360, 2nd paragraph, l. 3	nost	lost
p. 360, 2nd paragraph, l. 3	No saber	El saber
p. 370, l. 3	Biographical	Bibliographical

Page reference		
p. 115, note 75	stu-dies	stud-ies
p. 121, l. 4	sin decoro de palacio,	sin decoro, de palacio
p. 133, note 106, l. 12	Arceo	Arceo
p. 137, 2nd paragraph, l. 1	offig	offing
p. 138, bottom	pues ¿qué si a mí ....?	pues que si a mí ....
p. 141, 1st paragraph, l. 8	wond-er	won-der
p. 147, 1st paragraph, l. 10	favor de	favor of
p. 150, l. 2	in a century's time	in many centuries.
p. 157, note 14, l. 6	episo-de	epi-sode
p. 157, note 14, last line	associeated	associated
p. 178, 2nd paragraph, l. 2	ware	wore
p. 179, note 45, end of 1st paragraph	accasion	occasion
p. 180, last line	intremés	entremés
p. 187, note 57, l. 1	Asensiós	Asensio's
p. 189, l. 2	pedigüeno	pedigüeño
p. 189, l. 3 of verse	versifiquer	versifiquier
p. 196, 1st paragraph, l. 1	pasing	passing
p. 200, l. 9	passage	passage
p. 207, note 47, 2nd paragraph	199	299
p. 207, note 47, 2nd paragraph	los santos lugares	las santas leyes
p. 210, 1st paragraph in prose	Pimentels	Pimentel
p. 210, l. 12	cha-racters	char-acters
p. 211, 1st paragraph, l. 6	printsince	print since
p. 211, 2nd paragraph, l. 10	du-ring	dur-ing
p. 221, quotation, l. 1	es es	es

discreto. To comprehend his use of the word, we must go to the indispensable study of Professor A. A. Parker,[44] entitled "The Meaning of 'Discreción' in *No hay más fortuna que Dios*: the Medieval Background and Sixteenth and Seventeenth-Century Usages." This study starts out (p. 218):

> The primary meaning of *discreción* in the sixteenth and seventeenth centuries, when not used in a theological context, can best be understood by reference to its antonym. Damasio de Frías, writing in 1579, tells us that the opposite of "discreto" is "necio." The Academy Dictionary preserves the fundamental connotation of "necio:" it is applied to a man who is ignorant of what he could or should know. Frías emphasizes the fact that the word conveys a moral reproach.

Profesor Parker also points out (227-229):

> Throughout the Middle Ages Discretion had meant not only Prudence but also the use of reason — a meaning that survives in our phrase 'to reach years of discretion' ... Since intelligence is nourished by study, it was natural to identify Discretion with Learning. St. Isidore of Seville had made "discretus" synonymous with "doctus" ... This conception of Discretion as intelligence and learning, or a good education, was taken over by the Renaissance ... becoming essentially a social accomplishment in the well-educated gentlemen ... It was restricted to a worldly prudence or a courtly refinement ... For Castiglione, Discretion was the sense of fitness in the art of deportment that prevented a gentleman from making himself ridiculous in company ... In short, to be discreet was above all to *operare opportunamente.*

Here is the basis of the contrast on which Tirso insists: although Mendoza might be called "el discreto" (in the sense of Castiglione's *cortesano*), Tirso was the learned, intelligent man (the "doctus") of St. Isidore. What is more, — and here we have

---

[44] Alexander A. Parker, "The Meaning of 'Discreción' in *No hay más fortuna que Dios*: the Medieval Background and Sixteenth and Seventeenth Century Usages," 218-234.

the implied moral reproach cited above — Antonio Hurtado de Mendoza didn't even merit the term "discreto": he couldn't hold his tongue! For Tirso's first target is undoubtedly that court poet, as we shall prove shortly. His second one, at the moment, was one Lope de Vega Carpio; [45] but of the latter's role in this matter, we shall speak later.

Let us continue with the dialogue which is essentially autobiographic:

PORT. 2: Poeta debéis ser vos.
CAST. 7: Castigóme en serlo Dios.
PORT. 2: Y ¿escribís con agudeza?
CAST. 7: Dícenlo todos, que yo
no me tengo por agudo.
PORT. 2: ¿Llamáisos?
CAST. 7: Decirlo dudo,
que hasta el nombre me quitó
la envidia.
PORT. 3: ¿Satirizáis?
CAST. 7: No se hallará quien presuma
de mí que muerda mi pluma
a nadie; antes si miráis
lo que he impreso y lo que he escrito,
por modo y estilo nuevo,
solemnizo a quien no debo
buenas obras.
CAST. 5: Ya es delito
saber mucho.

The first half of the above passage is not easy to understand in the light of such facts as we have. Miss Margaret Wilson [46] interprets it in connection with the decree of the *Junta:*

The edict of the *Junta de Reformación* had referred to "M.º Téllez, por otro nombre Tirso," and it may be that

---

[45] Although Tirso returns over and over to Mendoza's role in this whole matter, I have found no further criticism of Lope, aside from the fact that, in dedicating his *Primera parte* (Sevilla, 1627), to Alonso Paz of Salamanca, he alludes satirically to those who assign a different patron to each of the twelve plays included in a volume, "adocenados los patrones". I feel sure Tirso had in mind some of Lope's later *partes.*

the use of this pastoral pseudonym, so reminiscent of profane literature, had been condemned along with the writing of frivolous plays.

Certainly, the spirit of the document that would banish Tirso from Madrid is almost contemptuous. The very stern tone of the *Junta*, [47] made up in large part of grave prelates who wore the cloth, suggests they would probably not have been impressed by the literary achievement of a priest who styled himself "Tirso," one who, in their opinion, was writing plays of "evil incentive and example," one whose case they labeled "notorious." However, Tirso is here merely saying that envy had destroyed his "reputation." In 1635, the word he used (in identical context) was "fama." [48]

The second half of the above exchange is even more puzzling than the first, for Tirso had, by 1625, certainly written (and even printed in his *Cigarrales*) highly satirical verse and prose. The *Cigarrales de Toledo* of 1624 [49] was undoubtedly in print, and it was full of satirical darts, directed against both the poets of the day and their literary schools. In *La fingida Arcadia*, of 1622 [50] but not printed until 1634, he had inserted a scene (III, iii) of brilliant satire that was, as we shall prove later, at the expense of Luis Vélez de Guevara and Olivares, though he calls neither by name. Moreover, play after play of 1622-23 is filled with satire of Góngora and gongorism. His *La prudencia en la mujer*, [51] composed in 1622,

---

[46] See her edition of *Antona García*, pp. xxiii-xxiv.

[47] Ángel González Palencia, in "Quevedo, Tirso y las comedias ante la Junta de Reformación", has given the background of the various members of the *Junta*. At least seven of the ten were priests. It was one made up of distinguished men who, from the modern point of view, were puritanical, but it must be remembered that Spain was fighting a war on more than one front and that many Spaniards believed that their country's condition was due largely to moral decay. Tirso, though he satirizes over and over Mendoza, never condemns the *Junta*.

[48] In the "A ti a solas", of the *Parte IV*, Tirso tells Mendoza: "...impórtame el secreto lo mismo que *la fama, que se desploma con las murmuraciones*". He is clearly referring back to what Mendoza's "murmuraciones" had cost him in March of 1625.

[49] See below, "Tirso's Relations to Lope and his Theatre Reappraised."

[50] Fort the date of *La fingida Arcadia*, see Ch. IV, p. 211, n. 54.

[51] See "*La prudencia en la mujer* and the Ambient that Brought it Forth," in particular, 1173-1175.

THE ELMER E. RASMUSON LIBRARY
UNIVERSITY OF ALASKA

was a harsh denunciation of the new regime, though again he calls no names. Possibly he was thinking of such long "sátiras" as Lope had written against Torres Rámila around 1618, or of the *vejámenes* of the "Academia de Madrid," filled with highly *personal* invective, with which that "casa de locos" was amusing (and destroying) itself in 1625. More probably still, he was, in his own mind, limiting himself to the two envious poets whom he believed to be the cause of his troubles with the *Junta*.

The Fourth Portuguese is not yet sure that part of the blame does not lie with the accuser. He probes further:

PORT. 4:   Debéis ser
soberbio; hacéis menosprecio
de los otros.

CAST. 1:   Solo el necio
al discreto osa morder;
que yo venero de modo
a los de mi profesión
que el menor me da lición;
pero ni lo alabo todo
ni de todo digo mal.

PORT. 1:   De bobos es alabarlo
todo; y todo despreciarlo,
de perverso natural;
mas, *castigad su porfía,*
hablando bien siempre dellos,
que esto, para convencellos
es socarrona ironía.

That Tirso was *soberbio* on occasions, this critic has no shadow of doubt. Certainly he had shown contempt for both Alarcón and Vélez de Guevara before this passage was written in 1625, however softened in tone may be the verbal portrait of self that he chooses to present here.

In remarking that "*sólo el necio al discreto osa morder,*" Tirso's mind has apparently reverted to Mendoza. That "discreet" poet (to Tirso a "necio") was quite capable of "biting" his literary enemies, as we have seen in the characterization given above, and he must have exercised his suavely satirical tongue against the Mercedarian at this time. Tirso had, moreover, praised this court poet. In the miscellany that was the *Cigarrales*, he had written of Hurtado de Mendoza (I, 137): "Los entremeses [i.e., those played with *El vergonzoso*] fueron de don Antonio de Mendoza, cuyas sales y concetos igualan a su apacibilidad y nobleza." However, this praise is admittedly ambiguous. That the "émulo sin e," who had the reputation of being "discreet" *was* Antonio Hurtado de Mendoza, let us now prove.

Aside from the verses in *Antona García*, there is, in Tirso's theatre, other evidence of bad blood on the part of the Mercedarian toward Mendoza. At this point, let us take up such as is found in Gabriel Téllez's *El melancólico*. [52] This play is much concerned with *discreción;* what is more, one finds in it a curious bit of dialogue which confirms the jokes that Mendoza's position as *guardadamas* occasioned. The *gracioso*, Carlín, is determined to enter the Palace willy-nilly (**II, vi**):

CLEMENCIA:	Dejalde [entrar].
CARLÍN:	Pues ¿por qué no había de entrar?
	... Ni el alcalde
	ni el cura me quita a mí
	que no entre, si se me antoja,
	en la igreja.
CLEMENCIA:	¿Quién te enoja?
CARLÍN:	*Un viejo,* [53] porque entré aquí.
CLEMENCIA:	Es aquése el guarda-damas.

---

[52] Princeps: *Primera parte,* Sevilla, 1627. Sra. de los Ríos, who dated *El melancólico* 1611 (see "Cronología biográfica y dramática de Tirso de Molina", I, p. cx), saw in it and in *El vergonzoso* Tirso's "dos comedias más autobiográficas" and sought with them and other plays to prove her thesis that Tirso was an illegitimate son of the house of the great Téllez-Girón, Duque de Osuna. Concerning the original date of this play, see my "Studies for the Chronology of Tirso's Theatre," 17-27.

I suggested at that time "...the possibility [exists] that *El melancólico* is the revised version [of *Esto sí que es negociar*] and that Tirso rewrote *Esto sí que es negociar* (which must have been done but a short time before) in order to include [in *El melancólico*] his satire at the expense of the 'opulent fools' who, wealthy, only in the coin of this world, would rob him of the nobility which he had acquired, not through inheritance, but with his own God-given talent and industry. The fact that the very scene which carries the burden of Tirso's song is the one in *silvas* [type I] strengthens the assumption which the versification suggests...".

[53] Like *El melancólico, Esto sí que es negociar* carries the passage satirizing Mendoza as *guardadamas*. Was it there in 1622-23? If not, when did Tirso insert it? Don Antonio de Mendoza was born in 1586 in Castro-Urdiales. He was, accordingly, five or six years younger than Tirso! But Tirso was, I am convinced, incredibly vigorous.

CARLÍN: ¡Válganos Dios! ¡que hay quien deba
                guardar damas y se atreva
                a que no quemen las llamas!
                Pues aun no puede un marido
                guardar sólo a su mujer,
            ╲   ¿y habrá quien pueda tener
                tanto pájaro en un nido?
                El tiene gentil tempero.

And Antonio Hurtado de Mendoza was *"guardadamas"* in the *Palace!* Carlín's words indicate that Mendoza was admirably suited for the role of *guardadamas* in that he was very resistant to feminine charms! It is a comment that interests, in view of the thesis of Pinardo, *ayo* to the protagonist of this play, Rogerio. When the *comedia* opens, we learn that the latter is in many ways the perfect *cortesano:* he excels at fencing, painting, music, dialectics, philosophy, architecture, verses, and astrology (in so far as study of it is "licit"); he is even acquainted with the art of flattery, so necessary to the *cortesano* at court. But he lacks one important essential for that role: the *cortesano* must not be made up of intellect alone, but of intellect *and* emotion, and Rogerio has never *loved.* He has "un entendimiento sabio y una idiota voluntad." How then, asks Pinardo, his mentor, can he send to court a man (if a man he is!) who can sleep in the midst of flames? It is a fault that Rogerio will remedy very shortly by falling in love with Leonisa, a *campesina,* who, it ultimately turns out, is of as good blood as he. Now, Antonio Hurtado de Mendoza did not marry until he was thirty-seven years of age; on July 25, 1623 he was married by proxy to doña Luisa Briceño de la Cueva, a woman of noble birth who had ties with such important families as the Houses of Infantado and Alburquerque. Her paternal grandfather was Jerónimo Briceño de Mendoza, *corregidor* in Laredo and other places in Vizcaya. [54] They had one child. As I showed some years ago, *El melancólico* must have been first written in late 1622 or early 1623.

Tirso, in *El melancólico,* indicates, as does the Seventh Castilian of *Antona García,* his contempt for the "necios opulentos" of this

---

[54] The name (as well as the general region of Spain) suggests the possibility that she was a relative of Mendoza's.

world. The Duke of Brittany has legitimized Rogerio and names him his inheritor; yet the latter now suffers from melancholia, although when he lived as Pinardo's son "con un mediano estado," he had been happy with his books and the simple pleasures of the countryside. He tries to explain to his father his disillusionment with the Palace (II, i):

> y mientras estudiaba,
> agradecido al cielo, me preciaba
> que, a pesar de la herencia
> en que en el mundo estriba la potencia
> *de necios opulentos*
> (que llamo *sabios* yo *por testamentos*),
> yo, con la industria mía
> lo que, no a la fortuna, le debía
> a la naturaleza,
> ambicioso de fama y de grandeza
> no heredada, adquirida
> con noble ingenio y estudiosa vida,
> que ilustra más la personal nobleza...

But now that he has realized that the Palace makes no distinction between the wise man and the ignorant fool:

> Agora, pues, que veo
> frustrados mis estudios y deseo,
> y que en fe desta herencia
> no hay entre mí *y el necio* diferencia,
> pues fortuna inconstante
> *con riquezas* me iguala al ignorante,
> ¿no te parece justo
> que cuando adquiero estado, pierda el gusto?
> ....
> A pocos poderosos
> he oído celebrar por *ingeniosos,*
> que en ellos, *de honras llenos,*
> es el ingenio lo que vale menos.

That Rogerio is speaking for Tirso there can to me be little doubt, but it is the Tirso of 1625-26, who had expected recognition of his genius in the Palace, not the Tirso of 1611; instead he has found that within those walls "es el ingenio lo que vale menos." This is the same complaint we have met in *Antona García;* and

here, as in that refashioned work, Tirso is thinking primarily of
don Antonio Hurtado de Mendoza.

El melancólico must necessarily have been reworked after it was
originally done in 1622-23. There is, at least, proof that it was before the public in the early months of 1625, for Pantaleón de Ribera starts his *Vejamen segundo* (II, 45) with satire that seems
meaningless until it is placed against the thesis and protagonist of
Tirso's *El melancólico:*

> He reparado en que me voy haciendo muy *discreto,* y
> pésame, porque recelo que he de dar conmigo en *me-*
> *lancólico,* que *es punto menos de figura;* pero *si el amor*
> *hace avisados,* derecho tiene a presumir de muy enten-
> dido quien tiene mucho amor.

Now Pantaleón had just recently become enamoured of "*Sirene*,"
and Rogerio, protagonist of *El melancólico,* who had prided himself on being "discreet," goes into melancholia after falling in love
and being separated from his Leonisa. His *ayo* had previously
denied the title of "discreet" to one who had "idiota voluntad."

There are three other plays in Tirso's theatre, which hark back
specifically to the same scenes of *Antona García* that we have been
studying (i.e., those taking place in the little inn of Mollorido),
though we have not, up to this moment, had occasion to use this
particular bit of dialogue and must consequently quote it now.
These allusions will prove that the dramatist is recording (in the
emendations he has made in *Antona García*) his very early reactions to events that had taken place in Madrid but a short while
before. The protagonist of the play, Antona García, has just reached the inn mentioned. At almost the same moment she enters,
some other travelers arrive who will carry on the following pleas-
antries with the inn-keeper's wife (III, ii):

> PASAJERO 1:   Y ¿qué hay más?
> VENTERA: Un conejo.
> PASAJERO 2:   No sea gato.
> VENTERA: No es desta venta ese trato.
> PASAJERO 3:   Si le comes, mayarás.

Background for the passage is, of course, the commonplace expression, "vender gato por liebre."

In *Palabras y plumas*,[55] a play first written in 1621-22, but retouched in 1625-26, one finds a curious passage in which Tirso not only refers to the bad reputation of the inn of Mollorido but also to Mendoza in his role as Secretary of the Inquisition. The very faithful lover, don Iñigo, has lost everything, partly through service to his ungrateful lady, partly through a devastating fire. He must consequently sustain himself and his servant, Gallardo, with the game he kills with his gun. This game Gallardo is to sell in nearby Naples:

DON IÑIGO: Diestro soy en la escopeta.
Aquí hay muchas codornices
y *conejos*.

GALLARDO: ¡Qué bien dices!
Mejor trazas que un poeta.

....

---

[55] *Palabras y plumas* was put on in the Palace on July 20, 1623, by Domingo Balbín (*Averiguador*, I, 9). Tirso presumably sold it first to Jerónimo Sánchez, who had a company in Madrid on March 27, 1623. After that date for many years we hear nothing of this *autor*, nor of any members of his troupe. His company may have failed financially. At any rate, he would appear to have sold the play very shortly afterward to Balbín, who put in on in the Palace. The play was suggested by Lope's *El halcón de Federico*, in spite of Sra. de los Ríos' belief to the contrary (*Obras dramáticas completas de Tirso*, I, 1157), and since Lope's play was first printed in 1620 (*Parte* XIII), *Palabras y plumas* would have been written between 1620 and 1623. There are literary allusions, references to costume, etc. that argue strongly for 1621-22, but complete proof must be reserved for another occasion. It is at least evident that the passage quoted from *Palabras y plumas wass added after Tirso learned of Mendoza's appointment as Secretary to the Inquisition* and before it went to press in 1627 in Tirso's *Primera parte*.

It could possibly be argued that the reference was to his appointment as secretary to the king on March 10, 1623 ("sin ejercicio"), but the fact that the scene is tied to that of *Antona García* and that its setting is Mollorido makes evident that the reference is to his appointment as secretary of the Inquisition, made in May of 1625. Moreover, Tirso would not have been concerned over Mendoza's appointment as secretary to the king, since his place as *guardarropa* to his Majesty already gave him easy access to the presence of the king.

The title of *Palabras y plumas* (including as it does the word *plumas*), together with the appointment of Mendoza to the position of *escribano* to the Inquisition, would have recalled to Tirso the scene in *Antona García*, where the inn-keeper was accused of selling "gato por liebre." Who can say whether Tirso knew Quevedo's *Las zahurdas de Plutón* in manuscript or whether Quevedo had read Tirso's *Palabras y plumas*, in print by 1627?

> Mas yo en mi vida he andado
> sino es a caza de zorros.
> DON IÑIGO : Sólo que lo vendas quiero.
> GALLARDO : ¡Ay Dios! ¡quién hubiera sido
> mes y medio en Mollorido,
> pupilo de su ventero!
> Mas no comerán sin pebre
> lo que cazare tu mano;
> cázame tú un escribano;
> venderé el gato por liebre.

The reference to the inn-keeper of Mollorido is a throw-back to the scene of *Antona García* wherein the *ventero* had the bad reputation of selling "el gato por liebre." Only, the "cat" that Gallardo wants his master to catch is an *escribano,* none other than don Antonio Hurtado de Mendoza. Gallardo's malicious intention is underlined by his master's reply: "Yo en sátiras no te ensayo, sino sólo en cazador." At the time Tirso left Madrid, Mendoza had not yet been appointed *escribano* to the Tribunal of the Inquisition.

In *El mayor desengaño* [56] (in existence by 1622-23), the *escribanos* are again linked with the *gatos.* Marción, without shelter for the night, asks Laureta for a corner in the kitchen amidst her pots and pans. Her answer is (I, iii): "Tengo ... en la cocina dos gatos con unas uñas de a jeme." Marción's reply is: "Buenas son para escribanos."

Now the tie between the *escribanos* and the *gatos* must have been traditional; and in linking Mendoza with them, Tirso was relying on the reader for a certain amount of background. Members of that profession (i.e., the *escribanos*) were suspect in various directions, as details from various works of Quevedo will make evident. In the first place, the *escribano*'s feather-pen (*pluma*) was symbol of his avarice; this is made evident in both *La visita de los chistes* [57] and in *Las zahurdas de Plutón.* [58] In the former work,

---

[56] *El mayor desengaño,* like *Palabras y plumas,* was first printed in the *Primera parte,* 1627.

[57] Francisco de Quevedo, *La visita de los chistes,* 189-298; in particular, 257-258.

[58] Francisco de Quevedo, *Las zahurdas de Plutón,* 87-187, in particular, 146-147. I should like to thank Prof. A. A. Parker for recalling to me this

published in mid-1622, Quevedo, when glossing the phrase, "Voláráse con las *plumas*," links it with both the *escribanos* and the *genoveses:* "Pensáis que lo digo por los pájaros y os engañáis ... Dígolo por los *escribanos* y *genoveses,* que éstos nos vuelan [i.e., hacen volar] *con las plumas* el dinero de delante." In *Las zahurdas de Plutón,* written in 1608 but not published until 1627, we find not only this connection but two others as well (146-147):

> ... pregunté, *como nombraron ladrones,* dónde estaban los *escribanos:* —¿Es posible que no hay [sic] en el infierno ninguno, ni le pude topar en todo el camino? ... ¿Sálvanse todos? —No —dijo— pero dejan de andar y vuelan con plumas. Y el no haber escribanos por el camino de la perdición no es porque infinitísimos que son malos no vienen acá por él, sino porque es tanta la prisa con que vienen, que volar y llegar y entrar es todo uno, *tales plumas se tienen ellos,* y así no se ven en el camino. — Y acá — dije yo — ¿cómo no hay ninguno? — Sí hay — me respondió— mas no usan ellos de nombre de *escribanos,* que acá *por gatos los conocemos.* Y para que echéis de ver qué tantos hay no habéis de mirar sino que, con ser el infierno tan gran casa, tan antigua, tan maltratada y sucia, no hay un ratón en toda ella, que ellos los cazan.

The *escribanos,* then, were linked, as is evident, not only with their *plumas,* but also with the *ladrones* and the *gatos.*

In a passage of the *Buscón,* [59] Quevedo actually spells out the relationship of the *escribano* to the *ladrón:* Pablos, when trying to carry out one of his amatory ventures, is crawling over a roof top. Suddenly he slips and is unlucky enough to fall onto that of an *escribano,* with unfortunate consequences: "Al ruido despertó la media casa, y *pensando que eran ladrones — que son antojadizos de ellos los de este oficio* — subieron al tejado." Pablos manages to free himself from "las fieras y crueles manos del escribano" only with a large bribe.

---

very important quotation from *Las zahurdas de Plutón.* I had read all of Quevedo's satirical prose and verse many years ago, but a filing-case can become a mausoleum with the passing of the years.

[59] Francisco de Quevedo, *Historia de la vida del Buscón,* 225.

On another occasion, in *La visita de los chistes*, [60] Quevedo
brings in even "el gato de Juan Ramos," who is complaining:

> ... voto a Cristo que los diablos me hicieron tener *una*
> *gata*. Más me valiera comerme de ratones, que no me de-
> jan descansar: "daca la gata de *Juan Ramos*," "toma la
> gata de *Juan Ramos*." Y ahora no hay doncellita ni con-
> tadorcito ... ni *secretario*, ni ministro, ni hipócrita, ni pre-
> tendiente, ni juez, ni pleitante, ni viuda que no se haga
> la gata de *Juan Ramos*. Y todo soy *gatas*, que parezco a
> Febrero.

Notes to this passage give such proverbial expressions as: "La
gata de Juan Ramos cierra los ojos y abre las manos;" "La gata
de Marirramos, que se hacía muertecina para cazar los ratos;" "El
gato de Marcos Ramos halaga con la cola y araña con las manos,"
etcétera.

Elsewhere he links the *gatos* not only with *ladrones* but with
venteros as well. In the *Buscón*, [61] Pablos and his young master have
reached "la siempre maldita venta de Viveros." He then states:
"El ventero era morisco y ladrón, que en mi vida vi *perro* y *gato*
juntos con la paz de aquel día ... " Américo Castro's note to the
combination of *perro y gato* is: "Tradicional era el tratar de *pe-
rros* a los moros. Gato: 'Ladrón'." The formula was: *escribanos*
equal *ladrones; gatos* equal *ladrones;* therefore, *escribanos* equal
gatos. Like *gatos*, they have long claws.

Tirso, as well as Quevedo, was, of course, aware of these traditional associations, and he relied on the background of his readers
to interpret his passage in the light of similar knowledge on their
part. But whereas Quevedo was apparently aiming at the profession in general, the Mercedarian was shooting at a specific *escribano*, i.e., don Antonio de Mendoza. Proof of it lies in various dis-
ections: Tirso very carefully linked his *escribano* with the same
inn of Mollorido and its thieving innkeeper who was accustomed

---

[60] Francisco de Quevedo, *La visita de los chistes*, 292-293. "La gata
de Mari-Ramos" is a secondary title for a play, "El jardín de Vargas".
Morley and Bruerton (*Cronología de las comedias de Lope de Vega*) reject
its authenticity in Lope's theatre. With its *silva* I, it was almost certainly
written after 1620-21.
[61] *El Buscón*, 64.

to sell "gato por liebre," a phrase equivalent to "engañar"; and
in that same inn, the dramatist — through the Seventh Castilian
— had complained of Mendoza, who (he felt) had won his title
of "discreet" through his money. The dramatist probably had in
mind, as well, the personality of don Antonio de Mendoza. In the
Cigarrales he had said, we remember: "Los entremeses fueron
de don Antonio de Mendoza, cuyos sales y concetos igualan a su
apacibilidad y nobleza." [62] Gallardo, the *gracioso*, believed that a
strongly-spiced sauce (*pebre*) would be necessary to give flavor to
this particular cat. Finally, this "gata," like Mari-Ramos', had "uñas
de a jeme," however placid its usual appearance.

---

[62] The comment was almost certainly phrased with equivocal intent. I do
not believe that Tirso had a very high opinion of Mendoza's "sales y concetos"; moreover, the latter's "apacibilidad" was probably, from Tirso's point
of view, "placidity." Corral will even label it "laziness" (52-53). See p. 333.
    I am not even sure that Tirso doesn't raise doubts as to Mendoza's
"nobleza." In *El vergonzoso en palacio* (for which Antonio de Mendoza
supplied the *entremeses*), there is a curious bit of dialogue, one in which
don Antonio de Barceló (when looking for an excuse to remain near Serafina)
wishes to apply to the Duke for the place of secretary which is open. With
his cousin, doña Juana, don Antonio urges his special qualifications for the
vacancy (II, vii). When later the Duke takes up don Antonio's application
with Figueredo, he states the requirements of the place (II, viii): "Ya sabes
que requiere aquese oficio / persona en quien concurran juntamente / calidad,
discreción, presencia y pluma." Figueredo's answer is strange: "*La calidad
no sé*; desotras partes / le puedo asegurar a Vuexcelencia / que no hay en
Portugal quien conforme a ellas / mejor pueda ocupar aquesa plaza." The
passage is so applicable to Antonio de Mendoza that one cannot help
wondering if Tirso inserted it in 1623 or early 1624—after Mendoza became
secretary to the king. When talking to his relative, doña Juana, don Antonio
de Barceló had even pointed out: "¿No te parece, *si en palacio habito* / con
este cargo [i.e., de secretario], que podré encubierto / entablar mi esperanza,
como acuda / el tiempo, la ocasión, y más tu *ayuda*?" Figueredo calls him
"hidalgo."
    It would have hurt Mendoza tremendously to have anyone call into
question "la calidad" of his ancestry. Nevertheless, G. A. Davies (*A Poet
at Court...*, 18) states: "...he was the son of a mere *segundón*, the title *Señor
de Salcedo* being the prerogative of his paternal uncle, Diego Hurtado
de Salcedo y Mendoza. ...Like other members of his family, Antonio de
Mendoza oriented himself genealogically by the House of Salcedo..." In
"A algunos varones ilustres y ricoshombres del linaje del autor" (*Obras poéticas*, III, 116-119), don Antonio states that the Mendozas were "de los
primeros señores de Vizcaya..." Could Mendoza have played the role of
Antonio de Barceló in *El vergonzoso en palacio* when it was given in "Buenavista"?

El mayor desengaño probably carries reference, as well, to Mendoza's inability to keep his mouth shut (II, xvii). When the frightened Marción "tells everything" under pressure, the First Soldier says: "¡Lindamente desbucháis!" Later he asks, "¿Hácenlo así *los discretos?*" Marción explains: "El temor causarlo pudo. / Haceos media hora mudo, / veréis después lo que habláis. / ... Para hinchazón tan odiosa / es medicina famosa / una gaita de secretos."

Let us now take the very important allusion to Mendoza found in *La huerta de Juan Fernández.* [63] Here Tirso will again inveigh against so-called "discreet" fools who are anything but "discreet" — as he had in *Antona García* and in *El melancólico.* Tomasa, the *graciosa* of this play that was being written in the first half of 1626, holds to the philosophy that those of modest means should not imitate their "betters." Each to his own economy: " ...cada cual / comiera como quien es, / el marqués como marqués, / como pobre, el oficial ... cada cual se vista, / según su estado, la ropa ..." She extends her philosophy even to her young ass. When doña Petronila, dressed in men's clothes, points out that the amount of barley which Tomasa (also dressed as a man) has just given her ass is hardly enough for an animal that has travelled three leagues, Tomasa's curt reply is, "coma paja." Later she agrees to become page to doña Petronila, and the latter promises her a mule in place of the ass; Tomasa [64] assures Petronila that whoever buys her animal will get Apuleyo's "ass of gold" for:

> sabe caminar,
> siendo jumento, *y callar,*
> *que es gracia de otros distinta;*
> que el jumento no merece
> nombre de tal, si se halla
> deste humor, pues *mientras calla*

---

[63] *La huerta de Juan Fernández,* I, 1.

[64] One may suspect, without being able to prove it, that Tomasa's role is as important as it is because Amarilis was in the cast. At least, Mansilla, the *gracioso,* describes Tomasa (II, iv) in the following terms: "Estaba una villaneja / oyendo entre los demás / tan carihermosa, que atrás / las Amarilis se deja." Tirso also praises Amarilis in *El amor médico,* written just shortly before *La huerta de Juan Fernández.* As *autora,* Amarilis may have chosen to take the role of Tomasa rather than that of the heroine.

el necio, no lo parece;
y hay otros mil que procuran
cobrar nombre de "discretos"
que contra ajenos defetos
rebuznan cuando murmuran.
¡Qué dellos ocupan sillas,
dignos de albardas!

Many *necios* who have sought to attain the name of *discretos* by talking about *others'* defects are really braying asses. Really they are not so wise as Tomasa's ass, which at least knows how to keep quiet! They shouldn't occupy seats of dignity; they are fit rather for the gross saddle of a beast of burden. These are the same charges that Tirso had made against Mendoza in *Antona García*, where he calls his literary enemies *mules*. (Only he has now reduced his enemy to the level of an ass!) Nevertheless, that "discreet" poet who doesn't have as much sense as Tomasa's animal, was now filling a seat [65] (i.e., "a silla curul") as Secretary of the Tribunal of the Inquisition, a position he had held only since May 17, 1625!

Let us continue on our way with Tirso as he headed for Seville to attend the *capítulo* of his Order, meeting there in the last days of April 1625. He would presumably have stopped in Salamanca and Trujillo, en route to that city; but if a visit to either place has left any impression in his plays, I have not found it, unless his dedication [66] of his *Primera parte* (1626) to "D. Alonso de Paz, regidor de Salamanca," should be a reflection of the dramatist's stay in that city. However, any stop that Tirso made in either place was necessarily of the briefest duration.

In Trujillo he would presumably have talked with the *comendador* of the Mercedarian convent, Diego González de Salcedo — as well as with some member or members of the Pizarro family, for in Trujillo he was in the land of the conquerors of Peru, to whom his Order was so deeply indebted. P. Guillermo Vázquez, [67]

---

[65] Tirso is contrasting in his mind the *silla curul* of a magistrate, one of great dignity, wth the rough *albarda* of an ass.

[66] For this dedication, see Alan K. G. Paterson's "Tirso de Molina: Two Biographical Studies," 54-55.

[67] P. Guillermo Vázquez, *Breve reseña de los conventos de la Merced*, 24-25.

in his *Breve reseña de los conventos de la Merced,* gives the history of Trujillo's house:

> En esta ciudad de Extremadura, patria de los Pizarros, conquistadores del Perú, fundó un convento de la Merced en 1594 doña Francisca Pizarro, marquesa de Charcas, hija de don Francisco Pizarro, y viuda de su hermano, don Hernando.

In founding it, doña Francisca speaks of "la afición particular que tengo a esta sagrada religión y la que tuvo el marqués, don Francisco Pizarro, mi padre, que tan devoto fue siempre desta Orden, llevando consigo a la pacificación y conversión de los reinos del Perú religiosos della, fundando casas ..." Doña Francisca also set up, out of her own estate, funds for its *upkeep* and made don Francisco Pizarro, her son, its patron. In Madrid, the Marqueses del Valle, [68] "descendientes de Hernán Cortés," would later become patrons of the *Capilla Mayor;* and the Cortés family was closely related to the Pizarros.

From Trujillo, Tirso would hasten on to Seville in order to attend the *capítulo* of the Mercedarians which would presumably decide his fate. But his Order took no action in that meeting on Tirso's specific case, nor would it until a year from that time, when the Mercedarians would again gather, this time in Guadalajara. It is logical to assume that they were waiting for Rome to give its decision on the accusations that had been brought against Tirso. Possibly, too, before acting, they wanted Rome's official backing on the very strong stand they had taken in the matter of judging all cases that involved their own members.

Before Tirso left Seville with his old friend, San Cecilio, [69] he would necessarily have held another long conversation with Fray don Gaspar Prieto, the General of the Order, for there was the question as to what Tirso should do while waiting for the meeting in Guadalajara. The General, who evidently recognized the rare talents of this son of the Order, presumably decided that there was no reason why Tirso should not go quietly to Toledo, as the

---

[68] *Ibid.,* p. 18.
[69] See R. P. Manuel Penedo Rey, "Tirso en Sevilla", 36-39.

dramatist was undoubtedly anxious to do — not to his convent
there, but to the *cigarral* [70] of a friend, where he could write more
or less *incógnito*. He would be free of conventual duties, could
continue to compose plays, without publishing that fact.

At least, the dramatist — after taking leave of his friend, San
Cecilio, in Fuentes, where the latter was *comendador* — continued
on to Toledo and began to write plays. And very good ones they
are! As I have shown in earlier studies, both *Desde Toledo a
Madrid* [71] and *No hay peor sordo* must have been penned in the
Imperial City, in the last half of 1625. *El amor médico,* [72] which
reflects his stay in Seville, as does *No hay peor sordo*, was likewise
begun in Toledo in December of that same year, and possibly
finished there; but if so, it was retouched after August 11th of

---

[70] I now feel virtually certain that it was in Buenavista that Tirso took
refuge in 1625-26. The *cigarral* had belonged at one time to the Archbishop-
Cardinal, don Bernardo Sandoval y Rojas. See my study, "Tirso's *No hay
peor sordo*: Its Date and Place of Composition", 272-273; also 275, n. 26.
There is a poem included in the *Obras poéticas de don Hurtado de Mendoza*
(I, 254-257) which the poet wrote from Aranjuez shortly after the new
Duque de Lerma had inherited his latest title on May 17, 1625 (he speaks
of him as "un tres-duque"). In this poem, Mendoza complains: "Tócame en
lo cortesano / que no me escribáis, ni habléis; / mas no responder me ha
dado / en todo lo montañés." Earlier Mendoza had asked: "¿qué ceño y
tibieza es ésta / que ya os llegan a escoger [sic]...?" Another quatrain
begins: "Yo os perdono el no escribirme..." It seems not improbable to me
that the young Duque de Lerma, whom Tirso praises so highly in a play
of late 1625, *No hay peor sordo* (I, i), may have broken off his friendship
with Mendoza because of the latter's denunciation of the dramatist to the
Conde-Duque de Olivares—and that the young Duque accordingly made it
possible for the dramatist to hide out in *Buenavista*. Mendoza's poem was
almost certainly written in late June, 1625, for it declares at one point: "Ya
sé que en Madrid por vos / cañas jugaban ayer / sarracinos y aliatares, / ocho
a ocho y diez a diez." This is presumably a reference to the "Máscara muy
lucida de setenta" which was celebrated in the new duque de Lerma's honor
in Madrid on June 26, 1625. See *Noticias de Madrid*, 120. This new Duque
de Lerma was evidently a remarkably fine person (see *Noticias de Madrid*
[163] for his generosity in another direction). Mendoza's action against Tirso
would have made him—for this newest scion of the houses of Sandoval and
Rojas—little more than a spy for Olivares. And this descendant of Lerma
and Uceda had no reason for liking that favorite.

[71] See "Tirso's *Desde Toledo a Madrid*: its Date and Place of Composition", published in the *Homenaje* to Prof. Fichter, 357-366. For "Tirso's
No hay peor sordo: its Date and Place of Composition," see *Bibliography*.

[72] For *El amor médico*'s date and place of composition, see the first
number of *Reflexión 2*, I, no. 1, 11-33.

1626, by which time Tirso was in Trujillo. This may explain the fact that the action of its last two acts takes place in Portugal.

Both *No hay peor sordo* and *El amor médico* make evident something else: Tirso heard, while in Toledo, something more about events that had happened after he left Madrid, "casi huyendo." His *Antona García* makes evident, as we have seen, that he blamed Antonio Hurtado de Mendoza (and Lope de Vega) for the accusation which had resulted in the *Junta's acuerdo*, but there is no indication whatsoever that he had, at that time, heard of the abusive *copla* [73] which linked his name with that of Ruiz de Alarcón. It was a *mote* which angered him so profoundly that it has left one bitter allusion after another in his theatre. Had Tirso known of it in days when he was retouching his *Antona García*, it would inevitably have found reflection there. However, we believe that this *copla* was primarily one of Luis Vélez de Guevara's "donaires" and must, therefore, be left until we can get to Tirso's relations with that Andalusian.

The exact time that Tirso left Toledo we do not know. He had to be in Guadalajara by the end of May in order to attend the *capítulo* of his Order which would decide his fate. That he stopped off in Madrid, en route to that city, is suggested by three things:

He managed to throw together for the rich *regidor*, Juan Fernández, a *particular* which he entitled *La huerta de Juan Fernández*. In it, as we have seen above, he managed to reduce his enemy, Antonio Hurtado de Mendoza, from the status of envious mule to that of a braying ass who hadn't even sense enough to keep quiet! Yet that "ass" had on May 17, 1625, been named "Secretario ... de Justicia de la Majestad del Rey don Felipe IV en la Suprema Inquisición" and in that position was occupying a "silla curul"! Tirso probably wrote, as well, during this time his swift-moving comedy of *tramoyas*, *En Madrid y en una casa*, [74]

---

[73] It is the *copla* which begins: "Vítor, don Juan de Alarcón / y el fraile de la Merced..." In Chapter VII, I quote it in full and discuss the various references to it that are found in Tirso's theatre.

[74] Sra. de los Ríos dates it 1637 or 1641 (*Obras dramáticas completas de Tirso*, III, 1253-1255). It was undoubtedly reworked around 1635-1637, but this play trails the trip that Tirso made from Sevilla to Toledo to Madrid in 1625-1626. Moreover, it is in type and spirit close to *Los balcones de*

one that would be refashioned shortly after Lope's death in August of 1635. But there must have been a third reason. Unless we are sadly mistaken, Tirso still dreamed of getting a *primera parte* into publication. If we are right in this supposition, then he was probably in Madrid some time before March 6, 1626, since that is the date of the *tasa, given in the capital,* which will appear in a later edition of 1631, put out in Valencia. The dedication of this volume of *sueltas,* gotten together in 1626, is to D. Alonso de Paz, who was evidently in Madrid at the time it was written, probably in connection with some official duty as *regidor* de Salamanca. D. Alonso de Paz, Dr. Alan K. G. Paterson [75] tells us, "seems to have been closely associated with Tirso's Order." He had fame, it would seem, "as an Amphitryon and helper of needy poets." Whether Tirso had spoken to him in Salamanca, as he passed through that city some months earlier, or whether he first sought his help in Madrid, can be a matter of surmise only. Playing over and over on the family name of this benefactor, Tirso stresses his *peaceful* intentions and hopes that with such a patron, "niño en la inocencia," his book can "win for him a truce and open up tribunals."

As the end of May 1626 drew near, Tirso necessarily said good-bye to his friends in Madrid and started for Guadalajara, there to attend the *capítulo* which would send him to Trujillo as *comendador* of the Mercedarian convent in that city. The decision could hardly have given pleasure either to those who sent him or to the one sent, but it was imperative that his Order should not anger further the man who was trying to dissolve it, [76] and Tirso could recognize that necessity as well as they.

In order to reach Trujillo from Guadalajara, he would have to go back through Madrid. Presumably, ho would have stopped off

---

Madrid, which, with its allusion to the *vítor* of Tirso and Alarcón, was either written or rewritten around 1626. I doubt very much that Tirso ever *wrote* a play after Penninghis *acto de contrición* (1630), though he probably retouched some.

[75] See Alan K. G. Paterson, "Tirso de Molina: Two Bibliographical Studies," 53-68, in particular, 63-64, n. 35.

[76] See Sra. de los Ríos, *Obras dramáticas completas de Tirso,* III (doc. LXXXI, 25-26), for the *Arbitrio de la Redención preservativa,* presented at the Cortes de Monzón in early 1626, "cuyo objeto era la supresión de las Ordenes Redentoras de la Merced y la Trinidad".

to see friends, among them don Alonso de Paz, who would have given him the latest news as to the probable fate of his *Primera parte* in Madrid. The ultimate verdict was unfavorable (proof of it lies in the volume's lack of *aprobaciones*), but the Lyra edition of Seville of 1627, when set against the Valencian one of 1631, seems to indicate that token copies (made up of *sueltas*) came out in Madrid. One of these presumably reached the printer, Francisco de Lyra, in Seville, as Dr. Paterson [77] has suggested; and the extra pages of this edition would be used in 1631 by Mey for a Valencian edition, one dedicated to Pérez de Montalván, instead of to Alonso de Paz. Just how all this came about requires more space than I can at this point devote to it.

Tirso was in Trujillo at least by July 13, 1626, since we have a document of that date, one signed by him in that city, as *comendador* of its Mercedarian house. Of the three years he spent there, we have known little, but the *ABC* (August 24, 1971) recently carried news that "15 notarial documents," signed by Tirso de Molina, had been found in the Ayuntamiento de Trujillo by Professor Alfonso Urtiaga [78] of Kalamazoo College. The duties of Tirso's new office could have left him little time for writing. Even so, I believe we can be reasonably certain that he penned in Trujillo *Escarmientos para el cuerdo,* [79] as well as the three plays

---

[77] Dr. Paterson suggests that Francisco de Lyra, of Seville, "pirated" it. See "Tirso de Molina: Two Bibliographical Studies", 63. My objections to the second half of Dr. Paterson's study have been printed in the homage volume which recently came out in honor of Prof. Arnold Reichenberger: "Did Tirso Send to Press a *Primera parte* of Madrid (1626) which Contained *El condenado por desconfiado?*" See *HR*, XLI (1973), 261-274.

[78] A letter, dated November 10, 1971, from Professor Urtiaga, includes a photostat-copy of an article published in *Ya* which is somewhat more detailed than was the notice printed in *ABC* on August 24, 1971. He states in it: "I am planning to publish a complete transcription of the documents as soon as I can. The article in *Studios [Estudios?]* gives an accurate account of their contents." I should like here to thank Prof. Urtiaga for his kindness, as well as Prof. Vern Williamsen, who sent me a copy of the notice that appeared in *ABC*. No document, discovered by Professor Urtiaga, would seem to be of earlier date than that of July 13, 1626, cited by Sra. de los Ríos as the first document signed by Tirso.

[79] See in the first number of the new review *Reflexión 2*, I, 1, 11-33, my study on *Escarmientos para el cuerdo* and *El amor médico*. For the date of *La ventura con el nombre,* see "Tirso's *La ventura con el nombre*: its Source and Date of Composition," 40 and 42.

dealing with the Pizarros and *Las quinas de Portugal.* What is more, he must have retouched in that city at least *El amor médi-co* [79] and *La ventura con el nombre.* [79] My guess is that he altered several others as well.

We have, up to this point, centered our interests squarely on Tirso's relations with don Antonio de Mendoza in 1625-1626. Let us now go to the years of 1634-1635 in search of what seems irrefutable evidence that Tirso held that *cortesano* responsible for his troubles with the *Junta de Reformación.* For, in the *Cuarta parte* (1635), Tirso again takes up cudgels against Mendoza, and this time he speaks more openly. This volume carries, as prologue, an "A ti a solas" that to me cannot fail to refer to his relations with that Palace poet: [80]

> Mil cosas tenía que comunicarte en puridad, y *impor-tame el secreto lo mismo que la fama que se desploma con las murmuraciones.* Pero tiénenme tan embarazado los traslados de mi *Quinta parte* de comedias, sucesoras de esta *Cuarta parte, y el recelo de que no eches en corro lo que en chitón te confiara, que mortifica, a pesar de mi gusto, mis afectos.*
> Con todo eso, *si me prometes imposibles, que es ser guardadamas de tu lengua,* y apeteces lo que todos, que es picar en faltas que en nosotros nos parecen aradores y en los demás ballenas, búscame, cuando haya salido de la cuna mi hermano, el quinto deste nombre. Hallarásme en la tienda de Gabriel de León, mercader destas sazo-nes, y *nos daremos un buen rato a costa de los abusos en especie, sin riesgo de los individuos.* Y, entretanto, haz ganas (si es que te faltan, que no puedo creerlo) *para la ensalada más sabrosa que jamás puso a su mesa la dis-creción, provocada de la envidia.* Vale.

How revealing this "A ti a solas" is of Tirso's and Mendoza's relations, after one finds the thread that winds through the maze of Gabriel Téllez's works! The Palace poet couldn't keep a secret! His failure to do so could occasion gossip that might plummet one's

---

[80] See Cotarelo, *Comedias de Tirso,* I, p. lxvi, n. 1. The "A ti a solas" is apparently a misprint. Tirso himself, in his *Quinta parte,* refers to this prologue of the *Cuarta parte* as "Señor, a ti sólo".

reputation (*fama*)[81] in the future (as it had destroyed Tirso's in the past). Téllez is getting ready his *Quinta parte* but dares not trust any promise from Mendoza to be *guardadamas* of his tongue [as he was *guardadamas* in the palace!], for the latter takes delight, says Tirso, in picking the mote out of the other fellow's eye — which to him looks as large as a whale! Tirso's *Fourth Volume* will be found in Gabriel León's book-store, as soon as the Fifth has come off press. [Tirso evidently feared his enemy might try to prevent the Fifth getting printed!][82] There, in the book-store, they'll have a good time *satirizing abuses in general*, avoiding *personal* criticism of individuals. Mendoza can make ready his appetite for the tastiest salad that "discretion" (Tirso's!) *provoked by envy* (Mendoza's) had ever put on a table. Here, in large part, we find summed up Tirso's complaints against don Antonio Hurtado de Mendoza.

He evidently felt, nevertheless, that he had not underlined sufficiently Mendoza's *envy*, and that shortcoming he remedies promptly in the "A ti sólo" of his *Quinta parte* — this before starting to satirize the faults of another *motilón*. The *dedicatoria* of this volume begins with an epigram from Marcial (the 10th of book four) which Tirso "adapts" in two *décimas*, then continues: [83]

> Señor padre [84] me dijo que te buscase en la librería de la calle de Toledo en la tienda [de León] alegada en mi *Cuarta parte,* y que te llamabas el "Señor a tí sólo"; y según las señas, eres el mismo. Pues ya que di contigo, has de saber que yo vengo (como su hijo) en nombre suyo, porque Su Mrd. anda *tan ocupado en repartir envidias cuanto sin embarazo de sus escocimientos.* Advirtióme te dijese de su parte que en *Sexto tomo* (de que ya señora

---

[81] See pp. 98-9.

[82] So did el Conde de la Roca! See p. 119.

[83] See Cotarelo, *Comedias de Tirso,* I, lxvii-lxviii.

[84] In his third, fourth, and fifth *partes* Tirso chooses to make his intermediary a nephew, one named "don Francisco Lucas de Avila." There undoubtedly existed a man of that name; he may well have been nephew to Tirso; but in these introductions, *Tirso himself* must necessarily be expressing himself! What is more, it is a Tirso who is *still* interested in saving his theatre for posterity and in keeping the promise he made to his enemies in *La ventura con el nombre.* For this promise, see p. 119. The last sentence of the quotation from the *Cuarta parte* makes that abundantly clear.

madre está preñada) te cumpliría los brindis que en *la Cuarta* te hizo ...

Then, at this point, Tirso seemingly starts speaking to Vélez de Guevara, Mendoza's friend since childhood — with only a semi-colon to indicate the change of aim! The two court poets were apparently that close together in his mind!

The *Sexto tomo* never came out. The prologues of the fourth and fifth *partes* apparently produced the very results that Tirso had feared. After urging Tirso to continue writing "forever," the Conde de la Roca had straightway given the dramatist, in his *Ragguaglio* of 1635, some very good advice that both Tirso (and his critics!) unfortunately ignored: [85] "Ma se gli auuertisca, che nelle Dedicatorie di sue Comedie faccia prima di stamparle, che sian passate per i Libri della ragione que lascio il Piedi concha." The Conde de la Roca knew only too well in the year 1635 of the dangers of Mendoza's enmity! Had not "el discreto del palacio" written, back in 1627, his letter to Olivares advising him against entrusting his biography to the Count? [86] The fact that the príuado chose to ignore the suggestion would seem to indicate clearly that at this point Olivares, also, had a low opinion of Mendoza and his *soplonería*. It was one he had even earlier, in 1625, had occasion to know when Mendoza took to the *Junta* (directly or indirectly) his accusations against Tirso. And Tirso, by March of

[85] Wido Hempel republished the *Ragguaglio di Parnaso* (with commentary) in *Analecta romanica* (Heft 13, 138-64) and well-nigh proved that the "Fabio Franchi" to whom it is attributed is none other than El Conde de la Roca. That he was correct in his deduction is confirmed by an independent study of Bruna Cinti which cites a secret report of Agostino Rossi to that effect. (See *Cuadernos hispanoamericanos*, LIV, 609-20). For Prof. Hannah E. Bergman's review of Wido Hempel's book, see *HR*, XXXIV (1966), 163-68. Wido Hempel says of "que lascio el piedi concha". "kann nur zu lesen sein". He found no satisfactory explanation of the phrase, nor do I. What seems evident is that the Count of la Roca knew of Tirso's satire of Mendoza and this implies a connection that is important.

[86] G. A. Davies printed the letter in the *Hispania* (of Madrid), XIX (1959), 82-91. Presumably what he sums up in his book of 1971 sums up what he had previously said there. Marañón's comment on the letter was (*El Conde-Duque de Olivares*, 159, n. 28): "Es digna de ser leída por lo que enseña sobre Roca, sobre Mendoza, y sobre la época." This historian held a favorable impression of Roca, a *very* unfavorable one of Mendoza. We have quoted above Mr. Davies' opinion.

the following year (i.e., 1626), was characterizing Mendoza's cat-
claws as "de a jeme." Why, then, we must ask, should our
dramatist have been so imprudent as to write the "A ti a solas"
of the *Cuarta parte* and thus test out once more the ill-will of
that "cortesano"?

At this point we must also ask if one finds in the work of
Mendoza any evidence of enmity toward Tirso. In the former's
comedia, Más merece quien más ama, there is excellent confirmation that *el discreto del palacio* had no very kindly feelings toward
Tirso. This play, like the quatrain painted on the wall of the
pastry-shop — with which we shall have occasion to deal later —
links the Mexican and the Mercedarian in literary disrepute. What
is more, it at the same time, glorifies Lope. Fernández-Guerra,
when studying the Mexican's theatre many years ago, pointed to
this defense of Lope which Mendoza had written as an answer
to a sarcastic comment of Alarcón, included in *Las paredes oyen.*
When Celia of this latter plays asks her mistress concerning don
Juan, "Declarástele tu amor?," doña Aña answers her with another
question, "¿Tan liviana me has hallado?" Thereupon the maid
contrasts her mistress' decorous conduct with the shameless behavior of Lope's "infantas de León": [87]

> ¡Liviana dices, después
> de dos años que por ti
> ha andado fuera de sí!
> Bien parece que no ves
> lo que en las comedias hacen
> las infantas de León.
> ... Con tal condición
> o con tal desdicha nacen,
> que en viendo un hombre, al momento
> le ruegan y mudan traje
> y sirviéndole de paje
> van con las piernas al viento.

Mendoza first defends the decorum of palace ladies in general: [88]

---

[87] *Las paredes oyen,* III, viii.
[88] All quotations from *Más merece quien más ama* are from the *princeps,*
Barcelona, 1630. See II, f. 10r. The later edition of the *Escogidas* strives
to correct some errors of the *princeps.*

> Culpa agora muy de espacio
> las comedias, en que tantas
> mal ofendidas infantas,
> sin decoro de palacio,
> se huyen cada momento,
> siendo palacio un sagrado,
> a donde no entra el cuidado,
> ni se atreve el pensamiento.

Then Burón, his servant, makes direct answer to Alarcón's charges against Lope:

> Un poeta celebrado,
> y en todo el mundo excelente,
> viéndose ordinariamente
> de otro ingenio murmurado
> de que siguiendo a un galán
> en traje de hombre vestía
> tanta infanta cada día,
> le dijo: "Señor don Juan,
> si vuesarced satisfecho
> de mis comedias murmura,
> cuando con gloria y ventura
> nuevecientas haya hecho,
> verá que es cosa de risa
> el arte; y sorda a su nombre,
> las sacará en traje de hombre
> y aun otro día en camisa."

But, granted the setting in which this defense is placed, Mendoza manages to censure Tirso together with Alarcón — at the same time that he exalts Lope. At least, Fernández-Guerra so reasoned, and I believe him right in his assumption: [89]

---

[89] For Fernández-Guerra y Orbe's quotation, see his *D. Juan Ruiz de Alarcón y Mendoza*, I, 379-388, in particular 386-387. Lope first claimed 900 *comedias* in his *Parte XIV*, which came out after June 12, 1620. He made his next claim of 1070 plays in his *Parte XX* (January, 1625). Then in the closing lines of *La moza de cántaro*, a play which was retouched after the siege of Cádiz in November of 1625, he claimed 1500. Fernández-Guerra believed that Alarcón had in mind *Los donaires de Matico* when writing this satire. There are nine chances to one that Alarcón would not have "had in mind" in the 1620's a play that had been published in 1604! The reference is possibly to the *Parte I* of Lope's *Los Tellos de Meneses* (dated 1620-1628 by Morley and Bruerton's *Cronología*). This play also has its "infanta de León" who flees from the Palace.

Para ello dispone [Mendoza] que el príncipe Rosauro se decida a tomar el disfraz de cazador y así poder
servir a la princesa Fidelinda; pero el criado, Burón, rechaza semejante vestido, oponiendo que la ley de los disfraces exige el de *jardinero*. Y *puestos los ojos en el fraile
de la Merced*, forja en relación el argumento de un drama donde el príncipe, con este traje (de rigor en las
comedias) ha de presentarse dentro del jardín y ser visto
de la Infanta, la cual se enamora de él sin remedio, y
sabe que es amada, descubriéndoselo el galán por los nombres de las flores de un ramillete. Resuelta la ... dama en
adorar al encubierto amante, le citará para hablarle por
la pared del jazmín; el príncipe mostrará desconfianza
cortés (**II**, fol. 9v.):

>   Señor,
> ¿qué dices? Si has de encubrir
> quién eres, decirte quiero
> que yerras en lo que haces,
> que *la ley de los disfraces
> es servir de jardinero.*
> Ea, la montera y sayo
> te pon; serás escondido
> en este jardín florido,
> verde ministro de mayo,
> que es forzoso que al instante
> esta infanta se enamore
> de ti, que lo encubra y adore
> y tú, mudo y tierno amante,
> después que, por mil caminos
> equívocos, declarado
> le digas nombre y cuidado
> entre dulces desatinos,
> de las flores en que empieza
> su nombre, harás alcahuete
> un florido ramillete ...

Now Tirso had at least two *comedias*, *La fingida Arcadia* and
Amar por razón de estado, in which the hero, disguised as a gardener, courts a heroine of high birth. What is more, both of them
were politically dangerous. In the former, don Felipe Centellas
courts the Condesa de Valencia del Po. This play, as we shall
prove later, has in the third act satire of Olivares for his *vellón*
and of Luis Vélez de Guevara for his plays of *tramoya:* both were

traitors, Olivares for putting out a spurious currency (i.e., *vellón*), Vélez for writing grotesque *comedias* which depended on trickery of stagecraft. The play was done in 1622 as a "particular" for the Pimentel family, but it now seems probable that Tirso may have had the temerity in early 1625 to put it on again in a magnate's private theatre, probably Juan Fernández's.

The second one was hardly less dangerous, granting the delicate political situation of the moment. *Sutilezas de amor*, which (with its comic plot removed) [90] became *Amar por razón de estado*, has to do with the Duke of Cleves, his wife, and their very forward daughters. In the role of *jardinero*, Enrique has won the love of Leonora, one of the two daughters of the pundonoresque Duque de Cleves — has, in fact, become her husband, though without benefit of clergy. As Prof. Wade [91] has shown, this play was probably written between October 7, 1624 and March 13, 1625 while the Duke of Cleves [according to Almansa y Mendoza, "el duque de Neoburg y Cleves y Tulieris (sic; Julieris)"] was in Madrid, seeking to get approval of his pact with Jorge Guillermo de Brandenburgo to bring about the removal of Spanish troops from his lands, troops which had occupied the city of Cleveris (i.e., Cleves) in 1624. Olivares, on the other hand, was striving in every way possible to keep the duke happy, while refusing him the two important things he was requesting. Such a play as *Sutilezas de amor* could hardly have pleased a pundonoresque father — or a *privado* who was hoping to keep content his political ally without yielding one inch in military matters.

---

[90] Hartzenbusch (*BAE*, V, p. xxxviii) thought that "la pieza manuscrita [dated January 1st, 1637] parece obra de primera mano y la impresa corregida... Téllez hubo de conocer que el jardinero estaba de más en la comedia; le quitó de allí y la tituló de otro modo con más propiedad". I agree that the *princeps* of this play (Sevilla, 1627) was taken from a manuscript—of which the one of 1637 is only a late copy—but Hartzenbusch could not have collated carefully *princeps* and manuscript without realizing that Tirso mangled badly his play in taking out the *gracioso*'s role.

[91] For the date of composition of *Amar por razón de estado*, see Prof. Wade's study, "El escenario histórico y la fecha de *Amar por razón de estado*" in *Estudios*, número extraordinario (1949), 657-670. As Sra. de los Ríos points out (*Obras dramáticas completas de Tirso*, II, 1091-1092): "El protagonista es un bastardo muy semejante a *El melancólico*." He indeed is!

The fact that Tirso removed the role of the salacious Bretón before publishing this *comedia* in his *Primera parte* may well argue that this was the play that caused Tirso's troubles with the *Junta de Reformación*. On the other hand, the hero's use of a "ramillete de flores" to reveal his identity suggests that Mendoza was acquainted also with Tirso's *La fingida Arcadia,* for in the latter play, Felipe gets his message to Lucrecia under cover of the flowers in his garden (II, iv). Lope, in his desire to please Antonio Hurtado de Mendoza, may well have outlined to the latter the political satire of that play (not then printed), wherein the hero also courts the heroine as *jardinero.* This would explain further Tirso's indignation against Lope as expressed in *Antona García* — if such should have been the case.

Difficulties of chronology seem at first glance to argue against Mendoza's *Más merece quien más ama* having satirized Tirso and Alarcón in 1625. It is on record that this play was put on in the Palace between October 5, 1622 and February 8, 1623. [92] Alarcón's *Las paredes oyen* was undoubtedly in existence by early 1618, in which year it was played in the convent of La Victoria. [93] Tirso's *El melancólico,* probably first written around 1623 — at which time it was called *Esto sí que es negociar* [94] — was before the public of Madrid in 1625, if we have interpreted correctly Pantaleón de Ribera's fears as to his own *discreción* and his *melancholy.* His *La fingida Arcadia* [95] — with the protagonist in the role of lover who courts his lady fair with flowers from his garden — was first written in the summer of 1622, but Pantaleón de Ribera was in early 1625 satirizing Tirso in the role of "jardinero del Prado." His *Amar por razón de estado,* with its hero from Lorraine who likewise paid court to his beloved in the disguise of gardener, was apparently penned during the Duque de Cleves' stay in Madrid in late 1624 or early 1625.

Tirso's three plays, then, seem to have ties with 1625, though the threads that bind *El melancólico* and *La fingida Arcadia* are

<hr />

[92] See Rennert, *The Spanish Stage,* 235.
[93] For date, see above, n. 2 of this chapter.
[94] See my study of *El melancólico* and *Esto sí que es negociar, HR,* XI (1943), 17-27. Much of it will have to be altered as a result of the discoveries I have made in this book.
[95] See below Ch. IV.

at the moment somewhat tenuous. Can further reasons be found to strengthen their bonds with that year? What of Alarcón's *Las paredes oyen* and Mendoza's *Más merece quien más ama?* Is there any justification for making connections between these two plays and that same year of 1625? The transformation of *Esto sí que es negociar* into *El melancólico,* as we shall see later, was due to an "*epístola*" which Lope wrote to don Antonio de Mendoza around September of 1623, [96] though it was probably not known to Tirso until it was in publication around early 1624. There is some reason, as we shall see shortly, for believing that *La fingida Arcadia* was played in the garden of a great magnate of Madrid in 1625, and there is even internal evidence to show that Mendoza's *Más merece quien más ama* was written after Tirso's *El melancólico* was in existence.

Las paredes oyen, originally written in late 1617 or early 1618, was performed for a second time in 1625, possibly on the eve of St. John's, since that *fiesta* plays such an important part in the development of the plot. Let us prove, here and now, that it is at least anchored to 1625. The cast of characters, found on the manuscript of *Las paredes oyen,* was one of 1625, not of 1617-18, as Fernández-Guerra thought. Of the fourteen actors listed on Alarcón's manuscript, all but three minor ones are included in the cast of Andrés de la Vega which put on Lope's *El Brasil restituido,* [97] an autograph signed on October 23, 1625. One of those dropped is the unknown "Frasquito," who played the very slight role of Ortiz, *escudero* to the *Conde;* another is a musician, Navarrete. The third is [Diego de] Azúa, who, for some reason, was

---

[96] See pp. 139-41.

[97] For the casts of *Las paredes oyen* and *El Brasil restituido,* see Rennert, *The Spanish Stage,* 367 and 372-373 respectively.

We supposedly have the company of Andrés de la Vega and his wife Amarilis for the Corpus of 1625, included in the *Revista de archivos, bibliotecas y museos,* XXIV (1955), 255-56. It was, aside from the two *autores,* made up of "Lorenzo Hurtado, representante; Sancho el Bueno; some 17 dancers and musicians, all named; and "tres niños, lindos representantes". This list is preceded by the statement: "Este documento no lleva fecha, y por tanto damos la del catálogo." The document is signed by "de la Vega". It is cited by Shergold's *A History of the Spanish Stage* as one belonging to the Corpus feast of 1625. Vega's actors for the special occasion of the Corpus evidently had nothing to do with his regular cast.

no longer in the company when *El Brasil restituido* was performed. María de Córdoba, Damián Arias, [Luis Bernardo de] Bobadilla, Pedro de Villegas, Dorotea [de Sierra], Gabriel Cintor, María de Victoria [Bobadilla], Francisco de Robles, Bernardino [Alvarez], Juan Mazana: all these had roles in both Alarcón's and Lope's play. Some of them — and among them such famous actors as Damián Arias, Luis Bernardo de Bobadilla, and possibly Gabriel Cintor — were not even known in 1617-1618. And on March 13th, 1627, the *autor* Juan Acacio numbered *Las paredes oyen* among the plays he was taking with him to Valencia. [98]

Fernández-Guerra, who had seen the manuscript of *Las paredes oyen* (now lost), recognized that Alarcón's play of 1617-18 had been performed in a re-run during Philip IV's reign, though he does not suggest any particular year. He likewise mentioned the play's having been retouched, but gave only one instance of it. In the manuscript, the concluding four lines are: "Y pues que los daños ven / de los necios maldicientes, / *sacratísimos oyentes*, / desta comedia hablad bien." The corresponding verses of the printed edition are: "Y pues este ejemplo ven, / suplico a *vuesas mercedes* / miren que oyen las paredes; / y a toda ley hablar bien." [99] The first *redondilla* was evidently directed to the listeners at the convent of La Victoria; the second, to the general public. Whether or not the satire of Lope's princesses of León was included in the manuscript, Fernández-Guerra does not tell us. It is logical, at least, that it should have been word of the public presentation which reached Mendoza's ears, not that of the convent. The passage against Lope's "doncellas de León" may represent a reprisal on Alarcón's part for Lope's satire of his personal defects in the prologue of his *Triunfos divinos:* "a quien ... formó la Naturaleza para irrisión y burla de las gentes, *de cuyos pechos se trasladó el plomo de sus juicios.*" Certainly, it could be so argued. It is, however, more probable in my opinion — since the *Triunfos divinos* did not come out until September of 1625 — that these words are Lope's vengeance against Alarcón for the irony he had expressed in *Las paredes oyen*. The prologue of the

---

[98] See Henri Mérimée, *Spectacles et comédiens à Valencia,* 170-171.
[99] Quoted from Fernández-Guerra, *D. Juan Ruiz de Alarcón...,* I, 333-384.

Triunfos divinos at least makes evident that Lope's and Alarcón's relations were again anything but good in 1625.

Más merece quien más ama has for its protagonist a "Duque de Lorena" and Tirso's *Amar por razón de estado* a "Duque Lotoringio" (i.e., de Lorena), and both plays paint for us *el tipo cortesano*. It should be remembered, too, that the Duque de Neoburgo y *Cleves* of Lorraine was in Madrid from October 7th, 1624 to March 13 of 1625. [100] But, aside from this coincidence, Mendoza's play has internal evidence that indicates it was written after *El melancólico* was before the public in early 1625. Its satire of Tirso and Alarcón was presumably added at that time, [101] i.e., shortly after Pantaleón de Ribera, in early March of 1625, had expressed the fear that he was becoming "discreet" and that he might go from "discretion" into "melancholy" — as had happened to Rogerio, hero of *El melancólico*. Mendoza's *Más merece*, in its second act, picks up the passage (quoted above) in which Carlín is having his problems with the "old" *guardadamas*. It should be remembered, as well, that Tirso's *gracioso* is openly contemptuous of a man so cold of temperament that he dares to guard women without fear of being burnt. (Why, the average husband can't even guard *one* woman, argues Carlín!) It is a point of view which echoes and underlines that of Pinardo (Rogerio's tutor), who had complained that his pupil had acquired all the graces of the perfect courtier except that of love; that he had, in fact, "idiota voluntad."

Rosauro and Burón of *Más merece quien más ama*, have wandered into the *quinta* of the princess Fidelinda. When the latter comes upon the stage, she orders straightway that the Palace be cleared. The following dialogue then takes place (II, fol. 11r.):

CLORINDA: Caballeros, despejar.
BURÓN: Damíssima zahareña,
mirad que es para una dueña
oficio de hacer pesar.

... ...

---

[100] G. Wade, "El escenario histórico y la fecha de *Amar por razón de estado*", 657-670.

[101] Tirso was not even in Spain when *Las paredes oyen* was being written and acted; nor is there any reason to think he knew don Antonio de Mendoza at that time.

BURÓN :   ¿Quién lo manda?
CLORINDA :   La princesa.
          ... ...
ROSAURO :   Obedecelle es muy justo.
          ... ...
BURÓN :   ¿No hay *un viejo gruñidor*
             que aquí *guardadamas* sea?
             Más bien en mujer se emplea,
             que ellas se guardan mejor.
CLORINDA :   *¿No más de "viejo" le llamas?*
BURÓN :   A no serlo, hallara en él
             que es oficio de ser cruel;
             es propio para las damas.

There is yet other material in *Más merece quien más ama* that links it with Tirso's *El melancólico* — as well as with his *Amar por razón de estado. Both* of Gabriel Téllez's plays are much concerned with "the perfect courtier." So is *Más merece quien más ama.* In the last-mentioned work, Mendoza chooses to give us *his* portrait of the type (II, fol. 14r.), one that bears much resemblance to the poet himself, commonly known, we remember, as "el perfecto cortesano." Burón, servant to the protagonist, when responding to the title of "hidalgo" (one by which Mendoza frequently designates himself), sketches for Clorinda a portrait of his master Rosauro (II, fol. 14r.). He is one "con valor de primero" but with "agrado de segundo"; one who is valiant in important things, can even face a bull in the bullring "con bizarría," a real test of courage, we are assured; he is one who prefers the role of intelligent amateur — Mendoza, we remember, was called "el lego" — when writing his verses, not that of inspired poet; one who is "estudioso con recato / más que hasta ser literato, / hasta no ser ignorante ... " (Góngora, as we have seen, tells us Mendoza was "poco adornado de estudios.") In his role as lover, "ama, sufre, calla, obliga, / si en una mujer se emplea, / que él sólo quiere que sea / y los otros que se diga." (Elsewhere in the play [I, fol. 5v.], Burón agrees with his master that one should even *love* with moderation.) Mendoza puts the last touches on his self-portrait by saying:

                No hay queja de su sombrero
                ni de su lengua un agravio,

> tan cuerdo, secreto, y sabio,
> cortés, galán, verdadero,
> que no hay bien que no le sobre
> para el grande y para el chico;
> y en fin *es un hombre rico*
> con buenas partes de pobre.

If I understand Mendoza aright, he is telling Tirso: "This is how the perfect *cortesano* really is, and not as you have painted him in *El melancólico!*" It is essentially a portrait of a rather indolent, complacent dilettante, a *discreto* who shunned the extremes of professionalism as he would the devil. Mr. Davies has noted Mendoza's attitude (193-194): "A deliberate amateurism was indeed ... the hall-mark of the palace poet." The *cortesano* that Tirso would like to see in the Palace was, on the other hand, the true *discreto*, as he saw it, that is, the scholarly man who had, before going to the Palace, lived with his books far from the court. This "gentil tempero," of which Mendoza boasted, was as irritating to the very active Tirso, as it was to Carlín. He could not pardon in Mendoza "the unlit lamp and the ungirt loin." He saw in him one of those who neither wanted to enter heaven nor let others of inspiration and will-power do so. Why? "Out of envy," says Tirso. "Out of laziness as well," his friend, Gabriel de Corral, will add.

In short, I am suggesting as a real possibility that Mendoza reworked his *Más merece quien más ama* in 1625 and added his satire of Tirso and Alarcón: 1) after the latter had (in *early* 1625) commented ironically, in a retouched version of *Las paredes oyen*, on the unseemly conduct of Lope's princesses of León — not with an eye on *Los donaires de Matico* (of 1604), but with one on the first part of *Los Tellos de Meneses*, dated "1620-28" [probably 1623]; 2) after Tirso's *El melancólico* — with its satire of an "old guardadamas" and its stress on the *discreet* (i.e., the learned) courtier — had been played in the public *corrales*; 3) after the protagonist of his *Sutilezas de amor* (later to become *Amar por razón de estado*) had (in the role of a *jardinero from Lorraine*) courted the play's very forward heroine, daughter to the Duke of Cleves; and 4) after Tirso's *La fingida Arcadia* — with its hero who gets over his message of love to the heroine through the symbolic language of flowers — had been put on for a second time in the private theatre of one of the great estates which faced the Prado.

For we have, I believe, in *La huerta de Juan Fernández* — with its satire of Mendoza as an "ass" who was occupying a magistrate's seat of honor — Tirso's defiant answer to the latter's irony at the expense of a lover who assumes the garb of gardener and uses bouquets of flowers to get his message across to his beloved. This *comedia*, which Tirso wrote in the second quarter [102] of 1626 as a *particular* for the private theatre of the *regidor* Juan Fernández (one situated at the entrance to the Prado), has for its protagonist one don Hernando Cortés of Málaga. In courting Laura, don Hernando says (I, iii): "Jardinero soy de amor"; then he adds: "Ven y haréte un ramillete / de matices que distintos / te interpreten mis afectos; / que flores tal vez son libros." Like *La fingida Arcadia*, this *comedia* has for its heroine an Italian girl who is "Condesa de Valencia del Po." What is more, any number of the lines of *La fingida Arcadia* (I, iv) has been carried over bodily to *La huerta de Juan Fernández* (I, ii), beginning with "Los propósitos jugamos / una noche." The very close relationship of the two plays, one that Tirso seems to underline *consciously*, even suggests the possibility that *La fingida Arcadia* may have been given *for a second time* in early 1625 in this very same garden of Juan Fernández [103] and that Tirso was recalling that fact to his audience of *La huerta de Juan Fernández*. If such were the case, Pantaleón de Ribera would then, in March of 1625, have had in mind primarily *La fingida Arcadia* when speaking of Tirso as "el jardinero del Prado." And Mendoza's satire in *Más merece quien más ama*, naturally enough, would have followed soon thereafter. It may

---

[102] R. P. Manuel Penedo Rey (*Tirso en Sevilla*, 58) proves that it must have been written between March and the end of May, 1626.

[103] The relationship of Tirso and Juan Fernández needs to be explored further. One finds much concerning this Juan Fernández in the *Actas de las Cortes de Castilla*. He was not only *regidor* but he was lender to a government that was ever in the red. As such, he probably had little fear of Olivares.

Antonio de Mendoza has a malicious poem entitled "A una señora que estorbaba a un galán que estaba con una dama, llamándole a cenar" (*Obras poéticas*, I, 283-287). The setting of the poem is the garden of Juan Fernández: "¡Oh jardín de Juan Fernández, / verde campo del amor / y encarnado desafío / de una a una y otra a dos; / derriba a tus cenadores, / destiérralos, que si no, / de tu presunción romana / seré segundo Nerón".

well have been given at the *fiesta* in honor of the Queen's birthday on July 9, 1625 — and with it a *loa* which satirized Tirso as another "Arceo," of whom we shall later hear much when studying Luis Vélez de Guevara's part in this intrigue. [104] The anonymous commentator of the *Noticias de Madrid* has left us a description of the ceremonies that celebrated that occasion (122):

> A 9 el Marqués de Eliche y de Toral [i.e., Olivares' son-in-law] hizo una comedia en Palacio para festejar los años de la Reina, nuestra Señora. Fue toda de chistes muy donosos. Compuso una jornada don Antonio de Mendoza; otra, don Francisco de Quevedo; y otra, Mateo Montero, criado del Almirante. Representáronla don Cristóbal Tenorio, Ayuda de cámara del Rey, y otros ayudas de cámara. Fue una fiesta muy entretenida, así por los dichos y chistes que tenía, como por los bailes y entremeses que tenía, de que salieron los Reyes muy gustosos.

It should be noted: 1) that the title of the play given on that July 9th, 1625 is not mentioned; 2) that it was an occasion "de chistes muy donosos." I suspect that some of those jokes, at least, were at Tirso's expense.

If Mendoza, like Pantaleón, learned of Tirso's *El melancólico* in early 1625, the play could not have failed to irritate him profoundly and may well have been the fuse that ignited the whole situation. Mendoza, determined on revenge, would have begun to gather information as to Tirso's attitude toward Olivares: from his friend, Lope de Vega, he could have learned of the satire against the *privado* in *La fingida Arcadia;* from perhaps another, something of the political dangers that *Sutilezas de amor* offered; from yet a third the heavy charge of political dynamite that *La prudencia en la mujer* and other plays of 1622-25 carried, etc., etc., Armed with such evidence, he would then have gone to Olivares to get his revenge through the *Junta.* What we don't know is how many verbal missiles he may have sent in Tirso's direction before taking such decisive action.

By way of summation, let us point out that Antonio de Mendoza's *Más merece quien más ama* is something of a revue of the

---

[104] See pp. 278-81.

theatrical world of 1625. He not only defends Lope against Alarcón's satire of Lope's "princesses of León"; he answers, as well,
Tirso's charges in *El Melancólico* that he was an *old guardadamas*
without any fire. He creates as counterpart to Tirso's *cortesano*
Rogerio (drawn in Tirso's own image), his own *cortesano*, Rosauro,
patterned to his own likeness. But Mendoza managed, at the same
time, to satirize two other Tirsian plays. By making his noble protagonist from Lorraine, one who planned to court the princess in
the role of gardener, he recalled Téllez's *Sutilezas de amor* which
had for protagonist a noble from the same country, one who had
as *jardinero,* paid homage to the daughter of the Duque de
Cleves. He even succeeded in tying in satire of *La fingida Arcadia,* where the hero, also a *jardinero,* gets over his message to
the heroine through a game of flowers. Mendoza's play, in its
satire, is really tremendously clever. He strikes *openly* at Alarcón,
who was satirizing Lope for the unreal world he had created; *cov-
ertly* he attacks Tirso and points to the Mercedarian's lack of
realism in such plays as *Las sutilezas de amor* and *La fingida
Arcadia.* Thus, as in the *copla* on the pastry-shop wall, Tirso and
Alarcón are linked in crime.

There is yet another reference to Tirso in Antonio de Mendoza's *Los empeños del mentir,* [105] a play that originally had the
title of *Quien más miente medra más* when it was performed in
1631. It was retouched (or rewritten) in 1634, for the work, as we
have it today, celebrates the Spanish victory at Nordlingen (September, 1634). In the third act, a servant comes in from the Palace
and says the "Condesa-Duquesa" begs Teodoro and Marcelo (both
rascals who have, according to their tale, brought news of the
victory) to attend the *fiestas* in the *Buen Retiro.* The following
conversation then takes place (III, 452):

> TEODORO: ¿Qué fiestas hay?
> CRIADO: Las mayores
> de a caballo, y después dellas,
> dos comedias.
> TEODORO: Iré a vellas,
> que huelgo de sus primores.
> ¿Cúyas son?

---

[105] *BAE,* XLV, 437-455.

CRIADO: Es peregrina
la primera, [106] *de un lucido*
ingenio grande, escondido
en lo Tirso de Molina.

MARCELO: La otra será mediana,
que es de un fidalgo, que en ellas
nada hace bien sino hacellas
muy tarde y de mala gana.

TEODORO: ¿Qué es la historia?

CRIADO: La tragedia
(bien que con lazos severos)
de dos grandes embusteros...
será cosa entretenida
... ...

DON DIEGO: Muy gran favor
destos señores ha sido.

TEODORO: ¿Quién mucho no ha recibido
de su grandeza?

Praise of Tirso de Molina as "un lucido / ingenio grande, escondido / en lo Tirso de Molina"; self-depreciation of himself as "un fidalgo, que en ellas [i.e., las comedias] / nada hace bien sino hacellas / muy tarde y de mala gana"; praise of the Conde-Duque and his wife who are giving the fiestas for the Royal Couple! How interpret all this from an Hurtado de Mendoza who had denounced Tirso in 1625 to the *Junta?* Does it indicate disarming repentance on Mendoza's part, admission of his injustice to the Mercedarian?

---

[106] One may suspect that the play of Tirso's was *La firmeza en la hermosura,* which must have been first written in 1621 but was retouched after the theatre of the Retiro was built. One finds in it the following words (I, 1): "El Buen Retiro entre flores / con que al Ebro el cristal bebe, / da el teatro en que se atreve / a hurtar a Plauto y Terencio / aplausos con que al silencio / admiraciones renueve". The play has its setting in Aragón; hence mention of the Ebro. If *La firmeza* should have been the play, I doubt that Tirso was consulted in the matter of its presentation in 1634. See chapter III of this book, "Tirso's Relations to Lope and his Theatre Reappraised," p. 181, n. 48. Professors Vern Williamsen and H. G. Jones III are putting out a longer edition of this play than the one now known.

The *loa* put on with it — one satirizing "Arcreo", whom Vélez de Guevara linked with Tirso in early 1626 — is highly important for any interpretation of this passage from *Los empeños del mentir.* See *Obras poéticas de don Antonio Hurtado de Mendoza* (III, 22-29): "Loa para la comedia de *Más medra quien miente más,* que se hizo en el Buen Retiro, día de San Pedro de 1634". We shall return to the point in chapter VII.

Or is it another of his "gaterías" in which he is hiding his claws, one with which Mendoza would recall to the Conde-Duque the events of 1625? Let us reserve until later our answer, pointing out here only that if Tirso knew of his rival's praise, it apparently did not stop him from writing the satirical "Señor, a ti sólo" of the *Cuarta parte!*

Mendoza would, in 1635 and again in 1636, put on in the Palace his *El galán sin dama*, a *comedia* first written in 1621-25, according to Prof. Davies. [107] The play was, we believe, re-worked after it was first composed some time before February 11, 1623. In the first act the characters are wearing *calzas* (above-the-knee trunks) and *cuello* (ruff); later, they will appear in *ferreruelo* (a long, flowing cape that replaced the short *bohemio*) and in *golilla*, the plate-like collar that would replace the ruff after the sumptuary decrees of 1623, decrees that brought a veritable revolution in costume. *El galán sin dama*, like *Más merece quien más ama*, has mention of the "900 plays" which Lope had written, a number Lope first claimed in 1620, and one that, strictly speaking, was applicable only until early 1625, when he was claiming 1070. [108] I doubt, however, that Mendoza bothered to keep up with Lope's claims: he did not, in fact, even trouble himself to change the number of 900 plays in *El galán sin dama*, when it was played in the Palace in 1635 (and again in 1636)! Yet Pérez de Montalván had claimed 1500 for his friend in his *Para todos* of 1632. In *El galán sin dama*, I find no satire of Tirso which might have been inserted in answer to the charges that the Mercedarian had brought in his "A ti sólo" of the *Cuarta parte*. It perhaps would have required more energy than Mendoza — with his some fifty years of age and his indolent temperament — would have cared to expend, just as it would have required too much to bring up to date the number of plays Lope had written before his death.

---

[107] *El galán sin dama* was published in *El mejor de los mejores libros que han salido de comedias nuevas*, Madrid, 1653. For Mr. Davies' opinion as to its date, see *A Poet at Court...*, 260.

[108] According to Rennert and Castro, *Vida de Lope de Vega* (345), he put forth this claim in his *Parte XX*.

At this point we must revert to the satire of Lope de Vega in *Antona García*. Tirso, in his revision of that play and in the very same passage where he accuses Mendoza, sets up an outstanding poet, possibly as a candidate for the role of fellow *soplón*, certainly as a companion in envy to Mendoza. Miss Margaret Wilson [109] believed that this second envious poet could only be Lope; I quite agree. The Seventh Castilian, having declared that he "dealt in Envy," continues his chat with the Portuguese. It is dialogue that we must analyse at length when studying Tirso's and Lope's relations. *Here*, the only thing that is important is that the two merchant-poets are *linked* in their envy.

We must accordingly study the ties that bound don Antonio Hurtado de Mendoza to Lope de Vega Carpio. What background had Tirso in mind that justified his charge? Mr. Davies, in *A Poet at Court* ... (19), calls Lope "a life-long friend of the poet" and suggests that the "don Hurtado de Mendoza," known to have stood as godparent at the baptism of Lope's illegitimate child by Micaela de Luján in 1607, may well have been our don Antonio. It could have been he, for in Lope's *Pastores de Belén* (1612), we find Mendoza's high praise of Lope. Referring to this book as "lágrimas de Dios," he asks: "Belardo, ¿qué lira humana / las cantara como vos?" The two were, moreover, associates in Saldaña's academy. However, there is, in the last years of Philip III's reign, less evidence of a close relationship between the two poets, if I am right in arguing that Mendoza's warm defense of Lope against Alarcón and Tirso must have been written, not around 1617, when *Las paredes oyen* was first written, but that it was inserted in *Más merece quien más ama* after March 6, 1625, when the *Junta de Reformación* recommended Tirso's banishment.

Let us get on to those first years of Philip IV's reign. Mr. Davies (*A Poet at Court* ..., 42) points to Lope's praise of Mendoza in his *Justa poética y alabanzas justas* (1620) as "the best contemporary exponent of the epigrammatic *décima*." Lope's *Jardín de poetas*, [110] finished before July 19, 1621, contains the following stilted praise of Mendoza:

---

[109] See her edition of *Antona García*, pp. xxiii-xxv.
[110] *BAE*, XXXVIII, 422-425.

Retratado en un mármol Arimaspe,
pudiera don Antonio de Mendoza
ser gloria del amante de Campaspe.

Just what led Lope to compare Mendoza to the one-eyed Scythian who is "represented as in constant strife with the gryphons for the gold represented by the latter," [111] I cannot say. Even less do I understand why he was the glory of Alexander the Great. Written possibly after Mendoza was appointed "guarda-ropa" to the king on May 23, 1621, it should possibly be counted as a bit of the incense that Lope was, in those first years of Philip IV's reign, laying at the feet of all who stood near that monarch or the Conde de Olivares. The poem of *El jardín* as a whole is dedicated to Francisco de Rioja, secretary and intimate friend of the favorite. It was in 1621, as well, that Lope retouched his *El premio de la hermosura* wherein he declared to the world in general — and to Olivares in particular, to whom he dedicated the play — that he wanted to become royal chronicler to Philip IV. [112] In our study of Tirso's relations to Lope we shall have occasion to quote the passage at length.

The relations of the two poets in 1622 are not entirely clear. Mendoza was one of the many who contributed poems in honor of San Isidro's canonization, and in Lope's "Panegíricos de los poetas que tomaron parte en las justas," it would appear that Mendoza had been complaining to Lope of the illfortune that attended him. Lope comments: "Escribe a la devoción [de San Isidro?] / que tan devoto le han hecho, / *tristezas de su fortuna* / y honor de sus pensamientos." La Barrera, having quoted Lope's observation, states (246): "No sabemos qué motivo pudiera tener Mendoza para estar por aquel tiempo descontento de su fortuna." But don Antonio's meteoric rise in the Palace had not yet begun; and to

---

[111] This could possibly refer to a *carta de poder*, dated March 14, 1619, in which Mendoza reaffirmed his "right to a salary of 600 ducats a year, payable to him as a charge on the property of don Sancho Díaz de Zurbano, Vice-roy of the Kingdoms of Peru". See G. A. Davies, *A Poet at Court...*, 26. I can not see, however, how it could explain the reference to Campaspe's lover, if the allusion is to Alexander.

[112] See pp. 164-65.

that melancholy, ambitious poet, Fortune probably seemed to be dragging her feet.

She was, however, already in the offig — with the Duquesa de Olivares as her emissary. The young Queen, Isabel, had planned a *fiesta* for her royal husband's seventeenth birthday. The entertainment, as scheduled, was to include 1) a court spectacle, *La gloria de Niquea*, written for the occasion by the Conde de Villamediana, and 2) a mythological one, by Lope de Vega Carpio, entitled *El vellocino de oro*. The latter work had been commissioned through the very intelligent Leonor Pimentel, "Dama de la Señora Infanta," to whom Lope had dedicated his *Filomela* of 1621. The roles in both productions were to be acted by the ladies-in-waiting of the Queen and the Infanta.

A fire broke out when Lope's *El vellocino de oro* was only well-started, one (it was whispered) that had been set by the Conde de Villamediana because he was head over heels in love with his young Queen and wanted the chance to rescue her. The Condesa de Olivares straightway took charge of the awkward situation and commissioned Antonio de Mendoza to write up the *fiesta*. He complied, in both prose and poetry, but neither the one *relato* nor the other makes clear what really happened, so obscure is the wording of the accounts written. But that they pleased the Countess and her husband — perhaps because of their very lack of clarity — is evident, for Mendoza's fortune was seemingly at that moment launched.

Of Lope's *El vellocino de oro*, Mendoza says absolutely nothing in his poetical account. Yet when this play came off press in *Parte XIX* of 1623 (but with *aprobaciones* of June, 1622), it was dedicated, not to his patroness, Leonor Pimentel, as one might logically have expected, but instead to doña Luisa Briceño de la Cueva, who would, on July 25, 1623, become wife to Antonio Hurtado de Mendoza *por poderes*. Just when Lope wrote his *dedicatoria* to doña Luisa (and her husband) is not certain. La Barrera believed it to have been done before the *aprobación* of the volume was given in June, 1622, not in 1623 before the volume came off press. In writing the *dedicatoria*, Lope says: "Bien conozco que a sus bodas debíamos *los que le tenemos* [a Mendoza] *por maestro* felices epitalamios..." This fulsome flattery could only have stuck Tirso as nauseating.

In early 1624, a new volume of Lope's came forth, entitled *La Circe con otras rimas y prosas,* one dedicated to "el excelentísimo Sr. D. Gaspar de Guzmán, Conde de Olivares." Its *censura,* of September 4, 1623, is by don Antonio Hurtado de Mendoza. Moreover, it contains an *epístola* in verse to this same don Antonio, entitled "A don Antonio Hurtado de Mendoza, caballero del hábito de Calatrava, secretario de su Majestad." [113] Let us now scrutinize that poem with utmost care, for it will tell us much concerning the relations of Lope and Mendoza — as it must have told Tirso much concerning them some two or three months before his *Cigarrales* came off press. It is, we believe, primarily this poem that explains the satirical scene in *Antona García.*

From the very first lines of the epistle, necessarily written after September 24, 1623 when Mendoza was received into the Order of Calatrava, it is made clear 1) that Lope had asked the king directly for a *merced* as a result of some advice given him, and 2) that this *merced* had been granted him shortly before Lope wrote this poem. He tells his friend Antonio of his change of fortune and attitude:

> Ya se pasaron, generoso Antonio,
> las iras del rigor de mi fortuna,
> si basta su mudanza en testimonio.
> ... ...
> *Consejo fue de Dios* que le rogase
> quien pretendiese de él [el Rey] alguna cosa,
> materia en que su forma dilatase.
> .. ..
> Ya salgo a nueva luz del necio olvido,
> y de la queja criminal me aparto.
> ... ...
> ¡Bien haya el siglo de Felipe IV!
> Pues ¿qué si a mí me preguntara Clío
> si era verdad que los poetas *premia?*
> ¡qué presto vieran el ejemplo mío!

---

[113] *BAE,* XXXVIII, 400-401.

TIRSO, ANTONIO HURTADO DE MENDOZA, LOPE, AND...

What was the *premio* that had brought about Lope's jubilant mood? It could hardly have been anything other than the yearly pension of 250 ducats, granted him by the king, if Rennert and Castro [114] are right in believing that "el único favor real que recibió [Lope] fue una pensión en Galicia de doscientos cincuenta ducados al año." Who had given Lope such God-sent advice? By all the laws of probability, none other than his old friend Antonio de Mendoza, who was so near the king and Olivares. This is suggested by Lope's willingness to renounce in favor of Mendoza his long-held dream of becoming court chronicler. Now, with a guaranteed yearly income at hand, he urges Mendoza:

> *Escribid las grandezas de Felipe,*
> *que falta a mi rudeza atrevimiento*
> ... ...
> ... vuestra dulcísima armonía
> afrenta las científicas escuelas
> con excelente y natural poesía.

Mendoza had evidently pointed to his *melancholy* temperament as an impediment to his success in writing the feats of the king — and perhaps as well to his lack of formal education — but Lope reassures him in this direction:

> No ponga en vuestro ardiente amor templanza
> *ese humor melancólico,* pues siento
> que más contemplación con él se alcanza;
> que mejor el pasible [115] entendimiento
> percibe las especies producidas
> en el agente por tristeza atento.

---

[114] Rennert y Castro, *Vida de Lope de Vega*, 278. His biographers believed, as do I, that Lope was referring in his *epístola* to Mendoza to the 250 *ducados* that had been given him: "El favorito [i. e., Olivares] no parece haber hecho gran cosa por él [Lope], prescindiendo de la pensión de 250 ducados, garantizada por la corona, que, según Montalván, obtuvo Lope, merced a su influencia. A tal merced debe aludir el poeta en la epístola a don Antonio de Mendoza, donde, hablando de Olivares, dice: 'Pintad un claro príncipe, que sabe, etc....'".

[115] "El pasible entendimiento", in contradistinction to "el entendimiento agente". Carlos Fernández Gómez, *Vocabulario completo de Lope de Vega*, quotes another example.

But, says Lope, Mendoza must sing the praises of Olivares as well as those of the king:

> Después de celebrar la valentía,
> las heroicas grandezas singulares
> deste divino sol vuestra Talía,
>   decid cómo laureles y *olivares*
> abrasaron su espléndida corona.
>
> ... ...
>
>   Pintad del conde la real persona
> dulce severamente, amable y grave,
> que el aspecto de Júpiter abona.

Lope at this point interrupts his praises of Olivares to tell something of his own youth and of his own feats in arms; but he grants straightway that his interest in things military had soon yielded to the claims of his "infused poetry" [116] and to economic necessity:

>   Necesidad y yo partiendo a medias
> el estado de *versos mercantiles,*
> pusimos en estilo las comedias.
>   Yo las saqué de sus principios viles
> ¡engendrando en España más poetas
> que hay en los aires átomos sutiles!

He will now use his God-given talents to praise the Count:

>   Ya siempre agradecido, estoy pensando
> qué hipérboles, qué versos, qué concetos
> irán mi amor y obligación mostrando.

With what emotions Tirso must have read that epistle! With his strong Biblical background, his first thought would perhaps have been: Esau and Jacob! Lope had sold his birthright for a

---

[116] The adjective "infuso" probably became popularized at this time by Lope's reference to "la ciencia infusa" in his *Filomela* of 1621. This phrase, of ancient theological lineage, is found not infrequently in Tirso's theatre *after that date.* See its use by doña María de San Ambrosio y Piña (Tirso's sister?) in her poem that prefaces Tirso's *Cigarrales.* According to her, "Gabriel" also has "infusa ciencia". Tirso himself uses it in *La fingida Arcadia* (I, i); in *La venganza de Tamar* (II, iv); and in *Santo y sastre* (III, xii). All three plays are of 1622, in my opinion.

mess of pottage! Lope, apologetic for having written his *come-dias*, a form of literature that was to Tirso "the princess of liberal arts"! Lope himself, under whose leadership Tirso had so proudly enlisted in 1621, considered his plays "versos mercantiles"; and just as evident it was that he was now bartering away his dream of becoming poet laureate for a price! What is more, the buyer was to Tirso a second rate poet who was tremendously inferior in talent to Lope. Quite a tidy, business-like arrangement! No wonder Tirso placed his setting in *Antona García* among a group of merchants whose philosophy was "Viva quien venza," one where each was telling of the "merchandise" he peddled! What was Tirso's "line"? What did he have "for sale"? Only envy, says the poet sadly, the envy that reigned in the literary circles of Madrid!

Lope trafficking with a poet who was for Tirso the very symbol of envy, one who was the creature of the evil Olivares, one whose fortunes had sky-rocketed with the support of the *privado* in spite of the fact that he had during many years been tightly linked to the old order that Tirso favored! What had been the *quid pro quo in that* relatinship? Well, if Lope had taken himself out of the running, Tirso would unhesitatingly enter the race against this inferior poet Mendoza; and thereupon he must have withdrawn his *Cigarrales* from the press and inserted the paragraph in it wherein he paints himself as striving for the laurel wreath — with *envy* coiled at his feet.

That miscellany came out with a very intriguing title page, one which Dr. Alan K. G. Paterson [117] has described as follows:

> The engraving [on the title page] represents an elaborate façade, flanked by two figures, one a king, covered with hands to symbolize "FAVOR," and the other a wise man, covered with wings, to symbolize "INGENIUM." A compartment separates these two figures in which the title of the book appears: *Cigarrales de Toledo*. [The word "utinam" appears as part of the design of symbolic figures.]

Just what did Tirso mean by his symbolic title page? Unless I am mistaken, he was saying to Philip IV: "You, as king, have favor

---

[117] Paterson, "Tirso de Molina: Two Bibliographical Studies", 42.

at your disposal; oh, that you would put at your command knowledge with her soaring wings [i.e., Tirso's]'." If I am interpreting
aright this bit of symbolism, then the poets of the inner court
circle, among others Mendoza, could hardly have failed to take
note.

In the *Cigarrales*, one finds what is apparently related symbolism which, when interpreted in connection with that of the title
page, was surely nothing less than an open challenge to some
one. Tirso describes at length in his miscellany an aquatic fête
that apparently took place on the Tagus in Toledo, one in which
his own boat represented the last entry (I, 116):

> Tirso, que aunque humilde pastor de Manzanares, halló
> en la llaneza generosa de Toledo mejor acogida que en
> su patria, tan apoderada de la envidia extranjera — llegó
> en un pequeño barco, aunque curioso, hecho todo un
> jardín que hallara lugar entre los hibleos, y en medio dél
> una palma altísima, sobre cuyos últimos cogollos esta-
> ba una corona de laurel. Trepaba el pastor por ella, vestido
> un pellico blanco con unas barras de púrpura a los pechos,
> marca de los de su profesión, y ayudábanle a subir dos
> alas, escrito en la una "INGENIO" y en la otra, "ESTU-
> DIO," volando con ellas tan alto que tocaba ya con la
> mano a la corona, puesto que la Envidia, en su forma acos-
> tumbrada de culebra, enroscándose a los pies, procuraba
> impedirle la gloriosa consecución de sus trabajos, aunque
> en vano, porque, pisándola, colgaba dellos esta letra que
> sirvió también para los jueces: *Velis, nolis.* Dicen que la
> dio en latín, porque no la entendiesen sus *émulos;* que
> hasta en esto quiso que campease su modestia, pues pa-
> labras en algarabía no agravian a quien no las entiende.

The very, very tall (royal?) palm from which was hung the laurel
wreath of fame — for which Tirso was climbing in his Hyblean
garden — should presumably be equated with the king and the
favors he could give. The placard which he put in place of
the laurel wreath bore the words, "Velis, nolis": this was his open
challenge to Envy, coiled at his feet.

The Latin phrase "velis, nolis" was possibly intended as well
to recall to Lope his own use of it in *El peregrino* (1604) — pre-

cisely in connection with Envy. Sra. de los Ríos, [118] referring to it as one of Lope's "indiscretos geroglíficos," labels it further "sus jactanciosos motes." She goes ahead to add: " ... está en latín para mayor autoridad. *Velis, nolis, envidia, Seianus mihi, Pegasus. Aut unicus, aut peregrinus*, que Hartzenbusch agrupó y tradujo así: 'Envidia, quieras o no quieras, Lope es (o yo soy) único o muy raro (*ingenio* se supone).' " Tirso would certainly seem to be mocking Lope at this point, perhaps even challenging him. Yet the *culebra* (a traditional symbol of "envy") which was coiled at Tirso's feet must refer to Mendoza — if one judges by other references in Tirso's theatre. Possibly Tirso included the Latin phrase without any memory of Lope's having used it in his *Peregrino*.

Two things are, in fact, not clear: 1) with whom should "Envy" be identified? and 2) in what particular form was Tirso wanting favor from the king? Tirso's answer to the first question would be forthcoming in *El melancólico* which we believe to have been before the Madrid public in early 1625, since Pantaleón de Ribera seems to make clear allusion to it. With its satire of the "necios opulentos" of the Palace, whom Tirso there contrasts with the "discretos" (that is, men of learning), and with its sarcasm at the expense of the "old" "guardadamas" of the Palace by way of further identification, don Antonio Hurtado de Mendoza could hardly have failed to suspect that he was, for the Mercedarian, the personification of Envy, on whom Tirso would not hesitate to tread in order to reach the laurel wreath of fame.

In time, envy would become, in Tirso's lexicon, a synonym for Mendoza, but one may ask whether it was so at the time this passage was being written. The matter is made the more difficult by the fact that these words could, theoretically at least, have been penned as early as the summer of 1621, when Lope was dedicating *Lo fingido verdadero* to Tirso, and was pointing to the "envy" that attended the Mercedarian. [119] Moreover, Tirso's book had gone to press shortly before October 8, 1621; normally, it should not have left the printer's hands until some time after March 6, 1624, the date of its *tasa*. Could anything have happened in the two and

---

[118] *Obras dramáticas completas*, I, 906.
[119] See p. 160 of this study.

one-half years that intervened? Why was its publication so long delayed?

Could Tirso have made any changes in his *Cigarrales* in that period? He could, and did, in my opinion. Among them was this challenge to Envy, which seems to indicate that Tirso had already suffered at some length from Madrid's envy: "Tirso ... , aunque humilde pastor de Manzanares, halló en la llaneza generosa de Toledo mejor acogida que en su patria, *tan apoderada de la envidia extranjera.*" Mendoza was, from Tirso's point of view, a "foreigner" [120] (apparently, one not born in Madrid); he had instead first seen the light in the province of Santander. Moreover, this same combination of *ingenio* and *estudio* is repeated in *El melancólico*, refashioned in early 1625. Rogerio, disillusioned with the Palace, explains his feeling by the fact that he had entered it "ambicioso de fama y de grandeza / no heredada, adquirida / con noble *ingenio y estudiosa fama*" — only to find that the Palace made no distinction between him and the "necios opulentos." There is a third reason why Tirso could not have left his first brain-child in press for over two and a half years without changes, a psychological one: Tirso had not "el gentil tempero" — to borrow Carlín's description of the "guardadamas" of the Palace — to let his book stay in press untouched that long. He would have had to let "el necio" know that he was well aware of what his enemy was doing in order to prevent the glorious realization of his (Tirso's) dreams.

At this point one must raise certain questions before proceeding to others: was there any possibility of Mendoza's getting to know the *Cigarrales* while it was still in manuscript? Could Tirso have believed that his enemy was holding up the publication of his *Cigarrales* out of envy, that he feared the undeniable talents of a man like Tirso, talents that were accompanied by hard work, unlimited energy, and driving ambition? I believe the answer is yes. When in 1620-1621 his *El vergonzoso* was put on in Toledo as a *particular* at Buenavista and Mendoza had written the *entreme-*

---

[120] La Barrerás *catálogo* says of Mendoza: "... su país natal fue la montaña de Asturias." See, however, G. A. Davies, *A Poet at Court...*, p. 18. For "extranjero" as equivalent to "de fuera de Castilla", see Martín Alonso (*Enciclopedia del idioma*).

ses for it, Tirso, we remember, had praised him courteously (if ambiguously), saying: "Los entremeses fueron de don Antonio de Mendoza, cuyos sales y concetos igualan a su apacibilidad y nobleza." But something had brought him to the conviction that Mendoza was Envy itself. The probability is that he became convinced that Mendoza was preventing the *Cigarrales* from coming off press. Books, apparently, went to an "escribano de cámara" for their *tasa*. The *Cigarrales*, when it finally came out in 1624, had one authorized on March 6th by "don Hernando Vallejo, Secretario del Rey nuestro Señor y *su Escribano de Cámara*, uno de los que residen en su Consejo ... " Similarly, the *Primera parte*, on November 20, 1626, received its *tasa* through "Diego González de Villa Roel, *Escribano de Cámara*." And as early as June of 1623, the *Noticias de Madrid* tells us Antonio Hurtado de Mendoza was made "Secretario de Su Majestad y de su Cámara." In the case of the *Cigarrales*, since it already had its *aprobaciones* of 1621, given by two such illustrious figures as Juan de Jáuregui (on October 27, 1621) and Fr. Miguel Sánchez (on November 8, 1621), and since Pedro de Contreras had already authorized for the king its publication on November 8, 1621, Tirso was, in some way, able to bring enough pressure to get it out of press. Murcia de la Llana attached the *erratas* on February 22, 1624, Hernando de Vallejo gave it its *tasa* on March 6 of that same year. Shortly after the latter date, it must have been released to the public. But it was to be otherwise with the *Primera parte* of 1626, which Tirso sought to bring out in Madrid: with the censure of the *Junta* hanging over *him*, he was not able to get the necessary *aprobaciones*, and so had to spirit it out to Seville. [121] Granting Tirso's convictions as to the envy of his rival, as expressed in the *Cigarrales de Toledo*, it seems highly probable that don Antonio de Mendoza was instrumental in holding up publication of that miscellany.

We still must ask: what was the specific wreath of laurel that Tirso wanted from the King as the reward of his knowledge and

---

[121] See my study, "Did Tirso Send to Press a *Primera parte* of Madrid (1626) which Contained *El condenado por desconfiado?*", homage volume to Prof. Arnold Reichenberger. I believe it was Tirso himself who saw to it that a copy-text of the *Primera parte* reached Lyra of Sevilla, *HR*, XLI (1973), 261-274.

his talents? At which of Mendoza's various positions in the Palace was he aiming? Why was Mendoza afraid? Góngora, we remember, tells us that Mendoza was "poco adornado de estudios." Tirso, on the other hand, was "discreto" in the sense of learned. Of the many roles that Mendoza filled in the Palace, there was, it seems to me, only one that could have interested Tirso: that of king's chronicler.

Tirso, as king's chronicler? Such an interpretation of Gabriel Téllez's symbolism can, at first glance, seem only to have been born of a critic's unbridled imagination. Yet, this idea of a place in the Palace bureaucracy was not new to Tirso in 1623-24. He had been toying with it since early in Philip IV's reign. Proof of it lies in *La república al revés*, a play he necessarily retouched in 1621. [122] In it Tirso makes clear that he would like to be "First Secretary" to the young king. Tirso's pastoral role in *La república al revés* was more active than it had been in earlier plays. It is a fair guess that the dramatist increased the importance of that role on refashioning the work — with a very definite purpose in mind. In the second act Tarso exchanges his shepherd's clothing with the Empress Irene to the end that she escape from prison, dressed in his rustic *sayo*. In doing so, he saves her life at the probable expense of his own. At the moment of her leaving, she can thank him only with words (II, xvii):

> Déte Grecia,
> Tarso, la palma y laurel
> por el más leal y fiel
> que el siglo presente precia.
> ... ...
> ¡Cielos, que entre tantos malos
> haya un hombre que es tan bueno!

When at the end of the drama his monarch is in a position to reward him for saving her life, she tells him (III, xx):

> De Secretario Mayor,
> Tarso, el oficio tendrás,
> y con el cargo darás

---

[122] A study of mine on this play is found in *Reflexión*, 2, II (1973), 39-50. In it I have given my reasons for believing the work revised in 1621.

indicios de tu valor,
digno que le envidió [¿envidie?] el mundo.
... ...
No estoy contenta con eso;
en premiarte más me fundo.

It will be remembered that in this same year of 1621 Lope had asked — in the role of *jardinero* in *El premio de la hermosura* — to be chronicler to the new king. As Lope's disciple, Tirso was, in that year of 1621, willing to play second fiddle. But when "the Phoenix" in 1623 renounced his claims to that position in favor de Mendoza, Tirso straightway moved up his sights! He no longer had any interest in the place of *secretario mayor;* Mendoza was welcome to it! He wanted to be Chronicler to the King! With either ambition he was, by the autumn of 1623, invading territory on which Mendoza had, in his mind's eye, staked out a claim.

This poem of Lope to Mendoza must, as well, explain the transformation of *Esto sí que es negociar* into *El melancólico* in early 1625. With its stress on *melancholy,* it probably even gave Tirso his name for the *comedia.* In the play, as transformed, the Mercedarian seems to say to Mendoza: The one who has a right to be melancholy is I, not you. It is the *truly discreet* man, the wise man, who is entitled to a place in the Palace, not the courtier of social graces." Just how truculent was his mood when he said it may be judged by the last lines of the play:

... Tirso la ha escrito;
a quien la juzgase mala,
malos años le dó Dios;
y ¡a quien buena, buenas Pascuas! [123]

That Mendoza understood the message is evident, for *Más merece quien más ama* includes — as we have pointed out above — a "discreet man," named Rosauro, who is formed in don Antonio's image, just as Tirso had sketched his "discreet man," named Rogerio, with himself in mind. And to Carlín's strictures as to the

---

[123] The final lines of the play indicate that it was to be played just before Easter. This means it coincides in time with the poem of Pantaleón de Ribera which refers to his melancholy. See above, p. 104.

"gentil tempero" of the "old" *guardadamas*, Mendoza answers through Burón: "Love, like everything else, should be tempered in its expression."

Lope, no doubt, felt he could accept his friend, Mendoza, as king's chronicler (in exchange for a pension of 250 ducats annually); but it is hardly likely that that very jealous poet could have borne with equanimity the thought of his disciple, Tirso, successful in attaining an honor to which he had aspired in vain. He would, then, form an alliance, tacit or otherwise, with Mendoza against this daring dramatist who thought to occupy the Master's shoes. He would give Mendoza such proof as he might have of Tirso's hatred of Olivares. This would include at least a history of *La fingida Arcadia* with its satire of Olivares.

From the Mercedarian's point of view, his aspirations probably seemed logical enough. The great Lope — for whose dramatic genius, as we shall soon see, Tirso had tremendous respect — was out of the running. Surely he, Gabriel Téllez, was a better poet than was Mendoza? Modern criticism would quickly agree he was superior in literary talent to that court poet, but one cannot imagine a forthright Tirso in the Palace, where he would have been called upon constantly to feed not only Philip's ego, but Olivares' as well. Perhaps Tirso dreamed, instead, of being near his young king and of telling him some much-needed truths, truths that could just have turned the direction of Spain's *razón de estado*. Perhaps he was not thinking *only* of literary glory. Perhaps he felt in himself a will of steel that would enable him to challenge Olivares and all his power. Did he perhaps see himself as David, sent by God to save his people, through destruction of Goliath? Or had he cast himself in the Biblical role of San Gabriel ("man of God") who saw approaching for Spain the Last Judgment and hoped to save her? Who can say? At least such plays as *Privar contra su gusto*, *La prudencia en la mujer*, and *La mujer que manda en casa* make evident Tirso's profound interest in the political situation of Spain. [124]

---

[124] I have in my files, ready for publication, long studies on *Privar contra su gusto* and *La mujer que manda en casa*. They (with others) will appear in a volume on Tirso's political theatre, together with a revised study of my *La prudencia en la mujer*.

A few words more on the interrelations of Lope and Mendoza after the events of early 1625. Their ties, strengthened in that year, would last until Lope died in 1635. In August or September, 1628, we find the latter writing a short note to Mendoza, [125] alluding to Alarcón's success in getting published his *Primera parte*. He mentions also the Mexican's complaint therein of the *vulgo* as "bestia fiera" and states further that the public had taken offense and had written in self-defense a "sonetada." He even promises to send Mendoza a copy of it, if he can get hold of one. It was in this same year, too, that Lope asked for Mendoza's *La vida de la Virgen* and, having read it, declared: " ... no he visto en la lengua castellana cosa tan bien escrita y se aventaja a todas las deste género." As Mr. Davies points out (50), "the letter's tone reveals friendship." By the fall of the following year, Lope's *Laurel de Apolo* was finished. In it, Lope praises Mendoza as

> Raro maestro del hablar süave,
> gallardo en prosa y verso,
> conceptuoso, fácil, puro y terso.

To appreciate the tone of real sincerity that lies behind this characterization, one has only to remember the conventional verses of his *Jardín* that praise Mendoza: such a comparison makes evident a very different relationship between the two poets. In a *loa*, written for San Juan's day (1635), Mendoza terms Lope "king of the theatre" and "de la lengua castellana el claro segundo padre." When Lope died, in August of that same year, Mendoza exalted him both as poet and human being:

> Tu ingenio, que celestial
> se mide, se cifra, o suma,
> de alma, que sobró a tu pluma,
> te fabrica lo inmortal.

That don Crisóstomo, of *El galán sin dama*, was speaking for don Antonio when he praised Lope so highly, I have no doubt. Claiming that "Lope is his friend," he states that one could "more easily

---

[125] Rennert and Castro, *Vida de Lope de Vega*, 289-290.

meet daily in this world a Plautus, Virgil, or Tasso than one could a Lope in a century's time." [126]

It is now time to study the relations that Tirso and Lope sustained over the years.

---

[126] See *El galán sin dama*, 185. Chrisóstomo has his points of contact with Guillén de Castro's *lindo* of *El narciso en su opinión*. He claims: "...es más fácil que se tope / en el mundo *a cada paso* / un Plauto, un Virgilio, un Taso / que *en muchos siglos* un Lope...".

III

TIRSO'S RELATIONS TO LOPE
AND HIS THEATRE REAPPRAISED

The pattern of Tirso's relations to Lope and his theatre [1] is, at present, far from clear. Too much, I believe, has been taken for granted. What real evidence is there, for instance, of any personal contact between the two poets in Toledo? When did the Mercedarian write his most eloquent defense of the Lopean comedy: i.e., the defense found in the *Cigarrales de Toledo?* When did he begin his active support of Lope's theatre, and when did the master of that *genre* first take cognizance of the gifts that Tirso came bearing? In what year did Tirso's faith in Lope begin to falter? What brought about a change of attitude on the part of both dramatists? What were their relations in the 1630's? These are some of the questions which we shall hope to resolve or, where

---

[1] This study, a chronological resumé of Tirso's relations with Lope, will eventually serve as background, not only for this book, but for Tirso's part in the literary wars which Lope waged against the Aristotelians and the Gongorists. Separate analyses of his relations to these schools, the one finished, the other well-started, will be published in a later volume of this series.

In the present study, all discussions of Tirso's borrowings from Lope, or Lope's from Tirso, will be carefully excluded. This is intended as a running summary of the personal and literary relations that existed between the two poets, nothing more.

This chapter was first published in *B.Com.*, XVII (fall, 1965, pp. 23-34) and XVIII (spring, 1966, pp. 1-13). I have, on reprinting it here, made more changes than I could have wished — partly to avoid repetition of material found in the following chapter (which was also in print) and partly because I have, since writing both studies, made other pertinent discoveries.

solution at this time seems impossible, to bring them into clearer focus for future investigation.

Tirso's theatre undoubtedly had its first fine flowering in Toledo; [2] and just as certainly that flowering sprang from the soil which Lope's formula had prepared. (What young dramatist of Spain, unless he were of classical persuasion, would not find fertile that same soil — regardless of his geographical provenance?) But the assumption that there existed close personal ties between the two men in Toledo rests on a very tenuous foundation. So, too, does that which would find in Tirso a defender of Lope's theatre before 1621. There is, in so far as I know, no historical proof whatsoever to show that a fledgling Tirso of 1604-1607 was friend to a Lope whose very name would soon become a household proverb for all that was excellent. The warm defense of the Lopean comedy, found in the *Cigarrales*, was certainly written after 1618, and, more likely still, in 1621. Moreover, as we shall soon see, it is not only possible, but even highly probable, that the glorification of the Lopean comedy which one reads in *El vergonzoso en palacio* and in *Tanto es lo de más como lo de menos*, should be ascribed to that same general period, not to 1611-12, [3] as has been argued. Even the apology of *La firmeza en la hermosura*, wherein Tirso has defended the *comedia* as licit entertainment for a young king, belongs, we believe, to 1621.

Documentary investigations [4] have shown that Tirso's presence in Toledo could have coincided with Lope's there only in 1604-1607 and again possibly in the summer of 1615. Lope's residence in

---

[2] A recent study by José López Navío, Sch. P., "Una comedia de Tirso que no está perdida", 331-347 [in particular, 345], argues that Tirso's dramatic composition extends back to 1602-3. Tirso's fame would seem to have reached Sevilla by May 23, 1610, for in a list of *ingenios*, found at the close of the *Letanía moral* (Sevilla, 1613, but with *aprobación* of May 23, 1610), one finds mention of "Padre Fray Gabriel Téllez, mercenario [sic], poeta cómico". Quoted from E. Cotarelo, *Comedias de Tirso de Molina*, I, xvii.

[3] See pp. 173-75.

[4] Such scholars as San Román, Sra. de los Ríos, and R. P. Manuel Penedo have all brought documentary evidence to bear on this matter. For summaries of their conclusions, see Sra. de los Ríos, *Obras dramáticas completas de Tirso*, I, xxxii-xxxiv and cii-ciii. Consult also R. P. Fray Manuel Penedo Rey, "Tirso de Molina en Toledo", *Estudios*, núm. extraordinario, dedicado a Tirso de Molina, 22-28.

the Imperial City is attested between 1604-1610; Tirso's between 1604-1607 and 1612-1615. In April of 1616, Tirso went to Santo Domingo, and having returned from that island in 1618, he was in Toledo on September 30 of that year, at which time he signed, along with the other Mercedarians of that city, a document affirming their "adhesiones al Misterio de la Concepción." [5]

It must have been about this same time that Tirso established, or reestablished, his contacts with some of the owners of the city's *cigarrales* — in particular with those of the lovely "Buenavista." For it was in that fine *cigarral*, whose description Baltasar Elisio de Medinilla, Lope's good friend, has left us, that *El vergonzoso* was put on as a *particular*, having first gained fame through long years (as the dramatist himself tells us) in the commercial theatres of Spain. Tirso, himself, was not present at this performance — he speaks of himself as "the *absent* poet" — but he evidently received a detailed description of all that occurred on that occasion, one that argues strongly that he was in close touch with the owners of that fine estate.

When Tirso wrote his first *cigarral*, certain things are evident: 1) the old Archbishop, [6] don Bernardo de Sandoval y Rojas, who had owned Buenavista, was now dead, but his inheritors, [7] "don

---

[5] See Sra. de los Ríos [*Obras dramáticas completas*, II, plate following p. 696] for facsimile of these signatures.

[6] José Sánchez [*Academias literarias del Siglo de Oro español*, 301] points out that the Archbishop had his *academia*, where he gathered together Toledo's gifted men as well as any literary visitors from without who might be in the city. His nephew, the Conde de Mora, likewise "celebraba academia en su palacio".

[7] The inheritors of the Archbishop —"don Alejo" and "doña Irene"— have not been identified with certainty. In a study entitled "Tirso's *Cigarrales de Toledo*: Some Clarifications and Identifications" (246-272), Prof. G. E. Wade gives a tentative identification. His study supplements the book of André Nougué, *L'Oeuvre en prose de Tirso de Molina*. In a later study ("Tirso and the Court Circle," 253), Prof. Wade concludes that the Duque de Lerma's grandson, Francisco Gómez de Sandoval Rojas y Padilla, must have been inheritor of *Buenavista*. In my "Tirso's *No hay peor sordo*, its Date and Place of Composition" (276, n. 26), I had discussed the identity of the inheritors of *Buenavista*. The identification that Prof. Wade makes had, at that time, seemed somewhat doubtful to me because the young inheritor of Lerma was seemingly one who favored the "cultos"; yet it was precisely don Alejo, owner of *Buenavista*, who defended the "absent poet" (i.e., Tirso) so ardently against the "pedante historial" who was commenting unfavorably on Tirso's

Alejo" and "doña Irene," were carrying on the tradition of literary support which had characterized that Maecenas; 2) the representation of *El vergonzoso* took place at a time when the Aristotelians were making war on the Lopean concept of the comedy; [8] 3) the actors for Tirso's play were noble *toledanos:* "los que entraban en ella eran de lo más calificado de su patria ...; mereció que uno de los mayores potentados de Castilla tentase sus musas ... con hacer la persona del *vergonzoso* él mismo." [9]

The fiestas described in the *Cigarrales* took place, presumably, in the summer of 1620, though Tirso's description of them was not put in final form until some months after Philip IV ascended the throne on March 31, 1621. The Archbishop, don Bernardo de Sandoval y Rojas, had died December 7, 1618, a death to which Tirso makes evident reference in the very early pages of his first *cigarral.* He tells us that the fiesta took place "en la mayor de las hermosas salas *que conservan la memoria de su ilustrísimo dueño.*" [10] It is inconceivable that his inheritors should have been having elaborate fiestas there without the fitting interim of at least a year's mourning, a fact that in and of itself rules out the summer of 1619 as a date for the representation of *El vergonzoso.*

But there is, as Mr. Nougué has pointed out in his very helpful study, *L'Oeuvre en prose de Tirso de Molina,* [11] a reference in the early pages of the *Cigarrales de Toledo* (ed. cit., I, 42) that

---

El vergonzoso en palacio, a play which had just been put on. See the *Cigarrales,* I, 135-40; 142-48. However, I am now less sure. See p. 113, n. 70.

The "pedante historial" could possibly have been Mariana, who had no enthusiasm for the theatre anyway, and would certainly have objected to the liberties that Tirso had permitted himself with history. If it is argued that Mariana would have been 81 in 1620, it should be remembered that he put out a *Sumario* of his history in 1619, one that brought his work up to the year 1600.

[8] See my study, "Attacks on Lope and his Theatre, 1617-1621", 57-76.

[9] Who could this "potentate" be, known in the play as Mireno? Sra. de los Ríos (*Obras dramáticas completas de Tirso,* I, 292), in discussing the origin of this pastoral name, says: "...tomólo [i.e., el nombre], no de la *Arcadia* de Lope, como solía, sino de la *Galatea* de Cervantes, entre cuyos personajes figura: 'Mireno, el Desdichado, amante de Silveria...' ". Prof. G. E. Wade's "Character Names in Some of Tirso's Comedies", does not identify him.

[10] *Cigarrales,* I, *ed. cit.,* 135.

[11] André Nougué, *L'Oeuvre en prose de Tirso de Molina,* 35.

makes clear that 1620 must have been the year in question. Speaking of the fiestas that were being celebrated in the famous hospital of don Juan Tabera, Tirso's character points out they were exceptional that year, "por ser aquel el día del santificado Lucero, honra del Jordán y precursor de Cristo — que aquel año había ocurrido con el de la octava del Corpus." Now St. John's day had coincided with that of the octave of the Corpus in various years, but, as Mr. Nougué has proved by elimination, the reference could hardly be to any other than that of 1620. Furthermore, the passage was presumably *written* in 1621 since the *Cigarrales* went to press in October of that year, [12] and Tirso, in commenting on those fiestas, uses the phrase *aquel año*.

The "Al bien intencionado" with which Tirso prefaces his *Cigarrales* gives further confirmation for this same year of 1620. In it, Tirso has given us the troubled history of his brain-child's trip through the press. Apparently, he had originally given his book to the printer of a small town whose "ignorante compositor ... tal vez añadía palabras, tal [vez] sisaba letras." He had, if I interpret correctly his metaphorical prose, left it there eight months ("ocho meses ha que estoy en las mantillas de una imprenta, donde, como niño dado a criar en el aldea, me enseñaron los malos resabios que en mí descubrieres ..."). He had evidently taken it from his printer — losing in the process the down-payment he had made of half the cost of its printing — and put it in the hands of one in Madrid. All this suggests that Tirso first *wrote up* the fiestas in the months immediately following their occurrence in 1620, that

[12] Dr. Alan K. G. Paterson has, I believe, proved that no 1621 edition of the *Cigarrales* ever came out. See "Tirso de Molina: Two Bibliographical Studies", 43-53. I had reasoned that there was an edition of 1621, pointing to the Seventh Castilian's statement, "lo que he impreso", in *Antona García* (III, iii); but, as Miss M. Wilson argued in the preliminaries to her edition of that play (xxii-xxv), the autobiographical elements of the aforesaid *comedia* must have been added after Tirso's banishment in March of 1625.

What Dr. Paterson does not tell us is whether Tirso made any further changes in the content of the *Cigarrales* during the thirty months it supposedly was lying in the press of Luis Sánchez's widow. I believe he did (see pp. 143-44 of this book) and that consequently the date of October 8, 1621 (when Fr. Miguel Sánchez gave his *aprobación*) can no longer serve as a safe *a quo* for the composition of everything appearing in that volume. We cannot even be sure that the dramatist did not retouch his three plays, included in that miscellany! See p. 109, n. 62.

his book lay in press in the small town mentioned through the winter of 1620, and possibly the early days of 1621, that Tirso then recovered his work in the first half of 1621, [13] and gave it to a printer of Madrid around October 8th.

That he made important changes in his manuscript before turning it over to the press in Madrid is certain: there is a poem (II, p. 93), clearly written after Philip IV had been king for some months and was shocking a thrifty Tirso by his too-open hand. One finds also in the *Cigarrales* his delightful short story, *Tres maridos burlados*, which was penned after young Philip's accession, inasmuch as Tirso makes figurative mention of an imperial Toledo which had "married" Madrid in turn (*sucesivamente*) to four world monarchs, "uno, Carlos Quinto y tres Felipes," necessarily Felipe II, Felipe III, and Felipe IV, as doña Blanca de los Ríos first pointed out (*Obras*, I, 301). The literary satire against the Gongorists and the Aristotelians likewise points in the same direction: [14] indeed, chances are nine to one in my opinion that

---

[13] Mr. Nougué, *L'Oeuvre en prose...* (34-37), having pointed to various allusions in the *Cigarrales*, argues that it was composed after May, 1621: "Tous ces éléments nous permettent de conclure que Tirso a dû commencer la rédaction de son ouvrage à partir du mois de mai de l'année 1621". Sra. de los Ríos (*Obras dramáticas completas de Tirso*, I, 301) declared in 1946: "El texto de esta célebre miscelánea [i.e., el de los *Cigarrales*] ... muestra por sí propio estar escrito, a lo menos en su mayor parte, en 1621". However, see the concluding sentences of the preceding note.

We must, moreover, take seriously Tirso's words which indicate that his work was in a small-town press for eight months; that he then withdrew it and gave it to the printer in Madrid. (In what region of Spain would that small town have been?) The *Cigarrales*, as originally written, must have been a *very* different book indeed from the one that finally came off press in 1624. It is worthwhile noting that from the very first of his literary career, Tirso was given to revision of his works. See n. 32 of this chapter.

[14] One may point out also that the second *Cigarral*, which has as its framework the "castillo de la pretensión de amor", could have been suggested by the "roca valenciana" which Mira de Amescua had used for the *fiestas* of San Isidro's beatification in Madrid [May, 1620]. Cotarelo (*Mira de Amescua y su teatro*, 29) having pointed out that this *roca* was "una imitación de las aventuras difíciles y peligrosas de los libros de caballerías", goes ahead to say: "Fracasan en la tentativa de llegar al castillo: un emperador romano, que representa la gentilidad; la secta de Mahoma, personificada en un turco; la herejía y el judaísmo, que vence y pasa la primera puerta, pero se despeña en la segunda jornada. Desciende a este tiempo

this satire was added (or greatly modified) after Tirso moved to his convent in Madrid.

At the time the festivities were taking place in Toledo, the Mercedarian was presumably at his religious house in Segovia [15] whereas Lope was in Madrid. The two dramatists would necessarily have known of each other's existence long before this — very probably had met in Toledo: Tirso inevitably had heard of Lope, as every man, woman, and child of Spain had heard of him; and we have words from Lope himself that make evident that as early as the summer of 1615 he knew of *Don Gil de las calzas verdes* and "the Mercedarian" who had written it. This play was put on in the "Mesón de la Fruta" by Pedro de Valdés' company. In a letter which Lope wrote the Duque de Sessa around July 25th of 1615, [16] he first comments amusedly on the jealousy of the actor, Salvador [Ochoa] and on the street scandal which the latter had provoked against a fellow-actor, one San Martín. Then he adds: "perdía el tal hombre [i.e., Salvador] el juicio de celos ... prometía no ir con ella [i.e., Gerónima de Burgos] a Lisboa; con tantos donaires, voces y desatinos, que se *llegaba más auditorio que ahora tienen con 'Don Gil de las calzas verdes,' desatinada comedia del Mercedario.*" In the summer of 1615, Tirso was for Lope "el Mercedario," and the play of intrigue which has delighted theatregoers for more than three centuries was for him "desatinada."

---

el oso con el madroño, brotando fuego. Sale dél Isidro y llega a probar la aventura". Tirso had only to adapt this general structure to his lovers.

André Nougué (*L'Oeuvre en prose...*, 59-67) has studied in detail the sources of Tirso's *Cigarral*. He traces the development of the theme from Boiardo's *Orlando innamorato* through the *Amadís de Gaula*, Jorge Manrique's *El castillo de amor*, and his *Escala d'amor*. Hearing of Mira's use of the episode would perhaps have suggested to Tirso the long literary tradition which associeated the castle with lovers and their attemts to scale it.

[15] I am indebted to R. P. Manuel Penedo Rey for calling to my attention the very valuable information as to Tirso's whereabouts at this time. In a letter of 1959, he wrote: "En la obra *Teólogo y asceta: Fray Juan Falconi de Bustemonte (1596-1638)* [publicada por E. Elías Gómez, de Nuestra Orden en Madrid, C. S. I. C., 1953, p. 72, texto y nota] tiene Vd. publicado el dato ...: en abril de 1620 ... está de Lector en Segovia Fray Gabriel Téllez". The note referred to reads: "El 29 de mayo, viernes, se le dan unos zapatos al lector Téllez".

[16] Amezúa, *Epistolario de Lope*, III, 206. On p. 204, Lope quotes Vélez de Guevara's couplet on the scandal.

Could one ask for clearer proof than this letter that Lope felt in 1615 no particular warmth for Tirso — such as one might logically expect on his part, had the Mercedarian written shortly *before* that date the eulogies of the Lopean comedy which are found in *El vergonzoso* or in *Tanto es lo de más como lo de menos?* No, the *rapprochement* of the two men would come later, at which time Lope's appreciation for Tirso's literary support would be expressed in very fervent terms indeed.

It was undoubtedly Tirso who made the first advance. His tribute will be found in a passage which was clearly being written around March 25, 1620, since it stands near a letter so dated. In *La villana de Vallecas* (I, vi), don Pedro de Mendoza meets up by chance with don Gabriel Herrera in a lodginghouse of Arganda and asks him for news of the court, from whence don Gabriel has just come. As we have seen in our first chapter, he receives from the latter that of the king's recovery from the severe illness which had overtaken him as he was returning from Portugal and of the great rejoicing of the people over the improved health of their beloved monarch. Then follows — in answer to don Pedro's specific question — a very significant conversation as to the state of the theatre (I, vi):

> DON GABRIEL: Todo lo ha desazonado
> la salud del Rey en duda;
> no hay quien con gusto a ella acuda.
> La corte había alborotado
> con *El asombro* Pinedo
> *de la Limpia Concepción,*
> y fuera la devoción
> del nombre, afirmaros puedo
> que en este género llega
> a ser la primera.
>
> DON PEDRO: ¿Y de quién?
>
> DON GABRIEL: De Lope; que no están bien
> tales musas sin tal Vega.
>
> DON PEDRO: Por mi opinión argüís.

Thus, as it happens, the first mention that Lope has made of Tirso or Tirso of Lope is one having to do with a specific play: Lope's is unfavorable; Tirso's, very complimentary. There is, almost certainly, in the observation, "Por mi opinión argüís," a hint of the clashes of opinion concerning the Lopean comedy that marked early 1620 — at which time such "Catones" as Agreda y Vargas and the author of the very eloquent "Diálogos de las comedias" were decrying the harmful influence of Lope's theatre.

The vividness of this scene, the Madrid setting of the play as a whole, the satire of Ruiz de Alarcón: [17] all suggest that Tirso had been in Madrid for a visit by March of 1620. He may well have paid a call on Lope while there. Such a visit seems even more probable when studied in connection with a passage found in *El Caballero de Gracia:*

> ... un poeta amigo
> que en la corte de Castilla
> es águila y maravilla,
> hablando una vez conmigo,
> me dijo, viendo el ensayo
> de una comedia famosa:
> "Ya, hermano, es cansada cosa
> que, entre fregona y lacayo,
> siempre empiecen su papel
> con esto: '—¿Y él? ¿no habla nada?
> '—¿Y ella? ¿es soltera o casada?' "
> porque esto de "ella y él"
> era sagrado y chorrillo
> de toda plebeya masa,
> *y ya en la corte no pasa*
> *lacayo con estribillo;*
> y temo, si así le trato,
> *y allá me ven algún día*
> *la grita y silbatería.*

The friend in Madrid who is "águila y maravilla" is probably Lope; and the "si ... allá me ven algún día," a reflection of Tirso's opalescent dream of being transferred to his convent of Madrid; at the same time it is evidence which suggests that this play was written before Tirso went to live in the capital. Similarly, the reception he envisions could be part of the medley of hopes and fears that must have accompanied him in that transfer. If the

---

[17] See pp. 299-306.

"eagle" is Lope, introducing a fellow-dramatist from the provinces to the perils of theatrical Madrid, then Tirso will, in his *Cigarrales*, reward such an interest by hailing Lope as the "Master," thereby including himself among his loyal pupils. An attractive glimpse this of two great literary figures; but a fleeting one, alas, for their friendship would survive but briefly.

The interim would, however, be filled with bows and counterbows. After Tirso's tribute of *La villana de Vallecas* and *El Caballero de Gracia*, the next step *should* have been Lope's, and Hartzenbusch would find it in the dedication of *Lo fingido verdadero:* "a tan completo elogio [i.e., el de *La villana de Vallecas*], hubo de contestar Lope con la dedicatoria de *Lo fingido verdadero* ... " The *princeps* of the play in question is found in Lope's *Decimasexta parte*, which carries Vicente Espinel's *aprobación* of September 24, 1620 and a *suma del privilegio*, dated October 24th of that same year. But the *tasa* was not affixed until September 27th of *the following year*, and the volume did not actually come off press until after December 15, 1621. As we shall see presently, there is *excellent* reason for thinking that Lope may have written his *dedicatoria* for this play in the summer of 1621, not in that of 1620, and that the stimulus which gave rise to it was much stronger than the graceful tribute that Tirso had included in *La villana de Vallecas* or the very probable one of *El Caballero de Gracia*.

In my opinion, no one was farther from Lope's thoughts than Tirso in the last half of 1620 and the first months of 1621. If Gabriel Téllez made a visit to Madrid in February-March of 1620, as we have surmised, he must have gone back to his convent in Segovia — taking with him, no doubt, vague dreams of dramatic triumphs in the capital — for there is documentary evidence that he was in his convent in that city (i.e., Segovia) on May 29th of that year.

The fact that Tirso's name is *not* found among those who took part in the *certamen* of Madrid that honored San Isidro's beatification (around May 15, 1620) is therefore, in *no* way significant for Tirso's and Lope's relations in 1620, even though Lope did preside over those festivities. But our Lope, and Lope only, could be held responsible for the very significant omission of Tirso's name in the former's *El jardín,* published with the *Filomela* in 1621, [18] which received its first *aprobación* on May 31st and its *tasa* on July 19th of that same year. In his "garden," Lope has offered tribute to 85 *ingenios,* some dead, most of them still in the flesh. In that list, which includes most of the outstanding writers of the time (as well as some nonentities), one finds no mention of Tirso, though there is every reason for thinking that the latter was by this time in Madrid. [19] It must have been a shock to Tirso — the more so since he would have been penning a short time before the warm praise of Lope which one finds in the Cigarrales. But the truth is Lope's thoughts were elsewhere those days — as we shall soon see.

After reading the *Filomela* and the *Jardín* of Lope, Tirso must have decided to get in touch with him. On that occasion, he no doubt took with him some "historias divinas" that he had written recently, together with a manuscript copy of his *Cigarrales de Toledo.* Very shortly thereafter, Lope must have written his *décimas* for Tirso's miscellany, so lavish in their praise of that work as to seem hypocritical, when we remember that he had found no place for him in his "garden" that went to press around late May of 1621:

> Con menos difícil paso
> y remotos horizontes
> hoy tiene el Tajo en sus montes
> las deidades del Parnaso.
> La lira de Garcilaso,
> junto a su cristal luciente,
> halló de un laurel pendiente
> Tirso, y esta letra escrita:
> "Fénix en ti resuscita,
> canta y corona tu frente."

---

[18] It is available, in longer form in *BAE,* XXXVIII, 422-425, and in shorter, in Pérez Pastor's *Bibliografía madrileña,* III, under the year 1621. All bibliographical information concerning Lope's *partes* which we have quoted in this study will be found in that same *Bibliografía madrileña.* The "Queja del Teatro contra las comedias de tramoya", is, for instance, given there, 65-66.

[19] See on this point my study, *"La prudencia en la mujer* and the Ambient that Brought it Forth", 1185, n. 95. Probably *El árbol del mejor fruto* is the first work that Tirso wrote after reaching Madrid.

> Digno fue de su decoro
> el ingenio celestial
> que canta con plectro igual
> tan grave, dulce y sonoro.
> Ya con sus arenas de oro
> compiten lirios y flores
> para guirnaldas mayores
> a quien, con milagros tales,
> los ásperos *cigarrales*
> convierte en selvas de amores.

In brutal prose summation, Tirso had found Garcilaso's lyre and with it the assurance that the Phoenix had been reborn in him. His "celestial genius" deserved the honor bequeathed him, for did he not possess a plectrum equal to Garcilaso's, one that was grave, sweet, and sonorous? For a wreath to crown one who had wrought the miracle of converting Toledo's harsh *cigarrales* into Love's forest, the flowers of the Tagus were competing with her sands of gold. Such elaborate praise! Yet it had not occurred to Lope de Vega Carpio, when he was paying warm praise to Garcilaso in his *Jardín*, [20] even to mention the inheritor of that poet's lyre! Tirso was, for Lope, still in the limbo of the unimportant when he sent to press his list of immortals in May of 1621.

The *Prólogo dialogístico* of the *Parte XVI* gives Lope's unconvincing explanation as to why this volume was so late in coming off press. In the dialogue which prefaces this *Parte* ("Queja del Teatro contra las comedias de tramoya"), Lope includes an imaginary conversation between "Forastero" and "Teatro" which begins:

> FORASTERO: ... ¿qué libro es éste que estás mirando?
> TEATRO: *La Parte diez y seis de las comedias de Lope,*
>   que no se acabó de imprimir por su ausencia, y
>   así viene después de la *Decimaséptima.*

---

[20] The list had possibly been compiled much earlier. E. Cotarelo y Mori (*Comedias de Tirso,* I, p. xv) says it was "compuesto en los primeros años del siglo XVII aunque publicado con *La Filomela,* en 1621". Nevertheless, there were evidently additions that were included just before it went to print, among others that of Olivares' name.

The explanation Lope gives can, at best, have been but partial. Both his *Décimaquinta* and his *Décimasexta* had gone to Vicente Espinel before September 24, 1620, and the *Décimaséptima* must have reached him shortly thereafter, for by October 31st of that same year, the *suma del privilegio had been granted.* The *Décimaquinta parte* was off press before the year was out; the *Décimaséptima* presumably reached the public shortly after its *tasa* was affixed on January 27, 1621. But the *Décimasexta parte*, even though the *suma del privilegio is dated* October 24, 1620, did not receive its *tasa* until September 27, 1621, and its *erratas* are dated December 15th of that year.

One can only venture a guess as to why this part was not issued between September 24, 1620 and March 31, 1621; but after the latter date, Lope himself had excellent reasons for holding up its printing. The political skies of Spain had changed within hours on that last day of March of 1621; there were new luminaries in the heavens. The Conde de Olivares was now *privado* (all-powerful) to a stripling king of sixteen years, and both monarch and minister were of a literary turn of mind. Moreover, the young monarch felt a very special devotion to the theatre, as did his French wife. Olivares, who came from a family that had long patronized the arts, was himself reputed to be a poet, and one of his earliest official appointments was that of the Andalusian poet, Francisco de Rioja, [21] as his personal secretary. What is more, the new *privado* began playing the role of Maecenas to many of the struggling poets of the capital, particularly to those of Andalusian background, such as Góngora. This new state of affairs did not go unmarked by the ever-alert Lope, who, naturally enough, wanted to be among the favored. By May 31, 1621, he had not only written in the *Jardín de poetas* a warm tribute to the new secretary, but had even dedicated to him the poem as a whole. What is more, among the "poets" included in Lope's "garden" is the Conde de Olivares himself.

---

[21] For this relationship, see G. Marañón's *El Conde-Duque de Olivares,* 141-142. The privado's very distinguished biographer wrote: "...fue no sólo amigo, sino sesudo abogado y confidente del primer ministro [i.e., Olivares], *a cuyo lado le vemos durante todo el tiempo de su mando...*". For Olivares' roles as Maecenas and as poet, see also Marañón's study, 138-139 and 140.

But there would be more: Lope needed yet another vehicle to carry his messages to the new favorite, and he would accordingly use the *Décimasexta parte*, still in press, for that purpose. The first play included in that collection is *El premio de la hermosura*, and it is dedicated to the Conde de Olivares, don Gaspar de Guzmán. In his preliminary words to this mythological play, Lope points out to Olivares that he had composed it some years before at royal command and that the royal children, including the recently-crowned Philip, had played roles in it:

> La reyna [i.e., Margarita], nuestra señora, que Dios tiene, me mandó escribir esta tragicomedia. La traza fue de las Señoras Damas, ajustada a su hábito, decencia y propósito: el Cupido y la Aurora a las dos mejores personas del mundo en sus tiernos años ...

Lope, will, as well, under the name of Fabio (a gardener) put himself in the picture and in this role ask for his own appointment as court chronicler. Addressing himself to the *privado*, he begs (III, 473-4):

> Y así, por merced os pido,
> pues tan humilde me veis
> pasar la vida entre flores,
> digáis al Emperador
> que mi talento, señor,
> ocupe en cosas mayores;
> que aunque como labrador
> y de esta huerta *hortelano*,
> gasto mi música en vano
> sólo en canciones de amores,
> *también sabría cantar*
> *las grandezas de sus glorias*
> *en elegantes historias.*

When the *privado* promises to pass on his request to Aurora (i.e., to Queen Isabel), Fabio continues his plaints:

> Ventura quieren las cosas;
> yo he visto más venturosas
> menos letras que yo sé.
> Canté, desde que nací
> del Júpiter español

las grandezas, y hasta el sol
mi humilde plectro subí.
¡Y no he merecido ser
su coronista siquiera;
y de la tierra extranjera
otros me vienen a ver!

With his usual perspicacity, Menéndez y Pelayo [22] understood the turn of events:

Quizá esta singular y candorosa ocurrencia sea una de las cosas que Lope añadió en la comedia impresa, como un memorial indirecto al Conde-Duque, que nunca le honró ni protegió como debiera, prefiriendo a ingenios muy inferiores.

But in that momentuous year of 1621 Lope had yet other preoccupations: he was already hard at war with both the Gongorists and the Aristotelians, as well as with Ruiz de Alarcón. Yet he was not so wrapped up in these battles that he failed to see danger looming to his supremacy in the theatre from another direction. The *tramoyistas,* captained by Vélez de Guevara, were forging ahead too rapidly for Lope's peace of mind. What made matters worse was that they were from Andalusia — and Olivares, good *andaluz* that he was, was showing a preference for that school. Not only had he appointed secretary Francisco de Rioja and favored Góngora and his poetry, but unto Vélez de Guevara he had given the commission of writing a play to glorify the Guzmanes, and Vélez had responded with a play of *tramoyas,* which had scenes that were written in extremely gongoristic style. As one who had previously been undisputed master of the theatre, Lope felt he had a right to point out that the theatre was taking a wrong turn. With such thoughts in mind, he wrote in the summer of 1621, as his *Prólogo dialogístico* [23] itself makes clear, his

---

[22] "Observaciones preliminares", Acad. ed. of Lope's *Obras,* XIII, p. cxxx.

[23] The reader will find discussed at greater length this *Prólogo dialogístico* in my "Literary and Political Satire in Tirso's *La fingida Arcadia*", first printed in *The Renaissance Reconsidered: A Symposium* (*Smith College Studies in History,* XLIV [1964], Northampton, Massachussets). It is reprinted in this volume as Ch. IV.

"Queja del Teatro contra las comedias de tramoya." Therein he laments the new popularity of plays of spectacle in which machinery and elaborate stage trappings were emphasized at the expense of delicate metaphors and lovely poetry. He ends that lament by stating that the public's delight in such claptrap could be understood, were the "inventions" managed cleverly, as in the days of Greek tragedy; but — he asks himself — how can the public content itself with the awkward *tramoyas* of the Spanish stage?

Similar strictures are found in the play *Lo fingido verdadero*, [24] together with what was possibly intended as a hint that its author would like to give, at court command, a performance that was typically Lopean: i.e., a play of romantic love, one filled with lovely poetry and charming metaphors. In *Lo fingido verdadero*, the impresario, Ginés — later to be included in the church calendar as San Ginés — is in the palace of Diocletian at the order of this Roman Emperor. He is outlining for the Emperor the plays he can put on, in a scene that Lope evidently fashioned to his purpose. In it, he manages to exalt his own *capa y espada* plays over not only those following Aristotelian canons but also over those of a Greek poet, dependent for success on his *tramoyas*. He even takes a slap at a rival, Corintio, [25] who writes "furious verses," but is

---

Lope began to sense that theatrical winds were shifting direction as early as 1620, in which year he was evidently feeling the competition of Guillén de Castro (Valencian) and Mira de Amescua (Andalusian). The latter had just been chosen by the City Fathers to take charge of the elaborate street celebrations honoring San Isidro's beatification, and as early as May 6th, 1620, Lope was writing to the Conde de Lemos in melancholy vein: "Paso ... entre librillos y flores de un huerto lo que queda de la vida, que no debe de ser mucho, compitiendo en enredos con Mescua y don Guillén de Castro sobre cuál los hace mejores en sus comedias". See E. Cotarelo y Mori, *Mira de Amescua y su teatro*, 31.

In the *Relación de las fiestas* for San Isidro's canonization (with its *tasa*, dated September 1, 1622), Lope describes the seemingly automatic ("semovente") *tramoya* which Mira de Amescua had ordered for the occasion, then points out that "Heron Alejandrino" had written of such a *tramoya*, even though it was "jamás vista en España". Indeed, the "tramoya" was "tan antigua que hace della memoria Homero en *La Ilíada*".

[24] See Acad. ed., IV, ii, 57-58.

[25] Just what contemporary poets Lope had in mind for "Corintio" and "the Greek poet", I am not certain. The first reference may be to Guillén de Castro, in whom Lope praised "el vivo ingenio, el rayo, el espíritu ardiente". In speaking of Guillén de Castro, Hurtado y Palencia (*Historia de la*

unfortunate in his plots. In the chapter following this one, we shall necessarily analyse this play in greater detail.

Significantly, I believe, Lo fingido verdadero is the play of the Décimasexta parte which Lope chose to dedicate "Al presentado Gabriel Téllez" in the following lines: [26]

> ... Algunas historias divinas he visto de V. P. en este género de poesía, por las cuales vine en conocimiento de su fertilísimo ingenio, pues, a cualquier cosa que le aplica, le halla dispuesto: y con la afición que de esta correspondencia nace (aunque a los envidiosos parezca imposible simpatía), quedé cuidadoso de ofrecerle alguna ... en reconocimiento de lo que a todos nos enseña ... Lo fingido verdadero, tragicomedia de la vida y martirio de San Ginés, representante, doy a la estampa con el nombre de V. P. y con muchas razones para que sea suya (a pesar de los que envidian sus obras, que tantos bien intencionados califican) haciendo elección de historia divina, así por su profesión, como por haberlas escrito tan felizmente ...

In 1621, who was envying Tirso's works? Was Gabriel Téllez feeling Mendoza's envy us early us that? Or is the reference perhaps to Alarcón's or Vélez's? What "historias divinas" (¿vidas de santos?) did Tirso show Lope? Could one of them have been his La república al revés? If so, did it contain at that time the passages in which Tirso suggests to Philip IV that he make him First Secretary? Or did this thought occur to Gabriel Téllez after he learned of Lope's own ambitions?

Lope almost certainly dedicated his Lo fingido verdadero to Tirso in the summer of 1621, i.e., after reading the "Al bien intencionado" which prefaces the Cigarrales de Toledo — a dedication which is much more concerned with those of evil intention (i.e., the envious) than with those of good will. In the manuscript

---

literatura española, 585) also commented on "la energía de un estilo enfático, a veces algo culterano, con el que buscaba asombrar la imaginación de su público" and "la flojedad en el desarrollo de la acción". The "Greek poet" (presumably Aristophanes) would probably represent, among Lope's contemporaries, Vélez de Guevara, long known as a dramatist of "comedias de espectáculo".

[26] See Pérez Pastor, Bibliografía madrileña, III.

[27] For the reference in La república al revés, see pp. 146-47.

proper of Tirso's miscellany, Lope would have read Tirso's master-
ly defense of the "New Comedy," the latter's proud enlistment as
"disciple" under the banner of its leader. He would have taken note
of the fact that Tirso had there taken up cudgels for him not only
against Góngora, leader of the *culteranos*, but against Suárez de
Figueroa and Torres Rámila, [28] who were captaining the Aristotelians. But he would, at the same time, have noted an omission:
Tirso had said nothing in his *Cigarrales* against the *tramoyistas*
who were making rapid strides in the favor of both court and
populace. Why should not this new paladin of his enter the lists
in his behalf against this group which represented the newest
threat to Lope's supremacy in the theatre? Tirso would — and
did — but, as we shall soon see, he would wrap his defense in such
coverings that it would make shiver an aging Lope who was intent
on capturing Olivares' favor.

By all the probabilities of logic and human nature, we must
conclude that Lope wrote in the late summer of 1621 not only his
laudatory *décimas* for the *Cigarrales* and his *Prólogo dialogístico*
with its complaints against the *tramoyistas*, but also the *dedicato-
rias* to *Lo fingido verdadero* and to *El premio de la hermosura*.
One can hardly say with complete certainty that Lope *substituted
these two plays for others* that the volume had contained when it
first went to press in 1620; on the other hand, it is stretching greatly the laws of chance to assume that two *comedias*, so entirely
suitable for his particular ends after Olivares' rise to authority,
should have been included in a single volume before that magnate
had assumed the reins of power. It should be noted, too, that *El
premio de la hermosura* is found at the very first of the collection,
Lo fingido verdadero at the end, precisely where substitution would
have been relatively easy.

True, the latter play — that of San Ginés' martyrdom — had
originally been penned around 1608 [29] when Lope, in conflict with

---

[28] Sr. J. de Entrambasaguas (*Una guerra literaria del Siglo de Oro, Lope
de Vega y los preceptistas aristotélicos*, included in *Estudios sobre Lope de
Vega*, I and II) has given us a superbly documented study of Lope's fight
with Suárez de Figueroa and Torres Rámila. I have in manuscript a long
study of Tirso's part in that fight.

[29] See S. G. Morley and C. Bruerton, *Cronología de las comedias de
Lope de Vega*, 326-27. They date it "ca. 1608".

the Aristotelians, could, and probably did, paint the emperor Diocletian as rejecting a play of Terence or Plautus which Ginés as
impresario had suggested and as preferring to it one of the general
nature of a Lopean *capa y espada*. But, in 1621, Lope needed only
to enlarge the framework of that scene and include criticism of
the plays of *tramoyas* that were evidently giving him concern.
After reading Tirso's perfervid defense of his *comedia* against both
the Aristotelians and the *culteranos*, he must have asked himself
who better than the Mercedarian could second him in this new
war that he was declaring against the *tramoyistas*. Had not Tirso
in his *Cigarrales* proudly declared himself one of the Master's
"disciples" and promised to defend him "constantly" against those
who were impugning his theatre?

> ...Y habiendo él [i.e., Lope] puesto la comedia en la
> perfección y sutileza que agora tiene, basta para hacer
> escuela de por sí *y para que los que nos preciamos de sus
> discípulos* nos tengamos por dichosos de tal maestro y
> *defendamos constantemente su doctrina* contra quien con
> pasión la impugnare ..., nosotros ... es justo que a él, como
> *reformador de la comedia nueva*, y a ella, como más her-
> mosa y entretenida, los estimemos lisonjeando al tiem-
> po para que no borre su memoria.

And so with his "Queja del Teatro contra las tramoyas" and the
scene in *Lo fingido verdadero*, Lope would nudge Tirso toward
new exploits in defense of the Lopean *comedia* at the same time
that he was seeking Olivares' favor.

Tirso, on his part, must have responded gladly, for the admiration he felt for Lope and his comedy in 1620 and 1621 recognized
few limits. Just *how* beautiful Gabriel Téllez considered Lope's
creation at that time has, I believe, been summed up for us in the
oft-quoted passage of *El vergonzoso en palacio* (II, xiv), one that
was almost certainly penned not around 1611, by which date the
play itself was undoubtedly in existence, but instead in 1620 when
it was put on by the noble actors of Toledo. It is a controversial
point, and since the date of *El vergonzoso's* composition is pivotal
for any discussion of Tirso's relation to Lope, I must now develop
at some length the reasons that have led me to such a conclusion.

Tirso himself, in giving the circumstances under which *El ver-gonzoso en palacio* was put on at Buenavista, tells us (I, 136) this play had been "celebrada con general aplauso (años había) no sólo entre todos los teatros de España pero en los más céle-bres de Italia y de entrambas Indias ..." In this passage of defense, Cotarelo y Mori saw Tirso's answer to Mariana's "virulent diatribe" of 1609, *De spectaculis*. [30] Doña Blanca de los Ríos argues that the play was revised between March and October of 1621 (I, 298): "Para mí es indudable que *El vergonzoso en palacio* ... fue redac-tada dos veces por su autor: la primera en 1611 y la segunda en 1621 (entre marzo y octubre, como indicaré)." Some pages earlier (p. 291), she had spoken of "la más que probable refundición, o mejor, intencionados retoques que el autor puso en su célebre farsa en 1621 antes de entregarla a la imprenta." Yet it does not seem to have occurred to her that Tirso's defense of the Lopean theatre may have been inserted at the time it was revised. Instead, she uses, as the very cornerstone for her argument that Cervantes was at war with Tirso because of his support of Lope, this same passage of the *Vergonzoso* (p. 295): "Importaba consignar ... que *El vergonzoso* 'marcó fecha' en la guerra por todas las obras de Cervantes ..." Much rests, then, on when this passage was written.

As Prof. Américo Castro pointed out many years ago, in his second edition of *El vergonzoso en palacio*, [31] there are in the Biblioteca Nacional at Madrid two manuscripts of this play. At first glance they would seem to create a serious hurdle for any as-sumption that Tirso added this passage when revising his play in 1620-1621; in reality, if they do not actually give support to this assumption, they at least in no way negate it. The two manuscripts, nos. 16912 and 14996, are, as Prof. Castro indicated, copies one of the other. No. 14996 has *all three acts* written in the same hand; in No. 16912, Act II is in the same neat script as are the three of No. 14996, whereas Acts I and III are in a much looser, sprawling hand. In *both* manuscripts there is found in the first act a letter dated July 15, 1611 — instead of the March 12, 1400, found in the *princeps*. The copyist of 1611 presumably wrote down, in absent-

---

[30] See Cotarelo, *Comedias de Tirso de Molina*, II, "Cat. raz.", xli-xlii.

[31] *El vergonzoso en palacio*, ed. Clásicos Castellanos, p. lxxiv.

minded fashion, the day, month, and year of the time he was making the copy rather than the historical one which Tirso must have originally written. The play, evidently then, was in existence by July 15, 1611.

I suggest the following history for these manuscripts: Tirso decided in 1620 to refashion [32] his old play and to include in it his defense of the Lopean theatre which was under particularly heavy fire that year from the Aristotelians and the stern moralists of the day. He worked from an old manuscript of 1611 (without noting the incorrect date attached to the letter), and, having revised considerably the second act, gave it to the copyist who made a copy of that act, which he then put with Acts I and III of the 1611 manuscripts (No. 16912). He thus kept the misdated letter of Act I. Manuscript No. 14996 (all in one hand, i.e., the same hand as Act II of No. 16912) would be merely a copy of No. 16912, made for another actor. [33] To those of us who have worked with the many patched copies of the Biblioteca Nacional, the assumption does not seem at all farfetched.

But there are positive reasons as well for believing that this passage was added in 1620-1621. Serafina, *mantenedora* of this

---

[32] I would not reject the possibility that he may have made still further revision in this passage (or others!) after going to Madrid. After many years of study of Tirso's theatre, I am convinced that we have relatively few of his works exactly as he first wrote them. We shall see, in this volume, that he altered play after play of his *Primera parte*, adding here a barb against his enemies, refashioning others in large part to reflect his attitude toward certain people after his banishment. See pp. 355-63.

While in his convent in Madrid, Tirso must have done his literary work under great pressure from his clerical duties. Therein must lie partial explanation of his considerable self-plagiarism; the two versions of a single theme such as we find in *El amor y el amistad* and *Cautela contra cautela*, or in *Esto sí que es negociar* and *El melancólico*; the comic scenes which he carried over from *El Caballero de Gracia* (I, i-ii) to *Santo y sastre* (II, i-ii); or those shared in common by *La vida y muerte de Herodes* (I, iv) and *Antona García* (I, iii), and even *Bellaco sois, Gómez* (II, ii); the sonnet in *La fingida Arcadia* (III, ii) which he had used earlier in *Doña Beatriz de Silva* (II, iii), etc., etc.

However, in transforming *Esto sí que es negociar* into *El melancólico*, Tirso was probably influenced primarily by his desire to add satirical material. See pp. 147-48.

[33] Various copies of the same manuscript were necessarily made for the different roles in a day when hand-copying was presumably cheaper than printing.

particular fiesta and actress in *El vergonzoso,* is playing one of
the two feminine leads in it. In the latter capacity, she acts out the
heroine's role in a play entitled *La portuguesa cruel.* It is, if I
mistake not, Tirso's hazy remembrance of Lope's heroine in *La
portuguesa y dicha del forastero,* [34] a play which can be dated
1615-1616. Like Lucrecia of *La fingida Arcadia,* Serafina is a
warm defender of the Lopean comedy. In a scene which is in
itself so delightful that we tend to forget its episodic nature, she
will gather together all the felicitous "epithets" that she has heard
concerning it (II, xiv):

> No me podrás tú juntar
> para los sentidos todos
> los deleites que hay diversos
> como en la comedia ...
> ¿Qué fiesta o juego se halla
> que no le ofrezcan los versos?
> En la comedia *los ojos,*
> ¿no se deleitan y ven
> mil cosas que hacen que estén
> olvidados sus enojos?

---

[34] In Lope's *La portuguesa y dicha del forastero,* the protagonist is a
Portuguese girl named Celia (of the Silva family) just as the heroine of
La portuguesa cruel (whose role Serafina is playing) is likewise a Portuguese
girl called Celia. Both heroines are "cruel." Tirso's doña Juana comments
to Serafina (II, xiv): "En ti el poeta pensaba / cuando así la intituló"
For the cruelty of Lope's Celia, see the Cotarelo edition, *Comedias de Tirso*
(xiii, 340, 348). Lope's play can be dated 1615-16, as Rennert and Castro
pointed out in *Vida de Lope de Vega,* 507. See also Morley and Bruerton,
Cronología de las comedias de Lope de Vega, 43. Tirso refers, as well, to
the "cruel portuguesa" in his *Doña Beatriz de Silva* (III, vi). As I had occasion to point out in note 9 of this chapter, Cervantes paints "Mireno, el
Desdichado" as "amante de Silveria", and in *En Madrid y en una casa* (III,
iii), one has a "Serafina, daughter to don Andrés de Silva" (of Toledo) who
has pledged his daughter's hand to don Gabriel Zapata. There was in Toledo
a branch of the Silva's (of the Condes de Cifuentes), one of the most powerful
clans in that city. Prof. G. E. Wade, on considering the identity of the "Serafina" of *El vergonzoso...* ("Character Names in Some of Tirso's *Comedias*",
30), declares: "so in conclusion, and in the light of the apparently conflicting
testimony, we are not able to decide whether or not Serafina was a real
person." I believe it almost certain that she really existed and that she was,
moreover, of the Silva family. Consultation of Luis de Salazar y Castro's
Historia genealógica de la casa de Silva (1685) should be helpful in solving
the problem.

La música, ¿no recrea
al oído? Y el *discreto,*
¿no gusta allí del conceto
y la traza que desea?
Para el alegre ¿no hay risa?
Para el triste ¿no hay tristeza?
Para el agudo ¿agudeza?
Allí el necio ¿no se avisa?
El ignorante ¿no sabe?
¿No hay guerra para el valiente,
consejos para el prudente
y autoridad para el grave?
Moros hay, si quieres moros;
si apetecen tus deseos
torneos, te hacen torneos;
si toros, correrán toros.
¿Quieres ver los epitetos
que de la comedia he hallado?
De la vida es un translado,
sustento de los discretos,
dama del entendimiento,
de los sentidos banquete,
de los gustos ramillete,
esfera del pensamiento,
olvido de los agravios,
manjar de diversos precios,
que mata de hambre a los *necios*
y satisface a los *sabios.*

As hostess for the occasion and actress in the play itself, it is
logical that Tirso should have wanted to make Serafina's role
important. These scenes of Act II — wherein she plays out various
roles and in the process defends the Lopean comedy — could
very well represent a padded role for her, one expanded for that
important occasion.

But they were as well an *actualidad* of the day. The passage
quoted above ends with the following two verses:

Mira lo que quieres ser
de aquestos dos bandos.

And doña Juana will answer, with Tirso, "el de los *discretos* sigo...
me holgara de ver la farsa infinito." With this answer, she joins

spiritual hands with don Pedro de Mendoza of *La villana de Vallecas* who had declared, when praising Lope's play: "Por mi
opinión argüís."

Both are making alliance with the defenders of the Lopean
theatre against those who were attacking it in 1620. This whole
question of the theatre was a "cuestión candente" in 1620-21, as
I had occasion to show in 1965-66. [35] Suárez de Figueroa had
drawn up lines of battle for the Aristotelians as early as 1617 when
he put out his *El pasajero*. By early 1620 the Lopean theatre had
become a topic for discussion that interested not only the Aristotelians and the stern "Catones," as Tirso would term them, but
even the casual *cortesano* who kept up with the literary scene.
Don Antonio, of Antonio Liñán y Verdugo's [36] *Guía y avisos de
forasteros* (1620), when asked for his opinion of the *comedia*
(p. 146), declares the matter so controversial ("hallo tan encontra-
dos los pareceres de hombres, no sólo buenos cortesanos pero
muy doctos") that anyone dealing with it, "si se muestra contrario,
ha de quedar odioso y, si favorable, en opinión de no muy
cuerdo." And Diego de Agreda y Vargas, on giving the daily
schedule of some young nobles who were chatting while awaiting
eleven o'clock mass, will in his *Novelas morales*, [37] declare (pp.
321-22):

"...Llegáronse a los teatros, que *hay pocas conversaciones de
mozos que no lleguen a ellos*... vituperaron su poca inventiva, la
frialdad de lo yocoso [sic], la falta del argumento y suspensión..."

Both writers quoted were among those who expressed their
disapproval of the Lopean comedy. Liñán y Verdugo, though an
admirer of Lope's great talent, was clearly perturbed at the
thought of the great *number* of plays being offered (*op. cit.*, 147-
148: "...[siento de las comedias] lo que de los coches: que si

---

[35] This material, in much more complete form, is found in my study,
"Attacks on Lope and his Theatre, 1617-1621", 57-76.

[36] The *aprobación* of Liñán y Verdugo's *Guía y avisos...* by Espinel is
dated July 19, 1620. I have used the *Biblioteca Clásica Española* edition,
Barcelona, 1885. On Liñán y Verdugo, see Sarrailh's study in *RFE*, VI
and VIII.

[37] *Princeps* of Agreda y Vargas' *Novelas morales*: Tomás Junti, Madrid,
1620, with *aprobación del ordinario*, dated February 1st, and *erratas*, May
26th of the same year.

fueran menos, fueran menos dañosas...; bastara que las hubiera
en los días que no sean de hacer algo." Agreda y Vargas not only
shared Suárez de Figueroa's very poor opinion as to the literary
merits of the Lopean *capa y espada*; he was scandalized that
priests should be writing and even attending their presentation!
He recalls, with apparent approval, the fate of a pagan priest
whom the Roman Senate ordered to be buried alive when it
learned that he had written a play and had it put on! Then he
asks (*op. cit.*, 322): "¿Qué dijéramos de algunos de los eclesiás-
ticos de nuestros tiempos, cuyas costumbres son tan depravadas
que lo más loable dellas fuera el escribirlas [i.e., comedias]?
Agreda y Vargas then concludes: "...pero quédese aquí, que son
amigos y dirán que somos ignorantes y que me meterán en alguna
farsa o entremés ... pensando armarnos caballero ..."

The grave Theologian of the anonymous *Diálogos de las comedias* [38] makes no pretense of being a friend to Lope. That dramatist was for him in 1620 (p. 225 b) "vuestro Lope o lobo carnicero de las almas." He evidently counts him (p. 215 a) among
"estos ingenios depravados, contagión general de la república,
parricidas de su patria, traidores, enemigos secretos de la Cris-
tiandad. ..." As for the theatres themselves, the saints have called
them (p. 213 b): "escuelas de vicios, universidad de maldades,
peste de la república, hornos de Babilonia, oficinas de pecados,
ferias de los demonios, y otros nombres semejantes. ..." And he
bluntly tells Lope (p. 215 a), "los poetas que ahora viven y han
hecho ... estas farsas tienen bien que temer el juicio de Dios y
bien porque hacer penitencia." What is more, he openly suggests
to the Bishops that if Lope's confessors cannot stop his writing
plays, they should, in order to bring him into line, use the power
which was theirs through the Council of Trent (p. 215 b).

Lope would answer his various critics by rushing his three
partes (XVᵃ, XVIᵃ, XVIIᵃ) to his old friend Vicente Espinel for
approval. He would take care specifically of Agreda y Vargas by
referring to him in *La discreta venganza* (I, i) as "un pedante,

---

[38] See E. Cotarelo y Mori's *Bibliografía de las controversias sobre ... el
teatro* (210-31) for this very remarkable dialogue. I have, in n. 19 of the
study, "Attacks on Lope and his Theatre, 1617-1621," shown that it was
necessarily written before March 31, 1620.

destos que cuentos de viejas llaman *Novelas morales.*" His friend, Salas Barbadillo, would also come to his assistance in *El necio bien afortunado.* There Agreda y Vargas' fears would be realized when Dr. Ceñudo receives the *pescozada* in novel form: thrice they strike him *with a volume of Lope's comedias in order to teach him discretion.* [39] And Tirso will get his revenge against this didactic short story writer by promising "*doce novelas,* ni hurtadas a las toscanas, ni ensartadas unas tras otras como procesión de disciplinantes, sino con su argumento que lo comprenda todo."

But the all-out attack of a grave theologian such as was the author of the *Diálogos de las comedias* — who was striving to close the theatre, or that being impossible, to bring it under strict supervision — was of far more serious concern, particularly since the matter of the theatre was to come up in the *regimiento* and the prelate counted as his special friend a *regidor* who states that he wishes the theologian's opinion in order to know how to cast his vote. The churchman was evidently in sympathy with the Aristotelians, was well acquainted with their manoeuvers against Lope, and shared their low opinion of his theatre, deploring, with them, its lack of didactic purpose. Suárez de Figueroa had, in *El pasajero,* denounced the Lopean creation as "todo charla, paja todo, sin nervio, sin ciencia ni erudición," and the theologian would echo that contemptuous judgment by declaring: "*todo es nada y todo es aire.*" He had, moreover, insisted that the *capa y espada* was having a pernicious effect on public customs (213):

> ... ¿Qué se puede seguir de ver un enredo de amores lascivos y deshonestos? ¿Otro de marañas y embustes y testimonios de un criado revolvedor y urdidor de males? ¿Otro de venganzas, pundonores vanos, enormes crueldades y todo esto azucarado con la agudeza del dicho, la sutileza y artificio del verso, adornado con el aparato y riqueza de vestidos ...? ¿Qué han de aprender allí las doncellas que en su vida tal vieron ni oyeron? ¿Qué, las casadas? ¿Qué vergüenza y recogimiento? ¿Qué, los mancebos que les está hirviendo la sangre ...?

---

[39] Salas Barbadillo, *El necio bien afortunado,* 321.

We cannot say for certain that Lope knew these particular *Diálogos de las comedias*, but he could hardly have failed to realize that there was in 1620 deep-rooted opposition to both his theatre and his irregular life among the more rigid-minded clergy — and that this group was hoping to include among the *premáticas* of 1620 a decree that would restrict dramatic fare. The year of 1620 and the early months of 1621 must have been a period of great strain for Lope. He was not only in conflict with such individuals as Alarcón and Agreda y Vargas; he was waging bitter war with Aristotelians such as Suárez de Figueroa and Torres Rámila [40] at the same time that his concepts of poetry were being called into question by Góngora. He was even having his trouble with the *mosqueteros* [41] in the spring of 1620, at which time "se intentó dar un escándalo en un estreno de Lope ..." To it Lope refers in a letter to the Duque de Sessa, one written in April or May of that year. To these was added the agitation of stern churchmen, such as was the author of the *Diálogos de las comedias*. Small wonder that Lope, in the fiestas of the beatification of San Isidro, was challenging all "poetdom", the born and the unborn: [42]

> Reto cuantos poetas tienen fama
> y reto los donados y pobretes
> con los que Calepino monas llama
> y los estafadores de concetos;
> reto de Apolo la rebelde rama,
> tusona Daphne, a *necios y discretos*
> sus versos reto, innumerables sumas,

---

[10] The *Spongia* had been directed primarily against Lope's long poems, specifically his *Jerusalén conquistada*. See p. 47. The study of Alfonso Sánchez de Moratalla may have influenced Tirso's defense of Lope, found in the *Cigarrales*.

The "Invectiva a las comedias que prohibió Trajano y Apología por las nuestras", written apparently in 1618, though not printed until Francisco de la Barreda included it in 1622 as part of his "Panegírico de Plinio a Trajano," should be published anew. Menéndez y Pelayo wrote in his *Ideas estéticas*, II, 316: "No se escribió mejor poética dramática en el siglo XVII... Apenas encuentro palabras con que encarecer el mérito de este olvidado discurso". Let me echo wholeheartedly Menéndez Pelayo's enthusiasm.

[41] See J. de Entrambasaguas, *Estudios sobre Lope de Vega*, I, 579-580.

[42] *Justa poética*, "Estancias de Maestro Burguillos", beginning f. 132v.

hasta los gansos que les dieron plumas ...
reto los por nacer y los que nacen ...

That Lope would have liked to challenge his fellow-churchmen I have no doubt, but this *he* was certainly in no position to do.

In the year 1621, there would come out of the North one who did dare and his name would be Gabriel Téllez. He ware the cloth, he was an established dramatist of the romantic school of thought — though he knew all the classicist's arguments. Above all, he came openly declaring himself a disciple of Lope, one who was eager to defend him against all "comers" and with all the "arms of his subtle genius." He would, in the *Cigarrales*, take on Lope's battles with Alarcón and Agreda y Vargas, with the Gongorists, with the Aristotelians, [43] and with the *discretos* against the *necios*. When Gabriel Téllez came bearing his gifts that summer of 1621, he must have seemed to a harassed Lope the very archangel Gabriel — Gabriel, "the strong man of God" — come to defend his own; and if not the archangel, at least a San Ginés, the *cómico,* who had won his place in the Christian calendar.

After the presentation of *El vergonzoso en palacio,* Tirso would refute in prose the arguments of the Aristotelians as to the mixture of comedy and tragedy, the unity of time, the respect due history, [44] etc. Through doña Serafina, he would, in the lines of *El vergonzoso* itself, point to the charm which such entertainment offered both eye and ear, to the universality of the *comedia's* appeal. Over and against the authority of the saints, which the theologian of the *Diálogos de las comedias* had cited against Lope

---

[43] Tirso's defense of Lope in the *Cigarrales* against various groups and individuals would, by all logic, have brought immediate responses from those attacked. Yet I find no reply in Góngora's works nor any in those of the Aristotelians, nor in Ruiz de Alarcón's. It is a negative argument, but, nevertheless, a good one, which supports Mr. Alan K. G. Paterson in his belief that the 1624 edition is the *princeps* of that miscellany. See n. 12 above. When finally the *Cigarrales* came out in 1624, Góngora was writing but little because of his bad health, Suárez de Figueroa was in Italy, and Ruiz de Alarcón had virtually ceased to write for the theatre. It was the court poets who were still very active, and it was they who would take offense. See pp. 65-8; also chapters IV and VIII.

[44] See *Cigarrales,* 140-147.

and his theatre ("escuelas de vicio, universidad de maldades, peste de la república, hornos de Babilonia, oficinas de pecados, ferias de los demonios"), Tirso would place the epithets of "the discreet." He would ask rhetorically:

> ¿Quieres ver los epitetos
> que de la comedia he hallado?

and would, by way of answer, give eight, among them:

> De la vida es un translado,
> sustento de los *discretos*, etc.;

and doña Juana would choose "el bando de los *discretos*," rejecting that of *los necios*.

In connection with the presentation of *El celoso prudente* (also included in the *Cigarrales*), [45] he would tell the Aristotelians and the churchmen that the *comedia* could serve as the mirror of customs which they were demanding, could meet their requirements that this genre should "teach" while "delighting." He would even supply his play with the *documentos* which Suárez de Figueroa and Agreda y Vargas had urged (ed. cit., 256-257):

> Afilen ahora ... los Zoilos murmuraciones en la piedra de la envidia ... ! Censuren los Catones este entretenimiento, que, por más que lo registren, no tendrán las costumbres modestas ocasión de distraerse. Aquí pueden aprender los celosos a no dejarse llevar de experiencias mentirosas; los maridos, a ser prudentes; las damas, a ser firmes; los príncipes, a cumplir palabras; los padres, a

---

[45] *El celoso prudente* was, according to Sra. de los Ríos, penned in 1615 (*Obras dramáticas completas de Tirso*, I, 1093). If she is right in her conclusions, then this play was refashioned in 1620-21, as I shall show on another occasion.

The "documentos", recommended for the short story by Suárez de Figueroa and exemplified by Agreda y Vargas in his *Novelas morales* (1620), are the didactic explanations of the author, which, placed at the conclusion of the story, point out exactly what is to be learned from the conduct of each character. Tirso, in his analysis of *El celoso prudente* (*Cigarrales*, II, 257), follows the example of Agreda y Vargas — almost certainly with tongue in cheek!

mirar por la honra de sus hijos; los criados, a ser leales; y *todos los presentes,* a estimar el entretenimiento de *la comedia* que en estos tiempos, expurgada de las imperfecciones que en los años pasados se consentían a los teatros de España, y limpia de toda acción torpe, deleita enseñando y enseña dando gusto. [46]

And don García will add further:

> — Apacibles predicadoras ... son las que, en alabanza de sus autores, no pasan de los límites honestos, pues persuaden y curan los ánimos que se quieren aprovechar de sus consejos disfrazados. ¿Qué píldora se atreverá a acometer desnuda la salud del enfermo, por más eficaz que sea su medicina, si no viene con la máscara del oro que hermosea su amargura? Y las verdades que no se visten con metáforas ingeniosas y versos deleitables, dan en rostro y son difíciles de digerir. Y aquí vienen tan bien guisadas que el más delicado estómago las recibe, siguiéndosele el provecho que no hiciera, a venir sin adorno.

Tirso thus turns the Aristotelians' own weapons against them; he answers the stern theologians by telling them frankly that the public will take its dose of virtue only if the pill has a sugar coating.

At this same general time, too, Tirso could have originally penned the defense of the *comedia* found in *Tanto es lo de más como lo de menos.* [47] The prodigal, Liberio, in providing entertainment for the *cortesana* Taida, tells her (II, iii):

---

[46] See *Cigarrales,* II, 256-257.

[47] José López Navío, Sch. P. ("Una comedia de Tirso que no está perdida", *Estudios,* XVI [1960], 331-347), argues convincingly that *Tanto es lo de más como lo de menos* is the play sold to Juan Acacio in 1612 as *El saber guardar su hacienda.* I have long suspected that such was the case, but if so, the play, as we have it today, has been greatly altered. Let me here anticipate a recent study, one written for *Studies in Tirso,* II. I can now say, with some sense of certainty, that this play was first written as an *auto* in 1612, was converted in 1621-23 into a *comedia,* was retouched anew around 1626 before it was included in Tirso's *Parte primera* (Sevilla, 1627). See also E. Asensio, *El itinerario del intremés,* 128-131.

A ella
puedes por mí convidar
cuantos entretenimientos
alegran Alejandría:
bailes, juegos, bizarría,
juglares, y encantamientos.
Haya comedias discretas,
que es el mejor ejercicio,
suspensión de todo vicio
y martirio de poetas.

To these same days must belong as well the defense of the comedy as *royal entertainment*, found in *La firmeza en la hermosura* [48] — only, we are now in the early dawn of Philip IV's reign. The Count of Urgel, having just seen a play written by his young king, Juan II, will argue (I, vi):

Confiésote que tiene
el Rey buen gusto y *que es este recreo*
de príncipes empleo,
porque a cifrarse en la comedia viene
cuanto entretenimiento deleitoso
es alivio del noble y ingenioso.

---

[48] This play (Cotarelo, *Comedias de Tirso*, II) was first published in *Doce comedias nuevas de diferentes autores, Parte XLVII* (Valencia, 1646), at the expense of Juan Sanzoni. E. Cotarelo y Mori (*Comedias de Tirso*, II, xxi-xxii) stated that he had not been able to see it and reproduced the text as Hartzenbusch had given it in his *Teatro escogido de Fr. Gabriel Téllez*. Of this text, Cotarelo says: "Pero este texto, aunque no malo, es ya una refundición, porque se habla en él del Palacio del Retiro, construido en 1629 [sic], y en esta época ya apenas escribía Tirso comedias de este género. Hartzenbusch cree también que en esta obra anduvo otra mano que la de Téllez". So does this critic, though she believes that Tirso must have written the lines quoted above in the first months of Philip IV's reign when that young monarch's vassals were discussing which amusements were "licit" for a young king and which not. It must, too, have been done originally in 1621, before the Mercedarian's implacable antagonism for the new regime had been aroused —several months before *La prudencia en la mujer*, with which it shares an Aragonese setting, as well as the episode of the falling picture (cf. *La prudencia en la mujer*, II, ii and *La firmeza en la hermosura*, III, xvii).

A good guess is that *La firmeza en la hermosura* was the Tirsian play put on in the Buen Retiro, together with Antonio Hurtado de Mendoza's *Los empeños del mentir*, shortly after the battle of Nordlingen in September of 1634. See mention above of a play of Tirso's in Mendoza's work (*BAE*, XLV, III, p. 452). Dr. Vern Williamsen and a colleague are publishing a longer version of this play.

Tirso is not, then, as doña Blanca de los Ríos argues, defending Lope's theatre against Cervantes and others who were protesting it in 1611-12; he is shielding it against its critics of 1620-21 who were making an all-out attempt either to close the theatre or to make it a didactic instrument such as they felt the theatre of classical tradition to be.

The summer of 1622 would bring new festivities in honor of San Isidro, this time for his canonization. Lope would again preside over the literary *certamen,* and Tirso would offer *octavas* and *décimas* for the occasion — only to lose out, respectively, to Guillén de Castro and Mira de Amescua. [49] Lope wrote up these literary events in his *Relación de las fiestas,* including therein a composition entitled "Premios de la fiesta." In discussing the awards, he declares: "Secretario fue desta justa el que lo es mayor en el ayuntamiento, *no yo, como quieren los descontentos;* él recibió los papeles y los trajo a los jueces, que lo fueron el señor Luis de Salcedo del Consejo y Cámara de su Majestad ... y el señor don Alonso de Cabrera, asimismo del Consejo y Cámara de su Majestad ..."

Tirso was possibly, among the "discontent" who saw in Lope the real judge of the poems that were entered in that contest. At least, it is evident that Gabriel Téllez had been told by the summer of 1622 that one should expect little gratitude from Lope for any support that was given him. Lucrecia, in *La fingida Arcadia* (I, i, 435), has just paralleled Lope's prose with Cicero's and Boccaccio's and his poetry, with Ovid's "en la suavidad y lisura de sus versos, / sonoros, limpios, y tersos"; thereupon Angela comments, "Si él ese favor oyera / ¡qué bien le correspondiera! / ¡qué bien supiera estimallo!" Thereupon Lucrecia asks, "¿Agradece?" Angela's answer is highly suggestive (I, i, 435):

> ... *Aunque hay alguno* [50]
> *que apasionado lo niega,*

---

[49] For Cotarelo's unfavorable estimate of Tirso's contribution on this occasion, see *Comedias de Tirso,* I, xxxv. It should be noted, however, that the awards went to poets who were acceptable to the Palace.

[50] When I first wrote this study, I suggested that the very intelligent doña Leonor Pimentel was possibly the "some one" alluded to, for she had, as "dama de honor" to the Princess María, given into Lope's charge the

> es tan fértil esta *vega*
> que paga ciento por uno.

And Tirso will, en *La fingida Arcadia*, then make a defense of Lope that is so effusive that it at times seems an ironic burlesque. [51] He ends his play by putting the *tramoyistas* among the irredeemables — where they will be tormented by the "sierpes, / arpías, grifos, salvajes / que son los que en sus comedias / introducen ignorantes ..." and by crowning a Lope who, with his sweet verse, could entertain an audience for two hours without other stage properties than "a note, two ribbons, a glass of water, or a glove." But as we shall soon see [52] — and in greater detail than we can here devote to the matter — Tirso had given Lope his defense in a form that must have made the whole exceedingly embarrassing and even dangerous. He had linked his tributes to the master—and his defense of him against his literary enemies—not only with praise of the Pimentels but with a vigorous attack on Olivares, all-powerful *privado* to Philip IV. Lope naturally could make no response to Tirso's glorification. How could he do so when his every dream of aggrandizement lay precisely with the new *privado*? Or so he thought at the time.

Such hopes Lope would not easily renounce. When Lope's epistle to don Antonio de Mendoza came out in early 1624, Tirso must have felt both rage and contempt: not only had Lope renounced his dream of becoming poet-laureate in favor of the

---

second half of the *fiestas* which were put on in Aranjuez in May 22, and Lope had, at her request, written for it *El vellocino de oro*. Lope then dedicated the play not to her, but to the wife of the sycophantic don Antonio Hurtado de Mendoza, doña Luisa Briceño de la Cueva. There are, however, chronological problems. That marriage did not actually take place (and then *por poderes*) until 1623. If these lines were originally in *La fingida Arcadia*, then Tirso must have had someone else in mind.

[51] See my study of *La fingida Arcadia*, found in this volume, which was first printed in 1964. The interpretation of Tirso's satire, given here, rests on that longer study.

Sra. de los Ríos, in her preliminary study to *La fingida Arcadia*, describes it (*Obras completas de Tirso*, II, 1378) as "un mentís a Rámila y una bibliografía de Lope dramatizada, pero, más que apologética, sutilmente satírica y habilísimamente irónica". Her interpretation can be supported with Tirso's own words. See p. 191, n. 14.

[52] See Ch. IV.

less worthy Mendoza, but he had urged that *cortesano* to praise Olivares as well as the king, and had promised, from that time on, that he himself would glorify that same *privado*. Worse still possibly, from Tirso's point of view, Lope had denied his own beautiful creation, had labelled his verses before the whole world as "versos mercantiles," and thereby cheapened a theatre which Tirso and others had defended so warmly. What is more, Tirso, after March 6 of 1625 may have *suspected*, at least, that he had yet other reasons for anger against the envious Lope — as well as against the equally envious Mendoza and his protector Olivares. Where, if not from Lope, had Mendoza gotten some of the information he had passed on to Olivares?

The collection of *La Circe y otras rimas* was, *as a whole*, dedicated to that magnate. It contained, not only Lope's offending "epistle" to Mendoza but praise of Olivares' daughter as the "white rose" and a short story entitled "Guzmán, el Bravo" which glorified further the Guzmán name. In 1625 Lope put out, under the name of the countess of Olivares, his *Triunfos divinos con otras rimas,* but in 1629 he was again burning incense to the privado *himself*: his *Isagoge a los reales estudios de la Compañía de Jesús* has lines of praise for that "Guzmán generoso". Even in the last years of his life, he was still striving to gain the favor of the Guzmanes: he dedicated to the Duke of Medina de las Torres, son-in-law to Olivares, his "Egloga panegírica al epigrama del serenísimo infante Carlos."

Antona García [53] would seem to reflect, somewhat ambiguously, Tirso's feeling toward Lope in 1625. One finds in it — following

[53] For the original date of *Antona García* (1623), see my study "On the Date of Five Plays by Tirso de Molina," 198-208. I there pointed out that this passage must refer to Lope.

However, *Antona García* undoubtedly suffered *retoques* in 1625 after Tirso's banishment from Madrid was recommended by the *Junta de Reformación,* and not in 1623, as I thought when writing my study on its date. Miss Margaret Wilson caught my error in her edition of the play (1957). I have sought elsewhere in this volume to interpret Tirso's references to his flight from Madrid and to those whom he held responsible in "Tirso de Molina, Mendoza, Lope, and the *Junta de Reformación.*" There is further reference to the inn of Mollorido (in which part of the action of *Antona García* [III, iii] takes place) in *Palabras y plumas* (II, v), a play put on in the Palace on July 20, 1623, but retouched in 1625-26. See pp. 105-106.

the Seventh Castilian's statement that his wares are "envy," the envy that reigned in Madrid's literary circles — this significant bit of dialogue (II, iii):

PORT. 7:   ¡Buen caudal, por vida mía!

CAST. 7:   Bueno o malo, *ya lo gasta*
        gente que os admiraréis.

        ... ...

        ... véndese agora tanta
        envidia e [sic; ¿a?] ingenios diversos
        que *hay hombre que, haciendo versos,*
        a los demás se adelanta;
        y es tal (la verdad os digo)
        que quita el habla a su amigo [54]
        cada vez que escribe bien.

PORT. 1:   ¡Maldiga Dios tal bajeza!

Why did Tirso place this revised scene among merchants, merchants who had indicated that in the war between the Spanish and the Portuguese they held to a "viva quien venza" philosophy? Unless I am greatly mistaken, this dialogue represents, in part at least, Tirso's revulsion against the very "business-like arrangement" which Lope's epistle of September, 1623 indicated he had made with don Antonio de Mendoza. Even these Portuguese traders, with their very mercenary philosophy, were horrified at the wares in which the envious poets of Madrid were dealing. Envy! What a fine commodity! And when they learn that one of these

---

[54] The passage is far from clear. I interpreted it otherwise when writing "On the Date of Five Plays...", 206. Is Tirso using "quita el habla..." in the usual way or is he giving it a twist of his own?

Lope used the same expression ("quitar el habla a alguien") in *Las flores de San Juan* (III, 199), where it seems to have the rather literal meaning of "quit speaking to somebody." The anecdote in which it is found has to do with the friendship between two men — one don Alonso, an *hidalgo*, didn't ask his friend to borrow a certain horse because he was sure his friend would refuse him its use. He, nevertheless, became so angry over this imaginary refusal that "no le habló por más de un año entero". Thereupon Octavio, to whom don Alonso is explaining his position, comments: "Pues, sin pedirle / por sólo imaginar que os lo negara / le habéis quitado el habla?" Don Alonso justifies himself by asking: "¿Y no os parece ... que es muy justo, si había de negármelo?" The *Diccionario de Autoridades* gives another example from *El Caballero de Olmedo* (III) with the same meaning.

"envious poets" — one who, though he excelled over all others, would nevertheless refuse to speak to his friend whenever the latter wrote well — the First Portuguese is so shocked that he breaks forth: "¡Maldiga Dios tal bajeza!"

One has only to compare this stretch of dialogue with the high praise of Lope found in the *Cigarrales, El vergonzoso en palacio,* and *La fingida Arcadia* to realize just how deeply disillusioned Tirso had become with the man whom he had once hailed as master. And in the verses that follow — having first admitted that God had punished him by making him a poet — he then complains, as we have seen above, that envy had robbed him of his reputation. He insists as well, to his critics, that he is not proud; he can learn from the least among his fellow-poets. What is more, he had even glorified the work of those he shouldn't have praised. The very verb that Tirso uses, *solemnizar,* makes evident that he here has primarily in mind his tributes to Lope, not the one to Mendoza. The first Portuguese, having approved such an attitude on the part of the Seventh Castilian, counsels:

> ... castigad su porfía
> hablando siempre bien *dellos,*
> que esto para convencellos
> es socarrona ironía.

Crafty irony! Should Tirso's praise of Lope in *La fingida Arcadia* be so interpreted? Not a bad punishment for an opportunistic poet (a literary merchant) who, "haciendo versos a los demás se adelanta," yet deals in envy! Tirso had, by 1625, discovered about Lope what Alarcón had learned some years earlier: "... siempre se queja / de que es envidiado, siendo / envidioso universal / de los aplausos ajenos." [55]

In his *Laurel de Apolo,* [56] finished in the autumn of 1629, Lope gives his wreath to Tirso in words that at first glance mystify. The seventh *silva* of that poem pays tribute to Manzanares' sons. Having just sung (in eleven verses) the marvels of one Marcelo

---

[55] See Alarcón's *Los pechos privilegiados,* III, iii.
[56] For the *Laurel de Apolo,* see BAE, XXXVIII, 187-229, and, in particular, 213.

Díaz [Callecerrada], Lope then devotes all of six enigmatic ones to Tirso de Molina:

> Si cuando a Fray Gabriel Téllez mereces,
> estás, oh Manzanares, *temeroso*,
> ingrato me pareces
> al cielo de tu fama cuidadoso,
> pues te ha dado, *tan docto como culto*,
> un *Terencio español* y un *Tirso oculto*.

Exactly what Lope would imply in a "fearful Manzanares" and a "hidden Tirso," one cannot be entirely certain: Tirso had been in Trujillo for nearly three years (1626-29) when this was written in late 1629; he was in Salamanca in April of 1629, where he took an active part in the celebrations that his Order was putting on in honor of San Pedro Nolasco. Where he went after that we do not know; [57] apparently neither did Lope. The literary world of Manzanares, remembering the *Junta*'s harsh *acuerdo*, was, it would seem, still fearful to take Tirso to its heart, even though for Lope he was now the Spanish Terence, as "learned" (*docto*) as he was "polished" (*culto*).

In 1634, Lope approved Tirso's *Cuarta parte* in somewhat stilted terms: with his *aprobación* of that *parte* and with the tribute to Lope found in Tirso's *En Madrid y en una casa*, we shall be concerned later. [58]

---

[57] From Jaime Asenciós "A propósito de la primera edición de *Historia general de la Orden de Nuestra Señora de las Mercedes* (p. 105). We now know he made a trip form Salamanca to Conjo (Santiago de Compostela) in 1629-30.

[58] The last paragraph of the main text of this study, as originally published in *B.Com.* (XVIII [1966], 1-13) has been transferred to the final chapter of this study. See pp. 337-39.

IV

TIRSO, LOPE, LUIS VÉLEZ, AND THE CONDE DE OLIVARES: LITERARY AND POLITICAL SATIRE IN TIRSO'S *LA FINGIDA ARCADIA*

Tirso's *La fingida Arcadia*[1] is, on the surface, a pastoral play which exalts Lope de Vega while satirizing most of the groups inimical to him. The blows therein are directed primarily against the *tramoyistas*, though the Gongorists, and even the Aristotelians, come in for their share of pummelling.[2] What has not been suspected, in so far as I know, is that the satire of the *tramoyistas* in this *comedia* is directed specifically against Luis Vélez de Guevara — and, through him, at the Count-Duke of Olivares: in other words, Tirso's scenes have political, as well as literary, significance. In establishing this connection, we shall not only point the way to further understanding of Tirso's attitude toward Philip IV's favorite — an attitude which in 1625 was to result in the Mercedarian's banishment from Madrid — but shall get a glimpse into his relations with the palace clique of Andalusian poets who looked to that magnate as their Maecenas at court.

That there were bad relations between Tirso and Vélez de Guevara has scarcely been noted, and the bases on which I assert

---

[1] This study on *La fingida Arcadia*, whose *princeps* was in *Parte III* (Tortosa, 1634), was first printed in "The Renaissance Reconsidered. A Symposium," which was published in *Smith College Studies in History*, XLIV (1964, 91-110), Northampton, Massachussetts. The notes have been changed in a few instances to bring them up to date.

[2] For satire against the *tramoyistas*, see III, iii, and xii; for that of the Gongorists, III, iii; and for that of the Aristotelians, I, i.

their existence will at first seem very slight indeed. In January of
1626, as the king was setting out for Zaragoza, Véliz, *pedigüeno*
as always, [3] begs his sovereign for a new suit in order that he may
accompany him. In return for the favor, he promises to be: [4]

en todo el Pentecostés,
de las alabanzas vuestras,
eterno versifiquer,
más digna haciendo su musa
del siempre verde laurel.

And he ends this promise with the following curse:

Malos años para Arceo
y *el fraile de la Merced!*

With the enmity that existed between Vélez and *Arceo,* we are not
here concerned; with that he felt for *el fraile de la Merced* [5] (i.e.,
Tirso) we are.

In Tirso's theatre are likewise two lines which have on occasion
been interpreted as a possible slap aimed in the direction of Luis
Vélez de Guevara. *La celosa de sí misma,* written in late 1622 or
early 1623, [6] includes the following satirical verses of the *gracioso*
Ventura, made when the veiled doña Magdalena approaches his
master, don Melchor (II, iv):

Sé sumiller de cortina:
descubre aquesa *apariencia,* [7]

[3] Vélez's habits in this direction were so well known that Lope, on
asking his patron, the Duque de Sessa, for a *sotana,* comments: "Parece cosa
de Luis Vélez". See Amezúa, *Epistolario de Lope de Vega Carpio,* IV, 17.
  [4] Quoted by Rodríguez-Marín in "Cinco poesías autobiográficas de Luis
Vélez de Guevara", 62-78; more specifically, 75.
  [5] The term, "el fraile de la Merced", was used also in the abusive
quatrain that tied Tirso's name with Alarcón's. See p. 267. Tirso complained
in his play *Antona García* (III, ii:), as we have seen above, (p. 98): "que hasta
el nombre me quitó la envidia". But, as I have also shown above (p. 99,
n. 48), he is using "nombre" in the sense of "fama".
  [6] See my "On the Date of Five Plays by Tirso de Molina", 209-214.
However, this play, printed in Sevilla in 1627, suffered "retoques" in 1625-26,
as we shall see later in this volume.
  [7] This term, *apariencia,* must originally have referred to a stationary
setting which could be revealed to the audience by running or raising a

tocarán las chirimías;
que en las tramoyas pareces
poeta de Andalucía.

Don Emilio Cotarelo, pointing to the last two lines of this
quotation, declares [8] in connection with Vélez's love of the
spectacular: "... parece ser influjo de la tierra. Por eso, decía el
personaje de la comedia de Tirso: 'en las tramoyas pareces / poeta
de Andalucía.' " I believe him eminently right in this assumption.

With these two slight leads to point the way — plus the
realization that Tirso was by 1622 bitterly critical of Olivares and
his regime [9] — let us see if we can unravel some fascinating satire
in *La fingida Arcadia,* as well as the literary and political tensions
that lay behind it. This play, which has as its general background
the war in the Valtelline — as do various other Tirsian *comedias*
of this same general epoch — was clearly done as a *particular,*
one that was played in the confines of a private garden or patio. [10]

---

curtain. The *apariencia* probably first appeared in connection with *vidas de
santos,* wherein there was an apparition of the Virgin or of some saint — at
which moment *chirimías* were normally sounded. Apparently, when Rojas
was writing his *Viaje entretenido,* it was not an identical term with *tramoya,*
which implied stage machinery. Speaking of the *vidas de santos* and the
farsas de guerras, Rojas wrote: "Llegó el tiempo que se usaron / las comedias
de *apariencias* / de santos y de *tramoyas* / y entre éstas, farsas de guerra".
Quoted from Rennert, *The Spanish Stage,* 79, n. 1. Later, *apariencia, tramoya,* and *invención* seem to be used almost interchangeably.

[8] See E. Cotarelo, "Luis Vélez de Guevara y sus obras dramáticas,"
printed in *BRAE,* III, 621-652 and IV, 137-171, 269-308, 414-444. For the
quotation given, see III, 637. The word here probably refers not only to
Vélez's love of the spectacular, but to his trickery.

[9] For this enmity, see my study on *La prudencia en la mujer,* 1173-1175;
also "Notes on Two Interrelated Plays: *El amor y el amistad* and *Ventura
te dé Dios, hijo",* 212-213.

[10] See Felipe's comment (I, v): "No trocaré desde hoy más / estos jardines elisios / ... por la silla del imperio". The second act opens with scenes
that evidently take place in the garden: Felipe is *amante jardinero* and is
planting *maravillas, espuelas de caballero,* etc. Much of Act III must also
have been played in the open: scene iii has in its stage directions: "Y queda
un jardín lleno de flores y yedra" [symbol of envy?]. See n. 54 below.
    The hero of *La huerta de Juan Fernández* (1626) is, as we have seen,
fashioned on the protagonist of this play and even carries over into I, ii many
of the lines found in I, v of *La fingida Arcadia.* See above, p. 130.
    Both plays must have been given as *particulares.* That *La fingida Arcadia*
was not put on in the public theatres is suggested also by the fact that in

It was written, first to celebrate the marriage of don Felipe Centellas to an Italian countess, [11] named Lucrecia; and secondly, to
welcome the arrival of don Jerónimo Pimentel, [12] Captain-general
of the cavalry in northern Italy, who held that position under the
command of the great Duque de Feria. [13]

On writing *La fingida Arcadia,* wherein he exalts Lope in such
glowing terms that it almost seems ironic at times, Tirso has taken
his framework from the latter's novel, *La Arcadia* — a debt that
he acknowledges repeatedly within the lines of the play itself. [14]
The heroine of Tirso's *comedia* is a romantic young miss — one
who like thousands of other young girls of the time, found their
ars amoris in Lope's poetry. In the opening scene it is evident that
her bed-side table had, through the years, been laden not with the
various religious manuals recommended by Fathers of the Church
(which would make clear to her her role as future wife and mother)
but instead with Lope's *comedias.* She is his warm admirer, his
fervent defender, and in the first scene she names his works

---

the various lists of *comedias* we have of the twenties — those of the Palace
in 1622-1623, of Roque de Figueroa, Juan de Acacio, Amella, etc. — there
is no *Fingida Arcadia* listed. What is more, its *princeps* was in *Parte III*
(Tortosa, 1634), printed far from the court. The *Parte II* (with its four plays
of Tirso) came out in Madrid *after* the Parte III of Tortosa was available
to the public.

[11] My attempts in Italy many years ago to identify Lucrecia were unsuccessful, possibly because at that time I made search for the year 1621, not
1622. The Centellas were of the Counts of Oliva family and were linked up
with the Borjas by marriage. For a note on the Centellas, see my study
on *La prudencia en la mujer,* 1184.

[12] I have previously had occasion to deal with *La fingida Arcadia* and
the Pimentels. See "On the Date of Five Plays by Tirso", 191-199; and also
the one on *La prudencia en la mujer,* 1181-1186.

[13] The "Duque" in question was the third of that house. He had, as
family name, Lorenzo Suárez de Figueroa, the same as that of his father,
the second Duque de Feria, who had been ambassador in Rome and France,
Viceroy and captain-general of Cataluña and Sicily. The "Duque de Feria"
of whom Tirso speaks was governor of Milan and viceroy of Valencia and
Sicily. He died in 1634. See *Enciclopedia Espasa* under "Feria".

[14] See, in particular, I, i, ii and III, iii, xlii. Tirso himself recognized
the effect of excessive praise. At least, young Guillén, protagonist of *El
bandolero* —in a literary scene that must have been written around 1622-23—
tells his mistress Saurina, who has just praised his literary talent in glowing
terms (72): "No ponderes, te suplico, mis rustiqueces tanto que las ironices,
pues la alabanza en demasía suele traer consigo disfrazado el menosprecio."

almost one by one. What is more, she knows the basic issue involved in his fight with Torres Rámila, the classicist: having arrived at *La Filomela* of 1621 [15] — wherein Lope satirized that unwise grammarian — she even picks up, disdainfully, the phrase "infusa ciencia," which Lope had put into Torres' mouth (I, i):

> a él [i.e., a Lope] le da más alabanza
> lo que por su ingenio alcanza
> que a esotro su *ciencia infusa*.

Esotro is Torres Rámila, *el tordo*, and his *ciencia infusa* is a clear reflection of the battle between the Aristotelians, who were exalting literary training (*el arte*), and the *lopistas*, who chose to throw the emphasis on inborn talent (*el natural*). [16]

In the third act of his play (iii, 454), Tirso takes up the other two groups who were challenging Lope's supremacy. He first disposes of Gongora and the *gongorinos*. Amplifying the *Parnaso crítico*, which he had previously used in his *Cigarrales*, [17] Tirso here fashions a *Parnaso de Apolo*, made up of three parts: Purgatory, Hell, and Glory. He has assigned to Purgatory the followers of the Cordoban, "los más de ellos ... ignorantes." But Góngora himself, as the dogmatist who has introduced a new heretical sect, is in Hell, and with him the new Latinized words and metaphors he has coined such as: *candor, brillante, émulo, coturno, celaje, cristal, animado, hipérbole, pululante, palestra, giro, cerúleo, crepúsculos, fragantes*. With Tirso's satire of this group, we are not here concerned; our interest on this occasion must, like Tirso's, be centered upon a third literary group, i.e., the *tramoyistas*, who are likewise in Hell along with Góngora.

---

[15] The *aprobación* is Vicente Espinel's, dated May 31, 1621, and the *tasa*, July 19, 1621. It is dedicated to Leonor Pimentel.

For a study of Lope's relations with the Aristotelians, see Joaquín de Entrambasaguas' *Una guerra literaria del Siglo de Oro*.

[16] I have a long study in manuscript on Tirso's relations with this same group. If the Mercedarian says little here of the Aristotelians, it is perhaps because he had already expressed his disapproval of them, or was on the point of doing so, in the *Cigarrales, El bandolero*, and *Ventura te dé Dios, hijo*.

[17] *Cigarrales*, I, 113-117.

Before dealing with Tirso's satire against this group, we must first study its immediate sources. Again, we shall find them in Lope. The last *parte* of *comedias* which Lucrecia mentions, in checking off Lope's works, is his *Décimaséptima,* one whose *fe de erratas* is dated January 25, 1621. It came out some ten months before the *Parte XVI,* which could not have reached the public before the last two weeks of December, 1621.[18] Tirso makes no mention whatsoever of this *Parte XVI,* but he undoubtedly had read its prologue, as well as one play therein, before writing *La fingida Arcadia.* In the preliminary pages to this volume, Lope has included a "prólogo dialogístico", which takes place between *Teatro* and *Forastero.* Therein *Teatro* complains that he is maimed:[19] "Me ves herido, quebradas las piernas y los brazos, lleno de mil agujeros, de mil trampas y de mil clavos." His miserable plight, says *Teatro,* is due to the carpenters, by order of the theatrical managers. *Forastero* then protests that it is not the theatrical managers who should be blamed; rather, such conditions are due, as he sees it, to the dramatists who are like the physicians and barbers of the day: they give orders, and the patient bleeds. *Teatro* half agrees, but after all, what can the poets and managers do if all the great actors, such as Cisneros, Sandoval, and Cristóbal, are now dead, and if audiences come to *see* rather than to *hear?* If the public wants *spectacle* rather than poetry, the managers must necessarily take refuge in *tramoyas* and *volatines,* and the poets in conceits that are strained ('a los aros de cedazo'). *Teatro* adds that he could understand the public's delight in stage machinery, were it managed cleverly as in the day of Euripides, Aeschylus, and Sophocles; but how can it be charmed by such crude stuff as is being used for the Spanish *comedia* where the *figuras* rise and descend so awkwardly and where animals and birds appear in similar fashion?

But there is more, for this *Sixteenth Part* contains a play called *Lo fingido verdadero.* It is the life of San Ginés, an *autor de*

---

[18] Vicente Espinel approved it on September 24, 1620. Its *suma del privilegio* is dated October 24, 1620; its *tasa,* September 27, 1621; and its *erratas,* December 15, 1621.

[19] This dialogue is quoted from Rennert and Castro's *Vida de Lope de Vega.* I have eliminated such parts as are not germane to my purpose.

comedias in Diocletian's time, who was put in the calendar of the church's saints after being burned as a Christian. Significantly, this play carries a dedication to Tirso de Molina. [20] The protagonist of this *vida de santo,* first written around 1608-1609, [21] when Lope was defending himself in the *Arte nuevo de hacer comedias* against the attacks of the classicists, has been summoned to court to put on a play before the Emperor (II, 57-58). Ginés, as *impresario,* first offers to put on one of Terence or Plautus, but Diocletian rejects the suggestion, even if such plays do follow established precepts for the *comedias* and thus conform to Aristotelian canons. Ginés then suggests *La contienda de Marsias y de Apolo,* [22] whose author is Corintio, "hombre fantástico," he says, "en la pintura de furiosos versos ... digno de oír en lo que acierta pero infeliz en las trazas e invenciones." When this suggestion also proves unacceptable to the Emperor, he proposes one of a Greek poet, *"que las funda todas en subir y bajar monstruos al cielo."* [23] He adds (II, 58): "El teatro parece un escritorio / con diversas navetas y cortinas; / no hay tabla de ajedrez como su lienzo." And he closes his strictures with the following comment: "... suelen espantar al vulgo rudo / y darnos más dinero que las buenas, / porque habla en necio, y aunque dos se ofendan/quedan más de quinientos que la atiendan." Significantly, Diocletian ends up by asking for one of love, that is, one that conformed to the Lopean formula for the *capa y espada.* And this, as we shall see, is what both Lope and Tirso were still

---

[20] It may be read in Pérez Pastor, *Bibliografía madrileña,* III, 66.

[21] See Morley and Bruerton, *Cronología de las comedias de Lope de Vega,* 326. They date it "ca. 1608".

[22] *La contienda de Marsias y de Apolo* was a theme that Lope mentioned in his struggle with Torres Rámila. See Entrambasaguas, *Una guerra literaria del Siglo de Oro,* II, 43. I feel it virtually certain that Lope altered this passage at the time he sent it to print in 1620. "Corintio" is possibly Aeschylus. Among his contemporaries, Lope could possibly have been thinking of Guillén de Castro in 1620.

[23] Presumably Aristophanes. Did Lope have in mind also Vélez de Guevara? Spencer and Schevill, in *The Dramatic Works of Luis Vélez de Guevara* (p. xx), when commenting on Vélez's *comedias de ruido,* say: "They must have made exceptional demands on the mechanical and physical capacity of any stage of those days."

urging in the early 20's — against the play of *tramoyas* favored by the Andalusians.

Master of ceremonies for the *Parnaso de Apolo*, which Tirso has included in the third act of *La fingida Arcadia*, is the *gracioso* Pinzón, [24] who is palming himself off as a doctor, the better thereby to further the love affairs of Felipe Centellas and the heroine, Lucrecia. The lovers, in the guise of the *pastores*, Olimpo and Belisarda, are acting out Lope's *Arcadia*. Pinzón, the *gracioso*, makes it a play of *apariencias*: not only does he show them a magic cave wherein there are *apariencias* (III, iii, 453-454) —"porque *apariencias* no falten," he says — but the stage directions for the next to the last scene read (III, xii, 459): "Baja don Felipe en una nube y quédese abajo, y al mismo tiempo arrebata otra a Carlos, y vuela arriba." Thus Tirso, in broadest burlesque of the *tramoyistas*' methods, airily wafts his protagonist onto the stage — and just as summarily removes the *rival*.

The scene in question, is, nevertheless, directly based on one found in Lope's novel [25] which reads as follows: "[Anfriso] fue oído de un hombre rústico, que de aquellas soledades era dueño y desde sus tiernos años, estudiando el arte mágica, las habitaba ... [era] Dardanio, que así se llamaba el mágico." He tells Anfriso:

> ... yo soy aquel gran médico, Dardanio, famoso y conocido en todo aquello que el sol alumbra, temido y respetado en lo que nunca he visto; porque yo tengo fuerza sobre los elementos, templando el fuego, sujetando el aire, humillando la mar y allanando la tierra. *Hago domésticas a mi voz las más rebeldes víboras y sierpes destas horribles cuevas ...*

In the role of necromancer, Dardanio then conjures up for Anfriso, as examples to incite him, a long series of heroes beginning with

---

[24] Pinzón's role was perhaps taken by the actor, *Miguel Jerónimo* Pinzón (also Punzón). In 1623, he was with Vallejo, according to Pérez Pastor's *Nuevos datos*, I, 201. For further information on the two *Miguel Jerónimos*, see Hannah E. Bergman, *Luis Quiñones de Benavente y sus entremeses*, 495-496.

[25] It may be read in *BAE*, XXXVIII. For the stage directions given, see 84.

the names of Romulus and Remus, pasing through those of the Cid and Alonso Pérez de Guzmán el Bueno, [26] and ending with that of "el gran Gonzalo Fernández."

The stage directions of Tirso's plays are as follows (III, iii):

> Tocan trompetas, chirimías y toda la música; cáese abajo todo el lienzo del teatro y quede un jardín, lleno de flores y yedra. A la mano derecha esté un purgatorio y en él penando algunas almas. *Y a la izquierda un infierno y en él colgado, uno y otro en una tramoya ... una sierpe y un león a sus lados;* arriba, en medio de esto en otra parte, una gloria y en ella Apolo, sentado en un trono con una corona de laurel en la mano.

Asked for an explanation of this scene, Pinzón — with his background of a two years' stay in Salamanca, followed by military service in Italy — gives the following (III, iii, 453):

> El pastor, Criselio —
> que, aunque *pastor nigromante,*
> consoló en su cueva a Anfriso
> cuando lloraba pesares,
> en figura de romero
> (según cuenta en sus anales
> la *Arcadia,* tercero libro,
> folio ciento y cuatro) — *os hace
> ostentación de su ciencia.*

Having called the roster of military heroes — one that follows in abbreviated form the list which Lope had given — he concludes by saying:

> Este, pues, a instancia mía
> hoy os quiere hacer alarde
> *de sus mágicos secretos ...*

Asked concerning the scene which has opened up before their eyes, Pinzón explains (p. 454):

---

[26] Of don Alonso Pérez de Guzmán, el Bueno, Dardanio says (85): "Este es aquel valiente caballero, señor de la casa de Toral y cabeza de los Guzmanes, don Alonso Pérez, que mereció ser llamado 'el Bueno', título que tan pocos han merecido en el mundo, y que también dio España al que ves a su lado, que es el ilustrísimo don Esteban Illán, de tan notorias hazañas".

> Este es *Parnaso de Apolo,*
> y todos los circunstantes
> son poetas ...
> *El Parnaso* se compone
> de tres senos o lugares:
> gloria, infierno, y purgatorio
> ... ...
> los de la mano derecha,
> porque mejor se declare,
> en letras góticas dicen:
> *Parnaso crítico.*

There follows, then, the brief description of those in Purgatory, which has been outlined above. Pinzón, thereupon, turns to those in the Inferno, and we have the following conversation — for our purpose, on this occasion, the important part:

FELIPE:	Y ¿quién son los del Infierno?
PINZÓN:	Leed esas letras grandes.
FELIPE:	*Parnaso cómico dicen.*
LUCRECIA:	Y éstos, ¿no pueden salvarse?
PINZÓN:	No han de ir al cielo de Apolo
LUCRECIA:	¿Por qué culpa? ...
PINZÓN:	*Pues éstos venden*

> *a todo representante*
> *comedias falsas; con liga*
> *de infinitos badulaques*
> *han adulterado a Apolo*
> *con tramoyas, maderajes*
> *y bofetones,* que es Dios,
> y osan bofetearle,
> y están corridas las musas,
> que las hacen *ganapanes,*
> cargadas de *tantas vigas,*
> *peñas, fuentes, torres, naves,*
> *que las tienen deslomadas,*
> y así las mandan que pasen
> penas y cargas eternas
> a sus culpas semejantes,
> y las atormenten *sierpes,*
> *arpías, grifos, salvajes,*
> que son los que en sus comedias
> introducen ignorantes,
> dando el ingenio de palo.

and Lucrecia adds:

> *¡Quien tal hace que tal pague!* [27]

Having paid his respects to two other dramatists [28] who are likewise in Hell — with their identity we shall have to be concerned on another occasion — Tirso then enthrones Lope. Alejandra asks:

¿Quién es aquel que en la silla
tan autorizado y grave
tiene en la mano el laurel,
borla del Petrarca y Dante?

PINZÓN: Esa es la gloria de Apolo
y aquél, el dios que las llaves
tiene del entendimiento,
y premiar al docto sabe;
la corona es para quien,
escribiendo dulce y fácil,
sin hacerle carpintero,
hundirle ni entramoyarle,
entretiene al auditorio
dos horas, *sin que le gaste*
más de un billete, dos cintas,
un vaso de agua o un guante,
ése se coronará.

ALEJANDRA: ¿Y los demás?

PINZÓN: Que se abrasen,
pues, dándonos pan de palo,
los ingenios matan de hambre.
Los que quisieran saber
los misterios importantes
que el sabio Criselio enseña
a los pastores amantes,
a su cueva los convida.

---

[27] The last words that a criminal sentenced to death would hear. Rodrigo Calderón, who died on the scaffold as a result of the "strict justice" which Olivares had initiated, listened to them on October 21, 1621. The *pregón* is given in full by Andrés de Almansa y Mendoza's *Cartas*, 99. It ends: "[El Rey] le manda degollar, para que sea a él castigo y a otros ejemplo: *quien tal hace, que tal pague*". See below, p. 293.

[28] One is a "poeta vergonzante que pide trazas de noche de limosna"; the other is a "poeta de encaje" who puts in his plays "cuatro pasos de las viejas redondillas y romances". For the identity of both, see pp. 317-18.

LUCRECIA: Entremos todos a hablarle.
CARLOS: Satírico es el doctor.
ÁNGELA: Y sus burlas agradables.

In glorifying Lope over Góngora as a lyric poet, at the same time that he exalts him over those dramatists who are writing plays of spectacle that call for much stage machinery, Tirso is asking for a *comedia* that calls for simple stage properties, one that has easy musical verse. In other words, he is holding up the Lopean formula for the *capa y espada* play, which — with its sweet verses and its delicate metaphors — made its primary appeal to the *ear*; and he is decrying the popularity of the *comedia de ruido* which depended on stage effects and called for all kinds of elaborate machinery. In his denunciation, he picks up Lope's metaphor of the stage carpenters and elaborates it: the muses, loaded down as they are with "beams, boulders, fountains, and towers," have become mere "errand boys" whose backs are being broken under their load. The ignorant poets who are bringing on the stage serpents, harpies, griffins, and savages belong in Hell, there to be guarded by the very monsters they have introduced into their plays.

The *tramoya* was far from new when *La fingida Arcadia* was written in 1622,[29] but it assumed new importance at court with the accession of Philip IV and the rise to power of Olivares. Luis Vélez de Guevara, known to his contemporaries as *Lauro,* had for many years been writing plays that called for elaborate stage

---

[29] For date of *La fingida Arcadia,* see my "On the Date of Five Plays by Tirso," 191-97.

On the *tramoya,* see H. Mérimée, *Spectacles et comédiens à Valencia (1580-1630),* 186-89. The French critic says: "En fait, les premières mentions que j'en ai relevées datent de quelques années plus tard [than 1618]. Le 19 juillet 1621, la représentation habituelle ne put avoir lieu, parce qu'elle aurait empêché de dresser certaines machines pour la représentation du lendemain. Le 20 août de la même année, on fit à nouveau relâche dans les mêmes conditions; il s'agissait de préparer une 'invention' inédite. La mode des mises en scène compliquées se maintint en prospéra: on soigna les décors, on perfectionna la machinerie... Après le plaisir des yeux, le plaisir des oreilles".

The indispensable work today on Spain's stagecraft is the very remarkable study of N. Shergold, *A History of the Spanish Stage.* For comments on Tirso's use of *tramoyas,* see pp. 229-31.

machinery — *comedias de ruido,* they were ordinarily termed. When Rojas, around 1603, in his *Viaje entretenido,* speaks of "farsas de guerra" (and precisely in connection with *tramoyas* or *apariencias*), he probably had in mind such a play as Vélez de Guevara's *El capitán prodigioso y príncipe de Transilvania,* [30] as did Cervantes in 1615 when, in the introduction to his volume of *comedias* and *entremeses,* he spoke of "el rumbo, el tropel, el boato, la grandeza de las comedias de Luis Vélez de Guevara." Lope almost certainly wrote the pasage in which San Ginés describes the stage of one dramatist as "un escritorio / con diversas navetas y cortinas; no hay tabla de ajedrez como su lienzo," with the Andalusian school in mind — and even very possibly, Luis Vélez de Guevara. Suárez de Figueroa, in his *Pasajero* of 1617, satirizing plays of *tramoya,* mentions specifically Vélez's play on the Prince of Transylvania. [31] In 1620, Salas Barbadillo, in his *La sabia Flora Malsabidilla,* [32] laughs at a play whose stage decorations included "naves, galeras, casas de placer, selvas, elefantes, hidras ... panteras y salvajes." Here the satire is general in form, but in *Don Diego de Noche,* which was written before July 7, 1621, he has included an *Epistolario jocoso* wherein he sends *pésames* [33] to a "poeta cómico de que le silbaran una comedia." This *comedia* was — Salas makes evident — one of *tramoyas* which included in the last act an *apariencia de ángeles* and a horse

---

[30] Attributed both to Vélez de Guevara and to Lope de Vega. On these attributions, see Morley and Bruerton, *Cronología de las comedias de Lope de Vega* (541) and Spencer and Schevill, *The Dramatic Works of Luis Vélez de Guevara,* 368-72. The former study declares: "no creemos que Lope escribiese esta comedia"; the latter: "This drama, both by its content and by its language and its verse, is very characteristic of ... Luis Vélez". I heartily agree with these conclusions.

[31] Suárez de Figueroa says (*El pasajero,* 124): "En las de cuerpo [i.e., las comedias de ruido] que (sin las de Reyes de Hungría o Príncipes de Transilvania), suelen ser de vidas de santos...."

[32] *Princeps*: Madrid, 1621, with an *aprobación* and *licencia del ordinario,* dated October 31, 1620. The *tasa* is of February 8, 1621.

[33] Madrid, 1623. The *comisión del ordinario* is dated July 7, 1621; the *tasa,* November 7, 1623. The *epistolario jocoso* begins p. 53 and ends p. 63. I read it originally in microfilm; in the *princeps,* the *epistolario* begins on fol. 29v.

which unexpectedly bolted. The "poeta cómico" who wrote the play was none other than Vélez de Guevara, and it was acted by Roque de Figueroa, a fact which becomes clear, however, only when we study Salas' comments in conection with a satirical poem written by don Antonio de Mendoza. The poem is headed: [34] "Habiendo silbado una comedia de Luis Vélez, dijo don Antonio de Mendoza: 'Entre los sueltos caballos / de la mosquetera gente / que por el patio silbaron / entre lo Roque lo Vélez.' "

Tirso's satire of the *tramoyistas* in *La fingida Arcadia* is likewise *apparently* general, but in reality it is *very, very* specific. It, too, is directed against Luis Vélez de Guevara and a play (one involving *tramoyas*) which the Andalusian dramatist necessarily wrote shortly before Tirso penned *La fingida Arcadia*. [35] The

---

[34] Quoted from E. Cotarelo y Mori, *El conde de Villamediana*, 116. It might be argued that Salas Barbadillo's reference is to a play by Andrés de Claramonte, one in which a bolting horse led to the miscarriage of the actress, Ana Muñoz. But Ana Muñoz was in 1593 the wife of Antonio de Villegas, who died May 29, 1613. It is hardly probable that in 1621 Salas should have been alluding to an event which had occurred so many years before.

[35] This play, so evidently written to glorify the Guzmán family, should, by all logic, have been done not so very long after Olivares became official *valido* to Philip IV on March 31, 1621. There is internal evidence that points in general to that same time. The play contains *silvas* of type I (some 3.7%), a fact that, in and of itself, points to 1620 or later.

Aside from this, there is an allusion to the fight that Lope was waging against the triumvirate of classicists (Suárez de Figueroa, Torres Rámila, and Mártir Rizo) which began in 1617 and ended in 1623. Lope had satirized Suárez de Figueroa as "perro" and "abubilla"; Torres Rámila as "sastre", "culebra" and as "tordo" (in the *Filomela*); Mártir Rizo, as "gato". See Entrambasaguas, *Una guerra literaria...*, II, 325-406; in particular, 404. In the second *sátira*, printed by Entrambasaguas (II, 404), Lope promised a third one in the concluding lines: "Allí te diré yo del triunvirato / con que encubáis la fama de los buenos / juntándose *culebra, perro y gato*". The whole first *sátira* is given over to the theme of Torres Rámila as son of a Moorish *sastre*: it ends "Sastre fuiste y serás eternamente".

These *sátiras* led in 1622 to investigations that began March 24th of that year and ended in early 1623: Torres Rámila was asking for a vacancy in the Colegio Mayor de San Ildefonso (Alcalá), one calling for *limpieza de sangre*. Vélez, in *Más pesa el rey que la sangre* (III, 106a), puts into the mouth of his *gracioso*, Costanilla, the following neat reference to Lope's triumvirate and to Torres Rámila's supposed Moorish blood: "El *perrito* / que agora del foso sale / *gateando*, vive Dios / que le he conocido *sastre* / en Marruecos...". Yet Vélez swore hypocritically to the authorities on November

comedia in question was entitled *Más pesa el rey que la sangre y blasón de los Guzmanes.* [36] Let us prove the assertion.

Tirso, it will be remembered, begins his condemnation of the *tramoyistas* by asserting that they will never reach Apollo's heaven: they are traitors, guilty of "crimen lese [sic] majestatis" in that they are counterfeiting money (*moneda falsa*) by selling to the autores "comedias falsas"; they have, complains the dramatist, adulterated (i.e., cheapened) Apollo with the alloy of "infinitos badulaques," such as *tramoyas, maderajes, bofetones.* Tirso's metaphor, then, compares the traitors to Apollo with those of the realm who were "adulterating" the money, a clear allusion to the *moneda de vellón,* [37] i.e., money of silver adulterated with copper, and to the chief proponent of this policy, the Conde-Duque de Olivares, who was tampering with the coinage in an attempt to make money with which to finance the Thirty Years War. Elsewhere in this play (I, iv, 438a), Tirso calls it specifically "moneda vil de vellón."

The stage directions for this scene, it should be remembered, called for a *tramoya* on the side that was Hell, one on which were hung a *serpent* and a *lion.* Innocent though their presence may seem — they are apparently nothing but a bit of stage scenery which satirized the menagerie of animals which the *tramoyistas* were bringing on the stage — they, in reality, point specifically to the Guzmán coat of arms, and even more specifically to the recent play of *tramoyas* by Vélez de Guevara, *Más pesa el rey*

11, 1622, when they were making investigations concerning the charge of Moorish blood which Lope had brought in his *sátiras* against Torres Rámila (Entrambasaguas, *Una guerra literaria...*, 118): "...en cuanto a las sátiras, oio [sic] una vez leer una sátira, digo decir i referir a otro algunos fragmentos". He virtuously concludes his testimony, saying: "No solamente [no] se debe dar crédito, ni puede dar, pero siente que aun peca mortalmente contra justicia el que tal hace". Vélez's play was written, in all likelihood in the first months of 1622 — or even earlier in the new reign.

For the relation between *sastre* and *converso,* see Juan Rufo, *Seiscientos apotegmas,* ed. A. Blecua (Madrid, 1972), p. 63, *apotegma* 155.

[36] First printed as a *suelta* in the seventeenth century. See *BAE,* XLV.

[37] There are unfavorable allusions to *vellón* in ten or twelve other works of Tirso, written in his Madrilenian years. These references are important for Tirso's chronology, as I shall show in a later volume, one dealing with Tirso's political theatre.

que la sangre, which had made use of the Guzmán scutcheon in glorifying the feats of that noble family. And the scintillating light of that family at the moment was the Conde-Duque de Olivares, who, on becoming *privado* to Philip IV, had trampled ruthlessly under foot all those who had stood close to Philip III.

The origin of the lion and the serpent on the Guzmán coat-of-arms is made clear in a ballad which Durán included in his collection, one he took from a *Códice de la Biblioteca de Salazar, Genealogía de la casa de Guzmán.* [38] Its heading is "De cómo, estando Guzmán el Bueno a servicio del rey de Marruecos, mató una sierpe y domó un león que con ella combatía." Vélez, in his comedia, *Más pesa el rey que la sangre y blasón de los Guzmanes,* had developed this episode at great length (II, 102-140). The lion, already tamed when the curtain goes up, follows Alonso Pérez de Guzmán wherever he may go, on the stage and off it; and the winged serpent, "a terrible monster" that Vélez evidently took delight in painting, perished in the second act at the hand of Guzmán el Bueno. The stage directions for this scene are: "Don Alonso, armado con peto, espaldar y espada, y una rodela de acero a las espaldas, y el león..." Later ones add: "Sale don Alonso, con la rodela y espada llena de sangre, y Costanilla [i.e., the *gracioso]* con la cabeza de la sierpe." It was a *winged* serpent, that is, a dragon, Vélez tells us — one that would necessarily tend to link the Guzmán victory with that of St. George over the dragon.

Spencer and Schevill, [39] in analyzing this episode of Vélez's play, point to the dramatist's very evident familiarity with many incidents in the life of the hero, some of which he has slightly altered; then he suggests that Vélez must have utilized some history of the house of the dukes of Medina-Sidonia. The guess that Vélez had primary sources for his play is an accurate one, for almost certainly Vélez wrote this work at the behest of the Conde-Duque de Olivares (one branch of Medina-Sidonia's tree),

---

[38] Quoted from Spencer and Schevill, *The Dramatic Works of Vélez de Guevara,* 192. The reference is to the *Colección Salazar* (= D. Luis de Salazar y Castro), Biblioteca de la Real Academia de la Historia.

[39] *Ibid.,* 188-193. See in particular, 191-192.

who would naturally have put at the poet's disposal all available materials from the family archives, including the original patent of nobility from Sancho IV wherein are listed the *mercedes* that monarch had given the Olivares family. Nor does it require much stretching of the imagination to assume that it was played before an audience which included young Philip IV — all to the end that he be reminded of his great debt to the Guzmanes. The concluding scene of Vélez's play carries these significant lines, spoken by king Sancho IV after Guzmán's sacrifice of his son in defense of *Tarifa*:

> que sois el mayor, confieso,
> que a rey ha besado mano
> y éste ha sido el mayor hecho
> que ha celebrado la historia
> de romanos y de griegos;
> y, *cumpliendo con algunas*
> *de las finezas que os debo,*
> *estas mercedes os hago*
> y diga en el privilegio:
> "Por cuanto vos, Don Alonso
> Pérez de Guzmán el Bueno,
> imitasteis a Abrahán
> con más invencible esfuerzo,
> él, en el dicho no más,
> y vos, en el dicho y hecho,
> de una vez sacrifica[n]do
> a Dios y a mí el hijo vuestro,
> de *Niebla* os hago señor
> de *Sanlúcar y del Puerto*
> *de Santa María, Palos,*
> *Huelva, Sidonia y Trigueros;*
> y a la gran doña María
> Coronel le doy sin esto
> a *Olivares* y al *Algaba*
> para chapines.

These lines, and the man who penned them, i.e., Luis Vélez de Guevara, must have been a powerful irritant to Tirso, who looked with a jaundiced eye on the new *privado*, not only because of his cheapening of the coin of the realm, [40] but also because he

---

[40] Marañón (*El Conde-Duque de Olivares*, 314-315) treats Olivares' role in connection with the issues of *vellón* under the heading, "El desastre finan-

had been the recipient of so many *mercedes* from his sixteen-year-old king. Over and over and over again in his works of these years — beginning in 1621 — he has protested the debased coinage; [41] and on no less than three occasions, as I have had reason to show in a previous study, [42] he had protested the many *mercedes* that Olivares was receiving; in the *Cigarrales* (ed. cit., II, 93), in *Privar contra su gusto* (II, xxv, 357c), and in *La prudencia en la mujer* (III, i, 300b).

But, unless I am greatly mistaken, Tirso has, in this same scene of *La fingida Arcadia,* linked Olivares with another accusation that was being circulated in the capital in the summer and fall of 1622, one which was greatly perturbing officialdom and one which Marañón has dealt with in his chapter entitled "Las

---

ciero". He says: "...las grandes maniobras de este género [i. e., de *vellón*] se hicieron bajo el reinado de Felipe IV, y, por tanto, bajo la máxima responsabilidad de Olivares. En los primeros cinco años de su reinado, lanzáronse emisiones enormes de vellón cuyo valor estuvo, en adelante, sometido a las oscilaciones más bruscas y descabelladas".

[41] The first allusion I have noted in Tirso's works is in his short story, *Los tres maridos burlados* (*Los cigarrales*, II, 216). It must have been written after April, 1621, and probably before October 1, 1621. When the wife asks her husband (a *cajero* in the employ of a Genoese banker) if he is indisposed, the latter answers: "...si no es el enfado de haber contado hoy más de seis mil reales en *vellón*, no me he sentido más bueno en mi vida". See also my study, "Notes on Two Interrelated Plays of Tirso", 198, n. 20.

[42] See my study on *La prudencia en la mujer,* 1144-1147. However, Tirso's chief complaint here was the injustice Philip was showing his father's counselors.

By November 21, 1621, Olivares had recognized the resentment that the many *mercedes* given him were causing and had recommended to the king that he give him fewer. He says frankly: "Véome a mí más obligado al real servicio de V. M. que otro ningún vasallo...". (Quoted from Marañón, *El Conde-Duque de Olivares*). In his will, Olivares gives a complete list of his titles: "Conde de Olivares, Duque de Sanlúcar la Mayor, Duque de Medina de las Torres, Marqués de Eliche, Adelantado Mayor de la muy noble y muy leal provincia de Guipúzcoa, Gran Canciller de las Indias, Comendador Mayor de Alcántara, Comendador de Víboras y Segura de la Sierra y de Herrera, Sumiller de Corps, Camarero y Caballerizo Mayor de S. M. el Rey, de su Consejo de Estado y Guerra, Alcalde perpetuo de los Alcázares Reales de la ciudad de Sevilla, de la Casa Real del Buen Retiro y de la de Vaciamadrid y la Zarzuela, Capitán General de la Caballería de España y Sevilla y su Reino". One can hardly blame his contemporaries for not taking seriously his protestations against the *mercedes* he was receiving! See Marañón, *El Conde-Duque de Olivares*, 96, n. 3.

hechicerías de Olivares." [43] The Conde-Duque was a believer in witchcraft, as his modern biographer readily concedes: "...creía... en algunos disparates que su situación y cultura le debía impedir aceptar". Around September of 1622 such complaints, which had evidently been floating around from some time before, actually reached the President of the Royal council, don Francisco Contreras (*op. cit.*, 187): specifically, they involved one Leonorilla, who was urging certain philters on her customers with the argument that they were "los mismos que el conde de Olivares daba al rey para conservar su privanza". Thus the favorite was trafficking in witchcraft, and others actually accused him of possessing powers of black magic. The whole situation must have been known to Tirso in the summer of 1622 when he was writing this scene of *La fingida Arcadia*.

The *Parnaso de Apolo*, it is to be remembered, takes place at the entrance of a cave; and caves were, by long tradition, the abode of necromancers. Lope and Tirso were acquainted with that tradition, and so was the anonymous author of the malignant *Cueva de Meliso*, [44] who, at Olivares' fall from power, brought forth all the wild rumors that he had been collecting against this favorite in the more than twenty years that the latter had ruled Spain. In the very first note of the 72 which accompany the text of *La cueva de Meliso* — each accusation is annotated by the author — he comments on the evils of the time, adding (p. 552): "...no es la menor consultar al demonio para pedirle avisos..." Having pointed to the Marqués de Villena as an offender in this direction and also the tradition which associated the cave of Toledo with black magic, he brings in the name of Meliso, of whom Diógenes Laercio and Apolodoro had written; one who, he says satirically, gave admirable precepts of government. In the poem itself, don Gaspar de Olivares, i.e., Philip IV's *privado*, finds himself separated from his companions on a hunting trip in the Sierra Morena mountains and makes it an opportunity to enter the cave of Meliso, as Anfriso had entered Dardanio's in Lope's

---

[43] *Ibid.*, 185-190.
[44] "La cueva de Meliso", 543-552.

novel.[45] There Olivares' future is forecast, and there he receives from the wizard —whom he hails as "gran maestro, de toda ciencia mágica el más diestro que vieran las edades, oráculo mayor de las verdades" — the following promise, made supposedly in the dawn [46] of the favorite's rise to power (p. 544):

> que entre héroes has de ser el más perfecto
> que el mundo ha conocido,
> y poner los antiguos en olvido,
> manifestando el modo
> de gobernarlo y mejorarlo todo,
> y hacer, con nuevas leyes,
> reyes-privados y privados-reyes. [47]

The magician then recommends to him, one by one, all the Machiavellian acts with which Olivares was supposed to have brought Spain on evil days. He begins with the poison which the Count-Duke's father was reputed to have given to Sixtus V in August, 1616,[48] then passes to the philters which the *privado* had

---

[45] See above, p. 195.

[46] Olivares is there made to say (*ed. cit.*, 544a): "Si éste es Meliso, si de él guardo / el más cumplido aviso a mi privanza / para reinar en ella sin mudanza...".

[47] Marañón (*El Conde-Duque de Olivares*, 99, 100) has written: "Y Olivares sentía desde lo más hondo de su organismo, como uno de sus impulsos más eficaces, el afán del mando por el mando mismo...". The subtitle of the historian's book is "La pasión de mandar". Commenting further on this *privado's* love of power, he says: "Subir a los hombres de la nada es lo que más acerca a un hombre a la condición de Rey, *meta-subconsciente* del Conde-Duque". Later, he discusses his "emulación real". The desire to "govern everything": "...[de] hacer, con nuevas leyes, reyes-privados y privados-reyes" was early recognized, as was "the paralytic will" of Philip IV. Inevitable, then, was the fight between Olivares and the grandees of the realm! See Marañón, 87-95.
In a dialogue between two rustics, Ribato y Pascual, one attributed to Villamediana, we read (ed. Cotarelo, *Conde de Villamediana*, 199): "Y si al fin los santos lugares / nunca trocaran los dos / no queriendo el Rey ser Dios, / ni los ministros ser reyes...".

[48] Tirso promised in the closing lines of *La elección por la virtud*, a "segunda comedia", which normally should have dealt with Sixto Quinto's death. He apparently wrote it, for in H. Mérimée's *Spectacles et comédiens à Valencia* (173), there are listed, among plays Juan Acacio had in his possession on March 13, 1627, two entitled: "Sixto 5.°" and "2da parte de Sixto 5.°". [They follow, in that list of works, Tirso de Molina's *Martín*

used in 1622 in an effort to make secure his power over the king, and ends with the supposed assassination of don Miguel de Cárdenas, the alcalde of the court, who had first taken to the Royal Council the information about Leonorilla's powders and thereby linked Olivares' name officially with the use of black magic.

The very name which Tirso has given his necromancer must have some significance. Lope had called his wizard in the *Arcadia* "Dardanio", but Tirso, while retaining the other names of the original, has changed this one to Criselio. Now Criselio is the Italianate form of Klesl,[49] who had been the *privado* of Matías, Emperor of the Holy Roman Empire, until the latter's death in 1619. In that position the *privado* had urged on his sovereign a policy of peace between Catholics and Protestants. This tolerance, and the man urging it, were so unpopular in certain directions that in 1618 Maximilian had had him imprisoned in a castle in the Tyrol with Archduke Leopold as his jailer. When in 1621 Gregory XV became Pope, he was indignant at this treatment of one wearing the purple (for Klesl was a cardinal of the Church), and as early as January of 1622, he began his efforts to free the prisoner and to bring him to Rome. The attempt, not entirely successful until June, 1623, was opposed by the Archduke Leopold and also by the governor of Milan, who was no other than the Duque de Feria. Just what was Olivares' attitude in this particular matter of Klesl and just what Tirso had in mind on giving the name Criselio to his wizard,[50] I have not been able to discover, but the *Cueva*

Peláez, which must be his *El cobarde valiente*]. By the very nature of the theme, the *Segunda parte de Sixto Quinto* could hardly have failed to be a dangerous play which, if known to Olivares, would certainly have done nothing to improve relations between the Conde-Duque and Tirso. According to unfounded gossip, Olivares' father had poisoned Sixto V! See Marañón, *El Conde-Duque de Olivares*, 13.

[49] See this form of *Klesl* in Morel-Fatio's edition of "La guerra del Palatinado, 1620-1621", 331-332; also my study, "Two Interrelated Plays of Tirso: *El amor y el amistad* and *Ventura te dé Dios, hijo*", 206-207.

Klesl was in the spot-light from January, 1622 to October 23, 1622, and even until June, 1623, when the Pope managed to free him completely.

[50] I do not believe there could fail to be a reason —in a scene so carefully worked out as is Tirso's— for his changing the name of *Dardanio* to *Criselio*. If Klesl was being accused by his Spanish enemies of witchcraft, I have not been able to find mention of it. Certainly, Francisco de Ibarra, author of

de Meliso lists the death of the Duque de Feria among those supposed "muertes de grandes que se acumularon al Conde-Duque" (p. 557a).

Such tension, assuming that it existed as early as this, would necessarily have been known to don Jerónimo Pimentel, Captain-general of the Cavalry under Feria; and this is the Pimentel whom Tirso has glorified in *La fingida Arcadia* through the mouth of don Felipe Centellas. [51] The latter tells his beloved Lucrecia (I, iv, 438):

> Dióme el gran duque de Feria,
> milanés gobernador,
> una tropa de caballos
> debajo la protección
> de aquel Pimentel invicto,
> valeroso sucesor
> de aquel padre de la patria,
> de aquel Numa, aquel Catón ... etc.

There follows extended praise of the father, i.e., the 8th Conde-Duque de Benavente, who had recently died, and of his son, don Jerónimo, both of whom in Tirso's opinion had rendered such distinguished service to the father-land. Again, in the final scene of *La fingida Arcadia*, Tirso glorifies don Jerónimo, this time with Carlos as mouth-piece. What is more, in praising him, he probably mimics the last half of Vélez's title, *Más pesa el rey que la sangre y blasón de los Guzmanes* (III, xiii):

> Pastores, en nuestra casa
> tenemos el mejor huésped
> que honró en nuestro siglo a Italia:

La guerra del Palatinado (332), complains of "la ambición y avaricia del cardenal Criselio".

[51] Young Centellas evidently incurred criticism for his lack of responsibility in the conduct of the war. (See Pinzón's words, II, ix.) One may suspect that Suárez de Figueroa, in dealing with the lack of military discipline of the times (*Varias noticias importantes,* 159v.-174v.) had in mind just such casual conduct as Felipe Centellas' when he wrote (165v.): "No sé qué me diga de algunos *capitanes* destos tiempos, *a quien hace el favor empuñar la gineta en verdes años, sin prudencia y ejercicio*". He has in mind events in the Piemonte, for he says later (168v.): "durante la guerra de Piemonte".

> *don Jerónimo, famoso*
> *Pimentel, sol en las armas*
> *y blasón de Benavente,*
> *me da aviso en esta carta*
> *que hoy llegará a ser padrino,*
> *no de Anfriso y Belisarda,*
> *de Lucrecia y don Felipe*
> *Centellas, su camarada*
> *y amigo.*

Even though the setting of *La fingida Arcadia* is supposedly in Valenza del Po, Italy, Tirso was apparently welcoming don Jerónimo's arrival in Madrid in the summer of 1622. In fact, this play must have been finished by August 8, 1622, since in the *Noticias de Madrid*[52] we read, under that date, of the assassination of Fernando Pimentels (his brother) and of Jerónimo's rushing to the latter's aid. That the play was performed in the garden on a warm day of late spring or summer — probably in that of the Pimentel — [53] is almost certain, for most, if not all the scenes, are in the open, and there are at least two references which attest to the heat of the moment. Pinzón speaks (III, ii, 452b) of "el calor que el campo abrasa", and earlier, noting that some of the characters are seated on the ground, he, in his capacity as doctor, gives his comic stamp of approval with the comment (II, xv, 449b): "Si fuera en invierno, / disentería amenazaban / las humedades del suelo." Elsewhere, Felipe speaks specifically of spring (III, i, 451b): "La primavera, / a fiestas ocasionada, / la juventud novelera, / esta quinta celebrada, / estas selvas y ribera, / todo se junta al deseo / de ver mi condesa sana."

These allusions could well coincide with a literary event of May, 1622, which likewise seems to find reflection in *La fingida Arcadia*. Lope, as he presides over Apollo's Parnassus, is so strongly reminiscent of the literary fiesta that celebrated the canonization of San Isidro — over which he had presided in late May

---

[52] *Noticias de Madrid, 1621-1627,* 32. "Acudieron sus dos hermanos, don Gerónimo y don Vicente, puestas sobre las camisas sus sotanillas, y hallaron muerto a su hermano...".

[53] When I wrote this chapter as an article some years ago, I did not consider the possibility that *La fingida Arcadia* may have been put on again in 1625 in the *huerta* of Juan Fernández. See pp. 317-19.

of 1622 and from which he had excluded his enemies, the Gongorists — that it is logical to conclude that Tirso had in mind Lope's role on that occasion and that he began his play shortly thereafter.[54] In that literary event, interestingly enough, Vélez de Guevara had taken no part. As Lope's satire of the *tramoyistas*, found in *Parte XVI*, was already in printsince the preceding December, Vélez may well have understood that Lope was casting stones in his direction.

One may wonder that Tirso should have dared to satirize the all powerful Conde-Duque in any such fashion, but it is not necessary to go far for the answer. This play was done as a *particular*, and Tirso knew that in penning it for the Pimentels, he was writing for an audience that shared his sentiments about Olivares. Members of that family — originally of Portuguese origin — had been all powerful during Philip III's reign, and in many directions. The greatly respected eighth Conde-Duque de Benavente, so highly praised by Tirso in this play,[55] had, through two marriages, left numerous progeny, most of whom were, during that gentle monarch's life, holding high positions either in the royal household, in the church, or in the military. The father himself had been in charge of Italian affairs during the late years of Philip III's reign, and during that monarch's absence in Portugal he had virtually determined Spain's foreign policy. Don Jerónimo's wife, María Eugenia de Bazán y Benavides,[56] fourth

---

[54] In 1942 I wrote ("On the Date of Five Plays by Tirso", 197): "For the present, it is safe to say that this play was penned between November 8, 1621 and March 1, 1623, when the decrees against the collars [ruffs] and cuffs were put into effect. In all probability it was composed in late 1622 and early 1623". I now believe, on the strength of further study, that it was done between the *fiestas* given in honor of San Isidro's canonization, and the 8th of August, 1622. The "cartel" which was printed for the *Justa poética* that accompanied the *fiestas*, "se puso en el teatro que para dicha justa se levantó en el segundo patio de palacio el día 26 de mayo [de 1622]". See Pérez Pastor, *Bibliografía madrileña*, III, 130. Tirso had taken part in that *Justa poética*.

[55] See I, iv. He is "aquel padre de la patria / ... aquel Numa, aquel Catón / que fertilizando canas / a la Iglesia dio un pastor / un mayordomo a su reina, / tres columnas a su Dios, / tres Alejandros a Marte / a España, hijos veintidós / mil glorias a su alabanza / y a medio siglo un Hector".

[56] See García Carraffa, *Enciclopedia heráldica y genealógica*, under the name *Bazán*.

Marquesa de Santa Cruz, was maid-of-honor to the Queen in 1622. The new ninth Conde de Benavente (Juan Francisco Pimentel) was *mayordomo mayor* to the Queen, and on October 20, 1622, he married Leonor Pimentel,[57] maid-of-honor to the Infanta María, and sister to don Antonio Pimentel y Toledo (4th Marqués de Távara), who had for wife the Duque de Lerma's niece. This fourth Marqués de Távara had, before Philip IV's accession, even hoped to hold the very position in the new king's affections that Olivares now held. Villamediana's *Vita bona* makes clear that this had been his dream — at the same time it makes evident the tension between him and the Conde de Olivares. Two strophes of that *chacona* read as follows:[58]

> Olivares se desvela,
> con profana ostentación,
> por ser en toda occasión
> jefe de la parentela;
> Varelilla se las pela,
> que este señor andaluz
> le dejó entre cara y cruz
> y el de Tábara blasona ...
> En su pleito divertido
> de Tábara está el señor;
> él es muy grande hablador
> y con eso algo ha perdido.
> *Revienta por ser valido*

---

[57] *Noticias de Madrid*, 40. The notice reads: "A 20, se casó el Conde de Benavente con mi Señora doña Leonor Pimentel, Dama de la Señora Infanta y hermana del Marqués de Tábara. Fueron padrinos los Señores Infantes". The name was apparently pronounced at times with the accent on the middle syllable. I have preferred "Távara" because their ancestral home was in Távara (Zamora).

[58] See E. Cotarelo y Mori, *El conde de Villamediana*, 259, 262. The two strophes about Távara have by some mischance been separated, but they have to do with the same Távara, I feel sure. I have not been able to identify "Varelilla".

The line of the Marqueses de Távara is included under the "Pimenteles" in García Carraffa's *Enciclopedia heráldica y genealógica*. This branch was descended from Pedro Pimentel Vígil de Quiñones (the fifth son of Alonso Pimentel de Mayorga and doña María Vígil de Quiñones), who was "señor de la villa de Távara (Zamora). They were linked through marriage with the Enríquez family and the Toledos (of the House of Alba). This fourth Marqués de Távara became "Virrey de Valencia y de Sicilia". He died while holding the latter office in 1627. See *Noticias de Madrid*, 159.

y que la corte lo crea,
mas el alba que él desea
no se reirá en su persona.

Thus it is evident that there had been keen rivalry between this fourth Távara, a Pimentel of Valladolid, and the Conde de Olivares. What almost certainly made matters worse was that Olivares was also a Pimentel and that his mother, María Pimentel y Fonseca, was likewise from Valladolid. Still again, Olivares' wife was doña Inés de Zúñiga y Velasco, a fact which made him related through marriage to don Jerónimo (of the main branch of the Pimentels), for the mother of the latter was doña Mencía de Zúñiga y Requeséns.[59] This was, then, a family war.

The Pimentels must have realized early that their position under the new regime — with Olivares at the helm — was far from being as secure as it had been in the days of Philip IV's father. Their strength lay now in the favor they held with the Queen, the Infanta María, and the two Infantes, Fernando and Carlos.[60] All were supposedly inimical to Olivares because of his influence over the King.

---

[59] Jerónimo Pimentel was the son of the eighth Conde-Duque de Benavente by his second wife, doña Mencía de Zúñiga y Requeséns. Thus when Olivares' uncle, don Baltasar de Zúñiga (at one time *ayo* to young Prince Philip) was declared minister to the new king in 1621, he represented supposedly a link of peace between these two powerful houses. In reality, don Baltasar had been set up largely as a figure-head by the power-loving Olivares, and when Zúñiga died on October 6, 1622, it was said (without justification) that his death was due to poison from his nephew, the Conde-Duque. See Marañón, *El Conde-Duque de Olivares*, 49.

Don Jerónimo Pimentel, almost certainly through his wife's influence with the Queen, continued to flourish. Around October 15, 1622, we read in Almansa y Mendoza's *Cartas* (148): "A D. Gerónimo Pimentel, general de la caballería de Milán, dieron título y mil ducados de ayuda de costa"; later (155): "A don Jerónimo Pimentel, hicieron del Consejo de Guerra". And in the *Noticias de Madrid*, we are told (119): "A 30 de mayo [de 1625] dio el Rey título de Marqués de Bayona a don Gerónimo Pimentel, hijo del conde de Benavente, General que era de la caballería del Estado de Milán".

[60] As one reads the various *avisos* having to do with the Pimentels in these years, it would seem as if the Queen, the Princess María, and the two *Infantes* made special effort to honor members of the Pimentel family. As we have seen, it was to doña Leonor Pimentel, sister of the fourth Távara, that the second half of the *fiestas* of Aranjuez were, in May of 1622, entrusted.

Accordingly, Tirso must have known, on penning his satirical scene of *La fingida Arcadia*, that he was writing not only for an audience cognizant of all the gossip against Olivares that was floating about the court in 1622, but also for one which was entirely sympathetic to that gossip. To that audience he was criticizing the new *privado* for: 1) his monetary policy; 2) his glorification of his ancestors and the *mercedes* he was receiving for *their* deeds; and, (3) for his traffic with black magic.

As for Vélez de Guevara, he was, in Tirso's eyes, guilty not only of writing *tramoyas* and thus changing the *comedia* into one of spectacle, but because he was exalting with those *tramoyas* the new pride of the Guzmanes. And if Olivares was, for Vélez, the honor of the Guzmanes, Jerónimo Pimentel was, for Tirso, the glory of the Pimenteles.

When, in October, 1622, she married the ninth Conde de Benavente, *mayordomo* to the Queen, Prince Carlos and Princess María were their *padrinos*, and "his Majesty came from San Lorenzo el Real to be present at the wedding" (Almansa y Mendoza, *Cartas*, 148). Moreover, when the daughter of María Eugenia de Bazán y Benavides (wife to don Jerónimo) was married to her uncle, the Marqués de Xavalquinto, "comió la novia con los reyes en público, que fue de ver, en asiento aparte desviado de el de la Reina, nuestra Señora, cosa de una vara ... y el novio comió con el Conde de Benavente, Mayordomo Mayor de la Reina". See *Noticias de Madrid*, 36.

This ninth Conde de Benavente was having trouble with Olivares as early as June, 1622 (*Noticias de Madrid*, 27); and in the *Casa de los Condes de Benavente* (ms. 11569, B.N., f. 24v.), it is specifically stated: "...Murió de sentimiento de verse desfavorecido del Rey cuando la lealtad y amor con que sirvió y el querer excusar algunos lances, *de que dio cuenta al Conde de Olivares*, fue causa de mandarle retirar a su casa sin hacerle merced, ni habérsele pagado los gajes que le quedaron debiendo del tiempo que sirvió para satisfacer sus empeños, que fueron muchos". He apparently lost his father's title of "conde-duque" when the father died on November 8, 1621. I have heard that the "Conde-Duque de Olivares" — by which Olivares came to be known (Marañón, *El Conde-Duque de Olivares*, 95) after he was made "Duque de Sanlúcar la Mayor" in 1626 — was granted him to the end that he could boast of the same double title as that possessed by the eighth Conde-Duque de Benavente. I do not know of any proof that would justify such a conclusion.

TIRSO, LUIS VÉLEZ DE GUEVARA, AND JUAN RUIZ DE ALARCÓN

GENERAL FOREWORD

In studying *La fingida Arcadia,* we found clear proof that there was enmity, on Tirso's part, at least as early as the summer of 1622, toward Luis Vélez de Guevara. It behooves us, then, to find out as much as possible about this Andalusian — of whom relatively little is known — and then to see what more we can ascertain as to the relations of the two men. In doing this, we shall first strive to identify with Luis Vélez a series of satirical portraits, all of them written around 1625. One of these, the longest and by far the most detailed, may well be Tirso's own work. Even if he himself were not its author, he at least gave it a home, presumably of his own accord, when he reprinted it in 1635 in his *Segunda parte.* In addition to these portraits, all of 1625, we have three satirical passages, taken from as many works of Tirso, in which the latter has satirized a "corpulent" poet. It will be our purpose to show that all three of them, written between 1621 and 1626, refer to Luis Vélez de Guevara. We even have various other bits of Tirsian satire, directed against this same Andalusian, among others the "A ti sólo" of the *Quinta parte.* There are, as well, no less than five Tirsian plays — all composed, or else retouched, after the *Junta de Reformación* reached its *acuerdo* on March 6, 1625 — which contain Tirso's answers to a scurrilous *copla,* one written primarily, it would seem, by Luis Vélez, that appeared on the wall of a Madrid *pastelería,* and one which linked in ignominy Tirso's name with that of Juan Ruiz de Alarcón. Tirso would, by way of answer, satirize Luis Vélez and Alarcón together. To this barrage, found in Tirso's theatre, we know, at present, of only three counter-charges from Luis Vélez (two of them somewhat doubtful) and none from Alarcón. When more is known of Luis Vélez de Guevara's work, more may be uncovered. Alarcón had presumably ceased to write when Tirso began to link his name with that of Vélez.

V

TIRSO AND VARIOUS CARICATURES OF LUIS VÉLEZ
IN 1625; IN PARTICULAR, ONE FROM TIRSO'S
SEGUNDA PARTE (1635)

There exists, to my knowledge, neither oil portrait nor pencil-sketch of Luis Vélez de Guevara (1579-1644). Yet the Andalusian's residence in the Palace, as *valet de chambre* to Philip IV, coincided during many years with that of Diego Velázquez, who likewise was from the South. The lack is even more surprising because Vélez was, by any standard, a colorful figure. Tall and thin to the point of emaciation, he must have cast a strange shadow in the Palace, as long and as thin as did the lean figure of the Knight of La Mancha on the plains of that region. Despite the lack of any picture of Luis Vélez that could give us a retinal image, so many and so detailed are the vivid descriptions of this very flamboyant figure that a composite, made from them, would enable the least observant to identify him on sight.

These descriptions, covering a period of some forty years, extend from 1603-1604, the date of Vélez's appearance in Castile, to 1644, the year in which he died. Some of the various caricatures are signed and dated; others bear the name of the author, but it is not easy to establish their date of composition; still others are anonymous but can be placed in time with fair precision. In this last category belongs one of particular interest to this study since it is *linked with Tirso's name.* Whether or not it be the work of Gabriel Téllez, we shall maintain that it reflected in large measure his attitude toward the Andalusian from 1625 on and is therefore important in assessing their interrelations.

Shortly after returning to Spain from military service in Italy around 1603-1604, Vélez must have started toward the North of Spain. This we conjecture because Agustín de Rojas Villandrando's *El viaje entretenido* — with its *aprobación* given in Valladolid on May 15, 1603 and its publication in Madrid in 1604 — carries a laudatory sonnet, signed, by Luis Vélez de *Santander*. Now this was the Andalusian's rightful name, but he would soon discard it for the more illustrious one of Luis Vélez de *Guevara*. One Francisco de Quevedo quickly took note of this borrowing in his poem, "Milagros de corte son":

> que diga ser más soldado
> que en su tiempo el de Pescara,
> y que se llame *Guevara*
> el que no es más de *ladrón*,
> milagros de corte son.

The satire is too pat to the occasion, too perfect in its characterization of Luis Vélez de Guevara, for one to question seriously its reference to him. The Andalusian, newly arrived in the capital from the wars of Italy, struck the poet from Madrid as a *miles gloriosus*, who, in his craving for great ancestral background, had not hesitated to take unto himself the name of Guevara, one half of the grand old surname of Ladrón de Guevara. In reality, says Quevedo, it is the *other half* he should have appropriated.

By May of 1610 at least Vélez had attained some fame as a poet. His fellow-countryman, Andrés de Claramonte, had by that time written his *Letanía moral*, [2] though it did not come off press in Sevilla until 1613. In it he compares Luis Vélez's verses to precious stones. Interestingly enough, it is in this same book of Claramonte's that we find first mention of Tirso as a poet — Tirso who, as we shall see, came to detest this poet from the South (i.e., Vélez).

---

[1] Quevedo, *Obras en verso*, 84. Luis Vélez's name is here linked with that of Ruiz de Alarcón, who — says Quevedo — has also taken unto himself a name (that of "Mendoza") which does not belong to him any more than "Guevara" belongs to Vélez.

[2] See Cotarelo y Mori, *Comedias de Tirso de Molina*, I, p. xvii.

Miguel de Cervantes, in the years 1614 and 1615, penned two thumb-nail sketches of the Andalusian. Let us take first that of 1615. In the introduction to the volume of his *Ocho comedias y entremeses*[3] of that year, he characterizes Luis Vélez's theatre, mentioning "el rumbo, el tropel, el boato, la grandeza de las comedias de Luis Vélez de Guevara". The pomp, the bustle, the pageantry, the sheer "sweep" of Vélez's plays: with what exquisite precision Cervantes chose those nouns!

There is nothing here of Vélez's personal appearance nor of his temperament, probably because in the *Viaje del Parnaso* of the year before, Cervantes had given us their measure, which were evidently as flamboyant as are some of his dramatic works. Here Cervantes alludes to Vélez's "gigantic stature", as well as to his swash-buckling ways that were so annoying to Quevedo, to his *joie de vivre,* his "singular" temperament, the sheer quantity of his verse:

> Este, que es es escogido entre millares,
> de Guevara, Luis Vélez, es el bravo,
> que se puede llamar "quita-pesares."
> Es poeta gigante, en quien alabo
> el verso numeroso, el peregrino
> ingenio, si un Gnatón nos pinta, o un Davo.[4]

Encountering him again on his return from Parnassus, Cervantes mentions once more his joy-in-living, linking it here with his "discretion" and his courtliness of manner:

> Topé a Luis Vélez, lustre y alegría
> y discreción del trato cortesano ... ;

and this time he will close with six words that indicate the very real affection he felt for this giant of an Andalusian in spite of the many faults he saw in him: "y abracéle en la calle a mediodía."

---

[3] Cervantes, *Ocho comedias y ocho entremeses*, I, 8.
[4] *Viaje del Parnaso*, pp. 27-28. Gnaton and Davo were servants in Terence's plays. The former is a glutton. Thus, Cervantes stresses his talent in painting comic figures. Tirso will allude to the same characteristic in unfavorable terms. See pp. 288, 290.

If, in this last description, the phrase, "discreción del trato cortesano" [5] surprises, it was, nevertheless, eminently accurate. Vélez *was* and had been, a courtier from early youth. He had at 17 entered the household of the Cardinal-Archbishop of Seville, Rodrigo de Castro, where he remained some three years; and by 1608 at least, he was in that of young Diego Hurtado de Mendoza, [6] Conde de Saldaña. By this date, too, he was engaged to doña Ursula Ramisi y Bravo, who was a member of the household of doña Inés de Guzmán, Marquesa de Alcañices and fond sister to the proud Guzmán, the Conde-Duque de Olivares, who would, as we know, through his position as favorite to Philip IV, rule all Spain and her dominions after March 31, 1621. Such relationships would presumably have moderated to some extent Vélez's very exuberant personality and spread over it a patina of courtlines. In such relationships, too, he may have learned the obsequious ways of the hanger-on, the persistency in begging for which he later became only too well-known throughout Madrid.

Nevertheless, Vélez evidently played well his role as courtier: the events of his life prove it. When the fortunes of Saldaña fell with those of the Duque de Lerma in 1618, the dramatist became for a short time "gentilhombre de cámara" to don Juan Téllez-Girón, Marqués de Peñafiel, son of the great Duque de Osuna. [7] With Olivares' rise to power in 1621, Vélez's star was in the ascendant. For the new *privado*, he wrote in 1621-1622 as we have already seen, *Más pesa el rey que la sangre* wherein he glorified the great ancestor of Olivares, don Alonso Pérez de Guzmán el Bueno. [8] In turn, Vélez became: gentleman usher (*portero*) to the Prince of Wales in 1623, when that young man

---

[5] Cervantes here makes evident that he is using *discreción* in the sense of Castiglione's *cortesano*. See pp. 96-8 of this book.

[6] The family name of the Conde de Saldaña was Diego Hurtado de Mendoza y Salcedo. See p. 346, n. 46 of chapter.

[7] All the facts of Luis Vélez's life are taken either from the biographical sketch of Spencer and Schevill's, *The Dramatic Works of Luis Vélez de Guevara* or from E. Cotarelo y Mori's *Luis Vélez de Guevara y sus obras dramáticas.*

[8] See above, "Literary and Political Satire in Tirso's *La fingida Arcadia*", pp. 201-205.

came a-wooing Spain's princess; majordomo in 1624 to the gormandizing Charles of Austria, who lived only a few short months after his arrival in Madrid; [9] doorkeeper to the royal chamber of Philip IV himself in April of 1625, though the place gave him no stipulated remuneration until 1633. This last position he held until November of 1644 when he died — at which time he was able to hand down to his talented son, Juan, as tall, as thin, as bent as his father, [10] the official place he had held for so many years in the Royal Palace. On the occasion of Luis Vélez's death, all the nobles of the court attended his funeral; and José de Pellicer, having first praised the dramatist's "grande ingenio, agudos y repetidos dichos," goes on to call him "one of the finest courtiers of Spain." That he was the "hechura" at court of Olivares, [11] his fellow-Andalusian, can hardly be doubted, but that he had innate talent for his task is suggested by Cervantes' characterization: "lustre y alegría y discreción del trato cortesano."

Yet Cervantes, classicist that he was in his dramatic ideals, must have had some mental reservations about a theatre which he characterized with such nouns as "el rumbo, el tropel, el boato, la grandeza." For he had, as early as the first *Quijote*, [12] expressed

---

[9] Luis Vélez de Guevara did not marry María López de Palacios until November of 1626. The Archduke Carlos died in late December, 1624. One must ask how Vélez lived in 1625 and most of 1626. Judging by the poems that follow, he must often have gone hungry.

[10] See la Barrera, *Catálogo*, 461-462. He is there described in a *vejamen* of 1640 as "alfanje corbo", "pata larga", etc. What is more, he had a *very* large nose.

[11] His appointments as "valet de chambre" to the Prince of Wales, as Majordomo to Archduke Charles, and as door-keeper to Philip IV must all have come through Olivares. There are indications that Tirso thought the *privado* a very stingy patron. See p. 252, n. 10.

[12] The *cura*, in conversation with the *canónigo*, says (I, xlviii): "Pues ¿qué, si venimos a las comedias divinas? ¡Qué de milagros fingen en ellas, qué de cosas apócrifas y mal entendidas, atribuyendo a un santo los milagros de otro! Y aun en las humanas se atreven a hacer milagros, sin más respeto ni consideración que parecerles que allí estará bien el tal milagro y *apariencia*, como ellos llaman, para que la gente ignorante se admire y venga a la comedia...". Tirso, on writing his *dedicatoria* for *Deleytar aprovechando*, explains in very similar terms his reasons for avoiding the *comedia* as a vehicle for the *historias divinas* he planned to write. See Cotarelo, *Comedias de Tirso de Molina*, I, p. L.

apprehension over the *comedias de santos* and the *apariencias,* commonly used for their presentation. Such plays of spectacle, with their heavy dependence on stage machinery (and even on elements of the grotesque), were anathema to another classicist. Suárez de Figueroa, on writing his *El pasajero* [13] of 1617, satirizes the *tramoyas* used in what he terms comedias "de cuerpo que (sin las de reyes de Hungría o príncipes de Transilvania) suelen ser de vidas de santo." And Vélez was not only the author [14] of *El capitán prodigioso y príncipe de Transilvania,* to which Suárez was presumably alluding, but was famous at this time precisely for his "comedias de santos." In a letter dated August 6, 1616, one Jerónimo Dalmao y Casanate, on recommending Vélez to write the play on Santa Isabel de Hungría that was desired, stated: [15] " ... todos los autores me aseguran que [Luis Vélez] la hará muy bien ...; es en cosas a lo divino quien mejor hace agora." For Suárez, such *comedias* were nothing less than "espantavillanos," written for the express purpose of filling the pit of the theatre. Even so, the *tramoyas* were anything but dependable at this time as a further observation of that same satirist makes evident: "Hanse visto desgracias en algunas, que alborotaron con risa el concurso, o quebrándose y cayendo las figuras, o parándose y asiéndose cuando debían correr con más velocidad." Lope and Tirso, normally at odds with Suárez de Figueroa in their dramatic concepts, would, in this matter of *tramoyas,* [17] see eye to eye with him.

Within a few years the play of *tramoyas* would become more acceptable — at least to some [18] — and the nature of the satire, directed against Vélez, would accordingly change. The year 1625

---

[13] *El pasajero,* 124-126.

[14] The play is now generally attributed to Vélez, not to Lope. See Spencer and Schevill, *Dramatic Works of Luis Vélez de Guevara,* 368-372, and Morley and Bruerton, *Cronología de las comedias de Lope de Vega,* 540-41.

[15] See Cotarelo's *Luis Vélez de Guevara* in *BRAE,* III, 648, for Dalmao y Casanate's praise of Vélez as possible author for a *Santa Isabel de Hungría.*

[16] *El pasajero,* 126.

[17] See Ch. IV.

[18] Tirso was, by 1624-26, writing such plays of *tramoya* as *Los balcones de Madrid, En Madrid y en una casa,* etc. Lope, on the other hand, was still tilting against them.

would rain highly personal caricatures on the Andalusian poet. Most of them, probably *all* of them, had their origin among members of the *Academy of Madrid,* which in that year would seem to have been in a particularly satirical frame of mind. It is evident from the various word-pictures that were sketched at this time that the "giant" whom Cervantes had painted had grown thin to the point of emaciation, that his face appeared ludicrously long, and that he was nevertheless courting a young widow who was proving somewhat reluctant. Indeed, it would seem that he had even taken part in a tourney, presumably to do honor to his fair lady, on which occasion, though he fought right valiantly, he had ended up ingloriously by falling from his mount. Some of his fellow Academicians would have a field-day celebrating this contretemps.

Let us begin with the sketch of Gabriel de Corral, which we had occasion to mention in our first chapter. Around March 1, 1625, he pronounced his famous *vejamen* in the *Academy of Madrid:* it is a portrait which has the advantage of being labelled as to subject and signed by its author. What is more, it can, as I have shown on another occasion, [19] be dated with precision. In his *vejamen* Corral has left us a whole gallery of satirical portraits, for which the fellow-members of that organization had sat — most of them unsuspectingly, we should imagine. Corral paints the god Apollo as making his way through a mad-house of sick poets, i.e., Corral's colleagues in the Academy of Madrid. In the role of physician to these poets, Apollo passes by one sick bed after another, accompanied by his guide, don Lucido (i.e., one don Alonso de Oviedo). The very first patient they visit is "Lauro" (i.e., Vélez de Guevara), and by way of introduction to him, the reader is warned. "adviértase que Lauro era algo flaco." In view of the caricature that follows, the phrase "algo flaco" would seem to be magnificent understatement: [20]

---

[19] See my "Pantaleón de Ribera, 'Sirene', Castillo y Solórzano, and the *Academia de Madrid* in Early 1625", 197.

[20] For this *vejamen,* see Gabriel de Corral's *La Cintia de Aranjuez,* 173-198. The last of the "beds" is labelled "séptima cama", but it should be noted that "cama cuarta" has been omitted and that *eight* prizes (not seven) are awarded (199). Pantaleón's was probably "cama cuarta". Fileno's and Danteo's have also been omitted.

No vio Apolo bulto en medio, sino el que podía causar
una mano de carnero; a no ser la cabeza en la almohada,
la pasara en blanco. Pidió por el cuerpo de aquella cabeza Apolo y yo [dije]: Muy bien está dicho cuerpo, si
se entiende no sólo de difunto sino [de] algo más allá.
Esqueleto tan roído le tiene su enfermedad que, aunque
se muera en Viernes Santo, está la tierra segura de no
quebrar con el ayuno. Déjanle andar por acá los difuntos
sobre su palabra, para que, como mandadero, traiga y
lleve recados deste al otro mundo. Mas lo que hay que
admirar es que *ha pocos días* [21] que andaba este enfermo por el mundo batallando valientemente; mas ¿qué
mucho, si en faltándole lanza, daba los botes consigo
mismo?

Mandóle [Apolo] pues, que sacase lo que llamaba bra-
zo ... Luego que le tentó, creyó que era alguna fístula de
geringa ... y lastimado Apolo de su alma, que la conside-
raba aprensada entre dos zarzos, declaróle por hético y
tísico; y era así, porque se había desainado de consonantes y padecía flujo de sonetos y cólico de romances; a
cuyos achaques socorrió con esta receta:

> Para que por buen camino
>   engorde este cecinado,
>   esqueleto amortajado
>   en pieles de pergamino:
> Récipe: una gavioneta,
>   tan cortés y comedida,
>   que le quiera y no le pida;
> y absténgase de poeta.

Gabriel de Corral's very significant sketch stresses three things:
1) the great emaciation of Lauro at this time, so skeleton-like that

---

[21] I find neither in Almansa y Mendoza's *Cartas,* nor in the *Noticias
de Madrid,* nor in Alenda y Mira's *Solemnidades y fiestas...,* any reference
to a *fiesta* occurring at this time. However, it probably formed part of the
celebrations given in honor of the Marqués de Eliche's marriage to Olivares'
daughter, María. They were married on January 9, 1625, and private celebrations were still being given their honor at least as late as February 5th.,
1625. One reads in the *Noticias de Madrid* (113) under the date indicated:
"A 5, hizo el condestable de Castilla un gran banquete en una granja a los
Marqueses de Eliche; y serían los convidados más de treinta; hubo después
sarao y comedia". There must necessarily have been others, including a tourney, given in their honor. One of these could explain Corral's phrase, "ha
pocos días".

even if he should be buried on Holy Friday, the very earth which would consume him could not, in justice, be accused of breaking fast; indeed, Lauro was so near the other world that he was already acting as messenger [22] between this and the one beyond; 2) this emaciation was due *in part* to the many rhymes he had fashioned, to a constant flow of sonnets and to cholic resulting from the many poems in ballad-measure (i.e., *romances*) that he had fashioned (they had melted away all flesh from his bones!) and *in part* to the fact that he had need of a little bird (*gavioneta*) [23] who would love him, yet not ask him [for money]; 3) in spite of his emaciation, Lauro had, nevertheless, taken part *recently* in a tourney (presumably one he had entered in honor of his fair lady) in which he had the misfortune to lose his lance. But nothing daunted, this hero continued to fight valiantly, using his own thin body as a substitute weapon.

Keeping ever before us this word-picture of Gabriel de Corral's, let us go to other portraits which are undated and unlabelled. Sometimes, as we shall see, the author is lacking as well:

There exists a much less well-known *vejamen* than Corral's, one written by another member of the *Academy of Madrid*, named José Camerino. [24] Though it was not printed until 1655 in his *La*

---

[22] This is possibly a reference to some play, such as *El juicio final,* in which Vélez had taken the role of messenger.

[23] In Gabriel de Corral's *La Cintia de Aranjuez,* Elisa is paired with Lauro. She is unquestionably María López de Palacios, who is in the service of "Cintia", a Guzmán who marries "Fileno", of the House of Alba. Fileno says (307): "En Sevilla nací, rama de los excelentísimos Alvas...". As for Cintia, Lauro's *epitalamio* includes the lines (371): "Alto asunto a cuidados soberanos, Cintia Guiomar, que ilustra el apellido / de los héroes Guzmanes / repetido en valientes capitanes...". Elsewhere, when speaking of a poem, the author says (134): "Dedicóse a un héroe de los más insignes que tuvo el tronco de los Guzmanes, *de quien Cintia era hermosa rama*". I have not been successful in identifying the couple with such casual search as I have been able to make. With the proper books at hand, it should not be difficult to do.

[24] He was author of a book entitled *Novelas amorosas,* printed in 1624. For his *La dama beata,* see Willard F. King, *Prosa novelística y academias literarias en el siglo XVII,* 156-158. Camerino's *vejamen,* which followed a *comedia de repente,* puts last the characterization of Lauro, thereby giving him importance, as Corral had placed him *first* among the *locos.* This *vejamen*

dama beata, it was clearly done not so very long after Corral's. In the "fifth visit" of that book, the author is led by Fame to a small city called *Academia,* and even more specifically to the house of "un noble caballero de la ilustre progenie de los Mendozas." He sees there, among others, the very thin Prada brothers (Nicolás and Pedro), the dirty Corral (i.e., Gabriel de Corral), the furious Pantaleón de Ribera, "que en su escudo traía por insignia una pantera y un león [y] daba a cuantos se le ponían delante golpes de ciego." Then he comes on another member of "Academia," one described in the following terms (102):

> O quien pudiera hablar del caballero que se metió *en sacris,* subiéndose al prefacio; mas un corrimiento obliga a lo que el hombre no piensa. No puedo con esto cubrir, que, si bien era *hombre de mal pelo,* no dejaba que nadie le pusiese el pie delante, siendo *un desatado en las escaramuzas* y, como en pintar, fiero en la batalla; y confieso que hasta entonces no había visto pelear esqueletos, ni imaginaba que la Poesía tuviese sobrehueso de tanto provecho; y mirando su armadura, vi en ella estos versos:
>
> No soy profundo; bien sé
> que me podrás vadear,
> sin que te pueda faltar
> por más de una legua, pie.
>
> Murió en esta batalla un valiente campeón Andazul o Andaluz, y a éste dieron luego honrada sepultura; y en ella se leía *esta prosa:* "Aquí yace el desfigurado, de quien se persuaden los entendidos que no echase de ver su muerte, pues nunca supo si estaba vivo."

Here, as in Corral's *vejamen,* is reference to a skirmish (possibly "las lanzas") in which this skeleton of a man, this valiant Andalusian champion, had fought furiously, if unsuccesfully. He was one who was "*in sacris,*" had reached the "preface": [i.e., he was now in the Palace as doorkeeper to the king himself?]. Camerino recalls Baltasar del Alcázar's famous conceit which had apparently crystallized by this time into the form, "porque un consonante

---

was written after April when Vélez was made *valet de chambre* to the king: "se metió en sacris, subiéndose al prefacio".

obliga a lo que el hombre no piensa." [25] Thus Camerino must be equating "un corrimiento" with Corral's "un flujo": "se había desainado de consonantes y padecía flujo de sonetos y cólico de romances." Both Corral's and Camerino's allusions presumably allude, as well, to the fact that this quotation was one that served Vélez frequently as a crutch when he found it difficult to find his rhyme. The author had not previously realized that skeletons could fight, nor that Poetry could have a splint that was so helpful. On his armour were written verses that pointed both to his emaciation and to his very great height: he was more than a league long. They gave honorable burial to this "Andazul."

Pantaleón de Ribera, of whom Camerino says, "daba a cuantos se le ponían delante golpes de ciego," has also left us, in one of his *vejámenes* of 1625, a vivid sketch of Vélez in the role of Andalusian lover. In his "Vejamen que dio a los poetas de la Academia de Madrid" [26] — one necessarily written just after Corral's and shortly before Camerino's — this reckless young man stresses not only the great height of Vélez but also his exceedingly long face:

> Dígalo el poeta, que
> según le dura la cara,
> desde las ocho a las doce
> sólo en persignarse tarda;

This caricature of a man — with face so long that it takes him from eight o'clock until twelve just to cross himself — is supplemented by four more verses that are equally revealing:

> aquel que galanteando
> la deidad de una ventana
> suele arrobarse y se eleva
> de la tierra cuatro varas.

---

[25] For the conceit, see Bonilla's edition of *El diablo cojuelo*, 106. Bonilla cites (217) Baltasar del Alcázar's "Me fuerzan los consonantes / a decir lo que no quiero" as source of Vélez's favorite expression.

[26] *Obras de Pantaleón de Ribera*, "Vexamen que dio a los poetas de la Academia de Madrid", II, 167. It is in this same *vejamen* that Tirso is mentioned. Apparently, then, Tirso was a member of the Academy in 1625. The Mercedarian, like Pantaleón, paints Lauro as having a very strange face. See below, pp. 254 and 264.

Here is Luis Vélez in the role of ardent Andalusian lover. He is standing before the balcony of his deity, so tall that he rises up some thirteen feet as he ecstatically pays court to her in a veritable state of levitation. And, that Vélez was, at this time, courting doña María López de Palacios is highly probable. She must be the "gavioneta" whom Corral would recommend in his *vejamen* as part of his prescription for Lauro's cure.

That Corral was well acquainted with the course of Lauro's love affairs is made evident in his *La Cintia de Aranjuez.* "Elisa (i.e., doña María López de Palacios) finally accepted Lauro's hand and was united in marriage with him at the same time that her mistress, Cintia (evidently a Guzmán) was given to Fileno (of the house of Alba). "Lauro" wrote for the occasion a very long, very gongoristic marriage hymn, one which Corral printed in his *La Cintia de Aranjuez.* [27] Now Vélez's marriage to her is known to have taken place in November of 1626, but, as is evident from Corral's and Pantaleón de Ribera's *vejámenes,* he was playing the gallant as early as March of 1625 to some lady. And the fact that María López de Palacios was a widow of some means [28] who could help support the ever improvident Vélez fits in well with Corral's prescription of "una gavioneta, tan cortés y comedida que le quiera *y no le pida.*" La Barrera y Leirado, in his *Catálogo,* [29] quotes Joaquín M. de Ferrer as saying in his edition of the *Diablo Cojuelo* (1828): "fue [Vélez] excesivamente apasionado al bello sexo, pasión que ni la edad ni las enfermedades pudieron corregir en él." I do not know the basis of Ferrer's conclusions, but these *vejámenes* of 1625 attest its accuracy. Quevedo's "A Luis Vélez de Guevara," [30] fashioned on Marcial's epigram "Ad pannicum" (Lib. 6, epig. LXVI), also stresses this same weakness of the Andalusian.

---

[27] *La Cintia de Aranjuez,* 363-386.

[28] *Ibid.,* "Epigrama 50, de Elisa" (63-64), indicates that she was a widow: "Hazaña de hado inclemente / fue quitarla su marido / a Elisa; a quien como Dido / lloró atortoladamente. / Mas aunque el dolor fue tanto, / ya se entretiene y pasea; / ninguna cosa se orea / más fácilmente que el llanto".

[29] La Barrera y Leirado, *Catálogo,* 464.

[30] Quevedo, *Obras en verso,* 145.

There is yet another poem of this same time which seemingly refers to Luis Vélez. José Alfay included it in his anthology of 1654, one entitled *Poesías varias de grandes ingenios españoles,* [31] where he attributed it to Luis Vélez himself. This *romance, entitled* "A un hombre muy flaco", begins:

> Dígasme, tú, el esqueleto,
>   que haces la vida estatua,
>   hombre que al hambre pareces,
>   ¿a dónde te acaba el alma?
> El que de estoque de hueso
>   a linfarreta se pasa;
>   ¿a dónde tiene las tripas
>   quien nunca tuvo quijadas?
> El que es *caballete en pena,*
>   el que es pespunte de tabas,
>   longaniza de sepulcros,
>   y jeringa de fantasmas;
> El que es tu mismo cuerpo,
>   sombra de capa y espada,
>   sobre su conciencia vivo,
>   muerto sobre su palabra;
> El que fue dardo y virote
>   en la pérdida de España,
>   ¿qué hace de lo que bebe?
>   ¿dónde esconde lo que masca?

Of the skeleton, to whom these questions are addressed, the author states:

> Levantóse la estantigua,
>   que de un capullo de bragas
>   era gusano de tumba
>   que parce miquis hilaba,
> y enhebrando por las venas
>   en una aguja la [sic] habla,
>   con gárgaras de finado,
>   dio tal respuesta; escuchadla:
> "Asador soy de mí mismo
>   con tan poca carne humana
>   que traer puedo entre muelas
>   la pulga más ermitaña.
> Tan en ayunas los huesos

---

[31] José Alfay, *Poesías varias de grandes ingenios,* 121-22.

están de toda vianda
que soy vigilia perpetua
del sabañón y la sarna.
Tan buïdo soy de mío
que cuando salgo de casa
por notomía de esgrima
la zapatilla me zampan.
Zancarrón fui de Mahoma [32]
más de catorce semanas
y por flaco en demasía
me juraron de almarada.
Azote soy de cochero
para servir a las damas
y hombre, al fin, de pergamino
que con goma me embalsaman.
Porque el viento no me lleve
cuando se mueve, me amarran;
ten, caminante, el resuello,
que darás conmigo en Jauja."

This ghoulish sketch, made up of one long list of macabre epithets, is, I believe, a caricature of Vélez, but it can hardly have been drawn by him. The Andalusian was not given to self-depreciation. True, he likened himself on one occasion to Calatrava's pennant, "por lo luengo," [33] but he would never have handed to his merciless enemies — and precisely at a time when he was wooing doña María López de Palacios — any such string of repulsive metaphors as those found in this poem: "estoque de hueso," "caballete en pena," "pespunte de tabas," "longaniza de sepulcros," "jeringa de fantasmas," "dardo y virote," "estantigua," "gusano de tumba," "asador," "vigilia perpetua del sabañón y la sarna," "notomía de esgrima," "azote de cochero," "hombre de pergamino." These were coined by an enemy, a savage one whose taste leaves much to be desired. Not only does he satirize Vélez's emaciation, his great height, and his age, "el que fue dardo y

---

[32] For a note on "zancarrón de Mahoma", see Fernando de la Granja's "Milagros españoles en una obra polémica musulmana", *Al-Andalus*, XXXIII (1968), 341-46. Lope de Vega, in *Los esclavos libres* (III, 431-32), uses the legend.

[33] "Memorial de Luis Vélez de Guevara" (ms. 3797 of the B.N., ff. 253-56). The poem was written when Philip was planning to go to Zaragoza in early 1626.

virote / en la pérdida de España", but he suggests that behind Vélez's skeleton-like condition lay sheer hunger. He is a "whip-like lover" at the service of the ladies, at the very same time that he is a man of parchment ready for embalming. The emphasis on different sharp weapons (actually mentioned or implied) recalls Gabriel de Corral's phrase, "en faltándole lanza, daba los botes consigo mismo." Corral's metaphors "esqueleto de pergamino," and "fístula de jeringa," have also been carried over into this satire, fair proof that it was written around the same time as Corral's.

There remains one other caricature of Luis Vélez, done in this same year of 1625. Found in Castillo Solórzano's *Donayres del Parnaso, Parte Segunda,* (Madrid, 1625), [34] it is a rhymed poem, originally of 84 lines, entitled "A un poeta muy flaco y viejo, aconsejándole que se muera"; as subtitle, it carries the phrase, "romance en consonantes." The poem was necessarily written before April 12, 1625, by which time this book of Castillo Solórzano's was receiving its *erratas.* That it was penned in the same days as the *vejámenes* of Corral and Camerino is evident from its content, for it makes clear allusion to Vélez's unfortunate role in a tourney of the day that had taken place, we remember, just before Corral's *vejamen* was given on March 1, 1625 (*pocos días ha*). This rhymed attack, which in today's idiom, tells the thin old poet to "drop dead," begins as follows:

> A ti, el hombre más sutil
> que aguja de hacer filete;
> con más pliegues en la cara
> que de un obispo el roquete;
> A ti que traes el juicio
> puesto siempre al escudete
> porque no quiere estar fijo
> en barrenado casquete ...
> A ti que tienes el casco
> más débil que su copete,
> siendo veleta en la tierra,
> siendo en el mar gallardete;

---

[34] See Pérez Pastor, *Bibliografía madrileña,* III, 259.

A ti que atruenas hablando [35]
más que alemán pistolete
más que pieza de batir,
que trabuco o morterete:
Otro poeta de bien
que nunca ha puesto bonete
por hacerte algún favor
te escribe aqueste billete.

The satirist presents us the vivid portrait of a man thinner than
a needle, one with more wrinkles in his face than are to be found
in a bishop's rochet. The poet's poor brain is a mere patch, flutter-
ing about in the open spaces of his skull. He wears a poor
pompadour (*copete*). Because of his height and his bowed
shoulders, he reminds the satirist of a weather-vane on land or a
slender pennant at sea. [One recalls Vélez's somewhat later
description of himself as a pennant of Calatrava "por lo luengo."]

In other verses, the author of this satire taunts this thin old
poet with his poor intellect: "Que no debe ya vivir / un ingenio
tan pobrete, / que es la fábula de todos / y de la risa el sainete."
He apparently jeers at the poet's lack of courage when faced with
obstacles, at his lack of protective shell, his spiritual "softness"
"... a cualquier pequeña vaya / de cuitado se somete / por no
tener cortezón / sino miga de mollete."

Yet this old poet is a vain braggart, "a matasiete," (one
recalls Cervantes' term, "bravo"), a loud-mouthed fellow who
"thunders when he talks." He is a great gallant, decked out in his
armor, resplendent from crested-helmet to the greave that guards
his shin. Withal, he is a very poor horseman, one who should
"fall from his mount," though the satirist realizes that, with the
poet's great height, it would be as though Valencia's tower, the
Miguelete, were to come crashing down.

His reputation is on the wane: "tu fama llega ya a beber del
Lethe," an observation that suggests this poem was written before
April of 1625 when Vélez was made doorkeeper to Philip IV. It is
time he dies physically as well. The satirist goes ahead to suggest

---

[35] The four lines beginning "A ti que atruenas hablando" are omitted
in Tirso's version.

various forms of burial suitable for this very tall, thin poet: they could inter him, for instance, in the nest of a battering ram. (However humble, it was the thing that his vanity deserved!) Or they could wrap his machete-like body in an embroidered tapestry. Or if this luxury-loving poet preferred it, he might lie in a costly urn where he would be more famous than is the slice of orange or lemon (*luquete*) [36] with which wine is often flavored in southern Spain. At his death, all the poets would, no doubt, bring him from Parnassus (the Academy of Madrid?) epitaphs or satirical epigrams. Some one of them would probably lie awake at night (after downing a pastry!) to fashion for him — by way of praise — a banquet of his works. The lasses of Getafe [37] would pour from their gullets various songs to the rhythm of a love ditty. But this old poet, whose restless body could be stilled only in death, should die! "Muere, poeta caduco / porque tu cuerpo te quiete": Death, in fact, was, without remission, already preparing her butcher's scythe: "que sin remisión la Parca ha tocado ya a jarrete."

Mixed in with the many lines that deal with Vélez's physique are a few having to do with him in his role of poet. The satirist of *A un poeta muy flaco y viejo* ... calls into question the poet's originality by indicating that a "go-between" was essential before he could write:

> Jamás invocaste musa
> sin prevención de alcahuete.

Is the satirist, on bringing this charge, referring to Vélez's open collaboration with other dramatists, or is he alluding to Vélez's unacknowledged debts to such writers as Quevedo and Lope de Vega — in a word to his lack of creative imagination? Probably to the latter. It is instructive, in this connection, to remember that

---

[36] Tirso uses the relatively unusual word "luquete" in his *El amor médico* in a scene which has Sevilla as setting (I, iii). Tello has been struck by the beauty of the "sevillanas": "¡Cuántas topo por las calles / hermosas! de tres, las dos; / de cuatro, las tres; de siete / las cuatro y media: ¡más bellas ... que el vino tras el luquete!"

[37] The four lines which mention "las zagalas de Getafe" are omitted in Tirso's *Segunda parte,* as are the eight that precede them.

Rudolf Schevill, [38] in his study of Vélez, speaks with quiet humor of Vélez's borrowing as a "peculiar kind of collaboration with an unsuspecting fellow-playwright." His debt to Lope was one which the Conde de la Roca appears to have recognized (along with Vélez's unbridled spectacularism) as early as 1635. In his *Ragguaglio di Parnaso*, he says: [39] "Tell Vélez that in the matter of his hero's swashbuckling ("rodomontadas"), he should put on the great Lope's nosebag a month before writing for the theatre."

The satirist completes the two lines quoted above — i.e., "jamás invocaste musa / sin prevención de alcahuete" — with two others: "Y sin ayuda de amigo, / jamás hiciste motete." The term "motete" can hardly be used here in its musical sense; it must be rather a diminutive of "mote," i.e., an abusive epigram. With the depreciative ending "ete," the satirist is down-grading the reputation which Vélez undoubtedly enjoyed in that direction. Certainly Vélez wrote *motes*, which J. Pellicer [40] would call "agudos ... dichos."

There are yet other lines that clearly refer to Vélez as a poet, lines that are, however, not very clear:

> A ti relevante en prosa
> como tabla de bufete
> que daña su munición,
> más que la de algún mosquete.

Just what the satirist means when he describes the poet as "relevante en prosa como tabla de bufete, [41] is somewhat ambiguous.

---

[38] Spencer and Schevill, *The Dramatic Works of Luis Vélez de Guevara*, p. xxiii.

[39] *Ragguaglio di Parnaso* del sig. Fabio Franchi, 142. The passage reads: "Et al Vellez si dica, che alle sue ingegnose Rodomontate un mese auanti di meterse nel teatro, li metta la muserola del gran Lope, ò meglio serà dirgli che huomo, che seppe far la comedia chiamata, *Errore per Amor Fortuna*, peccarà di festa *duplex* sempre che fallirà in simile mestiero".

[40] Pellicer labelled them "agudos ... dichos". See Cotarelo, *Luis Vélez de Guevara...*, IV, 168.

[41] I should like to thank here Major General William A. Harris, Retired (of San Antonio, Texas), who referred my questions about Spanish mortars of the seventeenth century to William A. Knowlton, Lieutenant General, U. S. A., Superintendent of the United States Military Academy. The latter

No definition of "relevante" found in the dictionary can apply here: the general spirit of this jingle — one long string of abusive epithets — precludes the posibility of any such meaning as "outstanding." The word was evidently associated at this time with the *cultos* and the *críticos* — as a quotation from Quiñones de Benavente's *Las dos letras* [42] will make evident. The lady of that *entremés*, clearly an enemy of gongorism, asks her suitor in reproving tones, "habláis crítico, culto, y *relevante*?" And he will answer apologetically, "It is the fashion." The reference must, then, be in part to the inflated style of the so-called *críticos*. It is possible, however, that the satirist is, as well, calling the victim's prose harsh, so harsh that it proves more destructive than the rounds of a musket. And finally he may have had in mind the

---

put the problem up to the Curator of Arms of the West Point Museum, who was kind enough to search out the following information for me:

"...there was in use in the seventeenth century a mortar-tray which more than likely consisted of oak planks nailed to a frame on which mortar shells were ... stacked. Since the act of loading a cannon was termed 'serving the piece', the analogy made by the poet was not too far-fetched. As far as we know, there were no standard dimensions or name given to this piece of equipment. The slides of the tray would have been of sufficient height to retain the first tier of cannon balls.

As to loading a mortar, this was accomplished *standing up*. In fact an elevated plank was part of the mortar-bed, located in front of the muzzle on which the cannoneer stood in order to load and clean the mortar."

This suggests to me that the mortar-tray, apparently termed "bufete" in Spain, was possibly shoulder-high. The term "relevante" then refers to the unnaturally "elevated" style of the *críticos*.

I am indebted not only to Major General W. A. Harris, to Lt. General W. A. Knowlton, Superintendent of the United States Military Academy, and to the Curator of Arms at West Point, but also to my friend of many years, Mrs. Albert Sidney Williams, who put me in touch with General Harris.

[42] See Benavente's "Entremés de las dos letras", in *Colección de ontremeses*, II, 769-73; in particular, 771.

According to a quotation cited in Andrée Collard's *Nueva poesía* (110), Trillo y Figueroa, a *gongorino*, uses the term *relevante* when insisting that "el estilo [de una poesía] no sea llano ni común sino el más *relevante* y dificultoso, la frase menos usada, las voces las más pomposas, significativas y producidoras de menos común concepto". (Quoted from Trillo y Figueroa, *Obras*, 429-33.) When dealing earlier with this same question of poetic style, Collard (104) quotes Gracián as saying that Carrillo y Sotomayor "anunció a Góngora 'especialmente en su *Polifemo y Soledades*' por el 'estilo aliñado que tiene más de ingenio que de juicio, atiende más la frase *relevante*, el modo de decir florido'". Collard cites *Agudeza y arte de ingenio* (LXII, 510), included in Gracián's *Obras completas* (Madrid, 1960).

satirical qualities of this poet's work. All three charges would, in Vélez's case, have hit the mark.

Yet Vélez was, in his later years, more at home in prose than he was in poetry. His plays, particularly those written after 1621, often sin badly with their very gongoristic [43] language, which at times is harsh indeed. The truth is that Vélez, particularly in his later years, found the tyranny of rhyme more and more annoying. Gabriel de Corral, as we have seen, indicated this in having Apollo recommend that he "abstain from poetry." Vélez himself, will, around 1637-1638, make it even clearer. In a *vejamen* yet in manuscript, entitled "Juicio final de todos los poetas españoles vivos y muertos," one done in 1638 that is seemingly at present unknown to the critical world, the author [44] (Vélez himself probably) declares that he is sick as a result of what he calls "consonante lluvio." The picture we get is of an emaciated, bent-over figure who is tired of searching for rhymes for his *ovillejos*:

> En esto, entró, cayéndose de su estado, un poeta muy flaco, enfermo de consonante lluvio, que se iba de ovillejos como una canilla. Mandó Apolo que le diesen para los ovillejos conserva de Faraón, que es más dura que carne de membrillo, y que le restañen el consonante lluvio, me-

---

[43] Spencer and Schevill tended to separate Vélez's early plays from his later ones by their language. Of *La niña de Gómez Arias* they remark (*The Dramatic Works of Luis Vélez de Guevara*, 71): "Our play is in Vélez's early vein; it is relatively free from all traces of *culto*...". Of *Juliano Apóstata* their comment is (186): "From the language and technique, this play may be considered one of Vélez's later compositions. It has many ornate and *culto* traits...". Such partial studies of Vélez's versification as Prof. Carlos Félix (a former student of mine) has made tend to justify the norm. *Más pesa el rey que la sangre* (with such a gongoristic passage as that found in III, 1) has the following percentages: red. (19.6 %), dec. (4.9 %), rom. (68.6 %), silva I (3.7 %), oct. (3.2 %); and its three acts end in *romances*. *Los hijos de la Barbuda* (in print by 1612) has: red. (44.1 %), quint. (11.3 %), rom. (26.9 %), oct. (2.1 %), son. (5 %), terc. (6 %), suelt. (9.1 %). Its acts end in *rom.*, red., rom. The *silva I* has, in *Más pesa el rey*, replaced the *sueltos* of *Los hijos de la Barbuda*; we have 68.6 % of *romances* versus 26.9 % ; 4.9 of *décimas* vs. 11.3 % *quintillas*, etc.

I should like to thank Prof. Félix for his permission to cite their percentages. We need badly a complete study of Vélez's versification.

[44] It is found in the Lisbon library, and is, in my opinion, the work of Vélez himself. Prof. Hannah Bergman and I have transcribed the *Juicio final* and have studied it at some length.

tiéndole en la boca a San Bruno, que fundó la religión de el silencio, y que le acerasen y almacigasen las sílabas como el agua *y que comiese prosa esta cuaresma* y que él se juzgase cuando estuviese con salud.

The allusion to his *consonantes* makes clear that he found it increasingly difficult to write poetry. This is even clearer from his presidential address to the Academy in the preceding year. On that occasion, when he spoke in prose, he excused himself for so doing by saying that he had already sweated enough blood, what with the four hundred *comedias* he had written in verse: [45] "¿Qué pensarán vuesas mercedes que el Señor Presidente había de hacer en la Academia? ... ¿una oración *donde sudase consonantes de sangre?* Hartos he sudado en 400 comedias que he hecho..." In the *vejamen* quoted above, it is the suggestion, probably of Vélez himself, who is admittedly ill from a constant flow of rhymes, that they not only close tight his mouth with a San Bruno (San Bruno who had established the Carthusian order of silence) but that he *eat prose not poetry* that Lenten season. What is more, it is significant that Vélez chose to end his literary career with a satirical work *in prose, El diablo cojuelo,* a work which has brought him more fame than all his comedias together. [46] And there he would allude once more to Alcázar's famous lines: among the *ordenanas y premáticas* for the *vejamen,* given in Sevilla, was one that forbade poets from excusing themselves by saying, "porque un consonante obliga / a lo que el hombre no piensa." [47]

And finally it should never be forgotten that Vélez was before everything else a satirist, a fact that his contemporaries knew only too well. Rojas Zorrilla, [48] in the *vejamen* of 1638, said of

---

[45] See Cotarelo, *Luis Vélez de Guevara y sus obras dramáticas,* IV, 160.

[46] We should know more of Vélez's dramatic works, if for no other reason than to try to decide whether or not *La Estrella de Sevilla* is his play. At his all-too-infrequent best — for instance, in *Reinar después de morir* — he has produced one of the really moving *comedias* of the Golden Age; at his worst, he can be very bad indeed. Prof. William Whitby was working on a study of Vélez's works, but I believe he has abandoned the project. I have lately heard that Prof. Vern Williamsen will take it over.

[47] See *El diablo cojuelo,* 105. It is found also in *El juicio final,* referred to on p. 292.

[48] Quoted from Cotarelo, *Luis Vélez de Guevara y sus obras dramáticas,* IV, 161.

the Andalusian dramatist: "Luis Vélez no se daba lenguas a decir mal de todos, y todos no se daban palabras a decir mal de Luis Vélez." Cotarelo, his biographer, speaks of "la propensión ingénita de Vélez … a la sátira" and at one point he bluntly calls him (158) "maldiciente." I am inclined to think, therefore, that the author of "A un poeta muy flaco y viejo aconsejándole que se muera" was referring primarily to the keen edge of Vélez's satire which could "hurt its victim more than a round from a musket."

Indeed, Vélez prided himself on his satirical vein which he probably termed "donaire nativo." [49] In an unpublished *mojiganga* of 1638 that he apparently wrote, one which lies hidden away in the National Library of Lisbon, we find this dialogue between two of the maids-of-honor, Luisa Enríquez and one "Luisa María" whose last name isn't given:

> El Vélez volvióse atrás,
> y fueron sus chistes buenos.

To this Luisa Enríquez makes answer:

> Grande ingenio es; nadie llega
> a su donaire nativo,
> pero el chiste es tan esquivo
> que pocas veces allega.

This poem, "A un poeta muy flaco y viejo, aconsejándole que se muera" — with its subtitle, *romance en consonantes* — puzzles by its unusual metrical form, one to which the satirist himself would seem to be calling attention when he carefully labels it "*romance en consonantes*." By very definition, the "romance" has not "consonance" (i.e., rhyme of all consonants *and* vowels, beginning with the last-accented syllable) but instead "assonance," rhyme of vowels *only*. Moreover, the satirist is seemingly putting his victim on the alert as to the significance of this poem: in writing it (the satirist says), he is doing him a favor, a courtesy, one that the poet should note:

---

[49] Quoted from a photostat of the *mojiganga*. Dr. Hannah Bergman has made an excellent study of it in "A Court of Entertainment of 1638." *HR*, XLII (1974), 67-81. I am personally of the opinion that Vélez himself wrote it.

> Estima esta cortesía
> para ponerla en membrete.

Evidently he fears that his human target is so dull-witted (at least in matters of metrical skill) that the point of the poem will escape him unless he warns him in advance:

> Aunque teme de tu ingenio
> que sus versos no interprete.

What is it that the satirist is afraid this dullard will overlook?

In a poem comprising 84 verses, 42 of the words end in *ete: filete, roquete, escudete, casquete,* etc., on to *jarrete.* Now the ending *ete,* even though it is a diminutive which is normally depreciative, is not used so frequently as to make it a particularly easy one for which to find a rhyme. Moreover, I know of only a few other *romances en consonantes,* all of them of Torres Naharro's day. [50] It is as if the satirist were trying to demonstrate his own facility in finding rhymes (i.e., *consonantes*) to a Vélez "que se había desainado de consonantes."

For this portrait, it seems to me, must be one of Luis Vélez de Guevara, confirmed as it is by those of his contemporaries and/ or by the verdict of time itself: a Vélez who was so tall as to bring to mind Valencia's tower of the Miguelete; a Vélez who, with his relatively broad shoulders and his thin body, recalled a pennant at sea, one so wrinkled of face as to suggest a bishop's rochet; a Vélez so vain and so romantic that at his advanced age he had entered a tourney, only to fall ingloriously; a Vélez who loved spectacle and show; a Vélez who was so lacking in creative talent that he could summon his muse only with the help of others, could finish an abusive quip only if a friend came to his aid; a Vélez who was given to a gongoristic vocabulary, whose prose was so *culto* and so edged its satire that it did more damage than so many rounds of a musket.

---

[50] See Joseph E. Gillet, *Propalladia and Other Works of Bartolomé de Torres Naharro.* See I, 216-222, 224-227, etc. These *romances,* however, are all formed with past participles. I am indebted to Prof. Otis Green for this reference.

Who was expressing such derogatory opinions of Luis Vélez de Guevara in early 1625? The answer is not easy. This poem, first printed in the *Segunda parte* of Castillo Solórzano's *Donayres del Parnaso* (Madrid, 1625), was reprinted some ten years later in Tirso's *Segunda parte*[51] (Madrid, 1635). Now this latter volume, which went to press by November 20, 1634, is, like the *Donayres,* something of an anthology, one which comprises: twelve plays (only four of them Tirso's); twelve *entremeses,* including eleven that are presumably of Quiñones de Benavente and one of Quevedo; nine poems, all composed probably by members of the *Academia de Madrid.* This *sátira* against Vélez de Guevara is first among the poems there printed; the second and ninth are Pantaleón de Ribera's; the third is Castillo Solórzano's.[52] All nine had in 1625 been included among the "donayres" that go to make up Castillo Solórzano's *Segunda parte.* Yet variants make evident that the compositor of Tirso's *Segunda parte* did not use the *Donayres del Parnaso* as a copy-text; instead he must have worked from a manuscript, as had the printer of the *princeps* — a less accurate one, it would appear, than the one given the type-setter of the *Donayres.*

So there can be no assurance that this satirical poem, "A un poeta muy flaco y viejo ... " is Tirso's. In fact, when one remembers that this dramatist was a Mercedarian priest, one is hard put to it to explain the following lines found in it:

> Otro poeta de bien,
> que nunca ha puesto *bonete,*
> por hacerte algún favor,
> te escribe aqueste billete.

---

[51] This volume is a *rompecabezas,* as every student of Tirso knows. Let me insist once again that, in view of what we now know concerning the authorship of *La adversa fortuna* and *La reina de los reyes,* I can see no reason why we should question the truthfulness of Tirso's statement that only four of the plays are his works. I likewise can see no earthly reason for assuming that Tirso wrote any of his plays in collaboration with other dramatists. I have in press a long study on the two don Álvaro plays. For another on *Cautela contra cautela,* see *RABM,* LXXV, 1-2 (1968-1972), 325-353. All three of these plays are included in the *Segunda parte.*

[52] See my study, "Pantaleón de Ribera, 'Sirene', Castillo y Solórzano, and the *Academia de Madrid* in Early 1625", 189-200.

For the dramatist *was* a priest who, therefore, wore the biretta, ordinarily called *bonete*.

What is more, on reworking *Antona García* in 1625 [53] — shortly after this satire of "A un poeta muy flaco y viejo ... " was written — Tirso, we remember, declared roundly (III, iii), when asked if he wrote satires, "No se hallará quien presuma / de mí que muerda mi pluma / a nadie ... ," a statement that one finds difficult to equate with the facts. For Tirso had not only filled his *Cigarrales* of 1624 with satirical darts against Madrid's literati and their warring camps, but he had directed a broadside, specifically against Vélez de Guevara, in his *La fingida Arcadia* of 1622. There is every reason to think that the Mercedarian knew the Andalusian very well indeed by early 1625; and, of all the satirical poems written in that year, this poem is the most inclusive, the one which best probes Vélez's weaknesses. Yet again, many of the very shortcomings to which it points are the same as those Tirso has satirized in works undoubtedly his. [54] However, Tirso probably was acquainted with this poem by 1626, [55] and it could have served as source to some of the satire of similar nature found in his works.

Above all, this poem is, both in its satirical aim and the technical skill with which it is carried out, quite in keeping with Tirso's temperament and talents. If I have interpreted aright the spirit in which it was composed, then no vengeance could have been sweeter to a satirically-minded Tirso than to show a literary enemy, one "que se había desainado de consonantes," just how easy it was to find rhymes. No effort at all, says Tirso for the *real* poet! Nor would it have been for a Gabriel Téllez! Though the poem is a *tour de force*, one which required no little skill, even with a Rengifo at hand, the Mercedarian had such complete command of his poetic medium that it would have required a minimum of time for him to dash off "A un poeta muy flaco y viejo ..."

---

[53] See pp. 99-104.

[54] For instance, the statement: "Y sin ayuda de amigo, / jamás hiciste motete".

[55] Either Castillo Solórzano or Gabriel de Corral, both friends of his and both in the *Academia de Madrid*, could have given it to him when he went to Madrid in early 1626 — or even sent it to him in Toledo.

One has only to analyse the plan of the *justa literaria*, [56] which
was organized in Salamanca to celebrate the canonization of Pedro Nolasco in 1629, in order to realize that the dramatist was
extremely proud of his metrical skill as a poet. Tirso it was who
set the conditions for a "romance heroico," one which — while
arguing in eleven-syllable lines the question as to whether France
had done more for Spain in giving her Pedro Nolasco, or whether
Spain had made the greater contribution by giving Santo Domingo to France — should at the same time, incrust in it shorter lines
glorifying the life and deeds of don Jaime I of Aragon! The
dramatist presented a quite long poem that did just this! So
proud was he of his "versos cercenados" that he challenged other
poets to try *their* hands at this very difficult feat: "... examínele la
curiosidad ya bien intencionada, ya escrupulosa; quítele las sílabas que le desnaturalicen de Castilla, y si les pareciere fácil, agora
que les ha enseñado [el poeta] el camino, responda por su autor
el huevo de Juanelo."

This "egg of two yolks," as Tirso at one point terms it, had,
by way of background, other "eggs" that he had fashioned for
plays that were written earlier than was this strange poem. In
Amor y celos hacen discretos, [57] the Duquesa confounds don Pedro
by including "a sonnet in redondillas" (i.e., one of eight-syllable
lines) in one of the normal eleven-syllable verses. The Italian sonnet leads him to the false conclusion that she is in love with
Carlos, but don Pedro, Spanish secretary to this Italian, should
have had the wit to find the real truth, hidden though it was in
the Spanish sonnet of short verses: so argues the Duquesa. These
verses "en circunferencia," as Tirso here labels them, would, in
Quien calla, otorga (III, xvi, 107), take on somewhat different
form. In this latter play, Rodrigo gives Aurora what appears to
be a single poem of twelve-syllable verse; but it is one which
can be divided into two separate and complete poems of six-

---

[56] See *Deleytar aprovechando* (1635), 325v.

[57] See III, vii. This play was written before Tirso went to Santo Domingo
but was reworked in the 1620's. Romero, the *gracioso*'s name, suggests that
the role was taken by Bartolomé Romero, and the first mention we find
of him was in 1622-1623, when he was in Avendaño's company. In 1624
he was in El Valenciano's. The satire on gongorism (I, v) and on Alarcón,
as well as other details, suggest it was retouched around 1622-24.

syllables each. The poem has, therefore, three different meanings, according to whether one reads it as a whole, or whether one takes the meaning of the first half or the second half. In *Amar por arte mayor*, [58] Tirso will set himself an even more difficult task. For this late play, Tirso has used as the crux of his plot a love poem in *arte mayor* which is so fashioned as to have a different meaning for each of the three ladies who will read it. One reaches the inner meaning only by removing *two* surrounding layers of verse! Thus Tirso was not only capable of doing metrical stunts but he was reverting to a past when the twelve- and the fourteen-syllable lines were in vogue — just as the poet wrote "A un poeta muy flaco y viejo ..." had presumably been studying the metrics of Torres Naharro's day before fashioning his *romance en conso-nantes*.

In favor of Tirso's authorship is yet another fact. Of all the poems found in his *Segunda parte*, this *sátira* is the only one of the nine that suffered real alteration: Tirso retained, of the 84 verses which Castillo Solórzano had printed in his *Donayres*, only 72 on reprinting it in his *parte*. Such a fact could have origin in his willingness to cut a work of his own, and his hesitancy to alter poems belonging to others.

Finally, the salutatory "A ti," with which the first four stanzas of this poem start, was used by Tirso [59] in the prologues to both the *Cuarta parte* (1635) and the *Quinta*. In the highly satirical *dedicatoria* to the latter *parte*, addressed to "A ti sólo," he mocks (in the plural while thinking in the singular) "unos bobarrones, cicateros del gracejo" who have stolen from the printed prose of "el sazonado, discreto y leído don Francisco de Quevedo," the wit evidenced by "los parásitos de sus comedias ..." Tirso's contempt for this poet's abysmal ignorance of Latin knows no bounds. In

---

[58] The play was written or rewritten, in 1626-29. See pp. 269-75. Because of its setting (Oviedo and León), Sra. de los Ríos argued for 1635 (*Obras dra-máticas completas de Tirso*, III, 1163-1166). I shall return to the question of its date at an early moment.

[59] See Cotarelo, *Comedias de Tirso de Molina*, I, lxv-lxviii. Pantaleón de Ribera (*Obras*, I, 239-240), in a *madrigal*, "A don Juan de Vidarte", started each strophe with "A ti". I have not been able to date the composition of the poem. The first edition of Ribera's works was printed in 1631 so that Tirso could have known the poem in print.

fact, the man doesn't even know his mother-tongue well enough to realize that *ceática* is *esdrújulo*! As we shall hope to prove later, this *dedicatoria* is addressed to Vélez de Guevara. However, the long poem of 1625, "A un poeta flaco y viejo," — with its four "A ti's" in a row — was very probably known to Tirso, even if it should not have been his, by 1626, and it was sent to the printer of his *Segunda parte* by November 20, 1634. The "A ti" may, then, have been repeated in the *Quinta parte*, precisely because both poem and *dedicatoria* were addressed to the same person.

Even if Tirso should not have been the author of this *sátira*, it is a fair assumption that some one gave it to him [60] precisely because he knew that Tirso would recognize the subject and be in hearty accord with the poem's content. And since our dramatist sent it to press and even placed it first among the nine that are found in the *Segunda parte*, it is reasonable to believe that he included it there for the express purpose of bringing again to the attention of the reading public this satire against his enemy. By 1635, the poem had probably been almost forgotten, *and Tirso wanted it to live.*

If "A un poeta muy flaco y viejo ..." should be Tirso's — and in the case of a poem that departs so far from the normal, I find it impossible to reach any definite decision as to its authenticity among his poems — then one should note the change in tone between this satire and that found in *La fingida Arcadia* of 1622. When penning the play, Tirso wrote with brilliant literary malice, but always in high good humor. The poet of this satire has, on the other hand, slashed away with bitter abandon, as though moved by deep, dark anger. If Tirso's it should be, what had brought it about the change?

---

[69] See pp. 233-246, above.

VI

TIRSO AND THE "CORPULENT" POET

Tirso has, on three occasions, lashed out at a "corpulent" poet:
in his miscellany, *Los cigarrales de Toledo;* in his religious novel,
El bandolero; and in a Biblical play called *Tanto es lo de más
como lo de menos.* The satire of all three — of ever increasing
intensity — is, we believe, directed against Luis Vélez de Guevara. In establishing the identity of the "corpulent" poet, we shall
need to keep in mind three things: Tirso's attack on this Andalusian in *La fingida Arcadia;* the various portraits of Luis Vélez
(most of them drawn in 1625) which we have studied in connection
with a poem published in Tirso's *Segunda parte,* i.e., "A un poeta,
muy viejo y flaco ... que se muera"; the special meaning that Tirso chose to give the word "corpulento" in a play of 1625-1626.

The satire found in *Los cigarrales de Toledo*[1] occurs in connection with the discussion of a matter which López Pinciano[2]
had barely touched upon under the heading of "verisimilitude of
time," i.e., the question of anachronistic details of dialogue. When
talking of the reception first accorded his own play, *Como han de
ser los amigos,* Tirso mocks those who write "impropriedades tan
indigestas que ... provocan a silbos y a vituperios," and by way
of concrete example, he points to the case of a "corpulent" dramatist:

> Yo conozco uno de los más corpulentos y no de los
> más dignos, que en una comedia, sacada de un *Flos*

---

[1] *Los cigarrales de Toledo,* II, 205.
[2] López Pinciano, *Filosofía antigua poética,* p. 214.

sanctorum, en romance, — cuyo argumento fue la vida de uno de los jueces de Israel — se dejó decir, entre ciertas promesas que el gracioso hacía a no sé quién, 'que le traería el turbante del gran Sofí.' ¡Mirad qué gentil necedad [scoffs Tirso]: profetizar un pastor los Sofíes que vinieron a Persia más de mil años después del nacimiento de Cristo!

Don Vela then asks — with scant regard for the footlings — "¿Tragaría el vulgo ... con todo el aplauso y risa imaginable la turbantada que le dio el poetón?" Don Melchor,[3] equally scornful of both poet and *vulgo*, comments: "Como esas zarandajas caben en el buche ... de la ballena plebeya, llaman a la Tarasca "tragacaperuzas"; y ¿no queréis vos que el poblacho trague turbantes?" Don García closes the discussion with the remark: "¡Yo se lo colgara, después de muerto [él], ... sobre su tumba, como capelo de cardenal, graduándole de presumido, no con borla, pero con borlas!"

Tirso is clearly satirizing a fellow-dramatist (not one of the best) whom he terms first "corpulento," then later "poetón." This dramatist's very "indigestible improprieties" had occasioned catcalls in the case of a *comedia* dealing with one of the judges of Israel,[4] one whose plot he had taken from a *Flos sanctorum* "en romance," probably Villegas Selvago's.[5] The particular "impro-

----

[3] As to the identity of "don Melchor", see my study, "Tirso's *No hay peor sordo*: its Date and Place of Composition", 15-16, ns. 26 and 27; also above, p. 113, n. 70.

[4] The more important judges of Israel were: Deborah, with Barak, Gideon, Abimelech, Jepthah, Samson. Less important ones were Othniel, Ehud, Shamgar, Tola, Jair, Ibzan, Elon, Abdon. I know of no play of Vélez's in existence today to which Tirso could be referring, but if Vélez wrote "more than 400", as he claimed, then we have today only a small percentage of his plays. J. C. J. Metford apparently leans to the idea that the "corpulent" poet was Mira de Amescua — partly because he accepts Cotarelo's interpretation of Lope de Vega's reference in *El jardín de Apolo* as one indicating that Mira was of great bulk and partly because Mira was author of *La hija de Jepté*. See Metford's "Tirso de Molina and the Conde-Duque de Olivares", 26-27. I have sought to show, in a study now ready for press, that Cotarelo misinterpreted Lope's allusion.

[5] Whether this is one of his first volumes or whether it is one of the so-called "Extravagantes", it is not easy to say. Tirso has mentioned three times the *Flos sanctorum* of Villegas: in *La villana de Vallecas* (I, i), *El celoso prudente* (II, iv), and *Privar contra su gusto* (III, xiii). All are plays written

priety" that Tirso recalls was the promise that the "gracioso" (apparently a shepherd) had made someone to bring him the turban of the great Sufi, this although the Sufies did not reach Persia until more than a thousand years after the birth of Christ! Such a colossal error should live with the dramatist the rest of his life; should, in fact, be recorded on his tomb, proclaiming him, not a cardinal with *one tassel*, but a conceited fool with the *three* that characterized the court jester's cap. The listeners, on hearing of this "turbantada" are sure that the mob can swallow a "turban" quite as well as the Tarasca does "caperuzas." This dramatist's humor, it would seem, was directed toward the pit.

In *El bandolero*, [6] the life of Pedro Armengol, a young herdsman of inborn poetic talent, named Pedro Guillén, has just finished reading his long poem, *Píramo y Tisbe*, to a mixed audience. Thereupon, the listeners comment on the story's improbabilities. Why on earth, asks the shepherd Lorino, didn't the lovers use a few grains of common sense, and instead of wandering off into the woods and getting themselves killed, why did they not make use of the vicariate (*vicario*)? When it is pointed out to him that Pyramus and Thisbe were citizens of *pagan Babylonia, not of Christian Spain, and that* there was, accordingly, no vicariate, Lorino asks how was he to know whether the lovers were "cristianos" or "críticos." In substituting "críticos" for "paganos" and in juxtaposing it to "cristianos," Tirso not only calls the "críticos" heretical — "hablar en cristiano" even today means "hablar claro" — but creates for himself the opportunity to satirize again a "corpulent" poet:

> Yo he visto representar comedia de un poeta, *cuya corpulenta fama*, a poder de consonantes *arménicos*, nos

---

or rewritten in 1620-1621. In the last-mentioned play, he comments unfavorably on Villegas' *Extravagantes*. I have not been able to see a copy of the *Extravagantes*.

[6] *El bandolero*, 80. In identifying the *críticos* with the heretical, Tirso is possibly labelling them "extranjeros" (from a province other than Castile?), but I should doubt there were any religious overtones in his remark. See Andrés Collard, *Nueva poesía: conceptismo, culteranismo en la crítica española*, especially 43-51; when dealing in a later volume of this series with Tirso and Góngora, I shall consider the Mercedarian's use of such terms as *crítico, culterano, gongorino*, etc.

echa pullas, en que cuando le daba no sé que mensajero
cierta mala nueva a un rey moro, dijo, santiguándose —
'Válgame Jesu Cristo!, ¿Que eso pasá?'

Tirso recalls yet another inverosimilitude on this dramatist's part:
"Y, en otra, pintó a Caín, martirizando a Abel porque, en el
juego de los naipes, le quitó una primera con cincuenta y cinco
de copas."

Let us take up in reverse order the two complaints of Tirso
found in *El bandolero*. He points to a play wherein Cain is
quarreling with his brother, Abel, because the latter has taken
from him "una primera con cincuenta y cinco de copas." Here
again it is a dramatist who commits "gross anachronisms": he
has introduced a game of "primera" into a *comedia* whose setting
is placed in the dawn of time. Clearly this dramatist knew something of cards, clearly he stresses his comic roles. He is, apparently,
a "crítico" who has penned some "Armenian" verses (schismatic
ones?) in which he has satirized Tirso ("nos echa pullas").

In the case of the anachronism of *El bandolero* which Tirso
cites first, it is again a question of a "corpulent" poet who is
given to inverosimilitudes of time and language, to "indigestible
improprieties." This particular play is one of a Moorish king
(naturally a Mohammedan) who swears by Jesus Christ and cros-
ses himself as piously as any Christian ruler.

This last reference may be to Luis Vélez's *El negro del Se-
raphín*. [7] Though the manuscript of this play (No. 17317) carries
at the end a *censura*, dated February 8, 1643, that fact is, of course,
no proof that an earlier one did not exist, one that was known to
Tirso at the time he was writing *El bandolero*. [8] Unfortunately,

---

[7] Ms. no. 17317, B.N. I have seen the manuscript in photostat. It is
a revision of Lope's play, "El santo negro Rosambuco de la ciudad de Pa-
lermo", first published in Barcelona, 1611?-1612.

[8] There are many reasons for believing that the literary satire of this
play was written around 1622. Luis Carlos Viada y Lluch, in his edition
of *El bandolero* (p. xvii) states, as we have seen: "Estuvo, pues, Tirso en
Barcelona antes de 1621". Later, he declares (p. xviii): "...hay que descartar
lo de que Tirso retocó *El bandolero*, añadiéndole sus impresiones barcelonesas
(no niego que hiciese nuevos viajes) en el trienio de 1632-35". I suspect that
this novel was originally intended to find a place in the second part of the
Cigarrales that Tirso promised.

folio 16 of this manuscript has been removed and two pages have
been inserted in its place, pages which represent a revision of
changes demanded by the censor, Juan Navarro de Espinosa.
These inserted pages include precisely the negro's defense of the
monastery against some Mohammedans.

Something of *the general nature of the changes* demanded by
this censor may be seen in Act I (fol. 8): in the verses, "Y aun
sólo de referirlo / tanto horror el alma siente / que, vive Dios /
que me corro," the censor has marked out the word "Dios" and
substituted "Alá" and in the margin on the right, he has pointed
out to the dramatist: "Mirad que decís unas veces 'Dios' y otras
veces 'Alá'." In the first act, the negro is still an unbeliever and
so could not logically swear by Jesus Christ. In the action of the
third one, he is a convert to Christianity and his oaths should
indicate that change. Tirso, of course, may well have had in
mind some other of the many plays of Vélez's wherein Mohammedans appear, but this manuscript at least makes evident that
the Andalusian concerned himself little with verosimilitude of
detail. Tirso is condemning just such "indigestible improprieties,"
improprieties that, in his opinion, make the conceited dramatist
worthy, not of the cardinal's hat, with its one tassel, but of the
jester's cap with its three.

As a matter of fact, Tirso's condemnation is mild by comparison
with that of one of its censors: [9]

> Una comedia hay escrita del Santo *que tiene más
> mentiras que escenas;* allí se hallan bandos fingidos, mila-
> gros falsos, travesuras indignas, rodomontadas quiméricas,
> y en fin, se halla en aquella pieza del teatro cuanto no
> hubo en toda la vida del sujeto.

The satire in this novel of the "corpulent poet" suggests that it was
written around the same general time as the passage of the *Cigarrales*, whose
outside dates are 1621-24. There are yet other things that indicate it was
done around 1622, among them the fact that Tirso apparently started his
satire of the *tramoyistas* with *La fingida Arcadia* (See pp. 201-208), which was
written in 1622. In it, satire of Vélez is linked with that of Olivares, as here.
Moreover, the setting of this novel (Cataluña) argues that it was penned
around the same general time as the last part of the *Cigarrales* and as his
plays with that setting, i. e., *El amor y el amistad* and *La firmeza en la
hermosura*, both done in 1621. See pp. 133, n. 106 and 181, n. 48.

[9] Quoted by Spencer and Schevill, op. cit., 289.

As in *La fingida Arcadia*, Tirso will, in *El bandolero*, indicate his disapproval of the *tramoyistas*. Saurina has just, conferred on Pedro Guillén a handsome piece of jewelry by way of reward for his poem on Pyramus and Thisbe. She accompanies the gift with these remarks (p. 74):

> ... quiero premiar tu fábula con esta joya, que no han de ser tan desgraciados tus versos como los de muchos que, *encarecidos y no pagados, mendigan en los teatros la censura del vulgo idiota*, expuestos a la envidia de los interesados: miserable cuanto ingeniosa profesión de un arte, princesa de las liberales, *vuelta ya mecánica*, por obligarla la pobreza de sus dueños a hacer vendible lo que les concedió el cielo gratuito.

Tirso seemingly has in mind a poor dramatist, one so poor that he must run the risk of censure from the idiotic mob because his patron is "tight-fisted." This dramatist is a "tramoyista" because spectacular plays of mechanical effect are popular with the mob; thus he puts up for public sale the talents which Heaven had bestowed on him gratuitously. By implication, at least, one gains the idea that some play, or plays, of the dramatist had met with the mob's disfavor. These remarks could well apply to Luis Vélez de Guevara in his relation to the Conde-Duque de Olivares [10] —

---

[10] Olivares had the reputation of being grasping. Marañón (113-117) places it, however, among the "calumnies," and quotes his will (116) as proof of it: "Al Rey, nuestro señor le suplico que se sirva de honrar así y favorezca *a los criados que dejo,* porque voy con algún desconsuelo de lo poco que les he ayudado y valido y con pena de su descomodidad...". There is evidence in *Privar contra su gusto* (II, xv) that some of his servants, among them the "bufón Calvo", held different views from their master as to what they should logically expect from the king's favorite. When don Juan tells him, "Bástaos ser vos mi criado", Calvo first mimics him: "Bástaos ser vos mi criado", then adds angrily: "Pues vive Dios, que *no basta / a quien* de sus carnes gasta, / *y es ministro de un privado.* / Esto es: uno piensa el bayo... Et caetera: más razón / es, siendo el amo pelón, / que sea calvo el lacayo". I shall show, on another occasion, that don Juan represents Tirso's ideas of Olivares in the summer of 1621; Calvo is, in my opinion, the buffoon, Soplillo.

There is, in so far as I know, no evidence that Olivares was overly generous financially to any of the poets he befriended. We have a memorial of Luis Vélez (ms. 3796, ff. 341-343), entitled: "Memorial de Luis Vélez de Guevara, pidiendo al rey merced de ayuda de guardarropa en Madrid". It was written just before the king set out for Zaragoza in January, 1626. In

but there can be no certainty that Tirso had the two in mind, since the passage is separated by several pages from the one dealing with the "corpulent" poet. Nevertheless, the description here given is so applicable to Vélez's theatre that the chances are good that it refers to him.

In *Tanto es lo de más como lo de menos,* the picture is clearer. Here poet and patron necessarily refer to specific people, and those people are, in my opinion, Vélez and Olivares, [11] equally materialistic in their point of view. The scene is a vigorous one, made all the more so by the setting given it. Nineucio, the Biblical Dives, has been dressing for his wedding day, attended by servants who hand him his garments and by musicians who are playing for him songs, accompanied by flageolets. Dina, wife to a former majordomo of the miser, one who has been a thousand ducats short in his accounts, has come to plead for her husband. Though he is a relative of Nineucio's, he is in prison by the rich miser's order. She begs in the name of her two lovely children, that her husband be freed, points out that kings, on their wedding day, are accustomed to grant favors, but Nineucio is not moved: she can sell her children into slavery and pay him. By way of terminating the scene, he asks his musicians for a "new song." It proves to be one which runs counter to the stress of charity, the play's basic theme (I, x):

---

it he reviews his previous roles, among others that of "ayuda de cámara" to the Prince of Wales, then adds: "quedando por esos patios / la Alteza Bretaña ausente, / ujier de cámara en vago, / volvió a mendigar mercedes / a las generosas plantas / de aquel *Alcides prudente*...". That is, he was again dependent on the Conde-Duque for *mercedes* until he was given a place as majordomo to the Archduke Carlos. It must likewise have been the Conde-Duque who took care of him again between the death of the Archduke in December of 1624 and his appointment as "valet de chambre" to the king in April of 1625 — and even afterwards, for the appointment to the king carried no financial reward at first. Vélez had evidently tried to beg from some of the great nobles before sending his memorial to the king, for he complains: "...aunque con plagas les piden, / no darán un alfiler". Luis Vélez must have lived from hand to mouth between 1621-1626; in the latter year he married his "Elisa".

[11] I have now finished a long study of *Tanto es lo de más como lo de menos,* one which seeks to show: 1) that this play was retouched after Tirso was banished from Madrid in March of 1625; 2) that Nineucio is Tirso's portrait of Olivares in 1625-26.

Si el poder
estriba sólo en tener,
y es más el que tiene más,
tú que das
tus bienes, que son tu ser,
serás tu propio homicida;
pues mientras gastas sin rienda,
cuanto dieres de tu hacienda
tanto acortas de tu vida.

Nineucio, impressed by the philosophy of the song (so entirely in consonance with his own outlook) asks, "¿Cúya es esa letra?" The answer is:

Es
de un poeta corpulento,
en verdades avariento
y en los versos, calabrés.
Miente más que da por Dios;
tahur en naipes y en engaños,
viejo en pleitos, como en años,
y es en la cara de a dos.

Nineucio, thereupon, gives order: "Ese ha de estar en mi casa: / gajes desde hoy le señalo." The musician's comment is: "Este medra porque es malo, / que aquí la virtud no pasa."

Tirso's "corpulent poet" of *Tanto es lo de más como lo de menos,* sketched or resketched in 1625-1626 when the dramatist was preparing his *Primera parte* for the printer, has in common with the portraits he fashioned for the *Cigarrales* and the *Bandolero,* certain things: In all three instances he is termed "corpulento." In addition, it is here stated: "Es en la cara de a dos," a phrase that is ambiguous and could refer either to length or breadth of face. In all three works, he is a man of the literary world. Here he is referred to merely as a "poet," but according to literary traditions of Spain's Golden Age, that term could include not only a writer of plays (i.e., a *poeta cómico*) but even a prose writer on occasions. In *Los cigarrales* and in *El bandolero,* he is specifically a dramatist, though in the former he is termed, at one point, "poetón presumido." In both *El bandolero* and in *Tanto es lo de más como lo de menos,* he is a card-player: in the former, Cain is quarrelling with his brother over cards; in the latter work, he is "tahur en naipes." He is a *crítico (armenio)* in *El bandolero;* and in *Tanto es lo de más …,* he writes "Calabrian verses." The term is again ambiguous, but "calabriada" can, according to the dictionary, be a "mixture of things" (as well as "balderdash"). The reference is, then, presumably the same as the "vocablos hermafroditas" which Tirso satirizes in *El bandolero.* Saurina has requested that each and all present give her (p. 77): "un ejemplo o símil que pinte al vivo la escabrosa propiedad de estos ingeniosos modernos *que se intitulan críticos."* Lorino's "example" (p. 82) includes the following question:

> ¿qué otra cosa son los versos, hilvanados de tanto emplasto de vocablos hermafroditas, sino capa de pobre socarrón que con diferentes hilos cose retazos de todo color y materia … eslabonando cláusulas, ni en romance ni en latín, pendón de sastre, jaspeado de todo género de sisa?

That such verses were often harsh goes without saying; consequently "verso calabrés" probably suggested as well "verso que descalabra." [12]

The meaning of *corpulento* and Tirso's own use of the word at this time is clearly vital for this study. For the average American, the phrase, "a corpulent man," conjures up visions of a fat, even an obese one. Yet the most basic definition of a Spanish dictionary is even today, "que tiene mucho cuerpo." From a passage of *El amor médico* (II, viii), written precisely in 1625-1626, [13] it is evident that Tirso used the word, on occasions at least, to refer to a person of *tall,* rather than *broad* build, though one may be sure that he would not have excluded from "the corpulent" some one who was horizontally "de mucho cuerpo." Tirso, in fact, must have chosen this particular adjective precisely because of its ambiguity — just as he chose "es en la cara de a dos" for the very same reason.

---

[12] Cf. the portrait of "el culto de Ocaña", of whom Pantaleón says in his "Vejamen que dio a los poetas de la Academia de Madrid" (II, 169): "cuyos versos son tan duros, / que nadie de oírlos trata / sin aceite de Aparicio / porque luego *descalabran".*

[13] See my study of *El amor médico* in *Reflexión* 2, I, 1, 11-22.

In the play mentioned, i.e., *El amor médico*, the diminutive doña Jerónima from Seville, is dressed as a physician, and in her masculine role, arouses don Gaspar's jealousy by her attentions to doña Estefanía. The unhappy lover has, in fact, triple complaints against this doctor: he is "breve de persona, sin autoridad de barba, y la edad no muy dotora." Doña Jerónima, having first defended herself against the charge of youthfulness, then deals with her short stature before going on to the third accusation (II, viii):

> Ni de *mi estatura corta*
> menor alabanza espero,
> cuando el sabio las abona.
> Platón toda corpulencia
> hace al ingenio enfadosa:
> de aquí el adagio, *amens longus,*
> de aquí el filósofo axioma:
> *fortior est virtus unita*
> *se ipsa dispersa;* y oiga
> la causa en que esto se funda,
> porque o se enmiende o se corra:
> la humedad dilata miembros,
> cuya obediencia es más propia
> para el calor natural,
> que con su aumento la honra.
> Por esto el muy corpulento
> es muy húmedo, y no hay cosa
> de las cuatro cualidades
> que así destruya las obras
> de la ánima racional
> como la humedad, que borra
> las imágenes y especies
> del discurso y la memoria.
> Esto no hay en los pequeños,
> cuya sequedad corpórea
> no permite que la carne
> se dilate correosa,
> y no pudiendo extenderse,
> queda en su estrechez angosta
> el ánima más unida;
> porque es cualidad heroica
> que sutiliza el ingenio
> la sequedad, de tal forma,
> que dijo Heráclito della
> esta sentencia famosa:

"*Est animus sapientissimus
splendor siccus;* de forma
que la falta de mi cuerpo
en el espíritu sobra.

Sra. de los Ríos, [14] having quoted the first part of this passage, concludes that Tirso was of slight stature: " ... esto no lo hubiera escrito un hombre alto. ... De modo que Tirso, al defenderse a sí propio, defiende la brevedad de estatura; luego era pequeño ..." It should be noted in passing that the use of the word *corpulento*, as a synonym of *de alta estatura*, did not in any way bother Señora de los Ríos! She does not even raise the point!

In defending men of "brief stature" in *El amor médico*, Tirso was — so Sra. de los Ríos goes ahead to reason — defending himself specifically against Suárez de Figueroa who recommended in *El pasajero* that applicants for public office should have an imposing appearance: [15]

> " ... importa excluir de públicos oficios sujetos menores de marca, hombrecillos pequeños, sin que obste el brocardico del filósofo, "la virtud unida es más fuerte que la dilatada"; ... el chico, aunque bien formado y capaz, debe hallar repulsa en lo que desea ...; ha de representar autoridad con su persona ...

Sra. de los Ríos' suggestion that Tirso was answering Suárez Figueroa is, from my point of view, untenable. True, Tirso could have taken the classical quotation concerning small men from *El pasajero*, so far as chronology is concerned, but he could not have taken from there the arguments that he cites as a basis for accepting the theory: these had to come from Plato himself or some other interpreter of his philosophy. Equally true is it that Suárez de Figueroa, after Tirso's *Cigarrales de Toledo* came out, had ample reason for disliking Tirso, since the Mercedarian had, in that miscellany, defended Lope and his theatre while castigating harshly classical precepts for the drama, but Suárez de Figueroa had left for Italy in September of 1622, and it now seems well

---

[14] Sra. de los Ríos, *Obras dramáticas completas de Tirso,* II, 966.
[15] *El pasajero,* 313.

established that the *Cigarrales* did not come off press until 1624. [16]
What is more, Tirso had departed for Santo Domingo in April
of 1616 and did not return until the same month two years later.
Why should Suárez de Figueroa, in 1617, have had the Mercedarian in mind when penning his disapproval of small men? What
office was Tirso seeking from the New World in 1617? And why
should he have felt the need to defend himself on his return in
1618? The passage of Suárez de Figueroa against men of low
stature was almost certainly directed entirely against Ruiz de
Alarcón; and Tirso's defense of his own abbreviated stature was
written in 1625-1626, as one may see in a recent study of mine. [17]

Moreover, if we analyse the other characteristics of this "corpulent" poet, it is evident that Tirso could not have had Suárez
in mind, even though this *gallego* was, according to Lope, [18] "cari-
glorioso." This doctor of jurisprudence wrote primarily in prose,
not poetry, and his books tend to be encyclopaedic in content,
sententious of spirit, and pedantic in style. He penned a long
narrative poem in 1612, *España defendida,* but he wrote no
plays in so far as we know. With his Aristotelian outlook, he
would have been one of the last writers in all Spain to direct his
art to the pit — even had he written them. In *El pasajero* (p. 123),
when inveighing against the Lopean formula, he cried out in
violent protest: "Todo charla, paja todo, sin nervio, sin ciencia,
ni erudición. Sean los escritos hidalgos ...!" One cannot imagine
Suárez fashioning a scene in which Cain "martyrizes" Abel in
a game of cards; nor can one conceive of his committing gross
anachronisms of time such as characterized the plays of that
corpulent poet. Neither was Suárez a *crítico* in style, nor — in so
far as I can find out — a "tahur" at the gaming table. No, Tirso's
"corpulent" poet was not Suárez de Figueroa.

Neither was he Góngora, as I now see it, though for many
years I felt reasonably certain that the portrait of the "corpulent
poet", found in *Tanto es lo más como lo de menos,* must be

---

[16] Alan K. G. Paterson, "Tirso de Molina: Two Bibliographical Studies,"
43-53.

[17] See "The Dates of *El amor médico* and *Escarmientos para el cuerdo,*"
11-22.

[18] See Entrambasaguas, "Una guerra literaria del Siglo de Oro", II, 375.

one of the Cordoban. I believed during those years, that the passage had been sketched between the years 1620 and 1623, [19] not 1625-1626, as I now believe it to have been done. Nevertheless, arguments in favor of identifying the "corpulent" poet with Góngora are substantial. Velázquez's portrait of the Andalusian (for copy of it, see Prado Museum, No. 1223) shows him to have a quite long face ("es en la cara de a dos"), set against great hunched shoulders that could easily have suggested to Tirso the word *corpulento*. Góngora was given to "pleitos," as all the world knew, and was, even as an old man, notoriously fond of the gaming-table. Quevedo's sonnet, written around 1625 probably, counsels a Góngora who was evidently expected to depart this world shortly [20] (182):

> Tantos años y tantos todo el día;
> menos "hombre," más Dios, Góngora hermano;
> no altar, garito sí; poco Cristiano,
> mucho tahur, no clérigo, sí arpía.

This he concludes with an epitaph for Góngora, who had been chaplain to Philip III:

> Yace aquí el capellán del *rey de bastos*
> que en Córdoba nació; murió en *Barajas*,
> y *en las Pintas* le dieron sepultura.

In yet another epitaph (p. 182), Quevedo asserts that Góngora "vendió el alma y el cuerpo por dinero / y aun muerto es garite-ro." Money, certainly, is the constant theme of Góngora's letters [21] in the 1620's. He was, what is more, author of the well-known *le-trilla*, "Dineros son calidad," wherein the power of money is exalted, as it is in the song that the "corpulent" poet sings. The very fact that he had been chaplain to Philip III could possibly have suggested to don García of *Los cigarrales* his metaphor of

---

[19] See "Studies for the Chronology of Tirso's Theatre", 42-46. I shall give various reasons for believing the play reworked in 1625-26 when I write a long study for one of the volumes that will follow this.

[20] See Quevedo, *Obras en verso*, 182. Astrana Marín dates it ¿1625?

[21] See Artigas, *Don Luis de Góngora y Argote*, 285-342, also 157-160.

the fool's cap with its three tassels and that of the cardinal's hat with its one.

Góngora wrote a long poem on Pyramus and Thisbe, which Artigas [22] calls, "el mayor alarde de su ingenio." In this connection, one remembers that in *El bandolero* it was Tirso's poem on that same theme of Pyramus and Thisbe which led to the juxtaposition of *críticos (paganos)* with *cristianos*. Góngora's name had even given to the movement of *culteranismo* that of "gongorismo," as every undergraduate knows, and few are the plays of the Mercedarian written between 1621-1623 which do not satirize that movement. In fashioning his *Parnaso de Apolo* of *La fingida Arcadia* (III, iii) of 1622, Tirso, as we remember, had painted three levels: Heaven, Inferno, and Purgatory. "Purgatory" is labelled "Parnaso crítico," and there he places the *followers* of Góngora, most of them "ignorant fellows," he says, "who do not sin through malice." But Góngora himself he puts in Hell as a dogmatist who has started a new sect. He does not, it should be noted, call him "ignorant."

The Cordoban was, from the first, favored by the Conde-Duque and from him received *gajes*. In a letter to Francisco de Corral, dated April 13, 1621 — that is just two weeks after Olivares became *privado* to the new king — Góngora began: "Ayer, segundo día de Pascua, estando yo con el Señor Conde de Olivares [23] ...;" at the close of the paragraph, the poet adds: "Yo le debo mucha merced que me hace." On one occasion, the *privado* even embraced Góngora publicly. [24]

Marañón, biographer to the Conde-Duque, has devoted a long paragraph to this relationship of Maecenas and poet, one wherein he states: "Olivares tuvo amistad especial con Góngora y protegió al poeta, gestionándole las mercedes de los hábitos y los emolumentos que pudo entre los muchos que el gran poeta — gran pedigüeño también — solicitaba." Marañón even believed that gongorism was "toda una modalidad entrañable del alma nacio-

---

[22] *Ibid.*, 161.

[23] See *Obras poéticas de D. Luis de Góngora,* Hispanic Society edition, III, 190.

[24] See Marañón, *El Conde-Duque de Olivares,* 146. All quotations here given are from the same page of that history.

nal." What is more, he was convinced that the influence of this
movement extended not only to the political philosophy of the
Conde-Duque but had even colored Spain's outlook from that
day on:

> De espuma gongorina está llena, desde entonces, no
> sólo nuestra literatura sino nuestra vida entera. Y la po-
> lítica del Conde-Duque llena está también de la misma
> pasión, a la vez trémula y alambicada. En sus dichos y
> en sus hechos, don Gaspar fue uno de los más conspicuos
> personajes del gongorismo; y acaso lo presentía cuando
> abrazaba al poeta ... con ... efusión ...

If one accepts (as I do) Prof. J. C. J. Metford's thesis [25] that
Tirso has satirized the Conde-Duque in the figure of the avaricious
miser Nineucio, then it seems to follow naturally enough that
Góngora is the "corpulent" poet whom Tirso was attacking and
that the scene is a reflection of Olivares and Góngora's special
relationship. It even becomes easy to understand the bitter comment of the musicians: "Este medra porque es malo, / que
aquí la verdad no pasa."

There are, however, various reasons for rejecting Góngora as
the materialistic poet. We are fortunate enough to have a detailed
word-portrait of this poet, drawn in 1622 by the inimitable artist,
Quevedo, which begins (181-182):

> Esta magra y famélica figura,
> cecina del Parnaso, musa momia,
> cadáver de la infamia ...

Yet neither in this caricature nor in the various other satires that
Quevedo wrote against him do we have any indication that Góngora was tall enough for his height to occasion comment; nor
was his face sufficiently long to call it to the attention of his
contemporary.

The Cordoban, though primarily a poet, has left a few plays,
but they do not fall at all into the pattern of those that Tirso has

---

[25] J. C. J. Metford, "Tirso de Molina and the Conde-Duque de Olivares",
15-27. Miss Margaret Wilson, *Spanish Drama of the Golden Age*, comments
(112): "...here [i.e., in *Tanto es lo de más como lo de menos*] Metford
makes a good case for identifying the loathsome Nineucio ... with Olivares".

criticized in the *Cigarrales* and the *Bandolero*. Nor is there any reason to believe, as I have already pointed out, that Tirso thought Góngora ignorant, nor anything to indicate that he considered him capable of penning the stupid anachronisms that characterized the plays of the corpulent poet. His basic complaints against Góngora are, instead, his Latinized sentence structure and his Latinized vocabulary. It was only the *followers of Góngora* whom Tirso labels ignorant.

Finally there is in the satire of *Tanto es lo de más como lo de menos* a note of hot anger, of sharp bitterness, [26] which differentiates it from that of both *Los cigarrales* and *El bandolero*. It approaches, in general tone, that of "A un poeta muy viejo y flaco, ... que se muera." It is one that suggests a personal attack from this poet, "tahur ... en engaños," "en verdades avariento." Yet if Góngora ever attacked Tirso in his poetry, I have not been able to locate the passage. This would be surprising except for one thing: the *Cigarrales* apparently did not come off press until 1624, [27] and Góngora's health was probably such by that year that he had not the energy to answer the barbs there included. Though he did not die until 1627, he was "deprived of his memory in the last years of his life." Finally, if I am right in believing the passage in *Tanto es lo de más* ... to have been inserted in 1625-1626, when Tirso was preparing his *Primera parte* for press, then it is unlikely that the dramatist had in mind Luis de Góngora.

Let us pass on to another *Luis* — from the South, as was Góngora — i.e., Luis Vélez de Guevara. In *La fingida Arcadia,* as I have shown elsewhere, [28] Tirso had put him in the Inferno along with Góngora, though Vélez's particular sin was that he was writing spectacular plays that called for mechanical effects. Luis Vélez, like the poet from Cordoba, was in the employ of Olivares and had eulogized the house of Guzmán in *Más pesa el rey que la sangre*. Thus Tirso was aware of the bond that existed between Olivares and Vélez at least as early as 1622. And if the passage of

---

[26] Miss Margaret Wilson noted it also (112): "The note of bitter criticism sounds clearest of all in the only play to be based squarely on New Testament material, *Tanto es lo de más como lo de menos*".

[27] See above, n. 16.

[28] See above the study on *La fingida Arcadia*.

Los cigarrales, satirizing the "corpulent" poet, was written before
October 8, 1621 — when that miscellany went to press — and not
inserted at a later time, then Tirso was criticizing Luis Vélez in
1621. In *La celosa de sí misma,* [29] originally of late 1622, Tirso
again satirizes a dramatist for his use of *tramoyas* — as he does
the "corpulent" poet of *El bandolero* who was a *crítico* and had
turned the theatre, "princess of the liberal arts," into a mechanical
affair. In both *El bandolero* and *La celosa* ... he seemingly con-
nects Vélez with the *privado.* [30] We have seen, too, that the *sátira,* "A un poeta muy viejo y flaco, aconsejándole que se muera,"
which is a merciless attack on Luis Vélez de Guevara, may well be
Tirso's, and, that in case it isn't his, he at least chose to republish
it in a prominent place in his *Segunda parte,* thereby suggesting
his approval of it and extending the period of its influence. In it,
one finds satire of Vélez's gongoristic style, his harsh verses that
do more damage than the rounds of a musket, his inability to summon his muse without the help of a "go-between," his dependence
on friends for aid when fashioning an epigram.

There, too, as in various other satires of 1625, Vélez is painted
as abnormally tall; so tall, in fact, that on falling from his mount,
it would be as if the tower of the Miguelete were to come crashing
down. Camerino speaks of this "andaluz" in 1625 as more than
a league long; Anastasio Pantaleón gives us a picture, done
that same year, of a lover, rising up "cuatro varas de la tierra"
to pay court to his lady at her balcony. The anonymous poem of
Alfay's collection uses in 1625 such metaphors as *longaniza, geringa, asador,* in describing Vélez; and the poet describes himself in
1626 as "por lo luengo pendón de Calatrava." He was not only
very tall, but with his bowed shoulders, he must have given the

---

[29] See "On the Date of Five Plays", 209-214. I there promise a later
study. This play, published in his *Primera parte* of 1627 was retouched in
1625-26, as I shall show later.

[30] Ventura, seeing doña Magdalena with face covered by her veil, begs
her (II, iv): "Sé sumiller de cortina, / descubre aquesa apariencia, / tocarán
las chirimías; / que en las tramoyas pareces / poeta de Andalucía". Olivares
was "sumiller de corps" to Philip IV and was the one who pulled back the
curtains of his bed in the morning. Here "tramoya" can be "trick" quite
as well as a piece of stage machinery. Both doña Magdalena and Olivares
were playing tricks in Tirso's opinion. As I shall show on another occasion,
there are at least two other references to the Guzmanes in this play.

sensation of being somewhat massive. His face was so long that Pantaleón de Ribera says it took him from eight to twelve just to cross himself.

Tirso, in *Tanto es lo de más como lo de menos*, paints a "corpulent" poet of whom he says: " ... y es en la cara de a dos." In the years 1625-1626, i.e., the very years in which Tirso was retouching some of his plays for publication in his *Primera parte* — and among them, *Tanto es lo de más como lo de menos* — we have proof in *El amor médico* that Tirso used "corpulento" as the equivalent of "de alta estatura."

Let us get on to other details of this portrait of the materialistic poet: Vélez was a *crítico*, at least after entering Olivares' service. [31] Whereas his earlier plays tend to be free of gongorism, those written after 1621 often have very harsh passages. To modern critics his greatest fault is perhaps his lack of originality, a shortcoming that was recognized even in his own time by such a critic as the author of "A un poeta muy viejo y flaco ... " and by the Conde de la Roca. [32] His love of the comic at times got the best of him, and it is not at all difficult to imagine him fashioning a scene in which Cain "martyrizes" Abel after losing to him at cards nor one in which a Mohammedan king swears "by Jesus Christ." He treated history without respect (as did Tirso on occasions), and some anachronisms would certainly not have bothered him in the least, nor even some *mentiras* inserted in the lives of his saints.

Vélez was "viejo en pleitos," as Cotarelo's study [33] of his life makes evident. What is more, with his great height, his bowed shoulders, and his excessive emaciation, he must have seemed old in years around 1625-1626, even though he was in reality only 46 or 47 years old. He was unquestionably fond of the fair sex at that

[31] His *Más pesa el rey que la sangre* has scenes that are definitely gongoristic. See for instance, III, 1. However, *El caballero del sol*, "written to commemorate the dedication of the collegiate church of Lerma, ... was performed by members of the household (*criados*) of the court of Saldaña on Tuesday, October 10, 1617". Of it, Spencer and Schevill say (19): "...the language is stilted, pedantic, and abounding in far-fetched similes and numerous traces of *culto*".

[32] For what Fabio Franchi (i.e., el Conde de la Roca) tells him in the *Ragguaglio di Parnaso*, see p. 236, n. 30.

[33] See Cotarelo, *Luis Vélez de Guevara y sus obras dramáticas*, IV, 138-146.

age, was vain, loved fine raiment. The fact that he had been in his youth in service to Rodrigo de Castro, Cardinal Archbishop of Seville, could possibly have suggested to don García the metaphor found in *Los cigarrales de Toledo:* "yo se lo colgara [i.e., el turbante del gran Sofí] después de muerto [él] sobre su tumba, *como capelo de cardenal,* graduándole de presumido, no con borla, pero con borlas." To Tirso, at least, there was much of the court-jester, the *juglar* in Vélez. Quevedo early recognized his conceit.

Just how much the Andalusian gave to his church is, of course, not on record, but he was evidently improvident, was eternally begging money of his patrons and friends. Lope, having written a mendicant letter of his own to the Duque de Sessa in 1626, ends up shamefacedly, we remember, "Parece cosa de Luis Vélez." Whether the sentence, "miente más que da por Dios," refers to the "mentiras" he included in his "vidas de santos" [34] or to some Vélez had told against Tirso, one cannot say. For one detail only in the three word-portraits of the "corpulent" poet, I can offer no specific confirmation: "tahur en naipes." Vélez certainly knew his cards, but I have found no statement to the effect that he was an out-and-out gambler. Yet it is difficult to believe that a man who loved so well the glitter of life, as did Vélez, should not have tried, on occasion at least, to solve his pressing economic needs at the gambling table — especially since he had grown up in an age in which even the pious Philip III lost princely sums at such entertainment.

The "corpulent poet" of *Los cigarrales de Toledo,* of *El bandolero,* and of *Tanto es lo de más como lo de menos* must be Luis Vélez de Guevara. Yet one question remains to be solved: Why is the satire of the play, *Tanto es lo de más ...,* so different in tone from that of the two novels? Why is it so much more intense, so much bitterer? We believe the answer lies in an abusive *copla* which appeared on a pastry-shop wall of Madrid in early 1625, one which linked Gabriel Téllez with Ruiz de Alarcón and sought to reduce his accomplishment to nothing. With that *copla* and its reflections in Tirso's theatre, we shall be concerned in the chapter that follows.

---

[34] See pp. 287-88.

VII

TIRSO AND VÉLEZ'S (?) SCURRILOUS COPLA, TOGETHER WITH OTHER SATIRE

There is, I believe, still other satire in Tirso's theatre which is directed primarily against Luis Vélez de Guevara — though Antonio Hurtado de Mendoza will come in for his share of the blame, as will some *repentistas* of the day. While in Toledo, Tirso seemingly heard something more about events that had occurred after he left Madrid, "almost in flight." His *Antona García* makes evident, as we have seen, that he blamed primarily Antonio Hurtado de Mendoza and Lope de Vega for the accusations which had resulted in the *Junta's acuerdo;* but there is no indication in that play that he had, at the time, heard of the scurrilous *copla* which linked his name with that of Ruiz de Alarcón. Yet it was a *mote* which angered him so profoundly that it has left one bitter allusion after another in his theatre. Let me reiterate what I have said before: [1] had Tirso known of it in days when he was retouching his *Antona García,* there is, in my mind, no doubt but that it would have left reflection there.

Furthermore, one finds, in plays that were being written in late 1625, bitter denunciation of "Zoilos de los ausentes," of "human leaches who draw blood without ever drawing their swords," and his attitude toward these envious detractors is no longer expressed in the sad but essentially reasonable, tones that had characterized the scene of *Antona García.* By the time he was writing *El amor médico* in December of 1625, he had, I believe,

---

[1] See p. 114.

heard of the indecent *copla* which appeared on a pastry-shop's wall in Madrid, one where the season's plays were commonly announced, sometimes in charcoal, sometimes in ochre. The theatrical year began just after Easter Sunday, which in 1625 fell on March 30,[2] and apparently the white-washed wall had carried, during Lent, announcements of plays both by Tirso and by Alarcón. Near them would appear an unsigned epigram, "en forma de vítor," which was composed against both dramatists. It was one that could hardly have been written against a priest of that day, had not that grave body of the *Junta* already brought his name into thorough disrepute:[3]

> ¡Vítor, don Juan de Alarcón
> *y el fraile de la Merced,*
> por ensuciar la pared
> y no por otra razón!

This well-known epigram has never been dated, but, as we shall see later, it must have been written soon after Tirso left Madrid in 1625, "casi huyendo."

Just how deeply it burned can be surmised from an allusion in the *Ragguaglio di Parnaso*, written in Italian in 1635 by one "Fabio Franchi," who was none other than the Conde de la Roca.[4] This essay, penned in honor of Lope, passed in review most of the dramatists of the time. Of Tirso he wrote, in part:

> Prevéngase a Tirso, bajo censura particular aunque generalísima, que escriba siempre, aunque *pared* y *merced* sean consonantes; porque si bien puede una ballesta satírica[5] manchar con una redondilla la pared blanca de un pastelero, no así la fama digna... de un ingenio como el suyo, no menos docto que festivo.

---

[2] See the *Enciclopedia Espasa* under "calendario".

[3] This *copla* was first brought to the attention of the scholarly public by Hartzenbusch when publishing *La ventura con el nombre* (BAE, V, 520, n. 1). For the complete statement in the *Ragguaglio*, see 142-143.

[4] For Fabio Franchi as "El conde de la Roca", see p. 119, n. 85.

[5] "Ballesta satírica", as a phrase, may have recalled to Madrid the fact that Villamediana was murdered with a shot from a cross-bow, one opening a tremendous wound that killed him instantly. That political murder, which was, at the time, laid by his enemies at the door of Olivares, produced much resonance.

This "shot from a cross-bow," which had rhymed *pared* and *mer-ced* on the wall of a pastry-shop, is evidently the one which we have quoted above, as Hartzenbusch pointed out decades ago.

What is probably a relatively late reaction on Tirso's part to this epigram is recorded in *La ventura con el nombre,* a play that was, in my opinion, not retouched until Tirso was in Trujillo: [6] I must, however, take it up at this point, for there is in it an allusion not only to the *redondilla* but also to the bonds that he felt were binding him at that moment. The rustic Clora of this play (one originally written in 1621 but revised in 1626) will have nothing of the love that her swain is offering her. Thereupon Balón turns to Tirso, who, under his well-known pseudonym, appears as sexton in this play, and suggests (I, iii):

> Tirso puede sentenciallo;
> que, después que es sacristán,
> tiene seso y no le verán coprista.

Tirso's answer to Balón's *non sequitur* ("y no le verán coprista") seems equally disjointed:

> Yo escucho y callo;
> pero algún día habraré
> en dejando la trebuna;
> que *a fe que tengo más de una
> trabadura*...

He then lashes out with a threat against his enemies that is equally obscure as to meaning, though it is clear that he is referring to the abusive epigram to which the Conde de la Roca alluded:

> Sí, a fe;
> y que me lo han de pagar
> más de cuatro *motilones*
> que *ensuciando paredones*
> piensan que no he de tornar
> a dar a *plumas mestizas*
> *que envidiar y que roer.*

---

[6] See on pp. 347-48 my reason for believing *La ventura* retouched in Trujillo.

To Balón's question, "Y esto ¿cuándo tiene de ser?" Tirso answers evasively with the well-known proverb, "más días hay que longanizas."

The whole exchange is tantalizing because virtually every key-word in it admits of several interpretations that differ widely in meaning. So heavily has Tirso veiled the autobiographic in re-writing[7] this play that it is evident he felt at the moment the necessity of proceeding with unaccustomed caution. What does he mean by "después que es sacristán"? Is it merely a reference to the humble role of sexton he is playing in *La ventura con el nombre?* What does the expression, "en dejando la trebuna," signify? Can it mean "en dejando [de obrar] la trebuna" (i.e., the tribunal of Rome)?[8] Or could the Mercedarian be thinking of abandoning his Order, either through choice or necessity? I am very much inclined to believe that the words mean: "en dejando [de obrar] la trebuna," (i.e., the tribunal of Rome) or else "en dejándome la tribuna.

Without attempting, however, to give categorical answers to the questions raised, I believe that certain things can be assumed, with more or less safety, from the above passages·

---

[7] For proof that *La ventura con el nombre* was rewritten, see my article in *B. Com.,* XXI (Fall, 1969), 35-45; also the last chapter of this book, "Assessments and Reassessments". I pointed out in the article mentioned: "...all of the autobiographical in *La ventura con el nombre* must have been added, ... as I shall show on an early occasion. I agree with Sra. de los Ríos that *La ventura* has in it allusions not only to the abusive *copla* which so wounded Tirso's pride that he referred to it in some half dozen plays but also to the difficulties he was having in March, 1625 with the *Junta de Reformación.* A comparative study of this autobiographic material, one which links it up with the chronology of the *comedias* in which such allusions occur, makes evident that they were all done in either 1625 or in the years immediately following, not in the first half of the 1030's, as Sra. de los Ríos believed." Sra de los Ríos (*Ubras dramáticas completas,* III, 954) points to three other plays where Tirso refers to this "vítor" — precisely when she is studying *La ventura con el nombre.* Prof. Gerald E. Wade — in a study that has just reached me, one found in the most recent number of the *HR* [XL, 1972, 442-450] — gives his interpretation of the *coplu.* The article is entitled "Vítor, don Juan de Alarcón / y el Fraile de la Merced". For some reason, Prof. Wade does not consider, or even mention, Tirso's other allusions to the abusive *copla,* though it is clear that he has read the *preámbulo* to her study. Her allusions, together with others not pointed out by Sra. de los Ríos, are basic for any comprehension of the *copla's* meaning, as this chapter makes evident.

[8] See pp. 87-9.

1) Tirso is refusing, for the time being at least, to reply *in kind* to his aggressors *(no le verán coprista)*, but he expects to answer them in his own good time and in his own chosen way. In so doing *he will again give cause for envy* to those who had perpetrated this outrage, though they may have believed that they had ended once and for all such competition.

2) At the moment, he feels that there are bonds ("trabaduras") which tie him, bonds that make it impossible for him to speak out, a reference possibly either to restrictions that the tribunal in Rome or his Order had put on him.

3) Tirso believed the epigram on the wall of the pastry-shop to be the work of more than one man in the literary world, poets who were motivated by envy, who gnawed at each other's reputations.

4) The authors of this abusive epigram are some "motilones" with "plumas mestizas." Here we must ask whether the word "motilones" refers to "the untonsured brothers of an Order who customarily perform the humbler services in it." Could it not be instead Tirso's own coinage for those who write *motes* (i.e., abusive epigrams); or could it carry, by transfer of meaning from *pelón*, the idea of "those having little intelligence?" Not impossibly, Tirso had in mind both meanings. The expression "plumas mestizas" might be understood here to allude to the Gongorists: Tirso, for example, in *El bandolero*, [9] had applied the adjective to those who mix Latin words with their Spanish. More probably, as we shall see later, it refers here to the poets who, he believes, had written "de consuno": the *copla* was a work of collaboration on the part of some *motilones*. One of these "motilones" was, in Tirso's opinion, "el discreto del palacio," as we shall see straightway.

In *Amar por arte mayor*, [10] one finds, to this *redondilla*, another allusion, one which seemingly makes evident that the

---

[9] *El bandolero*, 77. In denouncing the "críticos", Saurina calls them "estos exagerados paladiones de Apolo ... que con lenguaje *mestizo*, adulteran la legítima pureza de nuestro idioma...".

[10] Ed. *princeps*: *Parte quinta*, Madrid, 1636. Sra. de los Ríos dated it 1635. It is undoubtedly a relatively late play, but as to whether or not it involves a trip to Oviedo, as Sra. de los Ríos argues (*Obras completas de Tirso*, III, 1163-1166), I must leave for future discussion.

dramatist believed that the epigram was the work of several: the "motilones" of *La ventura con el nombre* become here "*escribanos de yeso, que algunos llaman escribas.*" Once more Tirso's metaphor is conceived in terms of a "vítor," as it was in *La ventura con el nombre.* Bermudo, rejoicing over the love that Elvira has just declared for his master, expresses his delight in the following terms (II, vi):

> *Almagrícente paredes,*
> *rotulícente en esquinas*
> *los escribanos de yeso*
> que algunos llaman *escribas.*

In equating these *escribanos de yeso* with *escribas* (judges), Tirso is almost certainly recalling the evil reputation that Jesus gives them in St. Matthew, [11] where he links them over and over with the Pharisees and the hypocrites. Jesus counsels his disciples (and the multitude) that "whatsoever they bid you observe, *that* observe and do"; but then he adds straightway: "do not ye after their works, for they say, and do not." Addressing both scribes and Pharisees directly, he calls them hypocrites, saying "ye shut up the kingdom of heaven against men, for ye neither go in *yourselves,* neither suffer ye them that are entering to go in." Such people, continues Jesus, are blind fools *(necios)* who swear by the *gold* that is in the temple, though it is the *temple* that sanctifies the *gold,* not the *gold* that sanctifies the *temple.* They are like "whited sepulchres which indeed appear beautiful *outward,* but are, *within,* full of dead men's bones and of all uncleanness." Jesus then promises to send to these scribes and Pharisees "prophets and wise men and scribes," but adds straightway: "and *some* of them ye shall kill and crucify; and some of them shall ye scourge... and persecute them from city to city." [12] It should be remembered that Antonio Hurtado de Mendoza, in 1625, became Secretary to the Inquisition and was therefore a judge (did its members wear white robes?), that he

---

[11] St. Matthew 23, verses 3, 13, 16, 17, 27, 34.

[12] Tirso may well have remembered, too, in Mendoza's case, Ch. 15, verse 11: "Not that which goeth into the mouth defileth a man; but that which cometh out of the mouth, this defileth a man."

was famous for his *aseo*, that Tirso continued to think him a rich and envious fool who condemned in others what he himself could not do, that is, amuse the truly "discreet."

There are, as we shall now see, yet other allusions in Tirso's theatre to this same *mote*, found on the pastry-shop wall. One of the most significant is the one found in his *Las Amazonas en las Indias*, [13] where the dramatist, in using twice the word *mote*, suggests that the word "motilones," found in *La ventura con el nombre*, is his augmentative for those who write *motes*. In the play indicated, the Viceroy of Peru finds on his door a threat which orders him to leave the country at once (as Tirso had had to leave his). So indignant is he at this *mote* that he takes unwise reprisals, "como engendran fuego los carbones." Commenting unfavorably on both the author of the epigram and the anger that had led the Virrey (Blasco Núñez) to reprisals, Tirso's character observes (III, iv):

> *Imprenta es la pared de la locura,*
> *y el carbón, pluma y tinta del delito;*
> *juzgad si es imprudente el que se afrenta*
> *de motes en paredes de una venta.*

Such abusive epigrams as Blasco Núñez had found on his door should be disregarded — to become affronted is to be imprudent. Even if they do "set one on fire," they are in reality only proof of the madness, the crime of those who compose them. Tirso is evidently congratulating himself on his own restraint: he had not returned *copla por copla* ("no le verán coprista"). Such epigrams are here *motes* to the dramatist. The word *motilones*, used in *La ventura*, is then, logically, a depreciative augmentative that Tirso coined for those who write *motes*. Consciously or unconsciously, Tirso had equated the *mote* on Blasco Núñez's door with the one written against him that appeared on the pastry-shop wall *(en paredes de una venta).*

---

[13] Princeps of *Las amazonas...*, *Parte IV*, Madrid, 1635. Sr. Luis Escolar Barreño lists this play as one whose preamble he had to complete. He dates it "1629 o 1632." I believe it surely written while Tirso was in Trujillo, 1626-29 — probably nearer 1626 than 1629.

In *El amor médico*, [14] a play which, as we shall see, includes angry comments against *maldicientes* who write unsigned libels, there is also a highly significant reference to the *mote* that appeared on the wall of the pastry-shop. In this very delightful comedy, the maid Quiteria is summing up the position of her clever mistress. The latter has been so daring as to have attended the University of Coimbra, disguised in men's clothing, and there to have taken her degree in medicine. Indeed, she has, as a physician, become so celebrated in that university city as to occasion the envy of her colleagues: parenthetically, Tirso observes (II, xii) that in doctors and in poets, *"envy is an incurable itch."* She has passed her examination brilliantly — so brilliantly, in fact, that her fame has occasioned "vítores," painted on the walls about the city (II, xii): *Ya en paredes te rotula.* Then another thought occurs to Quiteria, one that leads to an unusual metaphor:

> aunque en esto decir puedes
> que a la vergüenza te saca
> tu fama, y de puro flaca,
> la pegan a las paredes.

The compliment is a questionable one, she reasons, for Fame causes the envy of one's competitors who can bring one to shame: "a la vergüenza te saca tu fama." Thus, the *vítor* that normally accompanied the student's success could become his shame, just as had happened in Tirso's case, or so he felt. This train of thought leads Quiteria to recall the writing-in-red which the lash left on the back of one condemned, as he was marched through the streets — as it leads me to memory of the curious notice that is found in the *Noticias de Madrid*, [15] under date of August 11, 1626:

> Este día llevaron preso al Conde de Puñoenrostro por el escándalo que daba con una *comedianta llamada*

---

[14] *El amor médico* was begun in December of 1625, probably in Toledo, but was either finished in Trujillo in 1626 (?) or retouched there. See my study, "The Dates of *El amor médico* and *Escarmientos para el cuerdo*," 11-22.

[15] *Noticias de Madrid*, 146-147.

Quiteria, por lo cual no hacía vida con su marido; *y a los padres de la moza, que eran los alcahuetes, los azotaron y encorozaron.*

Now "Quiteria" (as well as "Estefanía," who also plays a role in *El amor médico)* were real actresses, so named. The two were probably sisters, who had acted sometime before this date in Quiñones de Benavente's *El murmurador,* with Antonio de Prado as their *autor.* [16] Quiteria has before her eyes, as she speaks to her mistress, the punishment to which her parents had been subjected, as Tirso has before his the one which envious poets had forced him to endure. But the shame of Quiteria's parents occurred after Tirso had left for Trujillo in order there to carry out his duties as *comendador* of the Mercedarian house. [17] Either he returned to Madrid — in connection, perhaps, with his efforts to get published his *Primera parte;* or he received word of this episode by letter and wrote (or retouched) this play in Trujillo. Since Coimbra is the setting for much of the action of the play, it seems not improbable that the dramatist retouched it in western Spain.

There is, in *Los balcones de Madrid* [18] a final allusion to this epigram which so seared Tirso's soul. Its *gracioso,* Coral, when talking to his master, don Juan, makes clear his contempt for those who scribble on walls (**II,** x):

> Tuve envidia en las paredes
> a las letras de *carbón,*

[16] Quiñones de Benavente, *El murmurador,* included in Cotarelo's *Colección de entremeses,* II, 526-528. Antonio de Prado was acting in Madrid in 1623-24 and 1626. It ends in a dance, and, according to Tirso (*Tanto es lo de más como lo de menos,* II, vii), Benavente's earlier plays ended in *palos.* Hannah E. Bergman, *Luis Quiñones de Benavente y sus entremeses,* says (169): "...tres piezas pertenecientes a Prado —*El abadejillo, El borracho, El murmurador*— lo serán [i.e., posteriores] a 1622." It was possibly written in 1623-24, more probably in 1626.

[17] The first official paper we have from Tirso that was signed in Trujillo is dated July 13, 1626.

[18] *Los balcones de Madrid:* Princeps, apparently Grimaud de Velaunde's *Teatro antiguo español,* Madrid, 1837. Prof. Vern Williamsen is, I believe, studying the various manuscripts of this play, and putting out a critical edition based on the longer one of Parma. "Necio" is Tirso's usual adjective for Antonio de Mendoza.

> deseando transformarme
> en ellas, con saber yo
> ser cartapacio del *necio*
> y sátira del letor.

So frightened was the *gracioso* that he almost envied the anonymity of the *letras* (written in charcoal) which he saw on the walls about him and would have liked to transform himself into them — this, though he realized that such walls were but "fools' notebooks." Thereupon, Coral plays on the word "lector" (the one who reads) and *lector* (lecturer): Tirso was "lector en teología," even back in 1620 when he was in Segovia.[19]

Let us now add such knowledge as we have gained from study of these various allusions, found in plays written (or rewritten) after the epigram had appeared: some will confirm ideas noted in the well-known passage of *La ventura con el nombre;* others will add to the information that passage gave us:

1) "Motilones," by all logic, could be Tirso's coinage for those who wrote unpleasant *motes*. It would not be the only instance of such coinages in his work.

2) The dramatist continued to believe that the epigram was the work of envious poets (plural) who were venting their envy against him, an envy occasioned by their own failures to please their audiences. One such poet was Antonio Hurtado de Mendoza, as the reference to "scribes" in *Amar por arte mayor* seems to make evident.

3) He did not write a *copla* by way of answer to his enemies ("no le verán coprista"), but he could well understand the anger of those who were attacked by such epigrams. However, he believed reprisals imprudent. One should remember the unworthiness of the source.

4) This abusive epigram, this *mote*, brought Tirso far more suffering than had the *Junta's* actions. He was particularly indignant at the *anonymity* of his attackers; this we shall see when studying later his bitterness — so evident in *No hay peor*

---

[19] See p. 70, n. 81, where Tirso is referred to as "lector".

sordo (II, viii) and *El amor médico* (I, ii) — against the cowardly "mirones," who had not dared to sign their names to their libels.

5) Tirso had probably not been in Madrid when the *mote* appeared on the pastry-shop wall. Otherwise he would presumably not speak, now of letters in *black,* now of letters in *ochre.* This conclusion is seemingly further confirmed by a passage in *El amor médico* in which he will label his detractors "Zoilos de los ausentes." We shall later quote it in its entirety.

The author of the epigram that appeared on the wall — *mote* to Tirso, *ballesta satírica* to the Conde de la Roca — has never been identified. Cotarelo [20] suggested that it was possibly a shaft from Quevedo's bow, and Señora de los Ríos, convinced that Tirso had broken with the great satirist because of the latter's early support of the Conde-Duque de Olivares, eagerly accepted Cotarelo's hesitant attribution.

I doubt very much that Quevedo was in any way responsible for the *redondilla* that cut so deeply into Tirso's pride. True, the two poets were at one time on opposite sides of the political fence; true also, Quevedo was quite capable of fashioning such a cleverly abusive *mote;* true, he would seem to have been a friend of Mendoza. [21] But by 1625, the similarity of their problems must have drawn them together: Quevedo, even before Tirso, had been brought up before the same *Junta* which had recommended Tirso's exile. [22] That he should have attacked one who was victim of the same forces of reprisal as was he seems improbable.

---

[20] Cotarelo, in his introductory study to *Comedias de Tirso de Molina* (p. lx, n. 1), says: "...quizá sea de Quevedo." Sra. de los Ríos dates *La ventura con el nombre* as "posterior a julio de 1632." I have shown in "Tirso's *La ventura con el nombre*: its Place and Date of Composition" (42) that it was originally written in 1621, but that it was retouched later, at which time the autobiographical material was added by Tirso.

[21] He collaborated with Quevedo and Mateo Montero in a play put on July 9, 1625 to celebrate the Queen's birthday, one mentioned in the *Noticias de Madrid,* 122. See G. A. Davies (*A Poet at Court...,* 50-52) for Mendoza's and Quevedo's relations.

[22] See A. González Palencia's "Quevedo, Tirso y las comedias ante la Junta de Reformación," 73-77.

What is more, if there is in the works of either Tirso or
Quevedo any real evidence of enmity between the two, I have
failed to find it. In the "A ti sólo" of the *Quinta parte*, [23] Tirso
satirizes, as we have seen, some poets, some of "wit's pick-pockets"
who have stolen the witticisms of their *comedias* from the "sazonado, discreto y leído don Francisco de Quevedo." If Quevedo
wrote that *mote*, Tirso certainly *didn't know it* at the time, for
Gabriel Téllez was not, as we have made evident above,
forgiving the enemy (or enemies) who put it there. Moreover,
those two poets were in many ways kindred spirits, as Señora
de los Ríos [24] herself recognized. Both were extraordinarily intelligent, scholarly, wittily satirical, and above all, daring to the
point of temerity. I cannot see the fearless Quevedo, anymore
than I can see the outgoing Tirso, scribbling an *anonymous*
attack, such as was the *redondilla* that appeared on the pastry-
shop's wall.

But I *can* see Vélez de Guevara and Hurtado de Mendoza
doing it, with assistance perhaps from "Cristóbal el ciego" [25]
and possibly from some of the pranksters from the *Academia de
Madrid*. It is quite in the spirit of that talented body of satirists.
So given to lampooning one another was the group in 1625 that
Castillo Solórzano, their Secretary, speaks of the Academy of
Madrid as a "pernicious congregation." [26] He had in mind

---

[23] See Cotarelo, *Comedias de Tirso de Molina*, I, pp. lxviii.

[24] Sra. de los Ríos, *Obras dramáticas completas de Tirso*, I, 1401-1403.

[25] There was a bond between Cristóbal el Ciego and Mendoza. We
have a *romance de repente* of the latter (*Obras poéticas de don Antonio
Hurtado de Mendoza*, II, 37-38) which is entitled "A Cristóbal ciego,
poeta de repente con eminencia, que asistía en casa del Marqués de Siete
Iglesias, don Rodrigo Calderón." Mendoza had given him a discarded
black suit (which included a *ferreruelo* and was therefore probably bought
after the sumptuary decrees of February, 1623). It was one Mendoza had
promised him and was "punto menos de nuevo."
Mendoza also wrote "quintillas, imitando las de *ciego*, porque se pi-
dieron en este estilo." (*Obras*, I, 296-300).

[26] See "A los críticos" in *Tardes entretenidas* (Madrid, 1625); for
description, see Pérez Pastor, *Bibl. Madrileña*, III, 265. As he makes the
same type of criticism in two *romances*, included in the *Donayres del
Parnaso*, and copied in the *Bibl. madr.*, III (262-263), it is safe to say
he is aiming at his fellow-members of the Academy: "Hay en esta corte
insigne / una gran *congregación*, / que se llama el critiquismo / de quien
nos defienda Dios, etc."

primarily, one may suspect, the hard feelings that had followed
the violent exchange of personalities between don Gabriel de
Corral and Anastasio Pantaleón de Ribera, mentioned above; but
that there were others that went to form that "pernicious congregation" is made evident by the various satires of 1625, directed
against Luis Vélez.

———

We have some proof that Luis Vélez de Guevara returned,
at least in a measure, Tirso's dislike. This is evident from a
limping "poem" that he wrote in early 1626, one directed to
the king himself. In January of that year, Philip IV was heading
for Zaragoza in order to win from the hard-headed Aragonese
financial support for his conduct of the Thirty Year's War. Vélez
— a mendicant poet if there ever was one — wrote a rhymed
memorial to his sovereign, begging him for a new suit so that
he might not discredit him on the trip to Aragón that was
being planned. In return for this finery, he promised to chronicle
the feats of the king on his journey, [27] — to be for him, in fact,

> en todo el Pentecostés
> de las alabanzas vuestras
> eterno versifiquier,
> más digna haciendo su musa
> del siempre verde laurel.

And then, with what is for today's reader a complete *non sequitur*,
he closed his memorial with the words:

> Malos años para Arceo
> *y el fraile de la Merced.*

The *fraile de la Merced*, here, as in the epigram, is Tirso, but
who is Arceo? What had led Vélez to pair "el fraile de la Merced"
with "Arceo"?

If we are to understand Vélez de Guevara's allusion linking
Tirso with Arceo, we must go to Antonio Hurtado de Mendoza's

———

[27] Rodríguez Marín, "Cinco poesías autobiográficas de Luis Vélez de
Guevara", 62-78, specifically 75.

works. [28] In a "Loa para la comedia de *Más medra quien miente más*, que se hizo en el Buen Retiro, día de San Pedro de 1634," "Arceo, poeta ridículo," is defending to Roque de Figueroa, "autor de comedias," what he feels is his right to compose all *loas* in praise of the royal family: "la jurisdicción es mía," he declares furiously. His anger is directed primarily against Antonio de Mendoza:

> Todos los puestos me hurtan,
> y los conceptos me roban,
> y entrellos, más que ninguno,
> don Antonio de Mendoza.

He demands that

> el pulidísimo lego
> respete pluma tan docta
> que sus versos cortesanos
> son bernardinas airosas.
>   Déjeme, deje mi oficio ...

In what follows, it is evident that Arceo's lexicon is hopelessly old-fashioned, unbearably commonplace; that the compliments with which he would praise the royal family are laid on with such a heavy brush as to be ridiculous. His "alabanzas," in short, were lacking in the subtlety that the discreet Mendoza felt his possessed in such abundance.

The "Arceo" in question can only be Francisco de León y Arce who, in 1624, was "escribano de S. M." He had written up for Philip III his *Jornadas de Francia, Portugal e Inglaterra*, and, for Philip IV, the trip which this monarch had made to Sevilla (*La perla en el nuevo mapa-mundi hispánico*). This last pamphlet was dedicated to the king with an *aprobación* dated March 20, 1624. Gallardo, [29] who has afforded us the above information, says: "Al autor le dicen poéticamente *Arceo*." This

---

[28] *Obras poéticas de don Antonio Hurtado de Mendoza*, III, 22-29.

[29] Gallardo, *Ensayo de una biblioteca española...* IV, suplemento, cols. 1329-30. "Arceo" wrote as well, it would seem, a poem "sobre las mercedes de Felipe IV" and an *Alegórica* [sic] *chancilleresca*, both regrettably now lost. Olivares, no doubt, had his reasons for not wanting the first to become generally known. With what would the latter work have dealt?

escribano of the king was having his quarrels not only with Mendoza, Secretary to the king, but with the buffoons and *poetas repentistas* of his Majesty, for he addresses them in the following fashion: "Oh gitanos, que con surrepticias diligencias y extravagantes rodeos, *queréis ganar el rostro a la ventura que pierde este retirado avechucho y pensativo poetista, pobre sin haberle hecho rico 20 años que con realzada pluma vuela penetrando, cual águila real, el sol de los reyes...*" The "gitanos" would presumably include the blind Cristóbal, a *repentista* who is known to have had ties with Mendoza, and possibly Mendocilla. [30]

As early as January of 1626, Vélez de Guevara was, then, trying to harm Tirso by associating his name with that of a vain old poet who was the laughing-stock of the Palace. And this is the same subtle technique used in the abusive epigram which was painted on the white wall of the pastry-shop. What is more, Arceo's name is maliciously put before Tirso's, as was Ruiz de Alarcón's before "el fraile de la Merced"; and Tirso is here "el fraile de la Merced", as he was in the *copla* that linked Tirso's and Alarcón's names.

One even wonders if this *loa* of Mendoza may not be a reworking of one, written in 1625, which had linked *Tirso with Arceo.* If so, we might just have an explanation of Vélez's reference to both of them early in 1626, as we might have one also of Mendoza's choice of this particular *loa* to accompany his play, *Más medra quien miente más* (in which Tirso is *seemingly* praised). In fact, one may suspect, without actually being able to prove it, that the whole performance of 1634 was, in so far as Mendoza could make it, a *replay* of one of 1625 (one which had satirized Tirso's ambitions along with Arceo's) — the better to alert an Olivares who was in the audience to the fact that Gabriel Téllez was once more in Madrid.

---

[30] If the *Noticias de Madrid* is accurate, "Mendocilla" was also a *repentista.* One reads in the *Noticias* (125) under date October 8, 1625: "A 8, desterraron a Mendocilla cuarenta leguas de la corte. Fue célebre bufón y el que hacía *coplas* a los ciegos." But the anonymous author of these *Noticias* seems not to have had very accurate information about the buffoons of the Palace, for on p. 43, under date of December 5, 1622, he tells us: "A 5, quemaron por el pecado nefando a cinco mozos. El primero fue Mendocilla, un bufón." Presumably, royal authority saved him from the stake.

Let us examine further Vélez's doggerel of 1626 which ties Tirso to the "stupid Arceo." Analysis of its implications will give the reader no little knowledge of what our dramatist was up against in 1625 when he asked the king for the role of court chronicler: it presumably tells us, in the first place, that the particular laurel wreath for which Tirso was striving was none other than that of court chronicler, for Vélez de Guevara is stressing to the king *his* own talents to serve him in that same role and is cursing his two would-be competitors, Arceo and Tirso; 2) the king is quite well aware of Tirso's identity as "el fraile de la Merced," — as he was of Arceo's — and could be counted on to understand the curse; 3) a bond of understanding has already been established between the king and his doorkeeper by early 1626, a oneness of outlook that could bode ill for any one attacking the one or the other.

The alliance must, in fact, have been quadripartite, as we shall see. This relationship between monarch and poet had almost inevitably been forged through the king's all-powerful favorite, the Conde-Duque de Olivares, who was at the same time protector to this talented fellow-Andalusian. The ties between Luis Vélez and Olivares may well have extended back as far as 1608. In that year, we remember, Vélez had married doña Ursula Ramisi Bravo, [31] who was a member of the household of doña Inés Guzmán, marquesa de Alcañices, and fond sister to the Guzmán who, after March 31, 1621, ruled Spain. When Olivares took over in that year, he had, as we have seen, turned to Vélez de Guevara for a play which would glorify the monarchical loyalty of the favorite's branch of the Guzmanes and would recall to the king that the Spanish monarchy was in heavy debt to that family. Vélez had answered that request with his play *Más pesa el rey que la sangre,* and Tirso had satirized the relationship between favorite and poet in *La fingida Arcadia.* [32]

There is yet other proof of the bond that existed between Vélez and the Guzmanes. By February 4, 1628, Gabriel de Corral had sent to press his *La Cintia de Aranjuez,* a pastoral novel

---

[31] See E. Cotarelo, *Luis Vélez de Guevara y sus obras dramáticas,* III, 642-643.

[32] See pp. 201-208.

which celebrates the marriage of its heroine, "Cintia," to one "Fileno." At the same time as this marriage — apparently that of "doña Guiomar," of the house of Guzmán, to one "don Juan," of the house of Toledo — [33] similar ties were forged for her maids, among them, "Elisa's" to "Lauro." The last reference can only be to Luis Vélez's fourth marriage to doña María López de Palacios in November of 1626. For the various weddings, Vélez had evidently written an *epitalamio* (a very gongoristic one), for Corral states (363): "Lauro, de tan feliz... como fácil ingenio, escribió a tantas bodas un *epitalamio*, aunque en principal asunto a las de Cintia y Fileno." Vélez was, then, firmly entrenched in the good graces of various Guzmanes; and when in April of 1625, he was made door-keeper to the king, he was, potentially at least, a very dangerous enemy. It was only when Tirso was in Toledo or Madrid (1625-1626) and was reworking his plays for the *Primera parte* [34] that he could realize what the bonds of Vélez to Olivares had cost him.

The power that Olivares had over Philip IV is too generally recognized for one to need stress it. However, we have such clear proof of his influence *in the matter of appointments and in precisely 1626*, that it may be well to include it here. The *Noticias de Madrid*, [35] under date of April 14, of that year, carries information that indicates that Olivares was making every possible effort to surround the king with appointees on whose loyalty he could count:

> A 14, hizo su Majestad merced *al marqués de Eliche* de la tenencia del Oficio de Sumiller de Corps, en ausencia y enfermedades del Conde-Duque, *su suegro*. Sintiólo mucho el Almirante de Castilla, por ser *gentilhombre de cámara el más antiguo*, y dejó la llave. Su Majestad le mandó retirar a su casa hasta que se le diese nueva orden.

Nor was the matter to end there! On May 15, 1626, the *Noticias* [36] carries notice of what was probably the later fate of the Admiral of Castile:

---

[33] *La Cintia de Aranjuez*, 357-358, 360. See above, Ch. V, n. 23.
[34] See pp. 356-62.
[35] *Noticias de Madrid*, 134.
[36] *Ibid.*, 136.

> A 15, llegó el Almirante de Castilla a la Alameda, *que iba preso a Ríoseco*. Salieron a verle su madre y sus hermanas, las de Alburquerque y Lemus, y el Duque de Sesa y otros muchos señores.

Thus we may be reasonably sure that Vélez de Guevara's appointment as doorkeeper, in April of 1625, was with full approval of the Conde-Duque de Olivares. However, Antonio Hurtado de Mendoza may well have urged to both Olivares and the king that this appointment be made — by way of reward for favors done — for Vélez became doorkeeper [37] to his Majesty *less than a month after Tirso's troubles with the Junta began!* And Antonio Hurtado de Mendoza was, on May 17th of 1625, [38] made Secretary of the "Consejo de la Suprema y General Inquisición!" There may or may not be a relationship between the three events. At least, Tirso must have known by 1626 that the bonds between the *three* men were very close.

For there were intimate links as well between the two poets of the Palace, links of long standing between Luis Vélez de Guevara and don Antonio Hurtado de Mendoza. They had first known each other in the days when, around 1608, both were in the service of the Conde de Saldaña, Lerma's son. Luis Vélez de Guevara had written a *librito* entitled "Elogio del juramento del Príncipe, don Felipe Domingo, cuarto deste nombre..." (Madrid, 1608), and in it he included a poem of don Antonio de Mendoza, "paje del Conde de Saldaña, mi señor." La Barrera states: [39]

> Luis Vélez de Guevara estaba asimismo por aquel tiempo al servicio del de Saldaña en clase de gentilhombre. Nuestro joven, don Antonio, adquirió, pues, en aquella casa la amistad del célebre poeta ecijano, y acaso debió

---

[37] Spencer and Schevill, *The Dramatic Works of Luis Vélez de Guevara*, xvii. I have not been able to find the exact day in April when Vélez became doorkeeper to Philip IV.

[38] *Noticias de Madrid*, 118. One reads under date of May 19th: "A 17, se dio la secretaría de la Inquisición, que tenía don Antonio de Losa, a don Antonio de Mendoza; y a Losa, se le dio la secretaría del Patronato." Presumably, then, Alosa lost *both* positions "por una cosa bien niña." See above, pp. 80-81.

[39] La Barrera, *Catálogo*, 246.

mucho a sus lecciones y ejemplo para el desarrollo de
los talentos que le distinguieron.

I am inclined to believe that the relationship had even more
influence on Mendoza's character than on his poetry.

The friendship continued in days when don Antonio de Mendoza enjoyed the full favor of Philip IV. We have another beggar's
letter from Luis Vélez, written in the form of two *décimas*, to
don Antonio Hurtado de Mendoza: [40]

> Rey muy *discreto* señor,
> don Antonio de Mendoza,
> cuyo ilustre ingenio goza
> dignamente el real favor:
> Lauro, vuestro servidor,
> sin dinero ha amanecido,
> de una familia oprimido,
> cuyo peso extraordinario
> derrengara un dromedario,
> que es para bestia un marido.
>   Esta falta socorred
> con algo de lo que os dan;
> seréis de este Tetuán
> *mi fraile de la Merced:*
> *el criado conoced,*
> *que ha sido vuestro criado,*
> y con él a este sitiado,
> cualquier socorro enviad,
> y dad a la vecindad,
> culpa, Celio, [41] de este enfado.

He received a "hundred" [ducats?] from don Antonio and with
them a courteous *décima*, which suggests that this was not the
first time that Vélez had asked money of Mendoza:

> Lauro, jamás importuno,
> pues *siempre obligáis pidiendo,*
> ciento van y recibiendo
> vos nos dais ciento por uno:
> tan gran lisonja a ninguno

---

[40] *Obras poéticas de don Antonio de Mendoza,* I, 322-323.
[41] "Celio" would seem to have been Mendoza's *early* pastoral pseudonym.

> sino al amigo ofreced,
> y el servicio os prometed
> sólo, de sola hidalguía,
> que a cualquiera señoría
> hace susto la merced.

Tirso was, then, in 1625 up against a court clique, a closed corporation, that was determined at all costs to keep its power.

What is more, he was apparently up against the *repentistas*, the *motilones*, of the Academy of Madrid; and these were within the very shadow of the Palace, at least in their spirit, for the Palace, too, had its *repentistas*. [42] With his "donaires" Vélez de Guevara would seem to have been dean of the Academy poets. They held their meetings, from October of 1623 on, in the house of don Francisco de Mendoza, secretary of the Count of Monterrey, who was none other than brother-in-law to Olivares. His house was in *la calle de Majaderos*, and Pantaleón de Ribera termed the poets in Lent of 1625 "los majadericos." If José Sánchez [43] is correct in saying that in the *vejámenes* "a nadie se puede omitir... . todos reciben el mismo salpiqueo de picantes alusiones," then both Alarcón and Tirso belonged to that *academia* around Lent of 1625, for surely the identification of these two in Pantaleón de Ribera's "vejamen" must be accurate. [44]

Tirso certainly had little use for the *repentistas;* what is more, he let them feel the edge of his keen satire on more than one occasion. In *Cautela contra cautela*, a play that was in existence by early 1623, the *gracioso*, Chirimía, in need of a rhyme for "hipocrás," finds it in the verse (I, ii), "y trescientas cosas más"; thereupon he comments satirically on his find: "que es socorro y estribillo / de poetas de repente." The Duquesa, of *Amor y celos hacen discretos*, exclaims bluntly (I, vi): "No hay poeta de repente / que escriba bien de pensado." In his novel, *El bandolero*, [45] Tirso alludes contemptuously to "those buffoons," "los

---

[42] See p. 280 with n. 30.
[43] José Sánchez, *Academias literarias del Siglo de Oro español*, 15.
[44] See pp. 89-91.
[45] *El bandolero*, 76.

que *de improviso* versifican, desautorizándose por juglares." Then
he adds:

> Ni el sol ... porque, sin trabajo de los vivientes se nos do-
> mestica, nace tan manifiesto que no le antecedan crepúscu-
> los ambiguos de la aurora; de suerte pido yo la lisura de
> un poema que no por vulgarizarse demasiado, pierda por
> sobra de plebeyo lo que el que llaman "crítico" por falta
> de digestivo.

In *Quien calla otorga* (II, x), don Rodrigo complains that his
lady had spoken "in cipher" and that she had left him "más
confuso que un poeta academista."

In *Escarmientos para el cuerdo* [46] (I, ii) Tirso again makes
reference to the *repentistas'* lack of clarity, and here he squarely
links them with the poets of an academy and presumably with
the bellicose atmosphere that characterized the *Academia de
Madrid* in the early months of 1625. He has, in this tragedy,
painted an academy meeting of Goa which recounts a surprise
attack *(rebato)* in which the various strophes are so many "shots."
Barbosa asks, "¿Cómo ha ido con tanto rebato?" To this Carballo
answers significantly, "Como tres con un zapato"; [47] and then
with manifest depreciation of those who had fired *redondillas:*

> Entre los tiros diversos
> hay unos llamados versos
> que arrojaban *redondillas.*

Others used ammunition "of greater esteem," *octavas* for example.
One of the poets, a *culebrón* (Tirso's augmentative for an envious
person) was a *culto*, hitting out recklessly in all directions with
his *sonnets:* "derribaba a bulto, / echando su consonante, /
cuanto topaba delante." The two *graciosos*, Carballo and Bar-

---

[46] Whether, in the phrase, "como tres con un zapato," Tirso had in mind
specific persons, I am not sure. I suggest, *as a possibility only,* that the one
who fired *redondillas* may have been Alarcón, a confirmed *redondillista*; that
he who used *octavas* ("of greater esteem") was Bocángel; that the *culebrón*,
hitting out in all directions with his sonnets, was Vélez (for his fondness for
sonnets in 1625, see pp. 226-27 of this study); that the *falconcillo* who wrote
"romances con estribillos" may have been Mendoza.

[47] See "Tirso against Juan Ruiz de Alarcón and Luis Vélez," pp. 317-18.

bosa, end their description of the Academy meeting in Goa in the following fashion:

CARBALLO: Pues ¿qué ciertos falconcillos
que *enramados* escupían
balas y piedras?
BARBOSA: Serían
romances con estribillos.
CARBALLO: Desto hubo abundantemente,
y más, que si disparaban
todos ellos se preciaban
de poetas de repente,
asombrándose de vellos,
en llegándose a entender.
Sátiras debían de ser
pues que todos huyen de ellos.
....
BARBOSA: Si en *versos de bronce* da,
toda Goa es academia.

This Academy meeting had ended in a *vejamen* apparently, one carried out by *poetas de repente* whose verses were "of bronze." They were surprised when they could understand one another.

Tirso apparently never wearied of a fight. In his *Deleytar aprovechando,* written in 1631-1632 and published in 1635, he seemingly takes time out to slap down [48] Vélez for his *comedias de santos,* with their concomitant *tramoyas.* When explaining in this religious miscellany his choice of the *novela* (instead of the *comedia)* as a medium for the lives of certain saints, he admits that he first considered dramatic form for them; but eventually he rejected it for various reasons, among others:

> lo contingente del aplauso, *lo peligroso de las ostenta-ciones carpinteras y pintoras* (a donde han dado en aco-gerse como a portería de convento *las penurias de las trazas y sentencias*), la poca fe que ganan las verdades con los *ensanches mentirosos* que en semejantes argumentos añaden las musas, pues no hay comedia de las desta es-

----

[48] See Cotarelo, *Comedias de Tirso,* I, p. L.

pecie en que no pongan más prodigios de su casa que
encierra un *Flos Sanctorum* (como les venga a cuento a
las tramoyas) sin que escrupulicen los poetas las censu-
ras que el Concilio sacrosanto Tridentino fulmina contra
los que fingen milagros nunca sucedidos... ¿Novelas?
¡Eso, sí!

Once again he is, I believe, satirizing Vélez for his failure to
find original "trazas," for his "mentiras," for his fondness for
tramoyas, with which he seeks to win the approval of the mob.

In the *dedicatoria* of the *Tercera parte,* the dramatist stresses
again his own creative ability — while pointing to the lack of
it in others. Supposedly his nephew [49] is speaking *(NBAE,* IV,
lvii):

> Gusano es su autor [i.e., Tirso] de seda: de su misma
> sustancia ha labrado la numerosa cantidad de telas, con
> que cuatrocientas y más comedias vistieron por veinte
> años a sus profesores, *sin desnudar, corneja, ajenos asun-*
> *tos* ni *disfrazar pensamientos adoptivos...* A todo les
> consta, *velint, nolint,* del caudal de su autor...

This is the same boast he had made in *La ventura con el nombre.*

In the *Quinta parte,* [50] Tirso renews his attacks on Vélez, after
having echoed once more the envy of Mendoza. With only a
semicolon to indicate his change of aim, he suggests that they
have a laugh together at the expense of an "ignorant" poet
who I believe to be Vélez:

> ... que entretanto nos riyésemos [sic] los dos a solas de
> unos bobarrones, cicateros del gracejo, que hurtando pro-
> sas impresas al sazonado, *discreto y leído don Francisco*
> *de Quevedo para los "parásitos"* [i.e., *graciosos,* but
> "a la latina"] *de sus comedias,* ignoran que nuestro idio-
> ma, con lo que connaturaliza de las otras lenguas, ... vie-
> ne a tener caudal copioso de voces y sinónimos; que ya los
> coronistas no llaman al socorro de municiones y comida
> sino "comboyes" y a los bastimentos "vivres." Tan pesa-
> rosos están estos zánganos de que se aproveche nuestra

---

[49] For "Tirso's nephew," see p. 118, n. 84.
[50] See Cotarelo, *Comedias de Tirso,* I, pp. lxvii-lxviii.

lengua de las que conquistadas son sus súbditas que *nos*
ocasionan a que maliciemos que hasta en las sisas quie-
ren ser los únicos.

Tirso had evidently been taken to task not only for his use
of "comboyes" and "vivres" but also for having formed the
verb "paralelar" from the noun, "paralelo." His answer is:

> ... que nos ahorremos de todas esas zarandajas de circun-
> loquios cuando en un solo vocablo hallamos significación
> proporcionada a nuestro intento sin ofender ni al *dialecto*
> [underlined by Tirso; presumably Vélez's word] ni al
> común modo de hablar de nuestra patria, pues ni se ante-
> ponen ni posponen los verbos ni adjetivos. [This last
> charge is directed against Vélez's Latinized sentence
> structure.]

Tirso continues his heated counter-charges:

> Pero no te entenderán, aunque se lo digas; porque
> *cojean del entendimiento y no saben que la "ceática" es*
> *esdrújulo,* satisfechos de que entre las almohadillas y
> ruecas se autorizan con achacar a señor padre que se viste
> de voces huéspedas, en cuyos regazos, *idiotizan* (este voca-
> blo vaya a contemplación de su descalabradura); que a
> hacer caso los lebreles de los *gozques caseros* que *los*
> ladran, no fuera difícil contarles una letanía de dispara-
> tes en la substancia de sus escritos que es pecar de cua-
> tro costados contra el entendimiento: v. gr., llamar a los
> coches "ruiseñores de los ramilletes de Provincia [sic] (ta-
> les se los depare su necedad a las almohadas, cuando ten-
> gan jaquecas).

He pokes fun again at Vélez's lack of learning:

> Decir que nuestros antípodas son los que tienen de-
> bajo de nuestras plantas sus cabezas de modo que andan
> de colodrillo y llevan las pantorrillas en el aire: ¡miren
> qué buenos latinos y qué bien entienden las significacio-
> nes del *anti* y del *pos-pudos* de los nominativos!

Tirso then points to Vélez's ridiculous metaphors and to
his difficulty in finding rhymes:

Vendernos que un valiente, luchando con un jayán, le congojó de modo que soltándole compasivo, necesitó "salir nadando por el piélago de su sudor"; que en la carrera de un Píramo "se desavecindó de la herradura de un bridón un clavo y voló tan Icaro que ya es estrella en el *octavo* firmamento, para lucir el consonante de *clavo* y *octavo*,

> Porque un consonante obliga
> a lo que un *bobo* no piensa.

Y tantas civilidades a esta traza, que, a atreverse a despinzarlas alguno, dieran en que entender a todos los pañeros de Segovia; buen provecho les hagan y con ellas este dístico que Marcial remite a los que se alaban de que de ninguno dicen mal, y los estrados y polleras los desmienten. Va [el dístico] como su madre le parió, porque en latín, no entendiéndole, no les para perjuicio; y es el 78 epigr. del libro III:

> De nullo quereris nulli maledicis (Avite)
> Rumor dit [sic; ¿ait?], lingua te tamen esse male.

Tirso concludes his defense and counter-attack with these words: "*Señor a ti solo,* dígales todo esto o no les diga nada, que están en el hospital de los precitos; y quédese con Dios hasta que mi padre y él asegunden vistas." And it should be noted that Tirso, having spoken previously in the plural, here ends in the singular: "hasta que mi padre y *él* asegunden vistas"!

Again we have the same charges against Vélez that we have met time and time again: he is an idiot who borrows witty sayings for his *gracioso* (he learnedly calls him "parasite," as though he knew Latin comedy!) from the printed prose works of the very delightful, very discreet, and very popular don Francisco de Quevedo; yet Vélez has the consummate nerve (as though *he only* had the right to borrow) to reprove Tirso for using military terms from other languages such as "comboyes" or "víveres" — or for coining the verb "paralelar" from "paralelo." At least he (Tirso) doesn't use Latinized sentence order as does Vélez!

But "they" are so stupid, so slow of comprehension, "they" wouldn't understand, no matter what one told "them." "They" don't even know that *ceática* is a word accented on the antepenultimate syllable! Yet "they" raise their own authority *with the ladies* by pointing out Tirso's use of borrowed words! In their laps, "they" play the idiot (from *idiotizan:* another verb, formed on the stem of a noun, just to pay them for their "descalabradura").

Then Tirso lists a series of "disparates" culled from Vélez's works:

1)   his silly metaphor for "coches."

2)   his belief that "antípodas" signifies men who, on the opposite side of the world, walk on their heads with their feet in the air! He doesn't know what *anti* and *pos-podos* mean! A fine Latin scholar!

3)   his description of a lachrymose "valiente" who had "to wade through the high seas of his sweat."

4)   another one telling how a nail from the horseshoe of a rider flew to heaven like Icarus, there to form a star in the eighth firmament and all to the end, says Tirso, that the poet be able to rhyme *clavo* and *octavo.* Then the dramatist alters one of Vélez's favorite quotations (one from Baltasar de Alcázar) to read:

> Porque un consonante obliga
> a lo que un *bobo* no piensa. [51]

As he draws near the end of his harangue, Tirso quotes yet another Latin distych (Book III, 78th epigram) from Marcial: it won't hurt Vélez since he doesn't know Latin! He ends up in tones of mock despair —for Vélez is already in the hospital of the condemned - saying it is useless to tell him *anything;* and so, God be with him until the two of them have a *second* meeting.

---

[51] This favorite expression of Vélez's, we find in the *sátiras* written against him in 1625 (see pp. 228-29), in his *El diablo cojuelo* (105), and in his *Juicio final.* In the *Juicio final,* still in manuscript, the phrase is used when the many "Giles" protest a line of a *villancico*: "Mas no lo sepan los Giles," where "Giles" is used to rhyme with "abriles." Apollo excuses the injustice done the "Giles" on the basis that "había sido *fuerza del consonante,* porque un consonante obliga a lo que un hombre no piensa."

Did this end Tirso's war against Mendoza and Vélez? I doubt it. The *Sexta parte*, promised by Tirso in his Fifth *parte*, never came out, though the dramatist certainly had enough plays floating around Spain to fill another volume and, among them, some that are excellent. [52] Mendoza and Vélez, as well, possibly answered Tirso's challenge by doing just what he himself had invited: i.e., they spoke, behind the scenes, to Olivares and Philip. However, Tirso had not yet started his *Historia de Nuestra Señora de la Merced*, though he had been appointed chronicler of his Order when Remón died in 1632. [53] It could be instead that his superiors began pressure on Tirso to start his history of the Order.

Vélez, too, apparently felt the need of venting his spleen against Tirso once more. In 1638 someone (almost certainly Vélez) wrote a *vejamen* entitled *Juicio final* in which all the poets are summoned to final justice by Apollo. One of the judgments sounds very much as if it were directed against Tirso. The countless "Giles" had come and gone, among them "*Gil del Rábano*" (alcalde of Vélez's *La luna de la sierra*) and Tirso's "*don Gil de las calzas verdes*"; there next entered "unos poetas castellanos con un poeta portugués y el demonio y los siete pecados mortales" who met short shrift at Apollo's hands, whereupon, [54]

> Aquí metieron en una cama [a; sic] cuatro cirujanos a un poeta quebrando a gritos los corazones. Preguntó Apolo qué traían y dijeron los susodichos cirujanos que "mal de piedra" y que estaba acabando. Y mandó Apolo, viéndolo padecer con tanto exceso, que le abriesen, a vivir o a morir, pues estaba con tanto riesgo de la vida. Hiciéronlo los cirujanos y halláronle en el riñón congelada una comedia más dura que un diamante y el título della era "Quien tal hace que tal pague"; y a duras penas la tu-

---

[52] He could have there included, for instance, *La santa Juana (tercera parte)*, *Amar por señas*, *El burlador de Sevilla*, *La firmeza en la hermosura*, *La ventura con el nombre*, *Quien da luego da dos veces*, *El honroso atrevimiento*, *Desde Toledo a Madrid*, *En Madrid y en una casa*, *Los balcones de Madrid*, *El cobarde más valiente*, *Las quinas de Portugal*, and others.

[53] See Sra. de los Ríos, *Obras dramáticas completas*, III, 31-33.

[54] Prof. Hannah Bergman and I have transcribed and studied at some length this *Juicio final*.

vieron en las manos cuando se hundió el juicio a silbos y
a castrapuercos. El poeta quedó descansado pero con pesadumbre de ver chillada su comedia, casi antes de haber
nacida, y mandó Apolo que de allí adelante se tuviese en
la cura y en la dieta muy gran cuidado con él y que no
le dejasen pasar consonantes. Sacáronle como le tru-
jeron.

Lauro presumably had Tirso in mind when penning this bit
of satire from *El juicio final.* "Quien tal hace que tal pague"
was a favorite expression of Gabriel Téllez. He had used it in
at least six plays: in the *Santa Juana II* (II, vii); in his *Tan
largo me lo fiais* (III, xxi); in his *Burlador de Sevilla* (III, xxii);
in his *Doña Beatriz de Silva* (III, iii), and in *El mayor desengaño* (II, xv-xvi). More important for our purpose than any of
those uses is the fact that he had employed it in *La fingida
Arcadia* — and precisely in the scene (III, iii) where he was
condemning to a figurative hell both Vélez and Olivares. This
satire is the vengeance of Lauro against a Tirso who had sent
him to the nether regions and had pointed repeatedly to the
cat-calls which had greeted a play of Lauro's. And in referring
to the doctor's orders, "que no le dejasen pasar consonantes,"
Vélez is presumably recalling to Tirso the *Junta's acuerdo* which
forbade his writing further plays. The last word would seem to
have been Vélez's.

Let us admit frankly that, in this chapter on Luis Vélez, we
are handicapped by our lack of knowledge of the Andalusian's
theatre. Until such a time as we have for Vélez a penetrating
study of his plays, much of what we have written in this
chapter can be termed surmise only. Even after we have the study
indicated, we shall have to remember that we have today only
a small portion of the 400 plays [55] that Lauro claimed to have
written. I have therefore not been able to prove beyond a shadow
of doubt that Vélez was primarily responsible for the abusive
quatrain against Tirso and Alarcón which so irked the Mercedarian, though the presumption of guilt against him is, I believe,
quite strong. Let us, by way of conclusion to this chapter, sum

---

[55] See p. 239, where Vélez claims 400 plays.

up the evidence which indicates that Vélez, with the help of don Antonio de Mendoza and probably some *motilones* from the Palace or the Academy of Madrid, wrote the epigram that was found on the pastry-shop wall.

1) Tirso, in *La ventura con el nombre,* attributes the offensive *copla* to *más de cuatro motilones* who wrote with *plumas mestizas.*

2) Luis Vélez de Guevara was, in his day, well-known not only for his malice but also for his "donayres," his *sales,* his *motes.* However, he seems to have called on his friends for help in bringing them to perfection: "y sin ayuda de amigo, / jamás hiciste motete." He was, in the 1620's, a close friend to Antonio Hurtado de Mendoza, and had been one since 1608 when both were part of the household of the Conde la Saldaña. Mendoza also was given to writing "motes" and was, we believe, one of the "scribes" who, as Tirso tells us in *Amar por arte mayor,* was responsible for the *mote* that appeared on the *pastelería's* wall.

3) In early 1626, precisely when begging to be chronicler of the king's trip to Zaragoza, Vélez links Tirso with the ridiculous Arceo ("¡Malos años para Arceo y el fraile de la Merced!"), who had chronicled some earlier royal trips (in most inartistic verse, according to both Mendoza and Alenda!). [56] A *loa* of don Antonio — in which "Arceo" is painted as resenting any and all who usurped what he considered his prerogative of being royal chronicler — was put on with Mendoza's *Más medra quien miente más* in 1634, a play that was being sponsored financially by the Conde-Duque. In this same play Mendoza apparently makes an opportunity to praise Gabriel Téllez, "escondido en lo Tirso de Molina." Together with the *loa,* in which Arceo was painted as a ridiculous competitor to Mendoza, the performance

---

[56] Alenda y Mira (*Solemnidades y fiestas públicas de España,* 237-238) has this comment on *La perla en el mapa-mundi* (i.e., the description of Philip IV's trip to Sevilla): "Basta y sobra lo extravagante del título para contar *este opúsculo* entre *las peores y más ridículas* producciones del siglo XVII." By comparing him with the stupid "Arceo," Vélez and Mendoza thus downgraded Tirso! Guilt by association.

was guaranteed to recall to the Conde-Duque what had happened back in 1625.

4) Two bits of symbolism, [57] found in Tirso's *Cigarrales de Toledo* (1624), seem to make evident that Gabriel Téllez was also challenging Mendoza's credentials as chronicler of the king's feats, was indeed asking for his place. A passage in *La república al revés* [58] (retouched in 1621) makes clear that Tirso had been dreaming of a position in the Palace bureaucracy since 1621. The link that Vélez establishes between Tirso and Arceo seemingly confirms us in our interpretation of the symbolism found in *Los Cigarrales de Toledo.* [59]

5) There is abundant evidence that Tirso detested Luis Vélez de Guevara. He had, in *La fingida Arcadia*, satirized him, together with Olivares, and had put them both in the Inferno. On three separate occasions, he had painted the Andalusian as a "corpulent poet," sometimes alone, sometimes in combination with Olivares, his patron. In an anonymous poem which had first appeared in the second *Donayres del Parnaso* (1625) and was reprinted in Tirso's *Segunda parte* (1635), he (or another) had written a vitriolic poem against Vélez. In reprinting it, Tirso gave the poem a new lease on life. He would apparently attack Vélez again in the "A ti sólo" of his *Quinta parte*.

6) Vélez (?) — after Tirso's *La fingida Arcadia* had appeared in 1634 (a play wherein the Mercedarian had condemned Vélez to the nether regions with a favorite phrase, "quien tal hace que tal pague") — had, in 1638, written his *Juicio final.* [60] Therein he paints surgeons as removing a "play" from a poet, one who was suffering greatly from "mal de piedra"; it was one entitled, "Quien tal hace que tal pague." The sick poet, in my opinion, was none other than Tirso.

7) Tirso had, perhaps as early as 1622 in *La fingida Arcadia*, linked Vélez de Guevara with Ruiz de Alarcón. When that satire

---

[57] See pp. 141-42.
[58] My article on *La república al revés* — see *Reflexión*, 2, II (1923), 39-50 — makes this evident.
[59] See 57 above.
[60] See pp. 292-93.

finally became known in the Palace, Luis Vélez and Mendoza apparently tied the name of Tirso to that of Alarcón and declared both of them worthless as poets in the *copla* that appeared on the pastry-shop wall. Tirso would counter — after both Vélez and Alarcón held bureaucratic positions — by labelling them "Apollo's tailor and cobbler," as we shall see in the chapter that follows.

It is now time to study Tirso's relations with the Mexican-born dramatist, Juan Ruiz de Alarcón. Before concluding the chapter that follows, we shall strive to find out why Alarcón should have been brought into this whole affair.

VIII

TIRSO AGAINST JUAN RUIZ DE ALARCÓN
AND LUIS VÉLEZ

Hartzenbusch [1] was apparently the first to suggest that Gabriel Téllez and Ruiz de Alarcón were friends and collaborators. In the *Segunda parte* — a bibliographical conundrum which in 1635 was put out under the name of Gabriel Téllez — the dramatist, on dedicating that volume, indicated the intervention of other playwrights: " ... la dedico, destas doce comedias, *cuatro* que son mías en mi nombre y en el do los dueños *de las otras ocho* (que ño sé por qué infortunio suyo, siendo hijas de tan ilustres padres, las echaron a mis puertas) las que restan ... " Hartzenbusch — with this declaration on Téllez's part — would go in search of an author (or a co-author) for the plays that were not Tirso's; and, having at hand the ugly *copla* which linked the names of the two,

---

[1] See Hartzenbusch (*BAE*, V, xxxviii-xxxix) under his analyses of *Cautela contra cautela* and *Próspera fortuna de don Álvaro de Luna y adversa de Ruy López de Ávalos*. Fernández-Guerra y Orbe (*Don Juan Ruiz de Alarcón y Mendoza*, II, 46-47) attributed *Siempre ayuda la verdad* to Alarcón and Belmonte Bermúdez, but it has also been included in the theatres of Tirso and Alarcón. Francisco Medel's *Índice general* shows two plays of that name, one ascribed to Tirso and one to Alarcón. This possibly implies a *suelta* attributed to Alarcón, which was existent in Medel's time but is now lost to us. Ed. Barry, in making his edition of *La verdad sospechosa* (p. xviii), even suggested that Alarcón must have collaborated with Tirso in the writing of *La villana de Vallecas*: "...les deux collaborateurs s'unirent pour la défense et la présentèrent d'abord dans *La villana de Vallecas*." Sra. de los Ríos (*Obras...*, II, 785-786) emphatically rejects the idea, as does this critic!

For Tirso's statement, taken from his *Segunda parte*, see Cotarelo, *Comedias de Tirso*, I, lix.

he would find that collaborator in Juan Ruiz de Alarcón. This suggestion would influence critics for a century. As late as 1951, E. Abreu Gómez[2] wrote: "En medio de estas tormentas, es posible que haya encontrado alivio en la amistad de Tirso de Molina ..."

On this occasion, we cannot attempt to resolve the bibliographical history of the many attempts to place, in whole or in part, this or that individual play in Tirso's or Alarcón's theatre. What we shall strive to do in this study is: 1) show that the Mercedarian was an enemy of Ruiz de Alarcón, one who satirized him harshly and repeatedly, and that it is therefore highly improbable that the two should have written plays "de consuno"[3]; 2) find out why Tirso should have linked Luis Vélez and Ruiz de Alarcón after 1625-26.

Tirso's satire of Ruiz de Alarcón falls largely into three periods: 1620, 1622(?)-23, and 1625-26. It began, evidently, when our dramatist made a trip to Madrid in early 1620 and, on returning to Segovia, wrote his *La Villana de Vallecas*. Therein he has

---

[2] Abreu Gómez, Ermilo, *Teatro completo de don Juan Ruiz de Alarcón*, p. viii.

[3] There is, in so far as I know, no evidence whatsoever to bolster what was, for Hartzenbusch, only a guess. What reason is there for rejecting Tirso's own assertion, especially now that we have the autograph manuscript of *La adversa fortuna de don Alvaro de Luna*, signed by Mira de Amescua, together with clear proof that *La Reina de los Reyes* was printed by Hipólito Vergara as his work nearly ten years before it was included in Tirso's *Segunda parte*? Tirso indicated in the clearest terms that only four of the plays were his. The burden of proof for assuming otherwise now rests on those who do so, or so it would seem to me.

Critics are well-agreed that *Amor y celos hacen discretos*, *Por el sótano y el torno*, and *Esto sí que es negociar* are works of Tirso, but they disagree as to which is his "fourth" work: some believe it to be the magnificent theological drama, *El condenado por desconfiado;* others point to the fact that *Cautela contra cautela* is a *refundición* of *El amor y el amistad* and that it must be "the fourth play." As one who has spent the greater port of a lifetime working on Tirso's theatre, I should like very much to believe that he wrote *El condenado por desconfiado*. Unfortunately, I cannot. There will appeared in a recent issue of *RABM* a long study entitled "Tirso's 'Fourth Play' in his *Segunda parte* of 1635: *Cautela contra cautela*, not *El condenado por desconfiado*." It will later be included in some volume of this series. See also my "Did Tirso Send to Press a *Primera parte* in Madrid (1626), one Containing *El condenado por desconfiado*?" It has appeared in the *homenaje* to Prof. Arnold Reichenberger, *HR*, XLI (1973), 261-74.

criticized the Mexican in no less than three directions; in such satire he was but following the lead of other writers of Madrid. The year 1623 brought down on poor Alarcón a whole avalanche of abuse from his fellow-poets of Madrid, among them Tirso, when that dramatist was asked to write up the royal fiestas of August, given in honor of the Prince of Wales. The third period was, we believe, occasioned by the quatrain of early 1625, in which Tirso's name was coupled with Alarcón's in derogatory fashion. The pattern of Tirso's satire against Alarcón is now reasonably clear — as it was not when I first wrote this study.

Gabriel Téllez was in Madrid some time before March 25th, 1620. This we know because there is in the first act of *La villana de Vallecas* a letter of that date. What is more, don Gabriel de Herrera, when in the little inn of Arganda, gives don Pedro de Mendoza the news from Madrid. [4] This included, as we have seen above: the recovery of Philip III from the illness that overtook him in Casarrubios; the royal visit to Atocha to give thanks; the love and gratitude of his subjects for the blessings of his reign; the state of the theatre (Pinedo's production of Lope's *El asombro de la Limpia Concepción*), and praise of Lope. The whole picture is so vivid, even of the bad bedroom in that poor inn with its various religious chromos, not to speak of the demonstrations that took place when Philip III made his visit to Atocha, that it seems to me, impossible that don *Gabriel* de Herrera should not have been speaking for *Gabriel* Téllez.

The satire in *La villana de Vallecas* against Alarcón extends in three directions; that against *indianos* as gossips; that against men who assume the title of "don" without being entitled to it; that of Alarcón as lover of a *boba*. Don Pedro de Mendoza, recently returned from the Indies, is happy over the thought that his father has pledged him to "Serafina," [5] daughter of don Gómez de Peralta. Agudo, his servant, is somewhat skeptical of the evidence

---

[4] In the first chapter of this volume, I have used the news budget as a general forecast of Tirso's interests for the years he spent in Madrid. See above pp. 59-65.

[5] It should be noted that he here uses the same name for his heroine, "Serafina," that is found in *El vergonzoso en palacio* (reworked, in all probability, in 1620-21) and in the *Cigarrales*. See p. 172, n. 34.

that has reached don Pedro in Mexico concerning the many virtues
of his Serafina, but the groom-to-be points out (I, iv):

> Fama, Agudo, que ha llegado
> limpia a Méjico, y a prueba
> de las lenguas, ¡cosa nueva!

Agudo is convinced that she must indeed be a seraph and even
adds his bit of evidence:

> Y más, donde es tan usado
> el murmurar, que sin ciencia
> colige toda criatura:
> "¿Indiano? Luego murmura."

The satire probably goes back to Alarcón's *Las paredes oyen* and
the charge of *maldiciente* which he there brought against his
detractors (among them, Lope). At any rate Lope would answer
the charge in his *Tercera parte* (of 1620):

> ... A *los gibosos* pinta el mismo filósofo [i.e., Aristóte-
> les] con mal aliento ...; mal aliento, claro está, ... *ha de
> inficionar cuanto* tocare hablando. Es cosa ordinaria de
> tales hombres ... la *soberbia y el desprecio*... Tengan por
> cierto los *invidiosos* que han de temer su golpe de cuan-
> do en cuando.

And Serafina has her prejudices also (III, xi):

> Razón el que afirma tiene
> que cuanto de Indias nos viene
> es bueno, si no es los hombres.

But, before Lope and Tirso had expressed their dislike of Alarcón,
Suárez de Figueroa had, in his *Pasagero*, indicated outright antipa-
thy (225-226): "Notables sabandijas crían los límites antárticos y
occidentales!" He had as well, previously accused the Mexican of
being "siempre en la malicia."

Satire of Alarcón and his *boba* is found on two occasions in
La villana de Vallecas (III, ix and x). On the first, Violante will
speak of "bellacos que andan de noche / y engañan a troche y
moche / a quien de ellos se fio"; then will add, "Si no hubiera

tantas *bobas*, / no hubiera embeleco tanto." She will return to her
theme in the following scene. When speaking of "la dama india-
nesa" she asks: "Luego, ¿ella creyó que hablaba con el buen
señor *a bobas?*" I was, some years ago, skeptical as to the interpretation that should be given the various quotations concerning
bobas (or *bobos*) that one finds in 1620-21, but I am now
certain, in my own mind, that the literary world was, in those
years, satirizing Alarcón's love for a certain *boba*. I doubt, however,
that Fernández-Guerra's identification of the girl [6] in question as
doña Clara de *Boba*dilla y Alarcón is correct, however logical
such an identification seems at first sight: she had, it is true
contributed a poem of praise, along with Alarcón, to Agreda y
Vargas' *novela, Los más felices amantes, Leucipe y Cletifonte*
(1617); and, what is more, they shared in common the name of
Alarcón, a fact that suggests they may have been distant relatives.
However, it seems to me even more logical that the reference is
to doña Ana de Cervantes [mother of his illegitimate (?) daughter,
Lorenza]. Of her, Mrs. King [7] — in her very fine study, "La ascendencia paterna de Juan Ruiz de Alarcón y Mendoza," — can tell
us only that she was the daughter of don Pedro Cervantes and doña
María do Rojas, the *padrinos* being Juan Cervantes and doña An-
tonia Garcés. As to her efforts to verify the information
of this document, Mrs. King tells us frankly she had not been able
to do it. Whatever the woman's identity, we may be sure that as
early as 1617 Alarcón was being satirized in the role of lover of a
beautiful woman, one with literary talent. In *El pasajero* [8] of
1617, Suárez calls him "matante de las más hermosas"; and in
"... 1620, Salas Barbadillo [9] (in his *El sutil cordobés, Pedro de*

---

[6] See my study, "Contemporary Satire against Ruiz de Alarcón as
Lover," 149, n. 9.

[7] Willard F. King, "La ascendencia paterna de Juan Ruiz de Alarcón
y Mendoza," 54-55 and n. 14. Don Manuel de Perea, "secretario de su
Majestad," calls Lorenza Ruiz de Alarcón "hija legítima."

[8] *El pasajero*, 313.

[9] The *princeps*, here cited, has Alonso de Illescas' *aprobación*, dated
August 30, 1619, but the "conformidad con el original" was given January
6, 1620. See fols. 108r.-111r., 126r.-131r.

Mrs. King, in *La ascendencia paterna* ... (61-63) cites evidence to the effect
that *Violante* González, illegitimate ancestress of the dramatist and "vecina del
castillo de Garci-Muñoz" was "de gente de raza de judíos y, por haber judai-

Urdemalas) describes in detail a *maldiciente*," one "tan defectuoso que sus partes personales fueron cosquillas de la risa de los más severos." This little man, who was the possessor of a nose, "hebrea en lo disforme," one which "hizo la limpieza de su sangre sospechosa," who "... escribía versos y jugaba las armas," was, as usual, making love to "lo más bello, lo más discreto." Later, he tells us she was a "dama papelista" who was the daughter of a "maestro de escuelas." In his *Fiestas de la boda de la incasable mal casada*,[10] which went to press by July 7, 1621, he gives a far more detailed picture of this bluestocking, who was so proud of her intellectual attainments that she preferred marrying a hunchback, one don Sebastián with double hump, to subordinating her will to a husband whom she considered intellectually inferior.

From 1619 to 1621, then, some specific woman in Alarcón's life was being satirized as "la boba." For, not only do we have the three references I have named on another occasion: the "que no haya bobos," of Cortés de Tolosa's *Lazarillo de Manzanares*[11] (1620, but with *aprobación* of April 27, 1619); the list of Lope's *Justa poética*[12] (May, 1620), in which he enumerates any number

---

zado, la penitenciaron en el Santo Oficio de Cuenca ...," but Mrs. King's efforts to confirm the document were unsuccessful. She declares (62, n. 25): "Pese a las protestas del P. Sebastián Cirac Estopañón y otros que confirman lo contrario, el archivo no está abierto al público ni a los investigadores." It should be remembered that the *real* don Pedro de Mendoza of *La villana de Vallecas*, recently returned from the Indies, had reached the village of Arganda from Sevilla *by way of Cuenca*. He states (I, x): "Llegué de Cuenca a la famosa sierra, / antigua patria de mi padre ... Tenía en ella un tío que hallé muerto ... guié a la corte ..." He is, in the play, talking to *Violante*, who is forcing don Gabriel de Herrera to keep the promise of marriage he had made to her. Did Tirso know something of Alarcón's family background?

[10] Alonso Gerónimo de Salas Barbadillo's *Fiestas de la boda de la incasable malcasada* is mentioned in an *aprobación* of *El cortesano descortés*, which was in press by July 7, 1621. See fol. 37; also 164r.-165v.

[11] Cortés de Tolosa, *Lazarillo de Manzanares*, 29v.-33v. While the *erratas* are dated December 7, 1619, there is a note in the *Libro de la Hermandad de Impresores* which reads: "Capillas de mayo de 1620. *Dos Lazarillos de Madrid*. Possibly then it did not reach the Madrid public until the late spring of 1620. See Pérez Pastor, *Bibliografía madrileña*, II, 522.

I cited many years ago the three references of this paragraph in "Contemporary Satire against Ruiz de Alarcón as Lover," 156-157.

[12] Lope de Vega, *Justa poética*, fol. 133r.

of disagreeable things that have come to mind, among them, "juanetes y corcovas gordas, espesas, pedigüeñas bobas;" the *Corcovilla* of Quevedo (1620-21),[13] which asks "¿Quién anda engañando bobas, / siendo rico de la mar?" We have, as well, these references of Tirso from early 1620 and, in addition, one of Mira de Amescua from 1621. In the latter's *Próspera fortuna de don Alvaro de Luna y adversa de Ruiz López de Avalos,* Pablillos warns his master, who is for the first time entering the presence of the great *privado* (Act I, v):

> Entre tu buena fortuna,
> y no hagas por desdichas
> reverencias con corcovos;
> *encomiéndate a los bobos,*
> *que son dueños de las dichas.*

I am, then, convinced that Alarcón was being satirized as a *bobo,* in love with a *boba,* in 1620-21. What is more, when one remembers Alarcón's warm defense of his heroine, doña Ana de Contreras, against the gossip of don Mendo, in *Las paredes oyen* (by 1618), I believe we must seriously consider the possibility that the name of its protagonist is an anagram for Ana de Cervantes, one which differs by only two letters from that of Ana de Contreras, who was mother to a daughter of the poet, one baptized on January 6, 1617. If I am right in this supposition, then we have a great deal of information concerning the mother of doña Lorenza, though the details will, of course, all have to be weighed, one by one.

Tirso's satire of Ruiz de Alarcón in 1620 is not limited to his calling him "malicioso," nor to that of a "bellaco" who is deceiving a *boba.* He picks up, as well, the charge that the Mexican is using a "don" to which he is not entitled and that he has even

---

[13] The *Corcovilla* is dated 1631 by Astrana Marín, but this must be a printer's error for 1621. Alarcón was out of the fray by 1631. Cf. the lines of this poem (*Obras en verso,* 184), "Que su línea es de Corbera / y sus líneas corvas son ..." with those of Quevedo's sonnet (dated 1622-24 by Astrana Marín) which begins (*Ibid.,* 138): "Cuernos hay para todos, *seor Corbera* ..." For further study concerning the date of the *Corcovilla,* see my study, "Studies for the Chronology of Tirso's Theatre," 45, n. 87.

appropriated a noble old name to which he has no right. Quevedo [14] had probably first brought this latter charge around 1603:

> Que don Milagro afeitado
> ajeno linaje infame
> y que *Mendoza* se llame
> por lo que tiene de *Hurtado;*
> ... ...
> *milagros de corte son.*

This same satirist, or another, will summarize various sins that were still being attributed to Alarcón in 1623: [15]

> Los apellidos de don Juan crecen como los hongos: ayer se llamaba *Juan Ruiz;* añadiósele el *Alarcón,* y hoy ajusta el *Mendoza,* que otros leen *Mendacio.* ¡Así creciese de cuerpo! que es mucha carga para tan pequeña bestezuela. Yo aseguro que tiene las corcovas llenas de apellidos. Y adviértase que la "D" no es *don,* sino su medio retrato.

Tirso also twice makes this charge: the first one, in the plot itself of his play. *La villana de Vallecas* has to do with a certain don Gabriel de Herrera, who can, through a mix-up of *maletas* at the little inn of Arganda, usurp both the name *and* fortune of don Pedro de *Mendoza,* recently arrived from Mexico. When his master changes names, the *gracioso* Beltrán significantly changes his name to *Cornejo.* Tirso echoes, too, Alarcón's appropriation of a "don" to which he is not entitled. When don Juan would pay a compliment to doña Violante, he tells her, "Donaire tenéis." Her quick answer is (II, v):

> sin *don:*
> que en Vallecas más se usa
> el *aire,* al limpiar las parvas,
> que el *don,* que mos las ensucia.

This last challenge Tirso will repeat, and even underline, in *Averígüelo Vargas.* When reworking this play, the Mercedarian

---

[14] Francisco de Quevedo Villegas, *Obras en verso,* 84.
[15] The quotation given is from *Comedias escogidas de fray Lope Félix de Vega Carpio, BAE,* LII, 587-588.

mocks a "don lacayo" who, as we shall show later in this study, is undoubtedly Alarcón. Puffed up by his new finery, the *gracioso* jingles away (II, ii):

> Es tanta la presunción
> que destas quimeras saco
> que no he de ser más *Tabaco,*
> o le he de echar *el tacón*
> de un *don;* que no es mal ensayo
> que *don Tabaco* me nombren,
> aunque los dones se asombren
> de haber hecho un *don lacayo.*
> Mas, tantos los dones son
> que aun las campanas los dan,
> pues si tañe el sacristán,
> pronuncia *dan, dan, don, don.*
> Y si *dan don,* desde hoy quiero
> un *don,* aunque sea trabajo;
> que un *don,* dado de un *badajo,*
> bien está en un majadero...

Alarcón has taken unto himself a *don* that does not belong to him; he is a *majadero,* a talkative, foolish person *(badajo)* who gets his *don* from a bell-clapper [16]

---

[16] Cf with Quevedo's comment (in *La vida del Buscón,* 161-162) on the name of the *hidalgo,* Don Toribio Rodríguez Vallejo Gómez de Ampuero y Jordán: "No se vió jamás nombre tan campanudo, porque acababa en *dan* y empezaba en *don,* como son de badajo." Prof. A. A. Parker, in his *Literature and the Delinquent* (57), says concerning the date of the *Buscón*: "A close comparison of its style with that of other satirical works of his whose dates of composition are known would not be likely, in my opinion, to point to a date much earlier than 1620."

As to the date of *Averígüelo Vargas,* Sra. de los Ríos (*Obras dramáticas completas de Tirso,* II, 1023) places its composition in 1619-21. The date she suggests is not incompatible with the versification (*red.,* 43.2%; *quin.,* 32.6%; *dec.,* 3.9%; *rom.,* 14.8%; *oct.,* 5.5%). Such figures should be compared with those of *La villana de Vallecas* of March, 1620 (*red.,* 48.4%; *quin.,* 21.8%; *dec.,* 1.3%; *rom.,* 19.9%; *oct.,* 3.8%; *ter.,* 2.3%; *su.,* 2.5%). *Averígüelo Vargas* looks slightly later than *La villana de Vallecas.* However, study of references to costume in *Averígüelo Vargas* argues that the play was retouched after the sumptuary decrees of February, 1623. See R. L. Kennedy, "Studies for the Chronology of Tirso's Theatre," 37-38, n. 63. But it must have been retouched *once more* after June 17, 1626. See below, pp. 315-16.

Casual study of the allusions to costume in *El Buscón* would, on the other hand, indicate that *it was all done before the aforesaid sumptuary decrees* of 1623.

The very name that Tirso has given his *gracioso* in this play points to Alarcón's Mexican origin. The word *tabaco* is uncertain of origin, but the product itself, in the Spanish mind of the seventeenth century, was linked with America. Corominas points out, in his *Diccionario crítico etimológico*, that it has been argued that "el nombre viene de la isla de Tabago [also "Tobago"] en el golfo de Méjico," where the Caribs supposedly used tobacco freely. This island's surface, one reads in *Collier's New Encyclopedia*, "is irregular … *abounding in conical hills and spurs*." On naming his *gracioso* Tabaco, Tirso (who had spent from 1616-1618 in Santo Domingo) would remember the island's topography and its products, as well as Alarcón's humps! He will, as we shall see later, enlarge on this satire in 1626 [17] when he retouched *Averígüelo Vargas*.

Let us get on to the year 1623 when Ruiz de Alarcón suffered his second baptism of fire. The Mexican had been commissioned through the Marqués de Cea, later Duque de Lerma, to write up the royal fiestas which were given in August of that year to honor the Prince of Wales, who was returning to England in early September. Faced with a task which was for him by its very nature difficult — it had been stipulated that it should be in *lenguaje culto* — Alarcón was so unwise as to call on other poets of the court for their help. When the hodge-podge that resulted brought Madrid's jeers, not cheers, and when Alarcón would not share the financial reward with his collaborators, the latter brought him to burlesque trial with a series of satirical *décimas*. The one attributed to *Luis* Téllez — the copyist, no doubt, unconsciously anticipated the "Luis" of Vélez's *décima* that immediately follows — reads as follows (*BAE*, LII, 587):

> Don Cohombro de Alarcón,
> un poeta entre dos platos,
> cuyos versos los silbatos
> temieron y con razón,
> escribió una *Relación*
> de las fiestas, que sospecho
> que, por no ser de provecho,

---

[17] See pp. 315-16.

la han de poner entredicho;
porque es todo tan mal dicho,
como el poeta mal hecho.

The *décima* is undoubtedly *Gabriel* Téllez's, as we shall soon see, for not only will this *décima* find echoes in his theatre but also another one, written on that same occasion.

With two words only, "don Cohombro," Tirso has reduced to the absurd Alarcón's claim to the honorable old title of *don*. Sir Cucumber! But in order to know just *how* absurd it sounded to Madrid's ears of that time, one must keep in mind how ugly was that particular species of the cucurbitaceous vine. Covarrubias wrote in his *Tesoro* of 1611: "... los *cohombros luengos* que se crían en Castilla en tanta abundancia no se hallan en otras partes y pone [sic] a los extranjeros una manera de horror, pareciéndoles tiene [sic] alguna semblanza de culebra."

On labelling the Mexican "don Cohombro," Tirso had in mind, however, far more than Alarcón's twisted body or his assumed "don"; he was recalling to his contemporaries a proverb of the time: "Quien hizo el cohombro / que se lo traiga al hombro." It is found in Covarrubias' *Tesoro* and, with it, its usual application: "Algunos padres engendran hijos mal talladas y desproporcionados, *como es el cohombro, y a veces por su culpa, por estar ellos dañados* o ser mal regidos; y éstos deben tener paciencia y sufrirlos y alimentarlos." From Tirso's point of view, then, Alarcón had, in his *Relación*, engendered an offspring that was "tan mal dicho como el poeta mal hecho," and having done so, he must carry his burden with patience, be of long suffering, give it a home and care.

The whole idea of *don Cohombro* pleased Gabriel Téllez so much that he would develop his metaphor into a scene, not in one play but in two, [18] both of them written (or rewritten) in the

---

[18] Tirso skirts its use on a third occasion (*Todo es dar en una ocasión*, I, xiv) when he employs the same scene of an illegitimate child that is being handed to a passerby; but on this occasion, he chose to play, not on the metaphor of "don Cohombro," but instead on one taken from an anonymous *décima* (possibly Tirso's) of those same *fiestas*—or else from Lope de Vega's second *sátira* against Torres Rámila. He apparently takes the word "volamatriz" from the *décima* beginning, "En el cascarón metido /

same general period. In *Escarmientos para el cuerdo*[19] — which, as we shall see later in this study, carries yet other satire of Alarcón — the *gracioso* Carballo is being interrogated by Leonor's stern father, García de Sa, concerning the new-born child that has been thrust into his arms. He rightly suspects that it is his own grandson, born out of wedlock to his daughter, Leonor. Carballo, terrified of his master, will complain (II, iii, 67):

> ¿por qué he de pagar,
> pecador de mi, señor,
> si mi sa doña Leonor,
> tan bien supo aprovechar
> cosechas de su hermosura … ?
> Si yo no fui la *comadre*,
> si *yo no hice el cohombro,*
> ¿*es bien que me le eche al hombro?*
> ¿que muera yo sin ser padre … ?
> ¿y que haya yo de pasar
> dolores de la parida?

The very same metaphor, used under vitually the same circumstances, may be found in abbreviated form in *Quien da luego da dos veces*[20] (I, xi, 552):

---

el señor *Volamatriz* / para un *elogio* infeliz / octavas ha repartido …," and plays on it in the following fashion: "Un burujón / vino a empujar con su cola / redonda que llaman bola de Beatriz." Crespo will correct him: "Callad, simplón / bolamatriz debió ser." It should be noted that Tirso has retained here the implications of Cohombro and of Margarito when he says the new-born child is "neither boy nor girl."

Lope, however, in concluding his second *sátira* against Torres Rámila and Suárez de Figueroa, had used the word "molamatriz" (the correct spelling) to satirize the grammarian. Having promised a third *sátira* worse than the two he had finished, he follows the threat with the following lines: "¿A qué regañarás, borla cagada, / molamatriz del cuerno [¿cuervo?] Figueroa / por la boca de víbora engendrada?" See J. de Entrambasaguas, *Una guerra literaria del Siglo de Oro*, 405.

[19] Sra. de los Ríos left a note, dating this play 1619 (*Obras dramáticas de Tirso*, III, 217-220), including it in what she terms Tirso's "ciclo galaico-portugués." See my study, "The Dates of *El amor médico* and *Escarmientos para el cuerdo*," 22-32. Both plays were written, or rewritten, in 1625-29 — almost certainly in 1625-26 — after Tirso was in Trujillo.

[20] Some years ago I placed this play's composition between February 11th and March 22, 1623 (see "Studies for the Chronology of Tirso's Theatre," 34). At that time I saw in Calvete's declaration, "La ley lo

CALVETE: ¿Qué te ha dado?
LUIS: La criatura.
CALVETE: Bueno, *a quien hizo el cohombro*
    di que se le eche en el hombro...
LUIS: Miremos por el honor
    de Margarita, Calvete,
    que, al fin, la he querido bien.
    A *buscar una ama* ven...
CALVETE: Ajó, niño, ajó.
    Llamaráse Margarito.

It is possible — though I do not urge the point — that Tirso, in labelling the Mexican dramatist *don Cohombro de Alarcón* and in developing in two separate plays the physiological implications of this proverb, may have had in mind Alarcón's liaison with Ana de Cervantes and the child that was born to them. Alarcón was father to a girl, one who, at the time of his death in August of 1639, inherited the bulk of his estate. In the will, she is named

---

veda ...: será seda sobre seda," a reference to the decree of February 11, 1623 which forbade use of that elegant silk and to the quick withdrawal of most of the provisions of that law on March 22, 1623 in honor of the Prince of Wales' visit. I now know that those *pragmáticas* must have been declared in force again almost as soon as the Englishman had turned his back on Madrid. Hence the date *a quo* will hold, the one *ad quem* will not. The development of the proverb, "A quién hizo el cohombro ..." just two scenes later, strongly indicates that its composition (or its retouching) should be placed after August, 1623.

Sra. de los Ríos (*Obras dramáticas completas de Tirso*, II, 292) believed that this play was originally written "between 1606 and 1612 or 1624," but seeing in the comment of Margarita, "Tú eres el Diablo Cojuelo," a reference to Vélez de Guevara's novel, thought it retouched after the publication of that work in 1641. Her reasoning will not hold, for there is a scene in the third act of *La Estrella de Sevilla* (1, 2521) which likewise refers to "el Diablo Cojuelo," and that play was in print by 1635. Moreover, its composition (or its reworking) can, with reasonable certainty, be ascribed to the months following the August *fiestas* of 1623, given in honor of Charles of England.

As a matter of fact, *Quien da luego* ... and *La Estrella de Sevilla* are related: John Hill pointed this fact out some years ago in his fine edition of the latter play (ed. Reed, Dixon and Hill, 94-101). Compare with these pages others of *Quien da luego* ... (III, xi and xii): both are in assonance e-o; both take place in Hell; in both, there is madness, feigned or real; both refer to the Diablo Cojuelo; both satirize the *sastres* and link them with the poets. "Clarindo" is a reasonably good anagram for "Alarcón." I cannot prove it, but I suspect that *La Estrella* ... is the borrower.

310 STUDIES IN TIRSO, I

doña Lorenza de Alarcón, and it is further stated that she is living with her husband, don Fernando de Girón, in Barchín del Hoyo [La Mancha]. Antonio Castro Leal[21] suggested that she would have been born around 1620. We now know that she had been baptized by January of 1617.

The Mexican was, in 1623, enamoured of some lady at the very moment the *Relación* was being written. Whether or not she is the same one he loved in 1617 and in 1620-21 is not clear. Whatever her identity, she, too, was apparently a woman of literary interests, for one of the *décimas* makes evident that she has been invited to witness Alarcón's trial and humiliation: "Si a vistas me llaman hoy / a los ojos de mi bien ..."[22] Luis Vélez de Guevara gives us a glimpse of her appearance — and at the same time appropriates for Alarcón the metaphor of "camello," which he probably found in Quevedo's "Acúsanse de sus culpas los cuellos cuando se introdujeron las valonas."[23] In this poem, clearly written in February, 1623, Quevedo summons to judgment "todo cigüeño gaznate y *con corcova camello.*" Vélez's poem[24] reads in part:

> La dama que en los chapines
> te esperaba en pie, muy alta,
> diga tu sobra o tu falta,
> ¡oh padre de matachines!
> porque, por más que te empines,
> *camello enano* con loba,
> es de Soplillo tu trova,
> aunque son de Apolo hazañas...

Tirso, in a satirical passage directed against a hunchback lover, possibly takes over the metaphor of *camello*. In *Tanto es lo de*

---

[21] Antonio Castro Leal, *Juan Ruiz de Alarcón, su vida y su obra*, 52. The critic asks: "A pesar de que el poeta agradecido la endoña, ¿no habrá sido su ama de llaves en Madrid o alguna aldeana de Cuenca?" Her literary interests argue against such an identification.

[22] "Elogio descriptivo" and "Comento," *BAE*, LII, 587.

[23] Quevedo Villegas, "Acúsanse de sus culpas los cuellos ..." ed. Astrana Marín, 352.

[24] "Elogio descriptivo" and "Comento," *BAE*, LII, 587.

más como lo de menos,[25] he introduces a song in *seguidillas* which asks (II, ii):

UNA: Corcobados amantes, di ¿qué parecen?
       Hijos engendrados de muchas veces.
TODOS: Mas, si hay dinero,
       es como un pino de oro *todo camello.*

If I am right in my conjecture, then the play was possibly retouched somewhat later.

In *Amor y celos hacen discretos,*[26] the Mercedarian again satirizes a hunchback lover. He, here, either remembers the name of Cornejo which his *gracioso* had assumed in *La villana de Vallecas,* or he borrows the metaphor from Góngora's *décima* (which formed part of the same *vejamen*) and fuses it with yet other epithets taken from Quevedo's *Corcovilla.* Romero is servant to don Pedro de Castilla, who, in his capacity as secretary to the *gran mareschal* Carlos, writes the love letters of the latter. This

---

[25] *Princeps: Parte* I, 1627. For the play's date of composition, see my "Studies for the Chronology of Tirso's Theatre." 42-46, and E. Asensio, *Itinerario del entremés,* 128-131.

[26] *Princeps: Segunda parte.* Its heading declares: "Representóla Valdés, con que empezó en Sevilla." Sánchez Arjona (*Anales del teatro en Sevilla,* 178) concludes that it must have been put on in that city during Valdés' presence there either in 1615, 1616, or 1617. Sra. de los Ríos (*Obras dramáticas completas de Tirso,* I, 1399-1412) accepts 1615 as the year of composition, linking the protagonist don Pedro de Castilla ("que, cual todos los Jirones, se preciaba de descender del fiero monarca de Castilla") with the Duque de Osuna [i.e., the Téllez-Girón family] and his efforts in 1615-1616 to be appointed viceroy of Naples. She believed Quevedo and Tirso to be friends in those years and pointed to the *loa* which Quevedo wrote for *Amor y celos hacen discretos* (Astrana Marín, ed., *Obras en verso,* 600-602), as well as to the fact that González de Salas had declared with regard to it: "... se representó en una fiesta ... la recitó una comedianta a quien llamaban 'la Roma' [i.e., Jerónima de Burgos, wife to the abovementioned *autor*]." She did not die until 1641. See H. Rennert, *Spanish Actors and Actresses,* 438.
There are undoubtedly good reasons for linking this play with Tirso's early years: its versification (with 76.1% of *redondillas*) supports her arguments for an early date. On the other hand, the satire of the *cultos* (I, v); of the *repentistas* (I, v and vi); and of Ruiz de Alarcón (if I am right in believing the long passage quoted above to be directed against him), the verses "en circunferencia" (III, vii) — i.e., a sonnet in eight-syllable lines, encased in an Italian one of eleven-syllable verses: all these things proclaim that this play was reworked in the 1620's.

gracioso is indignant at lovers who urge their court with verses
that are not of their own making: why, he is like a hunchback
lover who has won his bride with false *galas*, says Romero (I, vii):

> Hablemos, ¡cuerpo de Dios!
> y salga la maula fuera.
> Si un novio engañar quisiera,
> fingiéndose *caudaloso*,
> galán, sabio y *generoso*,
> a una novia, y esto fuera
> todo al contrario; y llegase
> con las galas de alquiler
> a la inocente mujer
> y en fe desto le adorase;
> y admitidas norabuenas
> para ser enhoramalas, ...
> *al desnudar pantorrillas* [él]
> *las hallase de algodón,*
> *y el peto con el jubón*
> *supiese igualar costillas*
> *y estevaciones del pecho;*
> *descubriendo el tal Macías*
> *un alma entre dos bacías*
> *y a tortuga antes derecho:*
> ¿no era forzoso que a engaño
> la tal dama se llamase
> y que afligida llorase
> tan mal prevenido daño?
> ¿Con qué amor diera los brazos
> la pobreta, toda queja,
> a este *marido corneja*
> de maquilas y retazos?

Góngora [27] had, in his verbal indictment of Ruiz de Alarcón,
brought three charges against him: he was a *sastre* (an "oficial"),

---

[27] Góngora, *Obras.*

Antonio de Mendoza (*BAE*, LII, 587) likewise links the *corneja*'s thievery
with that of the *sastre* in his "Décima a un poeta corcovado que se valió
de trabajos ajenos": "Ya de *corcova* en *corneja* / se ha vuelto el señor
don Juan; / todos sus plumas le dan / para escribir su conseja ..." Moreover, Tirso himself, in his "Al bien intencionado," which precedes the
Cigarrales, having first painted a "lindo" with "bigotera, guedejas, peto,
valonas, pantorrillas," says: "Y viérasme corneja, si me ves gozque de la
China." What is more, he has, in lines just above this passage, linked his

not a poet; he was a *corneja* who dressed up in the feathers of others; he was a *galápago* of double conch and would always be one:

> Hoy de las *fiestas reales*
> *sastre* y no poeta seas,
> si a octavas como libreas
> introduces *oficiales*.
> ¿De ajenas plumas te vales,
> *corneja?* Desmentirás
> la que delante y detrás
> gémina concha te viste:
> *galápago* siempre fuiste,
> y *galápago* serás.

Tirso, on writing this satire of *Amor y celos hacen discretos*, apparently remembered also Quevedo's *Corcovilla* (184): "... y quién ... / se viste un escapulario / de *bacías de barbero*? / ¿Quién es cinco y vale cero, / pechuga con *pantorrilla*?"

In this same play, too, Tirso may well have recalled that Lope had discredited Torres Rámila in his two *sátiras* by linking him with the Tailor of Toledo. At least Tirso deepens Carlos' crime — so stupid as to use the poems of another to plead his suit — by comparing him to a "mecánico oficial," one who is possibly that same tailor-poet (I, v):

> ... en unos es discreto
> lo que en otros no es de estima:
> *un mecánico oficial,*
> *confesando natural,*
> *hizo comedias; que anima*
> *bajezas tal vez Apolo:*
> no eran las comedias buenas,
> pues, de disparates llenas,
> a otro las silbaran; sólo
> ver que un herrador osase
> desde los pies del Pegaso,
> coronarse en el Parnaso
> y que a sus musas clavase
> causar pudo admiración;

"mal intencionado" with "hijos corcovados." The reference is probably to Alarcón.

que aunque reído y importuno,
lo que es vituperio en uno,
en otro es estimación.
Hámela Carlos causado...

The reference to "Apolo" and the encouragement he gives to
poor poets is possibly a reference to the commission given Alarcón to write up the royal *fiestas*. If that should be the case, then
this play was retouched in 1623.

Sometime after June 17, 1626, Tirso began to link Alarcón not
only with "Apolo" but also with a poor poet, who is, we believe,
Vélez de Guevara. Only after Vélez had been made *valet de
chambre* to Philip IV and Alarcón had been appointed to a
place in the *Consejo de Indias* on the date mentioned do certain
passages make sense. In *Escarmientos para el cuerdo*, [28] where
Tirso has developed at length the proverb, "Quien hizo el cohombro...," Carballo would throw overboard two poets in order
to lighten cargo. Seeing shipwreck ahead, Manuel de Sosa orders,
"Echa al agua esas cajas / de drogas y pimienta," but Carballo
straightway protests (III, iv):

> Con ventajas
> juega el mar si está airado;
> ¿qué hará después, señor, salpimentado?
> Otras cosas le aplica,
> que la pimienta abrasa, enoja y pica.
> *Échale dos poetas*
> *de estos que silba el vulgo y son maletas*
> *de Apolo; de estos bromas*
> *que hacen andar los versos por maromas.*

The two *tramoyistas* who had received jeers from the pit — poets
that Carballo would throw overboard — are, in all probability,
Vélez de Guevara and Alarcón. They were both *maletas* in Tirso's
opinion: i.e., "personas torpes, despreciables." Both had written
comedias de tramoya which had been greeted with derision. Of
Vélez's troubles with the *vulgo* and of Tirso's disapproval of that
Andalusian in *La fingida Arcadia,* I have already written. [29] Alar-

---

28 *Princeps: Parte V,* 1636.
29 See above, "Literary and Political Satire in *La fingida Arcadia.*"

cón's brush with the *mosqueteros* — which, as in Vélez's case, grew out of a *tramoya* — was yet in the offing when, in the summer of 1622, Tirso composed his *La fingida Arcadia*. But in December of 1623, Alarcón's *Anticristo* would bring not only catcalls but stink-bombs. It was a play of *tramoyas*, one whose presentation made theatrical history. Vallejo was, in his role, supposed to climb a *tramoya*. When, with his very considerable weight, he faltered and Luisa de Robles took over for him, both Góngora [30] and Quevedo celebrated the event. The former wrote a sonnet: "A Vallejo, autor de comedias, que representando la de *El Anticristo* y habiendo de volar por una maroma, no se atrevió, y en su lugar voló Luisa de Robles." Quevedo [31] compuso *redondillas* of similar nature.

As I pointed out above, Tirso began in 1626 to couple the cobbler (Alarcón) with the tailor (Vélez), [32] both of whom "Apollo had lifted up." In *Averígüelo Vargas*, an early play which Tirso probably first reworked around 1620, we find this same combination. Immediately following the passage cited above which satirizes the *dones*, we find that "don Tabaco" allies himself with the tailors (II, ii) ı

> Don Tabaco es mi apellido,
> porque en estas ocasiones
> *la poesía y los dones*
> *a tanta baja han venido*
> que hay ya dones al soslayo,
> *y de agujas y banquetas*
> *levanta Apolo poetas,*
> *como dones de un lacayo.*

---

[30] III, 18-19.

[31] *Obras en verso*, 137.

[32] My study, "Tirso's Satire of Ruiz de Alarcón" (*B. Com.*, XVI [1964], 1-12) is, I regret, inaccurate. After having summed up correctly the evidence as to the "tailors" and the "cobblers" in Tirso's theatre, I then, for some inexplicable reason, wrote (p. 6): "The same tailor and cobbler will appear for a third time in Tirso's *Averígüelo Vargas*, and here the identity of the tailor [sic] at least, can be established with reasonable certainty." The last part of this sentence should read: "the identity of the *cobbler* ..." For Tirso, Alarcón is always the *cobbler*; Vélez always the *tailor*. This same distinction is not always observed by some other writers of the time.

We shall see that, in this same play, Tirso accused Alarcón of "tacking on the heel" of a "don."

But, not satisfied with this bit of satire against Alarcón, Tirso returns to his theme of the tailors and cobblers who are would-be-poets in *Quien no cae no se levanta.* [33] In a passage that is clearly autobiographical — one written in a moment of depression — he counsels himself to withdraw from the company of the poets (III, ii):

> Apartaos de los poetas,
> aunque hay tantos, que no sé
> si podréis, pues *ya se ve*
> *entre agujas y banquetas*
> *Apolo, por su desastre,*
> *y el zapatero* se mete
> a dalle con el *tranchete*
> y con su *tisera* el sastre.

This play (like *Averígüelo Vargas*) must have been written some years before. Originally penned in 1623, it was apparently retouched in 1626 after Alarcón received his long-delayed reward from the king, one which came through the favor of the Duque de Medina de las Torres, son-in-law to Olivares.

Alarcón is linked with the *sastre* in yet another play, where mention of Apollo is lacking. In *La fingida Arcadia* [34] of 1622 we

---

[33] *Princeps*: *Parte V*, 1636. For date of composition assigned, see "Studies for the Chronology of Tirso's Theatre," 27-29.

[34] *Princeps*: *Parte III*, 1634. For date assigned, see study above, p. 211, n. 54. There are many other references in Tirso's theatre to the *sastres* (in Hell and out of it), but I am reserving discussion of them for a study of Tirso's relations to the Aristotelians. It should be remembered that Lope, in his *sátiras*, had lambasted Torres Rámila unmercifully by linking him with the "Tailor of Toledo." He reminds the grammarian over and over: "Sastre fuiste y sastre serás eternamente." Lope had, moreover, in the closing lines of his second harangue against Torres Rámila and Suárez de Figueroa, cursed the former with a ringing "mala corcova de Alarcón te nazca," thereby establishing a connection between Torres Rámila, *sastre*, and Alarcón, *sastre*. As Lope's two *sátiras* were constantly before the literary public in 1622 and even in early 1623, it is not always easy to decide which figure is being satirized in the literature of the time. For the two *sátiras* of Lope, see J. de Entrambasaguas' *Una guerra literaria del Siglo de Oro*, II, 244-411. Prof. Entrambasaguas has not only printed the two sátiras, but has annoted them with great care. What is more, he has given the official investigation that resulted.

find this bit of dialogue, one just following the curse which puts
Vélez de Guevara in the Inferno (III, iii):

> CONRADO: ¿Quién es aquél que se quema?
> PINZÓN: Un poeta vergonzante
>   *que pide trazas de noche*
>   *de limosna.*
> CONRADO: ¿No las hace?
> PINZÓN: No es hombre de traza el pobre,
>   que hay poetas oficiales
>   que cosen lo que les corta
>   el maestro.
> ANGELA: No le alaben
>   de ingenio a ése.

Now this description fits Vélez so aptly that it is difficult to
believe that the reference is not to him. Yet one must ask, "Why
should Tirso consign Vélez to Hell for a second time?" He had
already put him there because of his plays of *tramoya*. Apparently
the dramatist is saying that the Andalusian is a *sastre*, as well
as a *tramoyista*, one therefore guilty on a second score, in that he
lacks the ability to construct his own plots. What is more, in
El melancólico,[35] a play written in 1622-23, but again before the
public in early 1625, the same charge is brought against a poet and
in the very same words. Carlín has just begged for a "traza" with
which to get even with the disdainful Firela. When Rogerio
refuses the request, the *gracioso*, almost without context (I, v),
again alludes to the poet we have previously met in *La fingida
Arcadia:* "Pues yo conozco poeta / que compra trazas de noche."
This lack of creative ability is a charge that was being brought
against Vélez de Guevara, specifically in early 1625.

With the tailor of *La fingida Arcadia* is a *cobbler*, one who
can hardly be other than Alarcón since the language is virtually
identical to that found in *Averígüelo Vargas*. Of this cobbler,
Tirso says in *La fingida Arcadia* (III, iii):

---

[35] *Princeps: Parte I,* 1627. For the original date of 1622-1623, see
"Studies for the Chronology of Tirso's Theatre," 17-27. For the date of
its *refundición,* see p. 104, of this book.

> No le llamen
> al tal sino remendón
> y cuando escriba le manden
> *sentar sobre una banqueta*
> *pues echar tacones sabe.*
> Llevan sus muchachos éstos
> que pregonan por las calles,
> en vez de "¿hay zapato viejo?"
> "¿hay comedia vieja?"

Now Quevedo had left Alarcón in *La visita de los chistes* [36] — which went to press by June, 1622 — in the company of tailors who were suffering punishment because of their thieving and their lies. There he first describes one Arbalías, a tailor; then he pictures for us immediately another little man, the busybody Chisgarabís, who "de hablar ... no paraba," of whom he goes ahead to add: "Y, como si le dispararan de un arcabuz, en figura de trasgo se apareció ... otro hombrecillo que parecía *astilla* de Arbalías, y no hacía sino *chillar* y *bullir.*" This is apparently Alarcón, for in the *Corcovilla*, Quevedo had asked concerning that dramatist: "¿Quién ... desnudo es una *astilla* ...? ¿Quién, siendo cabeza de ajos, tiene *bullicio* de ardilla?"

It should be remembered, as well, that Tirso, in fashioning his *Parnaso* of three levels in *La fingida Arcadia* — made up of Purgatory, Hell and Glory — had but elaborated his *Parnaso crítico* of the *Cigarrales*. But Quevedo's *Visita de los chistes,* no doubt, suggested the idea that he add a *Parnaso cómico,* to which to consign his enemies of the theatre. Tirso, accordingly, first condemns to this region of hell the *tramoyistas,* then goes on to describe the two other dramatists who are also there: one a *sastre,* the other a *zapatero.* Admittedly there is, in the description of the *zapatero,* a detail that is not in general keeping with our ideas of Alarcón as a dramatist. Having disposed first of the thieving tailor, Alejandra asks, "Y ¿aquél?" Pinzón's answer is (III, iii):

> Es un poeta de encaje
> que en una comedia mete,
> como [sic; ¿cual?] si fuera de ensamblaje,

---

[36] *La visita de los chistes,* 249-251.

> cuatro pasos de las viejas
> redondillas y romances,
> con todas sus zarandajas.

Lucrecia's comment will be, "vena estéril." Thereupon follow the
lines concerning the "zapatero remendón." Certainly Alarcón did
not, in general, insert bits of old *romances* in his plays (as Vélez
and Guillén de Castro undoubtedly did), but the Mexican has,
in such a play as *Las paredes oyen* (III, xi), used "Por mayo
era ... " I suggest the *possibility* that Tirso may have retouched *La
fingida Arcadia* around the same time that his *El melancólico*
was again before the public (i.e., early 1625) and that he may
at that time have added this passage satirizing the cobbler and the
tailor. Since Alarcón had not yet received his place in the *Consejo de Indias*, this would explain the fact that there is no mention
of "Apollo."

For a third time Tirso will, in his theatre, sneer at those who
have difficulty in spinning their yarns. In *La ventura con el nombre* [37] (III, xiii) and under his own *nom de plume* of Tirso, he
claims for himself, as we have already seen, imaginative power
("a vos nunca os faltan trazas") at the same time he points a finger
of scorn at those who steal their plots ("no las hurto como algunos"), only to have them scorned ("a la postre se silbatan") by
the public.

Tirso's satire of the Mexican lasted, it would seem, from 1620
to 1625-26. Granting the very considerable amount of it that one
finds in his theatre, it is to me highly improbable that he should
have been the Mexican's collaborator. As we have seen, he has
thrice mocked him for the assumption of a *don* which was not his
by rights. He is, as well, a *murmurador*. What is more, he is "a
rascal who is deceiving a *boba*." Tirso has repeatedly pointed to
the hunchback's malformed body: comparing him now to a twisted
cucumber of so ugly a variety as to inspire horror in those not
accustomed to it; now to a *camel;* now to a *tortuga;* now to
a soul "entre dos platos." He has held him up to ridicule as a
hunchback lover, a "Macías ... entre dos bacías," who, with borrowed finery, deceives his beloved in regard to his many physical

---

[37] *BAE*, V, 520, n. 1.

defects: he is a thieving *corneja* who steals from other writers, a *cobbler* who knows how "to tack on heels," one of Apollo's hacks who writes *comedias de tramoya* that the audience greets with cat-calls. (But, it should be noted, *Tirso* never calls him a "tailor.") Our dramatist would like to see him in Hell or at the bottom of the sea!

If I am right in my interpretation of the many satirical passages I have cited, then part of Gabriel Téllez's anger at the *copla* would arise precisely from the fact that it put him in the same category as Ruiz de Alarcón. Another part would come undoubtedly from its lack of respect for the cloth he wore. In *Quien no cae no se levanta* (where there is satire of Alarcón), Gabriel Téllez first tells himself he should withdraw from the company of the poets, then adds in tones of injured innocence (III, ii):

> ... aunque sois un *San Gabriel,*
> han de murmurar de vos,
> pues no perdonan a Dios,
> ni a sus *ministros* con él.

These verses were presumably added after the scurrilous *copla* appeared on the pastry-shop wall in 1625.

We must now go back to our question: why should Ruiz de Alarcón have been brought into this whole affair? Why, more specifically, should Luis Vélez's *copla* have linked Tirso's and Alarcón's names? Why should Tirso have tied Alarcón to Vélez?

We must first ask if Alarcón was perhaps another poet who in 1625 had hopes of becoming royal chronicler. There is no real evidence to that effect; yet it is a question that cannot for three reasons be dismissed with a categorical negative: 1) the Mexican had, in late August of 1623, been chosen [38] to write up the *fiestas* given in honor of the departing prince Charles of England; 2) he undoubtedly had been looking for a place in the government

---

[38] *BAE,* LII. Did the Marqués de Cea, later to become Duque de Lerma, make the choice, or did the future son-in-law of Olivares make it?

bureaucracy since the new regime began. [39] We read in Antonio Castro Leal's *Juan Ruiz de Alarcón, su vida y su obra* (p. 46):

> El 1.º de Julio de 1625 el Consejo de Indias lo pro-
> pone para una prebenda eclesiástica en América o para
> una de las relatorías en alguno de los Consejos de la
> Corte. El 17 de Junio del año siguiente es nombrado re-
> lator interino del Consejo de Indias.

Just when Alarcón turned his eyes in the particular direction of the Indies we do not know; he may, before doing so, have previously dreamed of a literary appointment. 3) And the third reason why we can't reject out of hand the idea that Alarcón may have hoped for the role of royal chronicler is that the prowerful Duke of Medina de las Torres was for many years his patron. Unfortunately we do not know exactly when that magnate, son-in-law to Olivares, first began to favor him. It had been the "Patriarca de las Indias" who had married him to the *privado's* daughter on January 9, 1625; on August 16, 1626, Medina de las Torres was himself made "Gran canciller de las Indias." It is not improbable, then, that Alarcón should have had the Duke's backing if (some time before July 1, 1625) he made application to the *Consejo de Indias* for a place in that council. The tie that first bound the two men would presumably have been their common interest in literature: the Duke of Medina de las Torres played Maecenas to more than one literary figure, was a devotee of the theatre, was in fact responsible for bringing more than one actress to Madrid. Alarcón dedicated to him in 1628 his *Primera parte* and, in so doing, declared that his *comedias* were nothing more than "virtuosos efectos de la necesidad en que la dilación de mis pretensiones me puso." It should be realized, too, that if Alarcón held any such ambitions, Antonio de Mendoza and Luís Vélez de Guevara were in a position to know that fact and with their derisive *copla* may well have linked Tirso's name to Alarcón on the strength of it — as they linked Tirso's to Arceo's in early 1626.

---

[39] One of the first works he wrote after the new regime began was *El dueño de las estrellas* which exalts Olivares in the role of Lycurgus. See I, 941. Speaking of his appointment to the bureaucracy in June of 1626, Castro Leal says (46): "¡Qué gusto que los que ... lo vieron pretender año tras año, sepan que el rey ha acabado por darle la razón!"

However, other explanations can be found for the connection that Vélez saw between the two poets. When writing his *décima* in 1623 against Ruiz de Alarcón, Vélez had labelled the diminutive Mexican a "dwarf camel" and his account of the royal *fiestas* as "of Soplillo's proportions" — Soplillo being the tiny dwarf who is found in the picture with Philip IV, one by Villandrando. Now Tirso, too, was almost certainly a very small man. Fair proof of it lies, as I have shown, [40] in a passage found in *El amor médico* — written precisely around Christmas of 1625 — when the tiny Jerónima defends her short stature by quoting Aristotle's well-known axiom: "Fortior est virtus unita / se ipsa dispersa." It can, with all logic, be interpreted as Tirso's answer to Vélez's *copla*, which had paired him with the dwarf Alarcón and reduced to nil the talents of both dramatists. Thereupon Tirso answered *both* charges with a single quotation from the authoritative Aristotle — for with the very same quotation he told the abnormally tall Vélez that great height implies "great humidity," which is most injurious to human intelligence in that it erases images formed and destroys the memory. Tirso would at this point have begun, by way of retaliation, to pair the gigantic Vélez with the ill-formed dwarf that was Alarcón.

There are, however, in *No hay peor sordo* and in *El amor médico* — both plays written in late 1625 — passages which could possibly offer yet another motive for Tirso's satire of Alarcón in 1625-26. News of exactly what had occurred to bring about his downfall must have reached Tirso in Toledo, soon after he wrote *Desde Toledo a Madrid* but before he started *No hay peor sordo*, for in the former play I find no autobiographical overtones, whereas *No hay peor sordo* and *El amor médico* are filled with satire of certain "mirones," the name given to the curious onlookers in the "Academia de Madrid." In *No hay peor sordo*, begun in November of 1625, [41] Tirso cries out in anger against the "cowards" who strive to rob one of his honor (II, viii):

> que ya gradúa el *vicio*
> por *discreción el bárbaro ejercicio*

---

[40] See pp. 256-58.

[41] See my study on *No hay peor sordo* in *Homenaje a Rodríguez Moñino*, I, 261-278.

de fiscales mirones.
Ya no se estiman las conversaciones
que no desautorizan
las honras, que sin causa *satirizan.*
... ...
que suele tirar piedras *quien no alcanza.*
... ...
ya que el fruto no goza, le derriba.

Here is satire on a "discretion" that is "vicious," as in the passage
of *Antona García.* Here, too, is condemnation of people who "satirize": the reason they do so is because they are "envious" and, not
being able to grasp for themselves success' fruit, they throw stones
at the one who has succeeded in order to strike him down. The
speaker continues angrily against such people (II, ix):

¡Que así *desacredite*
el honor una lengua! ¡Oh, qué convite
hiciera yo a la fama
si pudiera comprar de quien la infama
las lenguas maldicientes
destos cobardes, en quitar valientes
la opinión! ¡Oh, qué plato,
por mucho que costara, tan barato!
¡Mas, no sé si tuviera
vajillas para tantas, Talavera!

Tirso was, in late 1625, in a mood to cut out the tongues of his
cowardly detractors, valiant only in robbing him of his good name.
Such a dish would be cheap, however much it might cost! But
then so abundant would it be in quantity that Talavera probably
couldn't supply dishes enough to contain it.

In *El amor médico,* [42] (I, ii), begun almost certainly immediately
after *No hay peor sordo,* there is even stronger denunciation of
these "human leaches," these "*sanguijuelas de las honras* [que]
sin espadas sacan sangre ...," these "*Zoilos de los ausentes,* de los
ingenios *vejamen,* destos ... *mirones* ... en los templos y en las
calles, [que] todo lo malician." His anger is directed against
"hombres sin nombres, cobardes," who have made their accusations without signing their names. He continues:

---

[42] See study on *El amor médico* in *Reflexión* 2, v. I, no. 1, 11-22.

> Carta sin firma es libelo
> que contra sí mismo hace
> quien no osa poner su nombre
> por confesar que es infame.

Let me grant forthwith that the setting of these remarks, in both *No hay peor sordo* and *El amor médico*, is a completely natural one, i.e., one justified by the play's action. In the former, don García is critical of those who have, in his opinion, brought false charges against the virtuous "doña Dorotea," who, in point of fact, has sprung full-grown from the fertile imagination of the *gracioso*, Cristal. In *El amor médico*, it is don Gaspar, who is complaining of an *anonymous letter* which claimed he was receiving more favors from doña Micaela than were licit. These false charges had led to a duel, and having killed one enemy and wounded the other, Gaspar had had to flee the wrath of King Fernando and take refuge in one of Toledo's *cigarrales!* It is only the great wealth of detail of these descriptions and the very real intensity of tone that indicate that there is something autobiographic in the long *relatos*.

Whom did Tirso have in mind when penning these two passages? Was he thinking of the *motilones* who had written the *copla* or of those who had been instrumental in seeing to it that his sins reached official ears? The stretch of dialogue found in *No hay peor sordo* would certainly seem to be directed against Antonio Hurtado de Mendoza, but in that taken from *El amor médico*, Tirso possibly hints at a *vejamen* in the Academy, news of which some *mirones* had passed on (possibly to the Palace) in an unsigned letter. Who were these "mirones"?

The meetings of the *Academia de Madrid* were apparently open to the curious-minded (called "mirones"), and it was they who were least responsible and most censorious of all in attendance. As the very scholarly Mrs. Willard King[43] sums it up: "No contribuían sino con risas y comentarios maliciosos." In a poem — written precisely in February, 1625 — which is entitled "Dando principio a un certamen," Pantaleón de Ribera addressed the various groups attending, among others the *mirones* (II, 132):

---

[43] Willard F. King, *Prosa novelística*, 98.

Y vosotros, *o mirones,*
que en este certamen docto,
con vuestras manos lavadas,
venís a reírlo todo:
   dejad el castra-poetas,
que os saldrá el silbo a los ojos,
si no reponéis [sic; ¿deponéis?] severos
aquí *lo mosqueteroso,*
   porque el señor don Francisco,
a quien llamo "Vice-Apolo" [sic; ¿llamó?]
don Jacinto de Herrera,
tiene pensado que *al Zoilo*
   que a chistar se dispusiere
ha de *escupirle* furioso
de ciertos labios *de bronce*
cierta saliva *de plomo.*

And, this warning given, the *certamen* begins.

Seemingly, these "mirones," these "Zoilos," were the initial cause of Tirso's troubles. He will, as we have seen, twice inveigh against them. In *No hay peor sordo* (II, viii), of late 1625, don García complains: " ... ya gradúa el vicio / por discreción [44] el bárbaro ejercicio / de fiscales *mirones* ..." And in *El amor médico* (I, ii), he will return to his attack on these *mirones,* "sanguijuelas de las honras," who are "Zoilos de los ausentes, / de los ingenios *vejamen.*" He may possibly have thought that Alarcón (through Medina) and Vélez (through Mendoza) were informers. We are now, however, in the world of pure surmise. We only can guess as to who carried tales to the Palace. Tirso evidently held Mendoza responsible for his troubles with the *Junta.* By all logic, don Antonio would have taken his information to Olivares, and don Gaspar would then have asked the *Junta* to take action on it; on March 1, 1625 that body would return to question the Conde-Duque to find out the proper procedure to be followed. The *acuerdo* of the *Junta* would follow on March 6, at which time Tirso's troubles would begin.

---

[44] "El vicio," linked as it is with "discreción," refers presumably to Antonio de Mendoza. Cf. in *Antona García* where he has won the reputation of being "discreet" and Tirso adds: "Riquezas son estímulos de *vicio.*" See p. 96.

Vélez de Guevara, seeing Tirso under attack from the *Junta*, would thereupon fashion the ugly *mote* against him — but with some help from others, among them Mendoza, in all probability — for Vélez needed help on epigrams. The strange poem, entitled "A un poeta muy flaco y viejo, aconsejándole que se muera," makes this abundantly clear. Written before April of 1625, it is, as we have already seen, unquestionably a satire against Luis Vélez de Guevara, and its author declares in unequivocal terms:

> ... *sin ayuda de amigo,*
> *jamás hiciste motete.*

Tirso would get his story to the public as best he could by adding barbs to plays already printed. These *comedias* would be printed for the most part in *Partes* I and III, both of which he would print outside of Madrid!

CONCLUSION

IX

ASSESSMENTS AND REASSESSMENTS

One finds in Salas Barbadillo's *Los platos de las musas*,[1] dedicated to "los venerables ingenios, ornamento y felicidad de la patria," a *vejamen* of 1626 which throws light, some direct, some indirect, on the characters involved in this palace intrigue.

In *Los platos de las musas*, Apollo is giving a banquet of "great ostentation" to the poets of Spain, one at which he is honoring them "con su lado y mesa." Salas gives first the rules that the poets were obliged to follow, according to which each one pledged himself to be "humble" and "modest," to write "well of the talented poets of his time, without irritating them by infamous satires or impudent apologies...." The banquet table

---

[1] The book is entitled *Coronas del Parnaso y Platos de las musas*. The *Coronas ...* is dedicated to the Conde-Duque de Olivares and Salas signs himself "El más humilde criado de Vuestra Excelencia que su mano besa." In the "Al lector," Olivares is "aquel magnánimo príncipe protector constante de las musas." The book carries a "suma del privilegio," dated October 28, 1630, signed by Juan Lasso de la Vega; and an *aprobación* of July 1, 1630, which was given by Juan de Velasco y Azcuedo (?). It was not published until 1635, after his death.

The date of *Los platos de las musas* is made clear on f. 2 verso and f. 3 recto where Salas mentions Philip IV, adding "Al fin del quinto año de este dichoso imperio, salieron de España para el Parnaso, cuando entraba el Abril en ella, tres no menos floridos ingenios: don Rodrigo Alfonso, don Fadrique Francisco, and [apparently] el licenciado Francisco Mateo Fernández."

The "Banquete de Apolo," dedicated to Gabriel Bocángel y Unzueta, occupies from 31r. to 36r. Bocángel was a member of the *Academia de Madrid*, known both for his poetry and his painting. For a modern edition of his poems (1946), see that of Rafael Benítez Claros.

is beautifully set, and the fragrance that emanates from the "flores poéticas, lucidas y elegantes" is "el de la buena fama de sus
autores, que no hay cazoleta como una buena fama." Salas' very
first tribute (a thing apart, as we shall see) is to Lauro, i.e., to
Luis Vélez de Guevara (33 r.):

> El salero, en vez de sal, estaba lleno todo de donay-
> res y agudísimos chistes del siempre ingenioso y singular
> varón, Luis Vélez de Guevara, porque en el Parnaso no
> se conocen otras salinas sino las de su felicísimo ingenio,
> cortés y cortesano, pues, sin injuria de nadie, siempre ad-
> mira y siempre entretiene.

Apollo sits down; then all those "virtuous men of talent"
find their places. The first course includes: "seguidillas, villanci-
cos y glosas." Following it is the main course of "romances, décimas, redondillas, y todo verso español, de que Apolo comió con
mucho gusto y dijo dos veces que aquel plato tenía grande sazón
y gracia." There follows another course, made up of "sonetos,
madrigales, canciones y tercetos," of which Apollo partook spar-
ingly, because these were not so easy to digest.

There is, at one point, praise for those writers who translate,
either from Latin or Italian — with special tributes for don Juan
de Xáuregui and for don Gabriel Bocángel "por ser [éste] tan
atento imitador suyo, así en el pincel, como en la pluma." It is
now the turn of don Antonio Hurtado de Mendoza, and he is
presented to us in an unexpected role, that of *tramoyista:* [2]

> Pusieron otro plato, y alzando los ojos Apolo, porque
> había sentido que el maestresala que lo cortaba hacía
> grande ruido y que había rompido en él dos cuchillos y
> un tenedor, preguntó: — ¿De qué es este plato? Respon-
> dió el maestresala: — Señor, comedias de tramoyas. Ape-
> nas dijo "comedias de tramoyas" cuando colérico Apolo

---

[2] Mendoza was in general *not* a *tramoyista*. He had written *Querer
por sólo querer*, a palace spectacle-play of the same general type as *La
gloria de Niquea*. Gareth A. Davies states (*A poet at Court: Antonio
Hurtado de Mendoza*, 222) that it was done "sometime in 1622." Apparently,
Salas does not refer to that spectacle, put on at Aranjuez, but to some
comedia de tramoya that has not come down to us, one written to glorify
an ancestor of some noble family.

le habló así: —¡Majaderón! ¡Grosero! ¿Comedias de
tramoyas me servís vos en esta mesa, siendo manjar sólo
para los brutos? Decid, ¿con qué dentadura hemos de co-
merlas? Y después, ¿qué calor de estómago bastará a di-
gerillas? Quitalde luego de la mesa y advertid que os
mando que no le deis a ninguna persona humana....

Entonces un curioso ingenio de los que asistían al banquete deseó saber si Apolo se ofendía de todas las comedias de aquel linaje, y respondió que no; antes bien
le agradaban algunas en quien concurrían majestad de
versos y disposición de algún caso grande, que trujese
consigo admiración, porque estas tales (dixo), enriquecidas
con el ornamento peregrino de no vulgares galas y joyas,
suelen ser pompa y ostentación de los palacios de los
grandes príncipes. En este género ha lucido el cuidado con
grande exceso del ilustre don Antonio de Mendoza y sin-
tiera mucho el ver que ha desamparado nuestras musas,
si no considerara que se ocupa en ser ministro de más
benigno y más luciente Apolo.

The reader then finds, in turn: 1) mere mention of Mira de
Amescua, doctor Juan Pérez de Montalván, don Pedro Calderón,
don Jerónimo de Villaizán "y otros que tendrán en otra parte su
lugar"; 2) warm praise of Lope and his comedias de capa y espada; 3) great enthusiasm for an entremesista [evidently Quiñones de Benavente], this last a dish which pleased Apollo tremendously; 4) warm words for don Guillén de Castro as a tragic
dramatist, "cuya rara virtud, peregrino ingenio, humilde modes-
tia y generosa nobleza aplaudió [Apolo] con singulares hipérbo-
les"; 5) for "el divino Hortensio," Joseph de Valdivieso, and Juan
Pérez de Montalván, with his "singular talent" as a novelist; 6)
for three "poemas heroicos": those of el Príncipe de Esquilache,
Francisco López de Zárate, and Doctor Miguel de Silveyra.

For dessert, they have "epigramas yocosos [sic] ... epístolas fes-
tivas, entretenidas y alegres, así en verso como en prosa." At the
end of this most harmonious banquet, Apollo sends a letter of
praise to one don Rodrigo Alfonso [3] — by Salas, it would seem —
one carrying this meaningful message:

---

[3] Did a "don Rodrigo Alfonso" really exist?

... porque sé que *sois más bien intencionado* [4] *que buen* poeta, beneficio que debéis agradecer mucho al cielo porque la parte poética, de que estáis bien falto, la tienen hoy muchos, *más para injuriar y ofender con ella a los varones modestos y virtuosos que para ejercitarse en la alabanza de sus virtudes heroicas,* fin último y el más noble de la poesía. [5]

One may suspect that Apollo's letter was directed more to a *good* poet whom Salas Barbadillo was labelling "mal intencionado" than it was to Rodrigo Alfonso, a *poor* poet but "bien intencionado." In other words, I strongly suspect that Salas' "poet of evil intention" is Tirso, who is no where mentioned by name in this *vejamen.* Nor is Ruiz de Alarcón. Without them, all was serene that April of 1626 when this banquet took place: *they* were the trouble makers! If the banquet had taken place after June 7th of that year, when Alarcón became part of the Palace bureaucracy, would he have been at that banquet?

In general, it would seem that the literary world about Tirso gave, in 1625-1626, surprisingly little evidence of concern over the Mercedarian's personal tragedy. His disappearance from Madrid's intellectual circles would seem to have disturbed but little the surface calm of the "sea that was Madrid." Pantaleón de Ribera, as we have pointed out in Chapter I, called him almost a "figura" when commenting on the protagonist of *El melancólico;* and when Tirso was trying to get his case before Rome's tribunal, the same Academician compared the noise he was making to that of a rachet brace.

Pantaleón's opponent of the Academy, don Gabriel de Corral, [6] on the other hand, was apparently all compassion for Tirso.

---

[4] Tirso had directed the introduction of his *Cigarrales* "Al bien intencinado." Lope alludes to it (see p. 167) and Tirso again refers to it apparently in *En Madrid y en una casa* when mentioning Lope. See, as well, Montalván's use of it below, n. 12. It seemingly became a phrase of contention between his friends and his enemies. It is, of course, a commonplace today.

[5] One remembers with some amusement that Salas had at one time been banished from Madrid for his *sátiras!* See Hurtado y Palencia, *Historia de la literatura,* 471.

[6] Gabriel de Corral, *La Cintia de Aranjuez,* 52-53. Corral was chaplain to don Jorge de Tovar Valderama [sic] y Loaysa. By 1630 de Corral was

He wrote two epigrams that he published in his *La Cintia de Aranjuez* (1628), epigrams which can hardly fail to refer to Tirso's banishment. The first, labelled "A un amigo desterrado," reads as follows:

¿Destiérrate de tu hermosa
patria *alguna vil cautela*
porque la virtud desvela
a *la envidia perezosa?*
No llores, ni se te acuerde
de estimarla; que en perdella
nada pierdes; antes ella
te llore, pues que te pierde.

Tirso's banishment was due to a vile trick from a lazy, envious person, one who had been frightened by the vigor of his opponent. It was the birth-place of the banished one that should weep his loss, not he who should weep the loss of his *patria*. The second epigram, called "De las palabras," is equally revealing: [7]

Las palabras (cosa es clara)
no tocan al que es *discreto*,
que en el bien templado peto
del desprecio las repara.
Nadie *al sabio* le provoca,
que, como de los sentidos
es señor de sus oídos;
y *el necio* no, de su boca.

Here is the contrast on which Tirso so often insisted: that of the *necio* and the *discreto*. Tirso's lazy competitor, a "necio" who is

---

in Rome with an official position; there he served the Spanish ambassador, Conde de Monterrey, who was brother-in-law to Olivares. Could Corral, once he was in Rome, have helped to work out Tirso's problems with the Apostolic Tribunal? See pp. 88-89.

[7] *Ibid.*, 50. Corral's beard must have been something to behold. This recalls the fact that one of the *graciosos* in *Escarmientos para el cuerdo* is called "Barbosa" and that in his satire of the Academy of Goa, he interrupts himself in curious fashion to offer his hospitality to his friend, Carballo: "ahora bien, señor Carballo, / si no tiene alojamiento, / el mío estará contento / de serville y de hospedallo. / ... La amistad premia / con lo que tiene y acá / si en versos de bronce da / toda Goa es Academia." Is Tirso telling us with whom he stayed when in Madrid (in 1626) en route to the meeting of his Order in Guadalajara?

not "master of his tongue," has, through his lack of "discretion," managed to bring distress to a *discreto* (i.e., a man of wisdom). But fools' words can not really penetrate the wise man's breast-plate of contempt. The fool may not be master of his tongue, but the wise man does have control of his emotions and his ears. What is more, in his *Prólogo* to *La Cintia de Aranjuez*,[8] Corral makes evident where he stood in the struggle between those who wanted a "literatura cortesana" (as did Mendoza) and those who aimed at pleasing the *vulgo* (as did Tirso):

> ... no hablo [en este libro] con los *Patricios* de la cultura, sino con el *vulgo*, con quien Marcial se entiende tal vez diciendo, *Vobis pagina nostra dedicatur*. Y el nuestro Cordovés: "Popular aplauso quiero; / perdónenme los tribunos..." Yo, a lo menos ahora deseo agradar al pueblo y que se agrade de lo que escribo; que los puritanos de la erudición bastan que me lean las fiestas, sin ocuparles todo el ingenio.

This, taken together with el Conde de la Roca's advice to Mendoza, which we have quoted above (p. 84), seems to suggest that "el discreto del palacio" wanted, even in the 1620's, to establish a "comedia cortesana" (such as his own) in contradistinction to the "old comedy" of Tirso which made its appeal to the people. The analysis that Gareth A. Davies has made of Mendoza's work gives abundant confirmation to such a conclusion.

If anyone else spoke out at the time in defense of Tirso, I have found no proof of it. From Castillo Solórzano and Pérez de Montalván, Tirso, no doubt, had personal letters deploring his

---

8 *La Cintia de Aranjuez*, 22.

9 While in 1621 Tirso was still thinking of the Lopean comedy as the "comedia nueva," to a young king, not yet seventeen, who wanted to change everything from what it had been in his father's day, that *comedia* would probably have been a "comedia antigua." The decade of 1620-1630 was evidently fumbling, more or less consciously, for a "new court comedy," one which Calderón, with his great talent and diplomacy, could usher in. Gareth A. Davies states (*A Poet at Court: Antonio Hurtado de Mendoza*, 222) that "Mendoza felt that a court art, whether dramatic or lyrical, should differ from that offered the vulgar throng." In 1635, El Conde de la Roca felt that *el vulgo* was dead, but in time it would, of course, adapt itself to the "new comedy."

misfortune. I doubt very much that he heard from Lope, even though Tirso's troubles evidently arose in part from the fact that both addressed their theatre to the *vulgo*. To speak out at the moment would, no doubt, have been dangerous; at least it could have endangered Lope's very tenuous favor in the Palace. Even when writing his guarded tribute to Manzanares' sons in the *Laurel de Apolo* (1630), one we have already quoted, [10] Lope apparently believed that Tirso was still *persona non grata* in official circles: Manzanares, careful of her reputation, was *afraid* to recognize her own scholarly, talented son. Tirso presumably had not yet written his *Acto de contrición*,[11] something which seemingly clarified the Mercedarian's position for all.

On the other hand, the praise of Pérez de Montalván, [12] when the latter was approving his *Cuarta parte* at the end of January, 1635, is fervent and without stint:

> Por comisión y precepto del Señor Licenciado don Lorenzo de Iturrizarra he visto la *Cuarta parte* de las comedias del Maestro Tirso de Molina, cuyo nombre es el mejor crédito de su censura; porque siendo suyas (que con esto se dice todo), no necesitan ni de elogios para su alabanza, ni de advertencias para su corrección. Pero supuesto que es fuerza cumplir ... digo que no tienen cosa que disuene de la verdad católica, ni palabra que ofenda las orejas *del más escrupuloso cortesano;* antes bien, lo sentencioso de los conceptos admira; lo satírico de las

---

[10] See pp. 186-87.

[11] See Fray Manuel Penedo Rey, "Tirso de Molina, *El acto de contrición*," *RABM*, LXXI (1968-1972), 479-509.

[12] For Montalván's praise, see Cotarelo, *Comedias de Tirso*, I, lxv. Tirso had written laudatory verses for the *Orfeo* (1624). He would, in 1635, write an *aprobación* for Montalván's *Primera parte*. See G. Placer López's "Nuevos datos acerca de Fray Gabriel Téllez," *Estudios*, VI (1950), 349-352. It is worthwhile noting that Montalván goes ahead to call Tirso, "Maestro por su gran talento en las *Sagradas letras* y Apolo por su buen gusto de las curiosas Musas" and that he urges further: "... así me contentaré con asegurar que merece no sólo lo [sic; la] licencia que pide para imprimir esta *Quarta parte,* sino un género de premio honroso para obligarle a que dé muchas a la imprenta en gracia de la lengua castellana, en honra de Madrid, su patria, *en gusto de los bien intencionados y en pesadumbre de los maldicientes.*"

For Lope's *aprobación* of the *Parte IV*, see also Cotarelo, *Comedias de Tirso*, I, lxvi.

faltas corrige; lo chistoso de los donaires entretiene; lo enmarañado de la disposición deleita; lo gustoso de las cadencias enamora, y lo político de los consejos persuade y avisa, siendo su variedad *discreta* como un ramillete de flores diferentes, que además de la belleza y la fragancia, aficiona con la diversidad y la compostura.

Montalván was grateful for Tirso's dedication to him of the *Primera parte* (1631).

Lope, too, approved the *Cuarta parte,* though in more laconic terms:

> Muestra en ellas [las comedias] el autor vivo y sutil ingenio en los conceptos y pensamientos; y en la parte sentencia grave sus estudios en todo género de letras *con honestos términos,* tan bien considerados de su buen juicio.

The *Parte quinta* carries the *aprobación* of Pedro Calderón de la Barca, [13] one dated July 16th of the same year, 1635. It is expressed in words that make evident his admiration not only for Tirso's plays but for their author:

> [En ellas] no hallo cosa que disuene de nuestra Santa Fe y buenas costumbres; antes hay en ellas mucha erudición y ejemplar doctrina por la moralidad que tienen encerrada en su *honesto* y apacible entretenimiento, efectos todos del *ingenio* de su autor, que con tantas muestras de *ciencia, virtud y religión* ha dado que aprehender a los que deseamos imitarle.

The Conde de la Roca was urging him in the very same year to "write forever": "Prevéngase a Tirso, bajo censura particular, *aunque generalísima, que escriba siempre ...*" [14] And he goes ahead to speak of the poet's "fama digna ...," of his "ingenio ... no menos docto que festivo." Should one perhaps read in these encomiums both an attempt to pay belated tribute to Tirso's ability as the true *discreto* (i.e., the *sabio*) and a desire to clear him of the

---

[13] *Ibid.,* lxvii.
[14] See p. 119.

charge of "indiscretion" which Mendoza had apparently identified with "falta de honestidad"?

Tirso de Molina, it would seem, had come into his own at long last, so far as the literary group of Madrid was concerned. They now had the perspective that Time could give. That the *people* had taken him to their collective hearts long before this is probably to be deduced from Tirso's own boasts in *Antona García* and in *La ventura con el nombre.* The repertoire of plays, in Roque de Figueroa's possession [15] on March 1, 1624, confirms in a measure the dramatist's claim; four out of eighteen are certainly Tirso's: *Ventura te dé Dios, hijo; Quien calla, otorga; La celosa de sí misma;* and *Cautela contra cautela.* A fifth, *La infanta doña Sancha,* is probably the Mercedarian's *Averígüelo Vargas.* As Henri Mérimée comments: "un nom domine dans cette énumération, Tirso de Molina." Lope had only two in the same list; Mendoza and Vélez had none.

Death, like Time, brings its own reassessments. Let us review the later years and the demise of the characters involved in this literary *tragi-comedia.* In spite of the *Mal de piedra* (a play), of which Tirso was supposedly dying in 1638, [16] our dramatist would outlive all his enemies.

The first to go would be Lope de Vega on August 27, 1635. Among the countless eulogies paid to the memory of the "Phoenix" at his death, one finds none from Tirso's pen. Nor is it easy to attribute that omission to chance. It is on record that Tirso was in Madrid in 1635, [17] though I have not been able to find out in exactly which month. But his *Parte IV*, the one which Lope had approved, received its *tasa* on August 2nd of that same year and must have been ready for sale by the 27th. Tirso would surely have been in touch with his printers at that time; and it is inconceivable that they should not have informed him of the death of a national figure such as was Lope. But even granting that they did not for some inexplicable reason, Pérez de Montalván was the one who gathered together the more than 900 tributes which go to form the "Fama póstuma" of 1636. Montalván, who had long been a

---

[15] Henri Mérimée, *Spectacles et comédiens à Valencia,* 170.
[16] See p. 292.
[17] Cotarelo, *Comedias de Tirso de Molina,* I, lxiv-lxv.

good friend of both poets, would certainly have let Tirso know of Lope's death. When, just three years later, Montalván followed the Master, Tirso wrote a eulogy to his memory,[18] one in which he declared the *Para todos* would make eternal the fame of its compiler:

> ... eternizándose está
> ... ...
> su *Para todos* aquí
> y él para todos allá.

Did Gabriel Téllez perhaps regret that he had had no part in that volume of praise to Lope? I am inclined to think he did, for in his comedy, *En Madrid y en una casa,*[19] one finds a tribute to the poet's memory that suggests that the Mercedarian was remembering not only the very fervent praises which he had paid the Master in the *Cigarrales* but the equally warm ones of Lope (including his phrase, *los bien intencionados)* which Lope had borrowed in dedicating to him *Lo fingido verdadero.* Notice, too, that "don Gabriel" is speaking (I, xi):

DON GABRIEL:	¿Cuál es ésa [casa]?
PACHECO:	La casa de comedia...
DON GABRIEL:	¿Háylas buenas ahora?
PACHECO:	En ellas, como en todo, se mejora; puesto que, Lope muerto, dudoso está el teatro de su acierto.
DON GABRIEL:	¡Gran pluma ha faltado!
PACHECO:	Fue prodigioso y poco celebrado si con su ingenio miden sus alabanzas.
DON GABRIEL:	Nunca las olviden *los bien intencionados;* que sin él quedan viudos los tablados.

---

[18] *Ibid.,* lxx.

[19] *En Madrid y en una casa* was not included in any of Tirso's *partes.* It was printed under Rojas Zorrilla's name and under Calderón's as *Lo que hace un manto en Madrid,* though neither put forward a claim to it. I have no doubt that the original work was Tirso's. We need a critical edition of this play.

To Lope, in death, Gabriel Téllez could not, perhaps, after all, deny the praise that was his due — nor would he mention the Master's faults as an individual. *De mortuis nihil nisi bonum.*

The second enemy of Tirso's to go would be Juan Ruiz de Alarcón in 1639, an Alarcón who had, from the first, thrown in his lot with Olivares. The dramatist's *El dueño de las estrellas,* written shortly after the *privado* took the reins of power, glorifies this son of the house of Guzmán in the role of Lycurgus. [20] Later the dramatist won the favor of Medina de las Torres, son-in-law to the Conde-Duque. In 1626, through the influence of this patron, he was, as we have seen, given a position in the Council of the Indies. From that time on, he probably lived out his life in relative economic comfort. Through further favor of Medina de las Torres, he was able to get his first *parte* of plays through the press in 1628 — in spite of the decree of 1627 which sought to prohibit the publication of *comedias.* Court favor thus enabled him to do what had been denied to both Tirso and Lope. His second volume would not come out until 1634; but it, too, was dedicated to Olivares' son-in-law.

In spite of Alarcón's mal-formed body, a talented and beautiful woman cared enough for him to bear him an illegitimate (?) [21] daughter — for whom he, in turn, had enough love to leave her the bulk of his estate on August 4th of 1639. Not even in death could he escape the indignity of his poor humpback! Don José Pellicer, in his *Avisos históricos,* records with matter-of-fact conciseness: "Murió don Juan de Alarcón, poeta famoso, así por sus comedias *como por sus corcovas,* y Relator de las Indias." [22] Few today would deny him a very distinguished place in the House of Fame.

---

[20] This fact has not been generally recognized, but when the king, "en la edad de joven floreciente," asks direction from the oracle as to someone to direct his inexpert hand, he is told, "Pide a Licurgo el árbol venturoso." Thereupon the young king seeks "Severo's" aid in interpreting the oracle's voice and is told: "No hay árbol para un reino más dichoso / que *el de la oliva,* porque paz publica: / pues pedillo a Licurgo el luminoso / Apolo manda, claro significa / que si dél gobernáis *acompañado,* / aseguráis la paz de vuestro estado," etc. Is "Severo" Baltasar de Zúñiga?

[21] See Willard King, "La ascendencia paterna ...," 55.

[22] Quoted from Castro Leal, *Juan Ruiz de Alarcón ...,* 52-53.

One can not know why Tirso so disliked Alarcón. His
aversion may have first been born out of his loyalty to Lope; it
could even have been related to the feelings he had for the
New World. His satire of the Mexican, from that of *La villana
de Vallecas* to that of *Escarmientos para el cuerdo*, seems largely
personal. The Mexican was not ordinarily the cobbler who
patched up old shoes that Tirso would seemingly make him
out. I like to think that *Siempre ayuda la verdad* is Alarcón's
— and that Tirso included it in his *Segunda parte* by way of
reparation for his injustices to Ruiz de Alarcón.

Luis Vélez de Guevara did not depart this world until 1644.
His passing was surrounded by "el rumbo, el tropel, el boato,
la grandeza" which Cervantes had so unerringly noted in his
plays many years before. In life, he may have had at times not
enough food to fill his stomach — partly, no doubt, because of
his family responsibilities and in greater part because of his
own improvidence. So charmingly did he beg, however, that
one of his debtors, at least, would tell him "Siempre obligáis
pidiendo." [23] The grandeur which had meant so much to him
through out his life was his in death: the same José Pellicer, [24]
who had wasted so few words on Alarcón, described with some
detail Vélez's demise, saying that he was buried "con la propia
grandeza que si fuera título, asistiendo cuantos grandes, señores
y caballeros hay en la corte." He was buried in the family vault
of the Duque de Veragua. Moreover, he had sufficient influence
with Philip IV to be able to pass on his place as doorkeeper
to his son, Juan. Luis Vélez never got around to gathering up
his plays for publication, nor has any modern editor yet done
so; consequently, we do not know enough about them to be
able to assess his worth as a dramatist. If he should be the
author of *La Estrella de Sevilla*, [25] then there was more depth

---

[23] See Vélez's and Mendoza's poems quoted pp. 284-85.

[24] Quoted from Cotarelo, *Luis Vélez de Guevara y sus obras dramáticas*,
IV, 168-169.

[25] I have in my files a long study on *La Estrella de Sevilla*. Like *La
prudencia en la mujer*, it gathers up all the gossip that was floating about
in Madrid. Reed, Dixon, and Hill, in their edition of the play (Introduction,
xxx), wrote first: "Now, in the whole range of the *comedia*, scarcely a play
can be found in which the monarch is portrayed in a light so uniformly

to this dramatist's character than Tirso saw in it — but also tremendous concealment, for few plays have painted a *privado* in such unflattering terms as don Arias was there painted. Yet don Arias should, I believe, be identified, in general, with Olivares.

For Luis Vélez de Guevara, Tirso had only contempt. Just when that feeling was born and what gave occasion to it, I cannot say. As we have seen in this study, [26] the Castilian thought the Andalusian a pretentious fool. He couldn't fashion his own plots; was, in fact, a literary tailor who snipped from here, there, and everywhere. He took refuge in *tramoyas* and in the spectacular or grotesque because of his lack of creative imagination. He was really a *juglar* without a solid background of knowledge, one who didn't hesitate to introduce into his plays the most ridiculous anachronisms of time or dialogue. His verse was often harsh: he was a *crítico*. What is more, Tirso saw in him a gross opportunist, one who courted Olivares' favor by flattery, was given to deceit *(engaños)*. And, above all, he was a great, hulking fellow, an enormously tall, thin one whom Tirso couldn't abide, one whom he would like to throw into the sea of oblivion along with Alarcón!

What we know about Luis Vélez de Guevara leads one to suspect that Tirso may have had no little provocation for the repeated attacks he made on him. Cotarelo, [27] without hesitation, labels Luis Vélez "maldiciente," and we know not how many "alfilerazos" the Andalusian may have aimed at the Mercedarian. In *El bandolero* [28] of 1622, Tirso says "nos echa pullas." To judge by the few bits of satire we have from Vélez's pen — the jingle wherein he links Tirso's name with *Arceo*, the *copla* wherein he

---

unfavorable as is don Sancho in *La Estrella de Sevilla*." They then go ahead to point out: "For him [i.e., the *privado*, don Arias], hardly any exculpation is to be found until toward the end. Intervening but slightly in the direct action of the play, this character is to be found expressed in his advice to the king, advice sinister and nefarious, inciting his monarch to the indulgence of base passions, to the corruption of officials, and to the circumvention of pure justice." Prof. Hill was inclined to accept Vélez de Guevara as the dramatist who composed it. See edition cited, p. xix, n. 2.

[26] See pp. 289-91.
[27] Cotarelo, *Luis Vélez de Guevara* ..., IV, 158.
[28] *El bandolero*, 80. For date, see 191 n. 14.

joins the name "el fraile de la Merced" with Ruiz de Alarcón's, and the satire of Tirso and his *mal de piedra* in *El juicio final*, [29] if these two last are his — Vélez was a malicious enemy. What is more, his position in the Palace, as well as his place in the "Academia de Madrid," gave him ample opportunity to exercise his malice with telling success. Rojas Zorrilla [30] indicates that Vélez's evil tongue had created for him many enemies who took delight in speaking ill of him. Cotarelo calls him "above all else a satirist," and Bonilla, [31] when editing his *Diablo cojuelo*, warns his readers that they must be ever on the alert if they are not to miss the point of his satire. An unprinted *mojiganga* [32] which lies in Lisbon's national library — probably Vélez's own work — speaks admiringly of Vélez's native "donaire," but it was clearly at times such as to make his victim squirm. Something of his conflict with Tirso must have spilled over into the plays he has left us, but students of his theatre will probably have to read between the lines if they are to find it.

What would be the end of the very "discreet" *cortesano*, "el que se llevó al Palacio" in the 1620's and 1630's, he who was "guardadamas" in that Palace, yet couldn't (as Tirso saw it) be *guardadamas* of his tongue? Mendoza's last days offer sad contrast to those of his glory. His first wife had died by 1631; thereupon he married the very beautiful Clara Ocón Coalla de Pineda, who was of a noble family from southern Spain. She survived don Antonio, who died on September 22, 1644. Of his death, his modern editor, don Rafael Benítez Claros, [33] has declared: "todo nos hace suponer que [murió] más en el olvido que en la fama, como si el astro jocundo y cordial de su pluma no hubiese trascendido más que la mera circunstancia que cantara."

Mendoza's last years were plagued by insufficient income. He was complaining around 1635 that he was "obligado a sufrir el destemple de la demasiada razón de una mujer de pocos años,·

---

[29] See for the three bits: pp. 267, 278, 292-93.
[30] See pp. 239-40.
[31] Bonilla, ed. of *El diablo cojuelo*, xxx.
[32] For the *mojiganga*, see *Bibliography*, 375.
[33] R. Benítez Claros, *Obras poéticas de don Antonio* ..., I, pp. xi-xii.

muy noble, muy autorizada, muy rica y que en mi poder lo ve mal logrado todo." [34] At the time he married doña Clara, he penned a poem wherein he sketched for her a self-portrait. Gareth A. Davies, passing judgment on it, says: [35]

> Above all, we see a vain and fussy man, with great pride in his lineage.... The most revealing passage, however, is that in which he tells of the place which he has established for himself at court. We hear a hint of envy of the titled nobility who are his superiors, and the satisfaction he feels at having become "a minister's truthful shaft," a man with a reputation for brilliant conversation whose thoughts and expressions are culled by even the most famous of preachers, Hortensio Paravicino.

A *décima*, entitled "Al sepulcro de don Antonio de Mendoza," gives us a contemporary's unflattering view of the poet: [36]

> Yace en esta sepultura,
> sin saber cómo ni cuándo,
> el que sin andar tentando,
> *siempre halló la coyuntura.*
> Representó su figura,
> con ser tan mala, harto bien;
> vivió de ten y más ten,
> y tanto en flaquezas dio
> que al fin, de flaco, murió;
> *requiescat in pace.* Amén.

That the years Mendoza spent in the Palace were for him happy ones is doubtful. His health was anything but robust, as we have already seen. In a *romance*, evidently written in the last days of his life, one in which he refers to himself as "este hidalgo," he complains bitterly: [37]

> siendo en Argel tan duro
> como es el servir de esclavos,
> la Orden de las Mercedes

[34] Quoted from Gareth A. Davies, *A Poet at Court* ..., 38.
[35] *Ibid.*, 34.
[36] *Ibid.*, 41, n. 85.
[37] R. Benítez Claros, *Obras poéticas de don Antonio* ..., III, 14-17.

todos la esperan en vano.
Esta, que parece muerte,
es la vida y los milagros
de Palacio: vil castigo
y aun sepultura de tantos.

Some lines earlier in this same poem, he had described himself
as "manto de colegial ... el más roto, el más antiguo"; and,
earlier still, he had lamented (14):

y en esta sábana ya,
de canas amortajado,
siendo del tiempo paloma,
ya soy cuervo de palacio.

He was apparently a curious mixture of self-confidence and self-
distrust. When Rojas Zorrilla listed in his *vejamen* of 1638 a
series of "impossible things," one was: "¿Quieres que le haga
creer al Señor don Antonio de Mendoza que no es el mayor
poeta del orbe?"[38] He apparently had, as well, no mean opinion
of his own physical appearance, for we read of a poem that lies
manuscript in the Hispanic Society of America, one in which
"Leónida" and "Fenisa" "compete for the favours of an 'Adonis
de la Montaña,'"[39] who can hardly fail to be Mendoza. Yet fear
would seem ever to have dogged the footsteps of this melancholy
man — fear, above all, that some poet would supersede him in
the Royal Palace.

Gregorio Marañón,[40] after studying the many points at which
Antonio Hurtado de Mendoza's life touched Olivares', calls that
very "discreet" courtier "venal." He points out that in 1642 "adu-
laba entonces [Mendoza] a Olivares con el mismo desparpajo
con que le atacó a su caída." Elsewhere, as we have seen, he
mentions his *envy* in connection with a paper "que el falso y
torcido don Antonio de Mendoza, entonces en plena adulación del
Privado, escribió a éste [en 1627] persuadiéndole que no permi-

---

[38] Quoted from Gareth A. Davies, *A Poet at Court* ..., 108, n. 80.

[39] *Ibid.*, 47, n. 19. It is interesting to know that Tirso's heroine in *El
melancólico* is "Leonisa" and that she is quite capable of defending her
interests against her competitor, Clemencia.

[40] For the various quotations of this paragraph from Marañón's *El Conde-
Duque de Olivares,* see 143, 182, 290, 330.

tiese que escribiese su vida don Juan de Vera [i.e., el Conde de la Roca]. In 1636, the Conde had warned Tirso to be "discreet" (i.e., wise) in the matter of his prefaces. Roca knew of what he spoke, for Mendoza had sought in a secret letter to prejudice Olivares against him. On another occasion, Marañón comments on Mendoza's "soplonería," as we have seen above. Corral [41] says that he was not "master of his tongue." Even his editor, don Rafael Benítez Claros, [42] calls Mendoza "hombre superficial, fácil," and compares him with a bee, which having first announced its presence by a small, obscure noise, "zumba, redondea a la víctima, la clava y huye." His recent biographer, Gareth A. Davies, though he is clearly an admirer of Mendoza as poet and dramatist, calls him, as we have seen, "a vain and fussy man with great pride of lineage." Moreover, he terms the letter written to Olivares against the Conde de la Roca, one of calumny that is nothing less than "venomous." [43]

If such were really the characteristics of this man who sought to destroy Tirso, it is not difficult to understand Tirso's unremitting attacks against him. And it should be noted that the Mercedarian's charges against Hurtado de Mendoza bear a remarkable similarity to those of his modern critics: he was envious, he was a tale-bearer, anything but truly discreet"; his poetry was essentially light and frivolous. The Conde de la Roca [44] will suggest to Mendoza that, by "intriguing" his *comedias* a bit more (one would normally expect the word "complicating") he could make them appear less long [and boring?]. He indicates as well that Mendoza disdained the *vulgo* and was trying to set up a *comedia cortesana* in contradistinction to the "old comedy." Tirso thought him, above all else, envious, and lumped him apparently with the Biblical scribes who neither go into Heaven nor suffer those who are entering to go in. [45]

In his troubles with the *Junta*, troubles occasioned by Mendoza, Tirso realized that nothing less than his whole future as a

---

[41] See p. 333.
[42] R. Benítez Claros, *Obras poéticas de don Antonio* ..., xiv.
[43] Gareth A. Davies, *A Poet at Court* ..., 33.
[44] See p. 84.
[45] See pp. 271-72.

dramatist was at stake. He knew, as well, that Mendoza, like Vélez, was in a position to wield power irresponsibly. He believed that these men were determined to end the competition he represented, once and for all. That was why the Mercedarian says, in *La ventura con el nombre* (I, iii): "piensan que no he de tornar a dar *a plumas mestizas* que envidiar y que roer"; and that is one reason why Tirso was determined to get his plays into print! Besides, the drama, in poetic form, was, as we have seen, for Tirso, "princess of the liberal arts." Gabriel Téllez, unlike Lope, was never apologetic for his theatre as an artistic form.

Mendoza published virtually nothing of his own, and the first edition of his poems did not come out until one Antonio de Salcedo [46] put them together in 1666. Did he himself perhaps realize the ephemeral nature of such fame as might be his with succeeding generations? At least in his *Querer por sólo querer* of 1623, he stated in the prologue: [47] "Un día es siempre maestro de otro: contra lo que se escriba hoy, estará lo que mañana se sabe más." Only within fairly recent years has one been able to read in a modern edition the *Obras poéticas de don Antonio Hurtado de Mendoza.* [48] His plays have not even yet been gathered up; [49] and until 1971, with Mr. Davies' study, there was available no detailed critical analysis of the works of "el lego cortesano." That he irritated some of his contemporaries, among them Tirso, the Conde de la Roca, and Gabriel de Corral, is not surprising — if Marañón, Rafael Benítez Claros and Gareth A. Davies have judged his character aright.

What of Tirso? Our dramatist outlived all of his enemies by four years. He died in the little town of Almazán after some

---

[46] The name "Antonio de Salcedo" suggest he was a descendant of Antonio de Mendoza, for as Gareth A. Davies has pointed out (*A Poet at Court* ..., 13), "Antonio de Mendoza oriented himself genealogically by the House of Salcedo ..." His paternal uncle, Diego Hurtado de *Salcedo* y Mendoza, was "Señor de *Salcedo.*"

[47] Davies, *A Poet at Court* ..., 193, n. 5.

[48] R. Benítez Claros put out his edition in 1947.

[49] It is to be hoped that Mr. Davies, having studied the chronology of his plays and assessed their literary value, will follow up with a collection of his plays.

time in cold Soria. [50] Of the circumstances attending his death
we know nothing, but this critic has no doubt but that he met it
courageously and without a trace of the "pusillanimity" which he
so much despised: with serenity but humility, for he was facing
his Maker, and he realized, as *El mayor desengaño* makes evident,
that the great sin of the churchman, like that of kings, is more
likely to be *presumption* than *pusillanimity*. His death would
go unmarked by the literary figures of the capital. It is, in fact,
only recently (since 1945) that we have known the place where
he was buried. None of the pomp that characterized the funeral
of Vélez de Guevara could have accompanied Tirso's. Fellow-
Mercedarians only would have attended him on that occasion.
His grave may or may not have carried a simple marker.

But, in truth, it mattered not: Tirso had already made
arrangements for his monument, probably when he was in Trujillo. He foresaw that, in fashioning his theatre, he had ordered
his own "majestic tomb." It is the same majestic tomb that
Ventura, [51] as *alcalde* of a small village, orders for himself in
La ventura con el nombre (III, iii):

---

[50] R. P. Penedo Rey, "Tirso de Molina, comendador de Soria y definidor
provincial. Su muerte en Almazán," *Estudios*, (número extraordinario), 93-122.

[51] "Ventura" is a name that Tirso may have assumed for the first time
in 1621 when he was writing *La ventura con el nombre*. It is, however,
more likely that he took it ironically in 1626 when he was retouching both
this play and *La celosa de sí misma*. In the latter play, one finds this bit
of dialogue (II, vii):

DOÑA ANGELA:	¿Cómo os llamáis?
VENTURA:	Yo, Ventura.
DOÑA ANGELA:	Buen nombre. ...
VENTURA:	... aunque el nombre me alegra,
	es por ser mi dicha negra;
	llamar al negro, Juan Blanco.

This same comparison is used in *El amor médico* (of 1625-1626) when doña
Estefanía comments on the beardless state of the heroine (doña Jerónima),
dressed as a doctor, who has taken the name, "dotor Barbosa." There doña
Jerónima answers (II, viii): "Como el moreno, Juan Blanco."

Karl Vossler wrote in *Escritores y poetas de España* (65): "... conocemos
la poca estimación que sentía [Tirso] en el fondo por el valor artístico de la
poesía dramática ... y la poca estimación que daba a la fama póstuma ..."
I believe both conclusions of that distinguished critic are highly erroneous. I
don't understand how Tirso's critics could fail to recognize the autobiographical nature of this scene.

> se haga a costa del Concejo [52]
> un sepulcro majestuoso
> de mármoles, tan curioso
> que desde el niño hasta el viejo
> le admiren ...

He sends Tirso to the capital — Tirso is "discreet," whatever "fools" *(necios)* may say to the contrary — to choose this tomb which should be so fine that all would admire it (III, iii):

> Partiráse Tirso allá,
> y sin reparar en precios,
> del mejor hará elección,
> que en fin tiene *discreción*,
> aunque les pese a los *necios.* [53]

And then, by way of justifying the expense involved to the village, he points out that wise men have always honored themselves (III, iii):

> Si para mí
> se hace, quiérome honrar
> a mí mismo; que ésta es ley
> que los cuerdos procuraron,
> *y pues vivo me enterraron,*
> *haced cuenta que es el Rey*
> *el que murió y que me fundo*
> *en algo.* .

They had buried alive the king of the *comedia* in the little town of Trujillo, but fools notwithstanding, he would have his own splendid monument of enduring marble, one that would inspire admiration in young and old alike throughout all time. He would live for the future in the plays he had written. His legacy to it was in the form of his *partes. That was why he had to get printed his "primera parte" in 1626, why he had to get out*

---

[52] Tirso may possibly be playing on "concejo" (town council) and "consejo" (the Consejo de Castilla?), which was headed up by don Francisco de Contreras, who also presided over the *Junta de Reformación.* Browning's bishop was not the only prelate who ordered for himself a beautiful tomb while still living!

[53] Again Tirso insists on his "discreción" and his enemies' "necedad."

his four other "partes" between 1634-1636. They were the answer which he promised his foolish enemies in *La ventura con el nombre.* Posterity would avenge him. Tirso was, I believe, as conscious as was Cervantes of the literary legacy he was leaving humanity. God had cursed him by making him a poet, as he himself tells us in *Antona García* (III, iii) — but He had also given him the realization that that gift was for *all* people and *all* time. Mendoza, on the other hand, who had apparently dreamed of heading up an *escuela cortesana* and had rejected the approval of "el vulgo," could offer by comparison little to succeeding generations.

The moment has not yet arrived in which we can make definitive assessment of the actions of those poets with whom we are concerned in this study: we do not know, even now, where to place the blame for Tirso's quarrel with Mendoza and Vélez. We cannot, at the moment, be sure even of what Tirso was accused by Antonio Hurtado de Mendoza. Apparently, the latter had "reproved" Tirso's "indiscreet" appeal to his audiences, if we may judge by the phrases the Mercedarian uses in *Antona García:* "Pues ¿qué queréis vos que sea *quien se pone a reprender* lo que nunca acertó a hacer, *porque al discreto recrea?*" And in *La huerta de Juan Fernández,* he speaks contemptuously of those who "procuran / cobrar nombre de *discretos* / que *contra ajenos defectos / rebuznan cuando murmuran.*" The passage from *Amar por arte mayor,* with its Biblical implications, suggests that Mendoza's own literary impotence prompted his actions. Gabriel de Corral calls Mendoza lazy and indicates he was envious of Tirso's vigor. From the constant repetition of the word "discreto" in Tirso's complaints (a term which Tirso promptly appropriated unto himself) and from the fact that Tirso removed completely the comic plot of *Sutilezas del amor y el Marqués del Camarín* — before publishing it in 1627 as *Amar por razón de estudo* (the twelfth *comedia* in his *Primera parte*) — I am inclined to believe that the *charge* (or one of the charges) taken to the *Junta* would have been phrased as Tirso's "lack of discretion." In "lack of discretion," Mendoza would probably have included Tirso's broad humor. Gabriel Téllez's own words, "porque al discreto recrea" may possibly bear out such a conclusion, as do those of Montalván. The latter poet told the censor that Tirso's *Cuarta parte* had "not a word that *could offend the ears of the most scrupulous courtier.*" Lope, too, assured the censor that Tirso's plays of the *Cuarta parte* were written "con honestos términos." Even so, whatever defects the *Junta* may have seen in some of Tirso's characters and dialogue, I strongly suspect that Tirso was essentially right in thinking that Mendoza's move was actuated, in part at least, by envy — and by fear. Mendoza was surely sufficiently the poet to know that he was facing in Tirso not an "Arceo" but a real competitor.

When it was observed by the "Second Portuguese" in *Antona García*, after he has listened to the Seventh Castilian's complaints against the envy that reigned among the poets of Madrid: "Poeta debéis ser vos," Tirso's simple answer was: "Castigóme Dios en serlo." And, indeed, Tirso was the poet born, in some ways, *almost as much* so as was Lope de Vega. In the latter's fight with the Aristotelians over *natural* versus *arte*, Tirso would unhesitatingly seize the opportunity to glorify inborn talent over training. [54] Robles Dégano [55] places him right after Lope in the facility of his orthoepy. Certainly, Tirso was more at home in verse than he was in prose. So many of his plays link up with the years 1621-1626 that only someone who wrote with utmost ease could have penned so many. His third *Santa Juana*, of 1614, was apparently written within two weeks. [56] And this, though his dramatic work must necessarily have had to be fitted into such spare moments as the duties of his Order permitted!

On the other hand, Tirso was a proud man who must have been very difficult at times. He himself realized it and was not apologetic for it. In his "Al bien intencionado" of the *Cigarrales de Toledo,* he says to his reader: [57]

───────────

[54] I have in my files a long study on Tirso's relation to the Aristotelians. One of the points at issue was the one outlined in *La Filomela* of 1621: i.e., innate talent vs. acquired training, there phrased as "el natural" vs. "el arte."

[55] Robles Dégano, F., *Ortología clásica de la lengua castellana* (21): "Como ortólogo, no llega [Tirso] a Lope, aunque poco le falta."

[56] Sra. de los Ríos, *Obras dramáticas completas de Tirso,* I, 589-590.

[57] *Cigarrales de Toledo,* I, 11-12.

Ya juzgarás, por lo dicho, que me vendo soberbio por consumadísimo. Pero ni te engañas en todo, ni en todo aciertas. Mira, toda arrogante presunción es locura, y *todo abatimiento de sí mismo que no se ejercita por Dios es pusilanimidad.*

For the pusillanimous man [58] Tirso had no use whatsoever. He would, I repeat, have agreed heartily with Saurina of *El bandolero* (p. 213 r.) when she declared: "Mejor me acomodo al espíritu temerario que al pusilánime..." The dramatist was never one to run from a fight — nor to turn the other cheek to his enemy.

Moreover, his appreciation of a laugh undoubtedly got the best of him at times. One must admit that his humor often had, as did Cervantes' occasionally, a good deal of the "earthy" in it. That he imitated Sancho on more than one occasion is not surprising, for contrary to Señora de los Ríos' thesis, it can be shown, I believe, that Tirso greatly admired the creator of that inimitable pair. [59]

If Tirso was a bad enemy (and he probably was!), this critic is disposed to argue that he was also a good friend, a spiritually-generous one who stood by such as were in need of help. No writer ever exalted loyalty-in-adversity more than he. Over and over, he glorifies it: in *Cómo han de ser los amigos*, in *El amor y el amistad*, in *El honroso atrevimiento*, and in *Palabras y plumas*. Utterly revolting to him was the right-about-face of many of those who had once praised Philip III's ministers in the heyday of their power, yet abandoned them in their hour of trial. Of the "tortuous" Antonio Hurtado de Mendoza, who deserted Olivares in 1643, he would have considered such a shift as despicable as did Marañón, though Tirso certainly had no love for the *privado* whom Mendoza chose to forget in his moments of adversity.

---

[58] The *desconfiado*, whether in matters of love or faith, was "pusillanimous." Although I do not believe that Tirso wrote *El condenado por desconfiado*, his attitude in this matter, like that of most theologians of the day, would have been the same as that of its author.

[59] *Deo volente*, I shall hope to prove it some day. Tirso borrowed from Cervantes, not Cervantes from Tirso.

It should be remembered, too, that many of Tirso's barbs were penned in 1625-1626, after Mendoza succeeded in getting him banished from Madrid. In the months that followed the *acuerdo* of the *Junta*, Tirso's nerves were necessarily taut, and the bitter allusions can be understood aright only if we keep firmly in mind the events of those years affecting him personally, as well as those touching his Order. Let us put them in chronological sequence to the end that we understand the multiplicity of anxieties weighing on him: "A fe tengo más de una / trabadura," he declares (under his own pastoral name) in *La ventura con el nombre* (I, iii), which was reworked, probably in 1626. And, "a fe" he did, as we shall see from the tabular list that follows:

March 6, 1625. The *Junta de Reformación*, after consulting matters with the Conde-Duque de Olivares, acted on information which Tirso believed was relayed to him, or to that body, through don Antonio Hurtado de Mendoza; it recommended that Tirso be banished from Madrid to one of the distant houses of his religious Order (the Mercedarians) and that he be forbidden to write profane literature of any type, under threat of excommunication. In accordance with this *acuerdo*, Tirso left Madrid shortly thereafter.

March of 1625. Some "motilones," among them seemingly the same Mendoza, painted on the wall of a pastry-shop (where plays of Alarcón and Tirso were announced) an indecent *copla*. It was one which hurt Tirso not only by its lack of respect for the cloth he wore as priest, but also by the fact that it put him in the same class at the hunchback Alarcón and reduced them both, as dramatists, to the level of zero.

April of 1625. Luis Vélez de Guevara, a close friend to Mendoza for many years and an enemy of Tirso's, was made *valet de chambre* to the king, almost certainly at the recommendation of Olivares. As the position carried no stipend at first, Vélez must have received *gajes* from the *privado* — or others.

May 17, 1625. Mendoza was made secretary "del Consejo de la Suprema y General Inquisición."

January of 1626. Vélez wrote a jingle to the king in which he asked for new raiment with which to accompany him as chronicler on his trip to Zaragoza. He ends it with a slur at "el fraile de la Merced," linking him with "Arceo," a ridiculous figure of the Palace, who had been royal chronicler on occasions.

January of 1626. The so-called "Redención preservativa" was presented at the Cortes de Monzón. Its object was nothing less than "la supresión de las Ordenes Redentoras de la Merced [la de Tirso] y la Trinidad." Señora de los Ríos has summed up what this meant for Tirso by saying: "... la Orden de la Merced era su patria, su hogar y su familia."

March 12, 1626 - November 20, 1626. Tirso attempts to get his *Primera parte* published in Madrid, but is, after months of effort, unable to get the necessary *aprobaciones*.

Late May, 1626. Tirso's Order, in the meeting at Guadalajara, sent him to the convent at Trujillo as "comendador" there.

June 17, 1626. Ruiz de Alarcón is given a place in the "Consejo de Indias" (as *"relator interino"*) through the influence of the Duke of Medina de las Torres, son-in-law to Olivares.

Such a table makes evident not only how very many things were pressing on Tirso, in 1625-1626, but also how high was the tide that was seemingly carrying his literary enemies on to Fortune and at what very low ebb was his own. Yet we have only the passages in *La ventura con el nombre* to indicate spiritual despression on his part. Only a man with as stout a heart as Tirso's could have kept his bark from sinking. When, in 1631, Gerónimo Margarit [60] put out his edition of the *Cigarrales,* the shield of the title-page carried a "phoenix rising from the flames." Tirso had been reborn from his own ashes. Was his "Acto de contrición," of 1630, the document that made possible that rebirth?

Behind Tirso's troubles stood not only the envy of Mendoza and his literary cohorts, but the ambitions of a power-loving *privado*. One should never doubt that don Gaspar's *real* complaint

---

[60] Alan K. G. Paterson, "Tirso de Molina: Two Bibliographical Studies," 47.

against the Mercedarian was not the nature of the latter's theatre but his opposition to the regime of Philip IV and to the policies of his favorite. The half of that opposition has not yet been told. I am inclined to believe that Olivares himself dipped into Tirso's theatre after the action of the *Junta* on March 6, 1625. There is, in fact, some slight documentary evidence to suggest that Olivares became personally interested in Tirso's works just after he had advised the *Junta* on May lst in matters of procedure. Around this time, he may well have been reading in manuscript Tirso's *La prudencia en la mujer!* Under date of March 13, 1625, i.e., just one week after the *acuerdo* of the *Junta,* one finds in the *Noticias de Madrid* [61] this significant notice: "Este día comió el Conde-Duque de Olivares en platos de barro, por haber dado a su Majestad toda su plata y joyas; pero después se lo volvieron." Was Olivares taking a leaf out of doña María de Molina's *razón de estado?* Centuries before, that Queen-Regent had made ready to sell her silver and jewels in order to avoid levelling new taxes on her already overburdened people (II, v), an action made necessary by the rapacity of her great nobles. Meaningfully she tells them (II, vi):

> Con sólo un vaso de plata
> he de quedarme este día.
> Vajillas de Talavera
> son limpias y cuestan poco.
> Mientras la codicia fiera
> vuelve a algún vasallo loco
> *[Mira al infante don Juan]*
> pasaré desta manera.
> ... ...
> Si en platos de tierra como,
> no se destruirá mi tierra.

Olivares' [62] problem, like doña María's, was to get money with which to wage war against those he probably thought of as infidels. He almost certainly did not care a rap about this literary

---

[61] *Noticias de Madrid,* 116. Of course it is possible that he may have been reading history instead! Nevertheles, the fact that this bit of news is so near in date to that of the meeting of the *Junta* which recommended Tirso's banishment suggests a direct relationship.

quarrel as such, but he, no doubt, was only too glad to have an excuse which would justify him in bringing about Tirso's removal from Madrid. Here was a politically-minded dramatist, one favorable to the old regime, and one who had expressed his opposition to the new one in such powerful works as *La prudencia en la mujer, Privar contra su gusto, La mujer que manda en casa,* and *Los hermanos parecidos.* [63] What is more, in order to bring about Tirso's removal, he (Olivares) had only to sit still and let the *Junta* act in accordance with its own puritanical desires. Don Antonio's complaints against Tirso, then, must have seemed to the *privado* Heaven-sent, and Olivares would be grateful to him. One should accordingly not be surprised to read that, some two months after the *Junta* had discussed with Olivares Tirso's notorius conduct, Mendoza was named Secretary to the Tribunal of the Inquisition! And Tirso was out of his way!

Critics of Tirso and his theatre will, in the future, have to deal with this dramatist's actions in the months that followed the *acuerdo* of the *Junta.* And this means they will have to concern themselves with Tirso's *Primera parte* of Madrid (1626) and the implications of its publication. I have recently sent to press a study which analyses the bibliographical aspects of this *parte* and the circumstances under which it was printed. Let me here analyse its make-up and ask whether the plays it included on March 12, 1626 were the same that Tirso was promising in *Los cigarrales* of 1624. Phrases, taken from the *dedicatoria* of this volume to don Alonso de Paz, Regidor de Salamanca, suggest they *were,* or that Tirso wanted the authorities to *believe* they were. Playing again on the name of his patron (as he had already done in the first part of the *dedicatoria*), he ends with these words: [64]

---

[63] The second volume of this series will deal with Tirso's political theatre.

[64] See Alan K. G. Paterson: "Tirso de Molina: Two Bibliographical Studies," 55. Dr. Paterson believes that Tirso tried to get through the Madrid press of 1626 a volume that contained *El condenado por desconfiado.* He bases his assumption on a list of plays found in a manuscript of *Privar contra su gusto* (no. 15675, B. N.), which he argues is of 1632. For my answer to his conclusions, see my study, "Did Tirso Send to Press a *Primera parte*

> Todas estas doce salen en su nombre seguras, o a lo menos, *ejercitadas al sufrimiento,* pues habiendo pasado libres por los infortunios de el Teatro, *maliciado ya de la envidia* y ya maliciado *por la ignorancia, como soldados viejos,* gozarán la plaza muerta del sosiego *y paz* que les promete el nombre y agrado de V. M.

These plays are "old soldiers" who had escaped the normal misfortunes of the theatre (presumably the hisses of their audiences), and although they had been censured by *envy* and *ignorance,* [65] he expected them to enjoy peace at last under the protection of Alonso de Paz's name.

Tirso was almost certainly whistling in the dark in order to keep up his courage, for he, better than anyone else, had real reason to doubt that his patron could open the door of tribunals that were closed to him. The marvel is that he came as near as he did to getting his volume of plays through Madrid's bureaucracy. For the *names* of the plays that are found in the *Primera parte,* as we know it today, and those of the volume that went to press in 1624 may have been the same; but some of them, at least, had suffered significant changes before they went to the Madrid printer around March, 1626. Unless I am greatly mistaken, Tirso employed part of the year of grace which his Order had apparently given him in inserting barbs (and even broadsides!) against his enemies in Madrid. He may indicate in the dedication to don Alonso de Paz that he is a routed man *("un derrotado")* who, under the white flag of truce was asking only for peace, but let us examine the plays of that *Primera parte* (made up of *sueltas)* and see just what he was offering! The plays in the *Primera parte,* as we know them today, are, in the order named:

1. *Palabras y plumas:* the seemingly innocuous story of don Iñigo de Avalos, very symbol of the faithful lover, whose devotion to his lady fair is backed by deeds of self-sacrifice,

---

(Madrid, 1626), one Containing *El condenado por desconfiado?"* which appeared in the *homenaje* put out in honor of Prof. Arnold Reichenberger.

[65] I am very much inclined to believe that *envy,* by this time, was in Tirso's mind, synonymous with Mendoza, and *ignorance* with Vélez de Guevara.

not by words, as is that of his Italian competitor. To this *comedia* — played in the Palace on July 23, 1623 — Tirso has added satire of don Antonio Hurtado de Mendoza, in his role as *escribano* to the Inquistion, a place the latter obtained on May 17, 1625. Gallardo's suggestion (II, v), as we have seen above, was that his master bring down with his gun an *escribano* that he could then sell in the city as rabbit, even though in doing so, he would be palming off on his customers a cat for a hare. The scene goes back to the biographical material he had added in *Antona García* (III, i-ii).

2. *El pretendiente al revés:* a *comedia* written before Tirso went to Santo Domingo in April, 1616, one that is seemingly close to the original as Tirso first wrote it. It may, or may not, be significant that Carlos, *privado* to the Duke of Cleves and husband to the play's heroine, Sirena, declares at one point (I, xii): "Del rey, del sol, y del fuego / lejos; que de cerca, quema." Later in the same scene, he exclaims to himself (I, xii): "Por alcahuete, privado! / pero no seré el primero." Such comments, it might be argued, are possibly more in keeping with the situation in 1621 (at which time Tirso may have retouched it), than in 1625-1626. Yet the setting of "Cleves" gives pause. [66]

3. *El árbol del mejor fruto:* penned in 1621, this play is virtually as Tirso wrote it originally. I find in it no satire of the new regime.

4. *La villana de Vallecas:* This work (of March, 1620) has probably suffered few changes. It satirizes Ruiz de Alarcón and his *boba*, but satire of that relationship belongs to 1620-1621, not to 1625-1626.

5. *El melancólico:* Originally written in 1622-1623, it underwent some changes in early 1625, as we have seen above. [67] Not only does it include satire of Hurtado de Mendoza as

---

[66] Tirso hal put his *Amar por razón de estado* in Cleves. See p. 127 for the role of Lorraine in Tirso's theatre of 1624-25.

[67] See p. 124.

guardadamas of the Palace, but also Tirso's contrast of the "necios opulentos" who were in the Palace through favor and those who had gained their success "con noble ingenio y estudiosa vida." This contrast of Mendoza's lot and Tirso's must have been in the dramatist's mind since the *Cigarrales* of 1624, for its title-page, as we have seen, carries two figures, one a king, covered with hands to symbolize 'FAVOR,' and the other, a wise man covered with wings to symbolize 'INGENIUM,'... [separated by the word 'UTINAM' as part of the design of symbolic figures]. Did Tirso believe that Mendoza had held up publication of the *Cigarrales?*

6.   *El mayor desengaño:* This life of San Bruno must be the *San Bruno* [68] played in the Palace between late 1622 and early 1623. It is a plays in my opinion that is at once theological and political: *theological* because it deals with *presumption* (an extreme of *esperanza),* which condemns the Christian to eternal damnation, just as *desperation* (the extreme of *desconfianza)* consigns him to eternal flames; *political* because there were those from Olivares' camp who, in their attempt to denigrate all phases of Philip III's reign, were insinuating, both by word and in writing, that that gentle monarch's excessive *desconfianza* on his death-bed may well have sent him to eternal destruction. Tirso says dryly in

---

[68] Cristóbal de Avendaño played it. See H. A. Rennert, *The Spanish Stage* ..., 235.

[69] Matías de Novoa in his *Memorias* (II, 331-333), writing of Philip III's "desconfianza" on his death bed, says: "Hasta en esto quiso calumniar la malicia a nuestro católico Rey... Porque habló las cosas tocantes al remedio de su salvación, como rey religiosísimo y santo y que había de dar la cuenta que nos refiere Santo Tomás para ejemplo de sus hijos y de sus súbditos, *nuevamente atentos a recientes lisonjas,* interpretan esto y lo dejan escribir en algunos libros con no más razón de la que a ellos les parece ...; ser un enfermo a la hora de la muerte, tentado de fuertes desconfianzas en que espíritu, el más inculpable y que ha vivido el más ajustado a las reglas de la virtud, no se ve antes.... Lo que se había de atribuir a gran virtud, quiere la malicia que sea delito; y que no pueda un Rey que tiene tanto de que dar cuenta decir con ansias de cristiano y piadoso: 'No he acertado, erré; Señor, no me neguéis vuestro rostro, ni me cerréis las puertas de vuestra misericordia.' Tentar sobre desconfianza es argumento de que no lo está el tentado, porque a estarlo, es cierto que fuera vana la celada: a fortísimos baluartes suponen poderosísimas baterías, que a los flacos es escusado. Y de

effect to Philip IV and his theologians: "Kings, like proud theologians, have more reason to fear Hell, because of excessive *hope* (i.e., *presumption*) than they do through excess of *desconfianza* (i.e., *desperation*).

Like *Palabras y plumas*, *El mayor desengaño* contains satire of Mendoza as an *escribano:* he is a "cat," one with tremendously long claws. Similarly, there is probably satire (II, vii) of this same individual as a "discreet" person who talks too much, satire that is similar to what is found in *Antona García, La huerta de Juan Fernández*, and the "A ti a solas" of the *Cuarta parte*.

7. and 8. *El castigo del penséque* and its sequel, *Quien calla, otorga:* the former is an old play (probably of 1613) which was written before Tirso left for Santo Domingo. I can see no evidence of its having been altered in 1625-1626. The same will, in general, hold for *Quien calla, otorga*, written (or rewritten) in 1623 [70] after the sumptuary decrees of February came out. The satire of the *repentistas* of the Academy (II, x) could have been added in 1625-1626. So may a reference to a fat *pastelera* (I, vii).

9. *La gallega Mari-Hernández.* It was, in all probability, first composed after Tirso had been refashioning his *El vergonzoso en Palacio* for "Buenavista" (one of Toledo's *cigarrales*). It was put on in the Royal Palace on April 24, 1625 by

---

aquí sacamos que su confianza estaba en más altísimo lugar que ninguna de las otras virtudes de que siempre vivió adornado; que ésta se le procuraba derribar. Vivió con ella y con ella acabó, armándose continua esta guerra de la sangre del cordero, de la virtud de la que nació sin mancha, y de la de los escuadrones de los santos; ... pues no fuera para mí tan católico, tan religioso, bueno, ni tan grande, si no muriera con ostas ansias de la salud de su alma..."

Novoa was, no doubt, an unfair critic of Olivares, but as "ayuda de cámara" to Philip IV and as a one-time spy of the *privado* in the Palace, he was in an excellent position to know what the new regime had been saying in 1621 about the previous one. Moreover, Tirso was probably as implacable an enemy of the *privado*, at least after Rodrigo Calderón's execution, as was Novoa.

[70] I have not studied the matter of *El castigo*'s date, but see E. Cotarelo, *Comedias de Tirso*, II, xi-xii. For the date of *Quien calla otorga*, see my study, "On the Date of Five Plays by Tirso de Molina," 183-190.

Manuel Vallejo. It is, moreover, one of Tirso's *comedias* which carries his name in its final lines — whereas *Los balcones de Madrid*, presumably revised after the *acuerdo* of the *Junta*, ends:

> *Los balcones de Madrid*
> aquí dan fin; perdonadme,
> que si no os digo el poeta,
> *me han mandado que lo calle.*

Why should a play of Tirso's — one which Cotarelo [71] rightly terms "una de las que tienen lenguaje menos limpio" — have been put on in the Palace some month and a half after Tirso found it necessary to leave Madrid, "casi huyendo," because his was a "notorious case"? Could it have been through the influence of Mendoza and Vélez, and to the end that young Philip be convinced that Tirso's humor was so broad as to merit the punishment recommended?

10. *Tanto es lo de más como lo de menos:* The final history of this play's development — which, in its first form, was probably the now nost *comedia, No saber guardar su hacienda* of 1621 — is yet to be written. The play was probably rewritten, almost completely, in 1621-1622, and then retouched slightly in 1623. I agree with J. C. J. Metford's conclusions [72] that it is, in its final form, a work in which Tirso has satirized bitterly the Conde-Duque de Olivares under cover of the *rico-avariento*, Nineucio. However, I now am certain of what I failed to realize some years ago: that this play was *once again retouched* in 1625-1626 [73] after the *Junta de Reformación* (in conference with Olivares) reached its *acuerdo* of 1625: i.e., that Tirso should be banished from Madrid and forbidden to do further writing. I shall discuss the identification at length on an early occasion.

---

[71] E. Cotarelo, *Comedias de Tirso,* II, xxii.

[72] J. C. J. Metford, "Tirso de Molina and the Conde-Duque de Olivares," 15-27.

[73] The proof is long and involved. I shall have to ask the reader to await volume II of this series.

11. *La celosa de sí misma:*[74] This delightful work, first written around 1622-1623, was retouched (perhaps *revised* thoroughly) in 1625-1626. Like *La fingida Arcadia,* it probably satirizes (II, iv) the relationship of Olivares and Vélez de Guevara. But it also points (I, iii) to the omnipotent power of the Guzmanes (which extends to "naves, coches e iglesias"). Tirso's *gracioso,* Ventura, avoids entering the fashionable church, La Victoria — where members of the Guzmán clan must have been accustomed to hear mass — with the significant remark (I, iii): "... huyo de apreturas."

12. *Amar por razón de estado:*[75] a revision of Tirso's *Sutilezas de amor.* From the latter *comedia,* the dramatist has pulled out by the roots the important role of the *gracioso,* Bretón, with very detrimental results to this play, in my opinion. Comparison of the printed work with manuscript (No. 16695, BN) makes evident that, although the latter is dated "Madrid, 1 de enero de 1637," it necessarily goes back to another version (now lost) which had the *gracioso's* role, as Tirso originally wrote it — or at least very near to it. *Amar por razón de estado,* one of the least satisfactory of Tirso's capa y espada plays, was, I suggest, altered to meet the charge of immorality brought against the dramatist by the *Junta.*

Such, presumably, was the *Primera parte,* as Tirso offered it for the second time to the authorities of Madrid. Such was the "niño

---

[74] For the original date of 1622-1623, see my "On the Date of Five Plays by Tirso de Molina," 209-214. This play, like *Quien calla, otorga* (I, vii), has mention of a *pastelería* (II, ii). Ventura says to his idealistic young master who has fallen in love with a *tapada's* beautiful hand: "Y si fuese ... / en lugar de Raquel, Lía / con el un ojo estrellado, / y con el otro en tortilla, / los labios de azul turquí / cubriendo dientes de alquimia, / jalbegado el frontispicio / a fuer de pastelería / y como universidad / rotuladas las mejillas, / ¿qué has de hacer?" I believe that this reference was added in 1625-26 since Tirso evidently has in mind a "vítor"; and that was the form in which the *copla* was written. When studying the political allusions in *La celosa de sí misma,* I shall return to this whole matter.

[75] Hartzenbusch, in his *Comedias escogidas de Fray Gabriel Téllez* ... (Catálogo razonado; XXXVIII), felt that "el jardinero (i.e., *el gracioso*) estaba de más en la comedia; le quitó de allí y la tituló de otro modo con más propiedad."

STUDIES IN TIRSO, I

en la inocencia" which he was asking don Alonso de Paz to sponsor!

Or was it? Could Tirso, daring though he undoubtedly was to the point of rashness, have sent such a volume to *audiencias* that he knew were already on the alert? Could it be, instead, that, after the magic name of Paz had failed to get from these *audiencias* the very essential *aprobaciones* he had hoped for, that he recovered the volume of *sueltas* (a relatively innocuous one) and substituted for some of its plays such politically dangerous ones as are *Tanto es lo de más ...*, *El mayor desengaño,* and *El melancólico,* before sending it down to Sevilla? If this should be the answer to this bibliographical conundrum that is the *Primera parte,* as we know it today, then he repossessed his book sometime after November 20, 1626 (the date when the volume received its *tasa* from the *Consejo*); and this means in all probability that Alonso de Paz, or some other friend of Tirso's, must have taken it to the dramatist in Trujillo, for Tirso was by that date in that city as *comendador* of the house of his Order. [76] There he could have made the substitution of some *sueltas* for others and forwarded it to the bookseller of Sevilla, Manuel Sandi, who then guaranteed the costs of publication to Francisco de Lyra. Whatever the route of transmission, Manuel Sandi *did pay the costs,* and Francisco de Lyra *did publish* it in 1627. I doubt that literary piracy was involved, as Doctor Paterson [77] suggests; the logical thing is — given the contents of the volume and Tirso's determined efforts to get printed his *Primera parte* — that the dramatist himself was responsible for it; he was going to outwit his enemies in Madrid and "leak" to the world something of what had happened.

The meaningful changes which Tirso made in his plays of the *Parte primera* before sending it to press recall words that preface his *Tercera parte.* [78] In an *A cualquiera* that introduces the volume, his "nephew," don Francisco Lucas de Avila, is supposedly speaking. He points first to the success which his uncle's *Cigarrales*

---

[76] Tirso's first document in Trujillo, as we have pointed out above, is dated July 13, 1626.

[77] See Alan K. G. Paterson, "Tirso de Molina: Two Bibliographical Studies," 63. All the bibliographical information concerning Tirso's *Primera parte* is taken from this same study.

[78] See Cotarelo, *Comedias de Tirso de Molina,* I, lvi.

and his *Primera parte* had enjoyed, to the unwillingness of his "uncle" since that time to tempt fortune again: " ... él, en fe de la buena fama que adquirió, se ha echado a dormir no menos tiempo que el de diez años, escarmentado de trampas y mohatras." But he, don Lucas, has nevertheless gotten into his possessions such plays as he could get away from his uncle and is going to publish them anyway. He promises also: some *novelas* which he doesn't choose to name, "porque no se me amotine alguna en profecía"; a *Segunda parte* of the *Cigarrales;* and then, under the true family name of his uncle, another which he will baptize with the title of *Deleitar aprovechando*. The "nephew" then adds:

> Excuse Vm. averiguaciones sobre si de una y otra fábrica ha de ser el alarife mi tío, el maestro, o su sobrino; que cuando me arrojo a afirmar que entrambos, poniendo de su parte aquél cuadernos escondidos y olvidados y éste nuevas añadiduras, no será mentira que me ejecute en la restitución. Ello dirá; y *como Vm. se entretenga con provecho del entretenedor, ¿quién le mete en la legitimidad o bastardía de los inquilinos que no pretenden canonicatos ni colegios?*

I myself have no doubt that Tirso himself wrote the "A cualquiera," and that he also sent the plays of the *Tercera parte* to the little town of Tortosa to get them printed. Several of those found in this *parte* are quite as dangerous as are any that came out in the *Parte primera: Ventura te dé Dios, hijo, La prudencia en la mujer, La fingida Arcadia,* and *La huerta de Juan Fernández.* Tirso very wisely decided to bring this *parte* out far from Madrid — and from Olivares and Mendoza. One must ask why *La ventura con el nombre* and *Antona García* were not among those published in Tortosa? Who can say?

We still do not have satisfying answers to *many* questions concerning either the *Primera parte* or the *Tercera.* Further study of Tirso's plays, or of works of his contemporaries, may yet reveal allusions that will help to clear up some of the mysteries that attach to them, but such an undertaking must necessarily be left for younger scholars of Tirso's works. Let this critic admit frankly that the role which the "discreet" don Antonio Hurtado de Mendoza had in Tirso's life did not become evident until many years after she had begun study of the Mercedarian and that she has not, since making the discovery, reread *all* of his plays to see if there is yet further satire of Mendoza to be found in them. Her guess is that other barbs will be found. (It is logical to suspect that some of the changes that Tirso's supposed nephew made in the dramatist's *Tercera, Cuarta,* and *Quinta partes* consisted of satire emanating from a Tirso who in 1633-1636 was *again* warring with Mendoza and Vélez de Guevara.) Her interest in these studies has been necessarily limited to the years 1625-1626 — except for the preliminary material of the *partes* indicated, necessary as further confirmation of the struggle that took place between Tirso and Mendoza in 1625.

BIBLIOGRAPHY

(of books, articles, plays, manuscripts, etc., cited in this study)

Actas de las Cortes de Castilla (Madrid, 1861-1916), 40 vols.

Agreda y Vargas, Diego. *Novelas morales, útiles por sus documentos* (Madrid, 1620).

Alcalá Yáñez y Ribera, J. de. *El donado hablador, Alonso, mozo de muchos amos*, in *BAE*, XVIII, 491-584.

Alenda y Mira, Jenaro. *Relaciones de solemnidades y fiestas públicas en España* (Madrid, 1903).

Alfay, José (ed.). *Poesías varias de grandes ingenios españoles* [Zaragoza, 1654], ed. J. M. B[lecua], (Zaragoza, 1946).

Almansa y Mendoza, Andrés de. *Cartas de Andrés de Almansa y Mendoza, Novedades de esta corte y avisos recibidos de otras partes, 1621-1626* (Madrid, 1886).

Alonso Pedraz, Martín. *Enciclopedia del idioma* (Madrid, 1958), 3 vols.

Aristophanes, *The Frogs*, translated to English by Gilbert Murray (London, 1925).

Artigas, Miguel. *Don Luis de Góngora y Argote: Biografía y estudio crítico* (Madrid, 1925).

Asensio, Eugenio. *Itinerario del entremés* (Madrid, 1965).

Asensio, Jaime. "A propósito de la primera edición de *Historia general de la Orden de Nuestra Señora de las Mercedes,*" *Reflexión* 2, II (1973), 101-111.

Barreda, Francisco de. "Invectiva a las comedias que prohibió Trajano y apología por las nuestras", included in *El panegírico de Plinio en castellano* (Madrid, 1622), 249-293.

Barrera y Leirado, Cayetano Alberto de la. *Catálogo bibliográfico y biográfico del teatro antiguo español desde sus orígenes hasta mediados del siglo XVIII* (London, 1968). Facsimile of princeps (Madrid, 1860).

Benavente, Casa de los Condes de. BNM, MS 11569.

Bergman, Hannah E. *Luis Quiñones de Benavente y sus entremeses* (Madrid, 1965).

————. Review of Wido Hempel's ed. of *Il Ragguaglio di Parnaso* by "Fabio Franchi", *IIR*, XXXIV (1966), 163-168.

Bible, Holy (Philadelphia, 1905).

Bruerton, Courtney. "*La ninfa del cielo, La serrana de la Vera*, and Related Plays", in *Estudios Hispánicos, Homenaje a Archer M. Huntington* (Wellesley, Mass., 1952), 61-97.

Bushee, Alice H. "The Guzmán Edition of Tirso de Molina's *Comedias*." *HR*, V, no. 1 (January, 1937), 25-39.

——. "The Five *Partes of Tirso de Molina*," *HR*, III, no. 2 (April, 1935), 89-102.

Cabrera de Córdoba, Luis. *Felipe II, Rey de España* (Madrid, 1619).

Camerino, José. *La dama beata* (Madrid, 1655).

Campbell, Lily B. *Shakspere's Tragic Heroes* (Cambridge, 1930).

Campbell, O. J. *Comicall Satyre* (San Marino, Cal., 1938).

Carter, C. H. *The Secret Diplomacy of the Hapsburgs, 1598-1625* (New York and London, 1964).

Castillo Solórzano, Alonso de. *Donayres del Parnaso*, II (Madrid, 1625).

Castro, Américo. *El pensamiento de Cervantes* (Barcelona, 1972).

——. Edition of Tirso's *El vergonzoso en palacio*, in *Clásicos Castellanos* (Madrid, 1922).

—— and Rennert, Hugo A. *Vida de Lope de Vega, 1562-1635* (Salamanca, 1968).

Castro Leal, Antonio. *Juan Ruiz de Alarcón: su vida y su obra* (México, 1943).

Castro y Bellvís, Guillem de. *Obras*, ed. E. Juliá Martínez (Madrid, 1925-27), 3 vols.

Cervantes Saavedra, Miguel de. *Comedias y entremeses*, in *Obras completas*, ed. Bonilla y San Martín (Madrid, 1915).

——. *Don Quijote de la Mancha*, Parte I, ed. "IV Centenario" (Madrid, n. d.) by Luis Astrana Marín.

——. *Viaje del Parnaso*, ed. Francisco Rodríguez Marín (Madrid, 1935).

Collard, Andrée. *Nueva poesía: conceptismo, culteranismo en la crítica española* (Madrid, 1967).

Corral, Gabriel de. *La Cintia de Aranjuez*, ed. Joaquín de Entrambasaguas (Madrid, 1945).

Cortés de Tolosa, Juan. *Lazarillo de Manzanares, con otras cinco novelas* (Madrid, 1620).

Cotarelo y Mori, Emilio. *Bibliografía de las controversias sobre la licitud del teatro en España* (Madrid, 1904).

——. *Colección de entremeses, loas, bailes, jácaras y mojigangas* (Madrid, 1911), 2 vols., *NBAE*, vols. XVII and XVIII.

——. *El Conde de Villamediana. Estudio biográfico-crítico* (Madrid, 1886).

——. *Mira de Amescua y su teatro* (Madrid, 1931).

——. "Las comedias en los conventos de Madrid en el siglo xvii", *RBAM*, II (1925), 461-470.

——. "Luis Vélez de Guevara y sus obras dramáticas", *BRAE*, III (1916), 621-652, and IV (1917), 137-171, 269-308, and 414-444.

Covarrubias y Horozco, Sebastián de. *Tesoro de la lengua castellana o española* (Madrid, 1674).

Cueva de Meliso, La. BAE, LXIX, 543-552.

Davies, Gareth A. "Una carta inédita de Antonio Hurtado de Mendoza al Conde-Duque de Olivares", *Hispania* [Madrid], XIX (1959), 82-91.

——. "A Chronology of Antonio de Mendoza's Plays", *BHS*, XLVIII (1971), 97 et seq.

——. *A Poet at Court: Antonio Hurtado de Mendoza (1586-1644)* (Oxford, 1971).

Davies, R. Trevor. *The Golden Century of Spain, 1501-1621* (New York, 1967).
"Diálogos de las comedias", included in E. Cotarelo. *Bibliografía de las controversias sobre la licitud del teatro* (Madrid, 1904), 210-231.
Diccionario de autoridades (Madrid, 1726).
Entrambasaguas, Joaquín de. *Una guerra literaria del Siglo de Oro: Lope de Vega y los preceptistas aristotélicos*, included in *Estudios sobre Lope de Vega*, I and II (Madrid, 1947).
Escudero y Perosso, Francisco. *Tipografía hispalense* (Madrid, 1894).
La Estrella de Sevilla, with notes and vocabulary by Frank O. Reed and Esther M. Dixon, and introduction by John M. Hill (Boston, 1939).
Fernández Gómez, C. *Vocabulario completo de Lope de Vega* (Madrid, 1971), 3 vols.
Fernández-Guerra y Orbe, Luis. *Don Juan Ruiz de Alarcón y Mendoza* (México, 1872), 2 vols.
Fernández Navarrete, Pedro. *Conservación de monarquías y discursos políticos*. (Includes "La gran consulta"). *BAE*, XXV. Princeps by Sebastián de Cormellas (Barcelona, 1621), as *Discursos políticos*.
Gallardo, Bartolomé José. *Ensayo de una biblioteca española de libros raros y curiosos* (Madrid, 1863-89), 4 vols.
García Carraffa, Alberto and Arturo. *Diccionario heráldico y genealógico de apellidos españoles y americanos* (Madrid, 1919-47), 62 vols.
Gómez, E. Elías. *Teólogo y asceta: Fray Juan Falconi de Bustamante, 1596-1638* (Madrid, 1953).
González Palencia, Ángel. *Quevedo, Tirso y las comedias ante la Junta de Reformación* (Madrid, 1946).
González de Amezúa, Agustín. *Epistolario de Lope* (Madrid, 1935-43), 4 vols.
Granja, Fernando de la. "Milagros españoles en una obra polémica musulmana", *Al-Andalus*, XXXIII (1968).
Gregg, Karl. "A Metaphor in Mira de Amescua," *BCom.*, XIX (Fall, 1967), 36-38.
Green, Otis H. *The Life and Works of Lupercio Leonardo de Argensola* (Philadelphia, 1927).
Guastavino Gallent, Guillermo. "Notas tirsianas, I", *RABM*, LXVII (1959), 680-688.
———. "Notas tirsianas, II", *RABM*, LXIX (1961), 817-820.
Hume, Martin. *The Court of Philip IV: Spain in Decadence* (London, n. d.).
Hurtado y Gómez de la Serna, Juan, and González Palencia, Ángel. *Historia de la literatura española*, 6th ed. (Madrid, 1949).
Ibarra, Francisco de. *Relation des campagnes du Bas-Palatinat en 1620 et 1621*, included in *L'Espagne au XVIe et au XVIIe siècle* (Heilbronn, 1878).
El jardín de Vargas (La gata de Mari-Ramos). Suelta, British Museum. *Acad.N.*, VI, 580-606.
Kennedy, Ruth Lee. "Attacks on Lope and his Theatre in 1617-1621," *Hispanic Studies in Honor of Nicholson B. Adams* (Chapel Hill, N. C., 1966), 57-76.
———. "Certain Phases of the Sumptuary Decrees of 1623 and their Relation to Tirso's Theatre," *HR*, X (1942), 91-115.

Kennedy, Ruth Lee. "Contemporary Satire Against Ruiz de Alarcón as Lover," *HR*, XIII (1945), 145-165.

——. "Did Tirso Send to Press a *Primera parte* of Madrid (1626) which Contained *El condenado por desconfiado?*" Included in homage volume to Arnold G. Reichenberger, vol. 41 (1973), 261-74.

——. "Literary and Political Satire in Tirso's *La fingida Arcadia,*" published in *The Renaissance Reconsidered, Smith College Studies in History,* XLIV (1964), 91-110.

——. "Notes on Two Interrelated Plays of Tirso: *El amor y la amistad* and *Ventura te dé Dios, hijo,*" *HR*, XXVIII (1960), 189-214.

——. "On the Date of Five Plays by Tirso de Molina," *HR*, X (1942), 183-214.

——. "Pantaleón de Ribera, 'Sirene', Castillo Solórzano and the *Academia de Madrid* in Early 1625," *Homage to John M. Hill (In memoriam)* (Indiana University, 1968).

——. "*La prudencia en la mujer* and the Ambient that Brought it Forth," *PMLA*, LXIII (1948), 1131-1190.

——. "A Reappraisal of Tirso's Relations to Lope and his Theatre," *BCom.*, XVII (1965), 23-24 and XVIII (1966), 1-13.

——. "Studies for the Chronology of Tirso's Theatre," *HR*, XI (1943), 17-46.

——. "The Dates of *El amor médico* and *Escarmientos para el cuerdo* (Tirso's Supposed Trip to Portugal in 1619)," *Reflexión* 2, no. 1, vol. I (1972).

——. "Tirso's *Cautela contra cautela*: its Authenticity in his Theater and its Importance," *RABM*, LXXIV (1972), 325-59.

——. "Tirso's *Desde Toledo a Madrid*: its Date and Place of Composition," *Homenaje a William L. Fichter* (Madrid, 1971), 357-366.

——. "Tirso's *No hay peor sordo*: its Date and Place of Composition", in *Homenaje a Rodríguez-Moñino* (Madrid, 1966), I, 261-278.

——. "Tirso's *La república al revés*: its Debt to Mira's *La rueda de la fortuna,* its Date of Composition, and its Importance," *Reflexión* 2, II (1923) 39-50.

——. "Tirso's Satire of Ruiz de Alarcón," *BCom.*, XVI (1964), 7-12.

——. "Tirso's *La ventura con el nombre*: its Source and Date of Composition," *BCom.*, XXI (1969), no. 2, 35-45.

King, Willard F. "La ascendencia paterna de Juan Ruiz de Alarcón y Mendoza", *NRFH*, XIX (1970), no. 1, 49-86.

——. *Prosa novelística y academias literarias en el siglo XVII* (Madrid, 1963).

León, Antonio de. *Noticias*, BNM MS 2395.

Liñán y Verdugo, Antonio. *Guía y avisos de forasteros que vienen a la corte* (Barcelona, 1885).

López Navío, José, Sch. P. "Una comedia de Tirso que no está perdida", *Estudios*, XVI (1960), 331-347.

López Pinciano, Alonso. *Filosofía antigua poética,* ed. Pedro Muñoz Peña (Valladolid, 1894).

McCready, Warren T. *Bibliografía temática de estudios sobre el teatro español antiguo* (Toronto, 1966).

Marañón, Gregorio. *El Conde-Duque de Olivares (La pasión de mandar)* (Madrid, 1936).

Mariana, Juan de. *Tratado contra los juegos públicos*, BAE, XXX, 413-462.

Medel del Castillo, Francisco. *Índice general alfabético de todos los títulos de comedias*, ed. John M. Hill (New York, 1929).

Mendoza, Antonio Hurtado de. *Los empeños del mentir, Flor de las mejores doce comedias de los mayores ingenios de España* (Madrid, 1652), BAE, XLV, 437-455.

––––––. *El galán sin dama* (exists ms. in Sedó collection). Without attribution in index of *El mejor de los libros que han salido de comedias nuevas* (Alcalá, 1651), but attributed on f. 5v of the preliminaries to don Antonio de Mendoza.

Mendoza, Antonio Hurtado de. *Más merece quien más ama*, published without attribution in *Doce comedias nuevas de Lope de Vega Carpio y otros autores. Segunda parte* (Barcelona, 1630). Published later in *Primavera numerosa de muchas armonías lucientes* ... (Madrid, 1679), attributed to Antonio de Mendoza and Juan de Vera y Villarroel. Not modernly reprinted.

––––––. *Obras poéticas*, ed. Rafael Benítez Claros (Madrid, 1947), 3 vols.

Menéndez Pelayo, Marcelino. *Historia de las ideas estéticas en España* (Santander, 1947), 5 vols.

Mérimée, Henri. *Spectacles et comédiens à Valencia (1580-1630)* (Paris, 1913).

Metford, J. C. J. "Tirso de Molina and the Conde-Duque de Olivares," BHS, XXXVI (1959), 15-27.

Mira de Amescua, Antonio. *Adversa fortuna de don Álvaro de Luna*, ed. Cotarelo, NBAE, IV (Madrid, 1906). Princeps: *Segunda parte de Tirso* (Madrid, 1635).

––––––. *Próspera fortuna de don Álvaro de Luna y adversa de Ruy López de Avalos*, ed. Cotarelo, NBAE, IV (Madrid, 1900). Princeps: *Segunda parte de Tirso* (Madrid, 1635).

––––––. *La segunda de don Álvaro (Adversa fortuna de don Álvaro de Luna)*, ed. Nellie E. Sánchez-Arce (México, 1960), with "Estudio preliminar".

––––––. *Comedia famosa de Ruy López de Avalos (Primera parte de don Álvaro de Luna) Próspera fortuna de don Álvaro de Luna y adversa de Ruy López de Avalos*, ed. Nellie E. Sánchez-Arce (México, 1965), with "Notas preliminares".

Montoto, Santiago. "Una comedia de Tirso que no es de Tirso" [*La Reina de los Reyes*], *Archivo hispalense*, VII (1946).

Morley, S. G. and Bruerton, C. *Cronología de las comedias de Lope de Vega* (Madrid, 1968).

Museo del Prado: Catálogo de los cuadros (Madrid, 1952).

Noticias de Madrid, 1621-1627, ed. Ángel González Palencia (Madrid, 1942).

Nougué, André. *L'Oeuvre en prose de Tirso de Molina* (Toulouse, 1962).

Novoa, Matías de. *Historia de Felipe III*. In two vols. by the Marqués de la Fuensanta del Valle and José Sánchez Rayón (Madrid, 1875). Reprinted (with the same pagination) in *Colección de documentos inéditos para la historia de España*, LX and LXI (1966).

Parker, Alexander A. *The Approach to the Spanish Drama of the Golden Age* (London, 1957).

––––––. "The Meaning of 'Discreción' in *No hay más fortuna que Dios*: the Medieval Background and Sixteenth and Seventeenth Century Usage," Sonderdruck aus *Calderón de la Barca*, Seiten 218-234 (Darmstadt, 1971).

370 STUDIES IN TIRSO, I

Parker, Alexander A. *Literature and the Delinquent: The Picaresque Novel in Spain and Europe, 1599-1753* (Edinburgh, 1967).

Paterson, Alan K. G. "Tirso de Molina: Two Biographical Studies," *HR*, XXXV (1967), 43-68.

Penedo Rey, R. P. Manuel. "Tirso de Molina en Toledo", *Estudios*, número extraordinario (Madrid, 1949), 22-28.

———. "Tirso en Sevilla", *Estudios*, núm. extraordinario (Madrid, 1949), 29-74.

———. "Muerte documentada del Padre Maestro Fray Gabriel Téllez en Almazán y otras referencias biográficas", *Estudios*, núm. extraordinario (Madrid, 1949), 93-121.

Pérez Pastor, Cristóbal. *Bibliografía madrileña* (Madrid. 1891-1907), 3 vols.

Placer López, G. "Nuevos datos acerca de Fray Gabriel Téllez", *Estudios*, VI (1950), 349-352.

Quevedo y Villegas, Francisco de. *Anales de quince días*, BAE, XXIII, 193-220.

———. *Obras completas. (Obras en verso)*, ed. Luis Astrana Marín (Madrid, 1952).

———. *La vida del Buscón*, ed. Américo Castro (Paris, 1915).

———. "La visita de los chistes", ed. *Clásicos Castellanos* of *Los sueños*, II (Madrid, 1916), 193-298.

———. "Las zahurdas de Plutón", ed. *Clásicos Castellanos* of *Los sueños*, II (Madrid, 1916), 87-187.

Quiñones de Benavente, Luis. *El murmurador*, included in E. Cotarelo, *Colección de entremeses*, II, 526-528.

———. *Las dos letras*, in E. Cotarelo, *Colección de entremeses*, II, 769-773.

Rennert, Hugo A. *The Spanish Stage in the Time of Lope de Vega*, including "Spanish Actors and Actresses" (New York, 1909).

——— y Castro, Américo. *Vida de Lope de Vega* (Madrid, 1968).

Ribera, Anastasio Pantaleón de. *Obras*, ed. Rafael de Balbín Lucas (Madrid, 1944), 2 vols.

Righetti, Mario. *Historia de la liturgia*, Spanish ed. by C. Urtasun Irisarri (Madrid, 1955-56), 2 vols.

Robles Dégano, Felipe. *Ortología clásica de la lengua castellana* (Madrid, 1903).

Roca, Conde de la. (Vera y Zúñiga, Juan Antonio de.) *Il Ragguaglio di Parnaso* (Venice, 1636). Published under pseudonym of "Fabio Franchi" and included recently in *In honor de la Fenice Ibera*. Ed. Wido Hempel (Frankfurt am Main, 1964).

Rodríguez Marín, Francisco. "Cinco poesías autobiográficas de Luis Vélez de Guevara", RABM, XIX (July-December, 1908), 62-78.

Rufo, Juan. *Seiscientos apotegmas*, ed. A. Blecua (Madrid, 1972).

Ruiz de Alarcón y Mendoza, Juan. *El dueño de las estrellas*, in *Teatro completo de don Juan Ruiz de Alarcón*, ed. Ermilo Abreu Gómez (México, 1951).

———. "Elogio descriptivo a las fiestas que la Majestad del Rey Felipe IV hizo ... en Madrid a 21 de agosto de 1623 años ...", together with "Comento", BAE, LII, 583-592.

———. *Las paredes oyen*, in *Teatro completo de don Juan Ruiz de Alarcón*, ed. Ermilo Abreu Gómez (México, 1951).

Ruiz de Alarcón y Mendoza, Juan. *Los pechos privilegiados*, in *Teatro completo de don Juan Ruiz de Alarcón*, ed. Ermilo Abreu Gómez (México, 1951).

——. *La verdad sospechosa*, ed. Ed. Barry (Paris, 1918).

Salas Barbadillo, Alonso Jerónimo de. *El caballero puntual*, II, in *Obras* (Madrid, 1909).

——. *Coronas del Parnaso y platos de las Musas* (Madrid, 1635).

——. *Don Diego de noche* (Madrid, 1944).

——. *Fiestas de la boda de la incasable malcasada* (Madrid, 1622).

——. *El necio afortunado* (Madrid, 1626).

——. *La sabia Flora Malsabidilla* (Madrid, 1621).

Sánchez, José. *Academias literarias del Siglo de Oro español* (Madrid, 1961).

Sánchez-Arjona, José. *Anales del teatro en Sevilla desde Lope de Rueda hasta fines del siglo XVII* (Sevilla, 1898).

Sarrailh, J. "Algunos datos acerca de don Antonio Liñán y Verdugo ...", *RFE*, VI (1919), 346-363 and VIII (1921), 150-160.

Sempere y Guarinos, Juan. *Historia del lujo y de las leyes suntuarias de España* (Madrid, 1788), 2 vols.

Shergold, Norman D. *A History of the Spanish Stage, from Medieval Times until the End of the Seventeenth Century* (Oxford, 1967).

—— and Varey, John E. "Some Palace Performances of Seventeenth-century Plays", *BHS*, XL (1963), 212-244.

Spencer, Forrest Eugene, and Schevill, Rudolph. *The Dramatic Works of Luis Vélez de Guevara* (Berkeley, 1937).

Suárez de Figueroa, Cristóbal. *El pasajero*, ed. F. Rodríguez Marín (Madrid, 1913).

—— and Torres Rámila. *Spongia* (Madrid, 1617). No copy exists today. We known of its existence and contents only through the *Expostulatio Spongiae*.

——. *Varias noticias importantes a la humana comunicación* (Madrid, 1621).

TIRSO DE MOLINA (TÉLLEZ, FRAY GABRIEL)

Non-dramatic works

Acto de contrición (en verso) (Madrid, 1630). *RABM*, LXXV, 1-2.

El bandolero, ed. Luis Carlos Viada y Lluch (Barcelona, n. d.).

Los cigarrales de Toledo (Madrid, 1624).

——, ed. Espasa-Calpe (Madrid, 1942), 2 vols.

Genealogía del Conde de Sástago (Madrid, 1640). No copy is known to exist today.

Deleytar aprovechando (Madrid, 1635).

Historia general de la Orden de Nuestra Señora de las Mercedes, Redención de cautivos, Real Academia de la Historia, MS E-16 and 17. First vol., of 417 *hojas*, finished Feb. 5, 1639; second vol., of 460 *hojas*, finished Dec. 24, 1639. R. P. Manuel Penedo Rey has transcribed and is soon publishing this manuscript.

La vida de la santa Madre doña María de Cervellón, RABM, XVIII (1908), 1-17, 243-56; XIX (1908), 262-73; XXI (1909), 139-57, 567-70. Published by Menéndez Pelayo as "Una obra inédita de Tirso de Molina".

Dramatic works

a) Collections

Primera parte. Doce comedias nuevas del Maestro Tirso de Molina (Sevilla, 1627).

Segunda parte de las comedias del Maestro Tirso de Molina. Recogidas por su sobrino, don Francisco de Ávila (Madrid, 1635). [Tirso claimed only four of the twelve plays contained in this *parte*.]

Parte tercera de las comedias del Maestro Tirso de Molina, recogidas por don Francisco Lucas de Ávila, sobrino del autor ... (Tortosa, 1634).

Parte cuarta de las comedias del Maestro Tirso de Molina, recogidas por don Francisco de Ávila, sobrino del autor (Madrid, 1635).

Quinta parte de comedias del Maestro Tirso de Molina, recogidas por don Francisco de Ávila, sobrino del autor (Madrid, 1636).

Comedias de Tirso de Molina, ed. Emilio Cotarelo y Mori, *NBAE*, IV and IX (Madrid, 1906-07). Includes Tirsian plays not found in Hartzenbusch (*BAE*, V).

Comedias escogidas de Fray Gabriel Téllez (el Maestro Tirso de Molina), ed. Juan Eugenio Hartzenbusch, *BAE*, V, 1944.

Obras dramáticas completas de Tirso de Molina, ed. Blanca de los Ríos (Madrid, 1946-58), 3 vols. Vol. III has "complementos editoriales" by Luis Escolar Barreño.

b) Individual plays

Amar por arte mayor, Parte quinta. BAE, V, 423-441.

Amar por razón de estado, Parte primera. BAE, V, 166-183. [This play, before the role of *gracioso* was suppressed, was known as *Sutilezas de amor y el Marqués del Camarín*.]

Amar por señas, Varios autores: Parte XXVII (Madrid, 1667). *BAE*, V, 462-481.

Las Amazonas en las Indias, Parte cuarta. NBAE, IV, 551-578.

El amor médico, Parte cuarta. BAE, V, 381-401.

Amor y celos hacen discretos, Parte segunda. BAE, V, 150-165.

El amor y el amistad, Parte tercera, BAE, V, 328-345.

Antona García, Parte cuarta. NBAE, IV, 616-644.

El árbol del mejor fruto, Parte primera, NBAE, IV, 30-60.

Averígüelo Vargas, Parte tercera, BAE, V, 668-689.

Los balcones de Madrid, Teatro antiguo español (Madrid, 1837). *BAE*, V, 556-571. [There are in existence at least four manuscripts of this play. Dr. Vern Williamsen is studying them for an edition which he expects to publish shortly.]

Bellaco sois, Gómez. BNM, MS 16.920. *NBAE*, IX, 591-622.

El burlador de Sevilla, Doze comedias nuevas de Lope de Vega Carpio y otros autores (Barcelona, 1630). *BAE*, V, 572-590.

El caballero de Gracia, Varios: Parte XXXI (Madrid, 1669). *NBAE*, IX, 358-387.

El castigo del penséque, Parte primera. BAE, V, 70-89.

Cautela contra cautela, Parte segunda. BAE, V, 501-518.

La celosa de sí misma, Primera parte. BAE, V, 128-149.

El celoso prudente, in *Los cigarrales de Toledo* (Madrid, 1624). *BAE*, V, 612-632.

Cómo han de ser los amigos, in *Los cigarrales de Toledo* (Madrid, 1624). *NBAE*, IV, 1-29.

Desde Toledo a Madrid, Comedias escogidas: Parte XXVI (Madrid, 1666). *BAE*, V, 482-500.

Don Gil de las calzas verdes, Parte cuarta. *BAE*, V, 402-422.

Doña Beatriz de Silva, Parte cuarta. *NBAE*, IV, 489-517.

La elección por la virtud, Parte tercera. *NBAE*, IV, 343-374.

En Madrid y en una casa, Comedias escogidas: Parte XXXV (Madrid, 1671). *BAE*, V, 538-555. [Printed also under Rojas Zorrilla's name and under Calderón's as "Lo que hace un manto en Madrid".]

Escarmientos para el cuerdo, Parte quinta. *NBAE*, IX, 55-82.

Esto sí que es negociar, Parte segunda. *BAE*, V, 248-264.

La fingida Arcadia, Parte tercera. *NBAE*, IV, 434-459.

La firmeza en la hermosura, Doce comedias nuevas de diferentes autores: Parte XLVII (Valencia, 1646). *NBAE*, IX, 333-359.

La gallega Mari-Hernández, Parte primera. *BAE*, V, 109-127.

Los hermanos parecidos (auto sacramental), in *Deleytar aprovechando* (Madrid, 1635). *NBAE*, IX, 709-718.

El honroso atrevimiento, BNM MS 15.966. *NBAE*, IX, 467-490.

La huerta de Juan Fernández, Parte tercera. *BAE*, V, 633-681.

La lealtad contra la envidia, Parte cuarta. *NBAE*, IV, 579-615.

Marta la piadosa, Parte quinta. *BAE*, V, 442-461.

El mayor desengaño, Parte primera. *NBAE*, IV, 90-117.

El melancólico, Parte primera. *NBAE*, IV, 61-89.

La mujer que manda en casa, Parte cuarta. *NBAE*, IV, 460-488.

No hay peor sordo, Parte tercera. *BAE*, V, 265-286.

No le arriendo la ganancia (auto sacramental), in *Deleytar aprovechando* (Madrid, 1635).

Palabras y plumas, Parte primera. *BAE*, V, 1-20.

La peña de Francia, Parte cuarta. *NBAE*, IV, 645-678.

Por el sótano y el torno, Parte segunda. *BAE*, V, 228-247.

El pretendiente al revés, Parte primera. *BAE*, V, 21-43.

Privar contra su gusto, Parte cuarta. *BAE*, V, 346-363.

La prudencia en la mujer, Parte tercera. *BAE*, V, 287-306.

Quien calla otorga, Parte primera. *BAE*, V, 90-108.

Quien da luego, da dos veces, BNM MS 15.948. *NBAE*, IX, 542-567.

Quien no cae no se levanta, Parte quinta. *NBAE*, IX, 142-172.

Las quinas de Portugal, BNM MS, dated March 8, 1638. Not autograph as originally claimed. *NBAE*, IX, 568-590.

La república al revés, Parte quinta, *NBAE*, IX, 83-114.

El saber guardar la hacienda.
A play known to have existed in 1612, now lost. It may well have been a primitive form of *Tanto es lo de más como lo de menos*.

La Santa Juana (Primera parte), Parte quinta. *NBAE*, IX, 258-275.

La Santa Juana (Segunda parte), Parte quinta. *NBAE*, IX, 276-303.

La Santa Juana (Tercera parte), BNM MS, vitrina 3, 23. *NBAE*, IX, 304-332.

Santo y sastre, Parte cuarta. *NBAE*, IX, 1-26.

Siempre ayuda la verdad, Segunda parte. *NBAE*, IV, 207-234. (Medel's *Índice* attributes one play of this name to Tirso, another of the same title to Ruiz de Alarcón.)

374 STUDIES IN TIRSO, I

Sutilezas de amor y el Marqués del Camarín; see above, *Amar por razón de estado*.

Tan largo me lo fiáis. [A *suelta*, attributed to don Pedro Calderón. It is *El burlador de Sevilla*, with many important variants.] *NBAE*, IX, 656-682.

Tanto es lo de más como lo de menos, Parte primera. NBAE, IV, 118-148.

Todo es dar en una cosa, Parte cuarta. NBAE, IV, 518-550.

La venganza de Tamar, Parte tercera. NBAE, IV, 407-433.

La ventura con el nombre, Comedias escogidas: Parte XXVII. *BAE*, V, 519-537.

Ventura te dé Dios, hijo, Parte tercera. NBAE, IV, 375-406.

El vergonzoso en palacio, in *Los cigarrales de Toledo* (Madrid, 1624). *BAE*, V, 204-227.

————, ed. *Clásicos Castellanos* by Américo Castro (Madrid, 1922).

La vida y muerte de Herodes, Parte quinta. NBAE, IX, 173-207.

La villana de la Sagra, Parte tercera. BAE, V, 307-327.

La villana de Vallecas, Parte primera. BAE, V, 44-69.

Torres Naharro, Bartolomé de. *Propalladia and Other Works*, ed. Joseph E. Gillet and Otis H. Green (Bryn Mawr, 1943-1961), 4 vols.

Vázquez, P. Guillermo. *Breve reseña de los conventos de la Orden de la Merced* (Rome, 1932).

Vega Carpio, Lope Félix de. *Comedias escogidas de Fray Lope Félix de Vega Carpio*, ed. Juan Eugenio Hartzenbusch, *BAE*, 4 vols. (XXIV, XXXIV, XLI, LII).

————. *La discreta venganza*. Princeps: *Parte XX* (1625). H. XLI. M-B: 1615-22 (probablemente 1620).

————. "Epístola a don Antonio Hurtado de Mendoza, caballero del hábito de Calatrava, secretario de su Majestad", written around September, 1623. Published in *La Circe* (Madrid, 1624). *BAE*, XXXVIII, 400-401.

————. *Los esclavos libres, Parte XIII* (1620). *Acad.N.*, V. M-B: 1600.

————. *La Filomela*. Princeps: 1621. *BAE*, XXXVIII, 478-492.

————. *Lo fingido verdadero (El mejor representante)*. Princeps: *Parte XVI. Acad.N.*, IV. M-B: hacia 1608.

————. *Las flores de don Juan*. Princeps: *Parte XII* (1619). *Acad.N.*, XII. M-B: 1612-15.

————. *El halcón de Federico*. Princeps: *Parte XIII. Acad.N.*, XIV. M-B: 1599-1605 (probablemente 1601-05).

————. *El jardín de Lope*. Princeps: 1621 (with *Filomela*). *BAE*, XXXVIII, 422-427.

————. *Justa poética y alabanzas justas que hizo la insigne villa de Madrid al bienaventurado San Isidro en las fiestas de su beatificación* (Madrid, 1620).

————. *Laurel de Apolo con otras rimas*. Princeps: 1630. *BAE*, XXXVIII, 185-229 (praise of Tirso, 213; of Antonio de Mendoza, 198).

————. *La limpieza no manchada, Santa Brígida*. Princeps: *Parte XIX* (1623). *Acad.N.*, V. M-B: 1619.

————. *La moza de cántaro*. Princeps: *Dif.* XXXVII (1646). *Acad.N.*, XIII. M-B: written apparently before 1618; partially revised in 1625.

————. *La pobreza estimada*. Princeps: *Parte XVIII* (1623). *Acad.N.*, XIV. M-B: 1597-1603.

————. *La portuguesa o dicha del forastero*. Princeps: *Esc. III* (1653). *Acad.N.*, XIII. M-B: 1615-16.

Vega Carpio, Lope Félix de. *El premio de la hermosura.* Princeps: *Parte XVI.* *Acad.N.,* XIII. M-B: 1610-1618. "...Lope undoubtedly made changes in it before publication."

——. *Relación de las fiestas que la insigne villa de Madrid hizo en la canonización de ... San Isidro* (Madrid, 1622). El certamen se celebró en 28 de junio (de 1622). In *BAE,* XXXVIII, 148-158 ("Panegíricos" not included).

——. *Los Tellos de Meneses, I.* Princeps: *Parte XXI* (1635). *Acad.N.,* VII. M-B: 1620-28.

——. *Triunfos divinos con otras rimas.* Princeps: *Sept.,* 1625. R-C (275): "Casi todo el prólogo está destinado a censurar a sus enemigos, entre ellos Alarcón...".

Vélez de Guevara, Luis. *El diablo cojuelo,* ed. A. Bonilla y San Martín (Madrid, 1910).

¿——? *Juicio final de todos los poetas españoles vivos y muertos.* MS in BNL; date, almost certainly, 1638.

——. *Más pesa el rey que la sangre y blasón de los Guzmanes.* Princeps: *suelta* of 17th century. *BAE,* XLV.

¿——? "La mojiganga de la Boda que se trazó en Buen Retiro este año de 1638 ...", MS, BNL.

——. *El negro del seraphim.* BNM, MS 17317, dated Feb. 8, 1643. Presumably written after 1612, since it was taken from Lope's *El sancto negro Rosambuco, Parte III* (1613).

——. *El prodigioso príncipe transilvano.* (S-S: *Del capitán prodigioso, príncipe de Transilvania*). Princeps: *Ocho comedias,* I (in Schaeffer's library). *Acad.N.,* I. M-B: "hacia 1597".

Vergara, Hipólito de. *La Reina de los Reyes* in *Parte segunda* of Tirso (Madrid, 1635). (See under Montoto, Santiago, for attribution.)

Vossler, Karl. *Escritores y poetas de España* (Madrid, 1944).

Wade, Gerald E. "Character Names in Some of Tirso's *comedias,*" *HR,* XXXVI (1968), 1-34.

——. "La dedicatoria de Matías de los Reyes a Tirso de Molina", *Estudios,* VIII (Madrid, 1952), 589-593.

——. "El escenario histórico y la fecha de *Amar por razón de estado*", *Estudios,* núm. extraordinario (Madrid, 1949), 659-670.

——. "Tirso and the Court Circle," in *Homage to John M. Hill* (Indiana University, 1968).

——. "Tirso's *Cigarrales de Toledo*: Some Clarifications and Identifications," *HR,* XXXIII (1965), 246-272.

——. "Vítor, don Juan de Alarcón y el fraile de la Merced", *HR,* XL (1972).

——. "The year of Tirso's birth," *Hispanófila,* VII (1963), no. 19, 1-9.

Webber, Edwin J. "The Shipwreck of don Manuel de Sousa in the Spanish Theater," *PMLA,* LXVI (1951), 1114-1122.

Williamsen, Vern. "The Development of a *Décima* in Mira de Amescua's Theatre," *BCom.,* XXII (Fall, 1970), 32-36.

Wilson, Margaret. *Spanish Drama of the Golden Age* (Oxford, n. d.).

——. Ed. of Tirso de Molina, *Antona García* (Manchester, 1957), with introduction (vii-xxvi).

INDEX

(It is my hope that all names of authors mentioned in this book—whether in the text proper or in the notes—will be found in this Index. On the other hand, titles of works have been included only where they are of the seventeenth century or earlier. Exception has been made when various studies of the same author are cited repeatedly; the alternative was a string of numbers so long as to be virtually useless to the reader.)

"Amarilis" (María de Córdoba, wife of Andrés de la Vega), 110 n. 64, 125 n. 97.
Amazonas en las Indias, Las, 272 n. 13.
Amella, Juan Jerónimo, 190-91 n. 10.
Amezúa, Agustín González de, 157 n. 16, 189 n. 3.
Amor médico, El, 12, 69 n. 78, 70 n. 81, 93 n. 41, 110 n. 64, 113 n. 72, 114, 116 n. 79, 117, 235 n. 36, 255-57 n. 13, 258 n. 17, 264, 273-74 n. 14, 276, 322-25, 347 n. 51.
Amor y celos hacen discretos, 244, 285, 298 n. 3, 311 n. 26, 313-14.
Amor y el amistad, El, 62, 71 n. 82, 171 n. 32, 251 n. 8, 267 n. 3, 351.
Anales de quince días, 34 n. 20.
Anales del teatro en Sevilla, 311 n. 26.
Anticristo, El, 315.
Antona García, 15, 92 n. 39, 93-101, 95 n. 43, 98, 104-06, 105 n. 55, 111, 114, 124, 135, 141, 155 n. 12, 171 n. 32, 184 n. 53, 184-86, 189 n. 5, 243, 266, 325 n. 44, 337, 349, 350, 357, 359, 363.
Apologie for poetrie, An, 44 n. 32.
Árbol del mejor fruto, El, 161 n. 19, 357.
Arbitrio de la Redención preservativa, see under Mercedarian Order.
Arcadia, La (novela, Lope's), 154 n. 9, 191.
"Arceo" (Francisco de León y Arce), 23, 133 n. 106, 189, 278-81 n. 29, 294 n. 56, 341-42, 353.
Argensola, Lupercio Leonardo de, 23, 50-51 n. 42.
Aristophanes, 44 n. 31, 167 n. 25, 194 n. 23.
Aristotelians and lopistas, War between, 35, 39-50, 65, 174, 192. *See also* López Pinciano, Alonso.
Aristotle, 39-40, 43.
Artigas, Miguel, 259, 260.
Asensio, Eugenio, 180 n. 47.
Asensio, Jaime, 187 n. 57.
Asombro de la Limpia Concepción, El, 64, 158, 299.

Astrana Marín, Luis, 259 n. 20, 303 n. 13, 311 n. 26.
audiences (unruly) in early 1620's, 52 n. 44, 314-15.
Avalle-Arce, Juan Bautista, 15.
Avendaño, Cristóbal de, 244 n. 57, 358 n. 68.
Averígüelo Vargas, 304-06 n. 16, 323 n. 15, 337.
Ávila, Francisco Lucas de, 118 n. 84, 288, 362-63.
Ayo de su hijo, El, 52 n. 44.

Balbín, Domingo *(autor),* 105 n. 55.
Balcones de Madrid, Los, 57, 114-15 n. 74, 274-75 n. 18, 292 n. 52, 360.
Bandolero, El, 24 n. 6, 71 n. 82, 90 n. 35, 191 n. 14, 192 n. 16, 247, 249-51 n. 6, 250 n. 8, 252-53, 263, 265, 285-86 n. 45, 341 n. 28.
Barreda, Francisco de la, 48-50 n. 39, 50-51 n. 41, 89 n. 34, 177 n. 40.
Barrera y Leirado, Cayetano Alberto de la, 67 n. 72, 78 ns. 3, 10; 81 n. 18, 83, 90 n. 35, 95 n. 43, 136, 137, 223 n. 10, 230 n. 29.
Barry, Edouard, 297 n. 1.
Bazán y Benavides, María Eugenia de, 4th Marquesa de Santa Cruz (wife to Jerónimo Pimentel), 211, 214 n. 60.
Bellaco sois, Gómez, 171 n. 32.
Belmonte Bermúdez, Luis de, 297 n. 1.
Benavente *(entremesista), see* Quiñones de Benavente, Luis.
Benavente, 8th Conde-Duque de, 209, 211 n. 55, 213 n. 59.
Benavente, 9th Conde de, 212 n. 57, 213-14 n. 60.
Benítez Claros, Rafael, 321 n. 1, 342 n. 33, 343 n. 37, 345, 346 n. 42.
Bergman, Hannah E., 119 n. 85, 195 n. 24, 238 n. 44, 240 n. 49, 274 n. 16, 292 n. 54.
Bobadilla y Alarcón, Clara de, 301.
Bocángel y Unzueta, Gabriel, 286 n. 46, 329-30 n. 1.
Bonilla San Martín, Adolfo, 229 n. 25, 342 n. 31.

n. 45, 180 n. 46, 184, 192 ns. 16 and 17, 186, 205 n. 41, 243, 247, 250-51 n. 8, 257, 265, 295, 299 n. 5, 312 n. 27, 332 n. 4, 338, 350 n. 57, 353, 355, 358, 362.
Cinti, Bruna, 119 n. 85.
Cintia de Aranjuez, La, 223 n. 20, 227 n. 23, 230 n. 27, 281-82 n. 33, 332-34 ns. 6 and 8.
Cirac Estopañón, Sebastián, 302 n. 9.
Circe, La, con otras rimas y prosas, 37 n. 23, 138, 184.
Claramonte, Andrés de, 201 n. 34, 220.
"Clarindo," 309 n. 20.
Cobarde valiente, El, 207-08 n. 48, 292 n. 52.
Collard, Andrée, 237 n. 42, 249 n. 6.
"comedia nueva," 64, 169, 334 n. 9.
comedia de apariencias, 65, 188, 189 n. 7, 194 n. 23, 195, 199-200, 223-24 n. 12, 263 n. 30; *de intriga,* 57; *de repente,* 67; *de ruido o de cuerpo,* 65, 199, 224; *de santos,* 65, 223-24, 287-88; *de tramoya,* 57, 65, 114, 161 n. 18, 162, 165-66 n. 23, 169, 188 n. 2, 189-90 n. 7, 193-95 n. 23, 199-201 n. 29, 223-24 n. 18, 251 n. 8, 252, 263 n. 30, 287, 330-31.
Cómo han de ser los amigos, 62, 64 n. 64, 247-48, 351.
Condenado por desconfiado, El, 14, 55, 88 n. 30, 116 n. 77, 298 n. 3, 351 n. 58, 355 n. 64.
Condenado por dudar, El, 88 n. 30.
"Consonantes, La fuerza de los," 228-29 n. 25, 239, 291 n. 51.
"Contienda de Marsias y de Apolo, La," 194 n. 22.
Contreras, Francisco de, 31, 35 n. 21, 348 n. 52.
Contreras, Pedro de, 145.
"Corcovilla" (letrilla), 303 n. 13, 311, 313.
"Coriandro" (Gabriel de Corral), 89.
Corominas, J., 306.
Coronas del Parnaso y platos de las Musas, 329-32 n. 1.
Coronel, Fray Diego, 69.
"Corpulent poet," the: as character-

ized in *Los cigarrales,* 247-49; in *El bandolero,* 249-53; in *Tanto es lo de más,* 253-55; as *defined* in *El amor médico,* 255-57; not to be *identified* with Suárez de Figueroa, 257-58; nor with Góngora, 258-62; "corpulent poet = Luis Vélez, 262-65.
Corral, Francisco de, 260.
Corral, Gabriel de, 67, 73, 89, 91, 109 n. 62, 225-227 and ns. 20, 21, 23, 24, 230, 243 n. 55, 278, 281-82, 332-34 and ns. 6, 7; 349.
Corral y Arellano, Diego de, 27 n. 8, 28, 31, 34, 35 n. 1, 37.
Cortes sessions, 26 n. 8, 30 n. 12, 31 n. 13, 40, 47, 50, 58, 62, 115 n. 76, 353.
Cortés, Hernán: praise from Tirso, 71 n. 84; 111-112; his descendants (Marqueses del Valle) and the Mercedarian Order, 112 n. 68.
Cortés de Tolosa, Juan, 36 n. 23, 302 n. 11.
"courtier, the perfect," 71-72, 102, 128-29.
Cortesano, El, 222 n. 5.
Cortesano descortés, El, 302 n. 10.
Cotarelo y Mori, Emilio, 15.
Bibliografía de las controversias sobre la licitud del teatro en España, 50 n. 40;
Colección de entremeses, loas, etc., 274 n. 16;
Conde de Villamediana, El, 201 n. 34, 207 n. 47, 212 n. 58;
Introductory pages to *Comedias de Tirso,* 21 n. 1, 58 n. 56, 59 n. 58, 69 n. 79, 89 n. 32, 90 n. 35, 117 n. 80, 118 n. 83, 152 n. 2, 162 n. 20; 170 n. 30, 172 n. 34, 181 n. 48. 182 n. 49, 220 n. 2, 223 n. 12, 245 n. 59, 276 n. 20, 277 n. 23, 287 n. 48, 297 n. 1, 335 n. 12, 337 n. 17, 359 n. 70, 360 n. 71, 362 n. 78.
Mira de Amescua y su teatro, 156 n. 14, 166 n. 23, 248 n. 4.
Comedias en los conventos de Madrid, 79 n. 2.

394 STUDIES IN TIRSO, I

Ventura te dé Dios, hijo, 190 n. 9, 192 n. 16, 337, 363.

Vera y Zúñiga, Juan Antonio de, Conde de la Roca, 79 n. 12, 80, 84. 118 n. 82, 119 ns. 85 and 86, 236 n. 39, 264 n. 32, 267-68 n. 4, 334 n. 9, 336, 344-45. See also under Mendoza, Tirso and Vélez.

Verdad sospechosa, La, 297 n. 1.

Verdades para la vida cristiana, recopiladas de los grandes y santos autores, 45 n. 34.

Vergara, Hipólito de, 298 n. 3.

Vergonzoso en palacio, El, 48 n. 39, 64 n. 64, 84, 101 n. 52, 109 n. 62, 144, 153-54, 158, 159-74 n. 31, 172 n. 34, 186, 209 n. 5.

verisimilitude of time and language, 247-251.

"versos en circunferencia", 311 n. 26.

vetus comedia, 45 n. 33.

Viada y Lluch, Luis Carlos, 24 n. 6, 71 n. 82, 250 n. 8.

Viaje del Parnaso, 221 n. 4.

Viaje entretenido, El, 190 n. 7, 220.

Vida de la Virgen, La, 149.

Vida y muerte de Herodes, La, 56-57 n. 53, 171 n. 32.

Vígil de Quiñones, María, 212 n. 58.

Villamediana, Conde de, 37, 38, 79 n. 11, 137, 212, 267 n. 5.

Villana de la Sagra, La, 64 n. 64.

Villana de Vallecas, La, 59-65, 72, 158-159, 248 n. 5, 297 n. 1, 298-304, 305 n. 16, 311, 340, 357.

Villandrando, 322.

Villayzán, Jerónimo de, 81, 331.

Villegas, Antonio de, 204 n. 34.

Villegas Selvago, Alonso de, 248 n. 5.

Vergil, 150 n. 126.

Visita de los chistes, La, 106 n. 57, 108 n. 60, 318 n. 36.

Vita bona, 212.

Vítor (the *copla* linking Tirso's and Alarcón's names) Ch. VII, 266-85; also 23, 114 n. 73, 115 n. 74, 267 n. 3, 269 n. 7, 320. For allusions in Tirso's theatre to *copla,* see 266-275; for authors of *copla,* 266-67, 271, 275-76, 297-98, 294-96; for date and causes of *copla,* 268, 273, 320-26; for interpretation of *copla,* 269, 270, 271-72; for outline of events, 217; for relationships it implies between certain court figures, 278-80, 281-85; for results, 283.

Vossler, Karl, 347 n. 51.

Wade, Gerald E., 22 n. 2, 69 n. 77, 123 n. 91, 127 n. 100, 153 n. 7, 154 n. 9, 172 n. 34, 269 n. 7.

Wardropper, Bruce, 16.

Whitby, William M., 239 n. 46.

Williams, Mrs. Albert Sidney, 237 n. 41.

Williamsen, Vern, 14, 58 n. 55, 92 n. 40, 116 n. 78, 133 n. 106, 181 n. 48, 239 n. 46, 274 n. 18.

Wilson, Margaret, 15, 26 n. 7, 54 n. 48, 55, 56 n. 51, 99, 155 n. 12, 184 n. 53.

Xavalquinto, Marqués de, 214 n. 60.

Zahurdas de Plutón, Las, 105 n. 55, 106 n. 58.

"Zancarrón de Mahoma," 232 n. 32.

Zúñiga, Baltasar de, 29 n. 10, 213 n. 59.

Zúñiga y Requesens, Mencía de, 213 n. 59.

Zúñiga y Velasco, Inés de, 213.